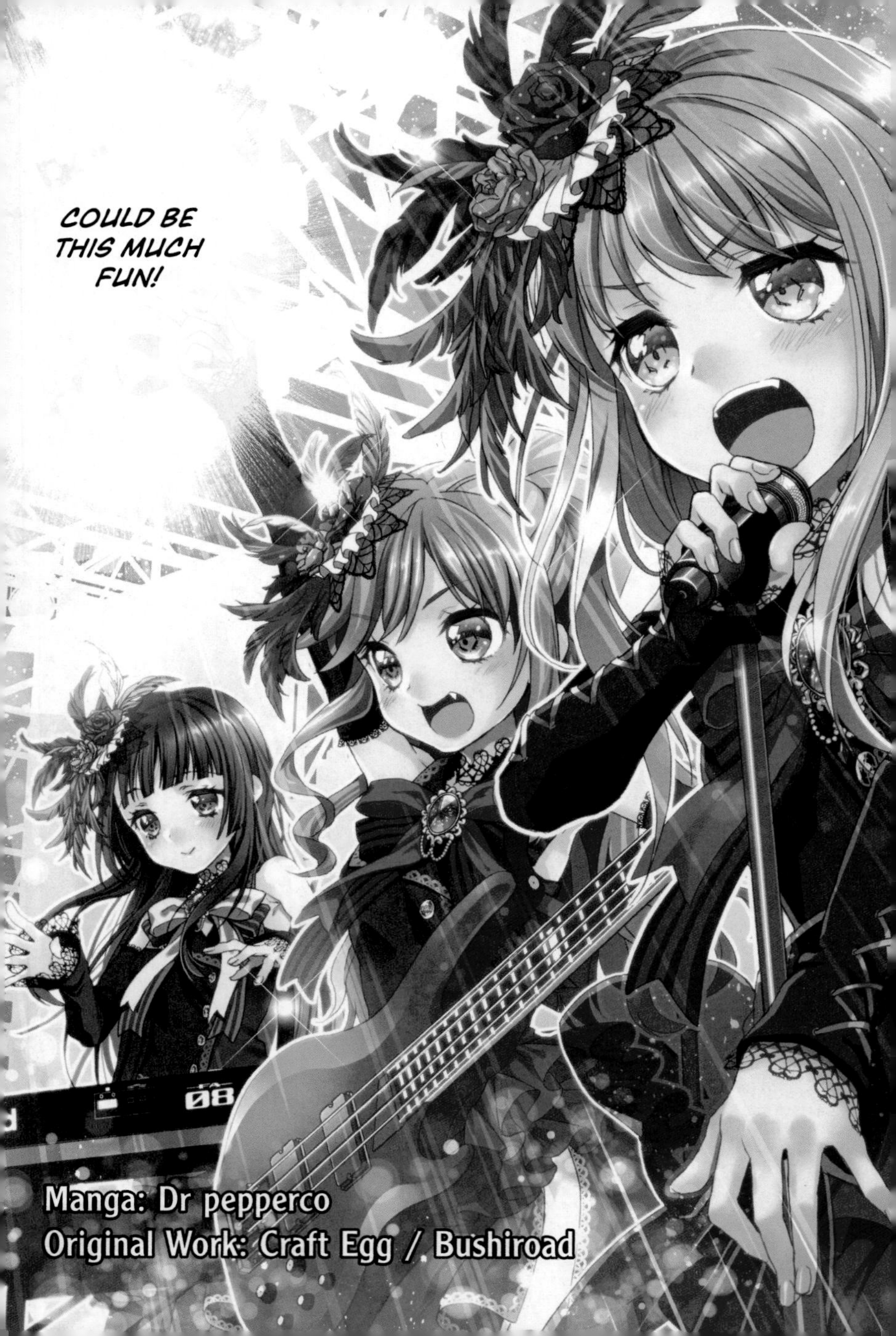
COULD BE THIS MUCH FUN!
Manga: Dr pepperco
Original Work: Craft Egg / Bushiroad

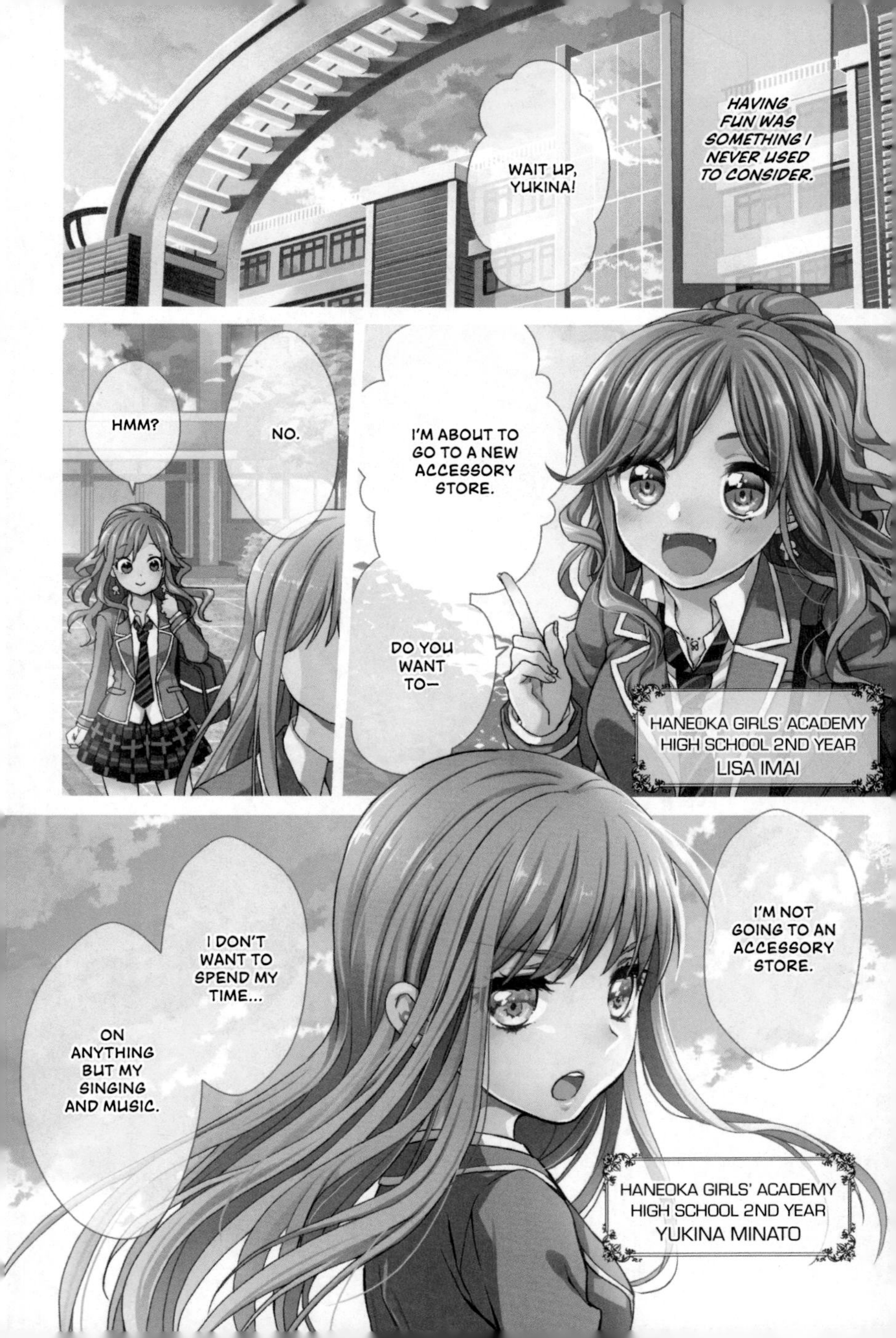
HAVING FUN WAS SOMETHING I NEVER USED TO CONSIDER.
WAIT UP, YUKINA!
I'M ABOUT TO GO TO A NEW ACCESSORY STORE.
DO YOU WANT TO—
HANEOKA GIRLS' ACADEMY HIGH SCHOOL 2ND YEAR LISA IMAI
NO.
HMM?
I'M NOT GOING TO AN ACCESSORY STORE.
I DON'T WANT TO SPEND MY TIME...
ON ANYTHING BUT MY SINGING AND MUSIC.
HANEOKA GIRLS' ACADEMY HIGH SCHOOL 2ND YEAR YUKINA MINATO

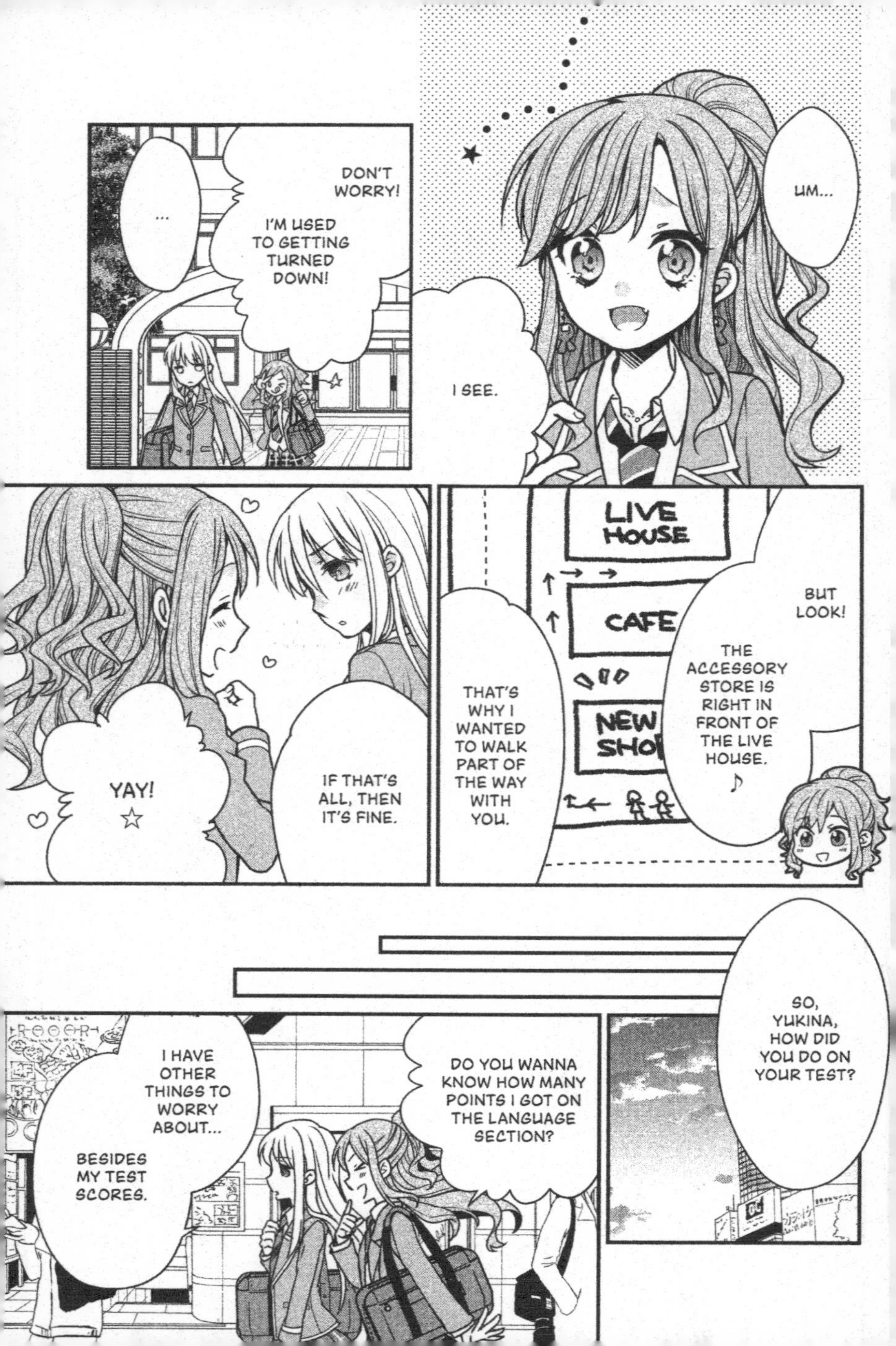
UM...
I SEE.
DON'T WORRY! I'M USED TO GETTING TURNED DOWN!
...
BUT LOOK! THE ACCESSORY STORE IS RIGHT IN FRONT OF THE LIVE HOUSE. ♪
LIVE HOUSE
CAFE
THAT'S WHY I WANTED TO WALK PART OF THE WAY WITH YOU.
IF THAT'S ALL, THEN IT'S FINE.
YAY! ☆
SO, YUKINA, HOW DID YOU DO ON YOUR TEST?
DO YOU WANNA KNOW HOW MANY POINTS I GOT ON THE LANGUAGE SECTION?
I HAVE OTHER THINGS TO WORRY ABOUT... BESIDES MY TEST SCORES.

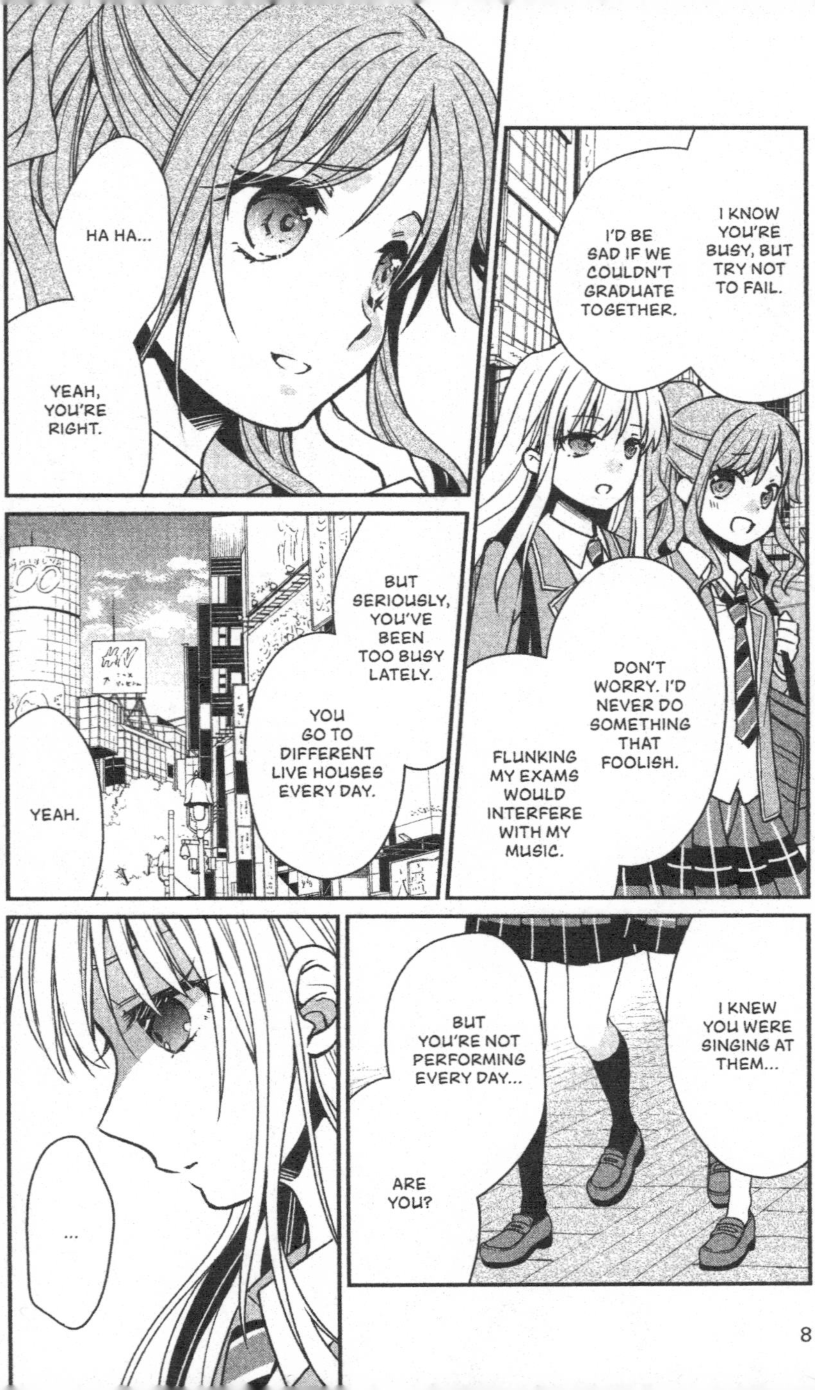
I KNOW YOU'RE BUSY, BUT TRY NOT TO FAIL.
I'D BE SAD IF WE COULDN'T GRADUATE TOGETHER.
DON'T WORRY. I'D NEVER DO SOMETHING THAT FOOLISH.
FLUNKING MY EXAMS WOULD INTERFERE WITH MY MUSIC.
HA HA...
YEAH, YOU'RE RIGHT.
BUT SERIOUSLY, YOU'VE BEEN TOO BUSY LATELY.
YOU GO TO DIFFERENT LIVE HOUSES EVERY DAY.
YEAH.
I KNEW YOU WERE SINGING AT THEM...
BUT YOU'RE NOT PERFORMING EVERY DAY...
ARE YOU?
...

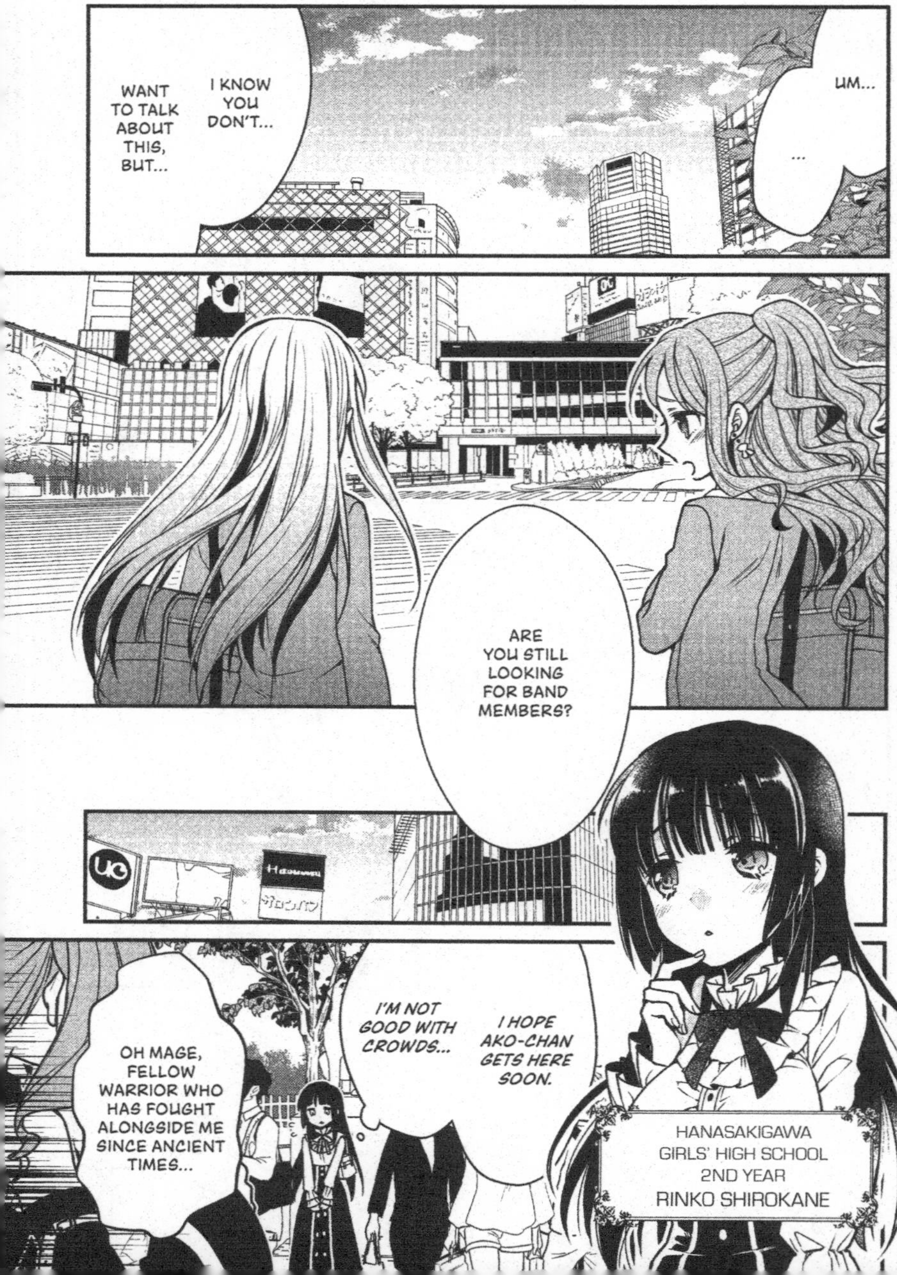
UM...
...
I KNOW YOU DON'T...
WANT TO TALK ABOUT THIS, BUT...
ARE YOU STILL LOOKING FOR BAND MEMBERS?
HANASAKIGAWA GIRLS' HIGH SCHOOL 2ND YEAR RINKO SHIROKANE
I HOPE AKO-CHAN GETS HERE SOON.
I'M NOT GOOD WITH CROWDS...
OH MAGE, FELLOW WARRIOR WHO HAS FOUGHT ALONGSIDE ME SINCE ANCIENT TIMES...

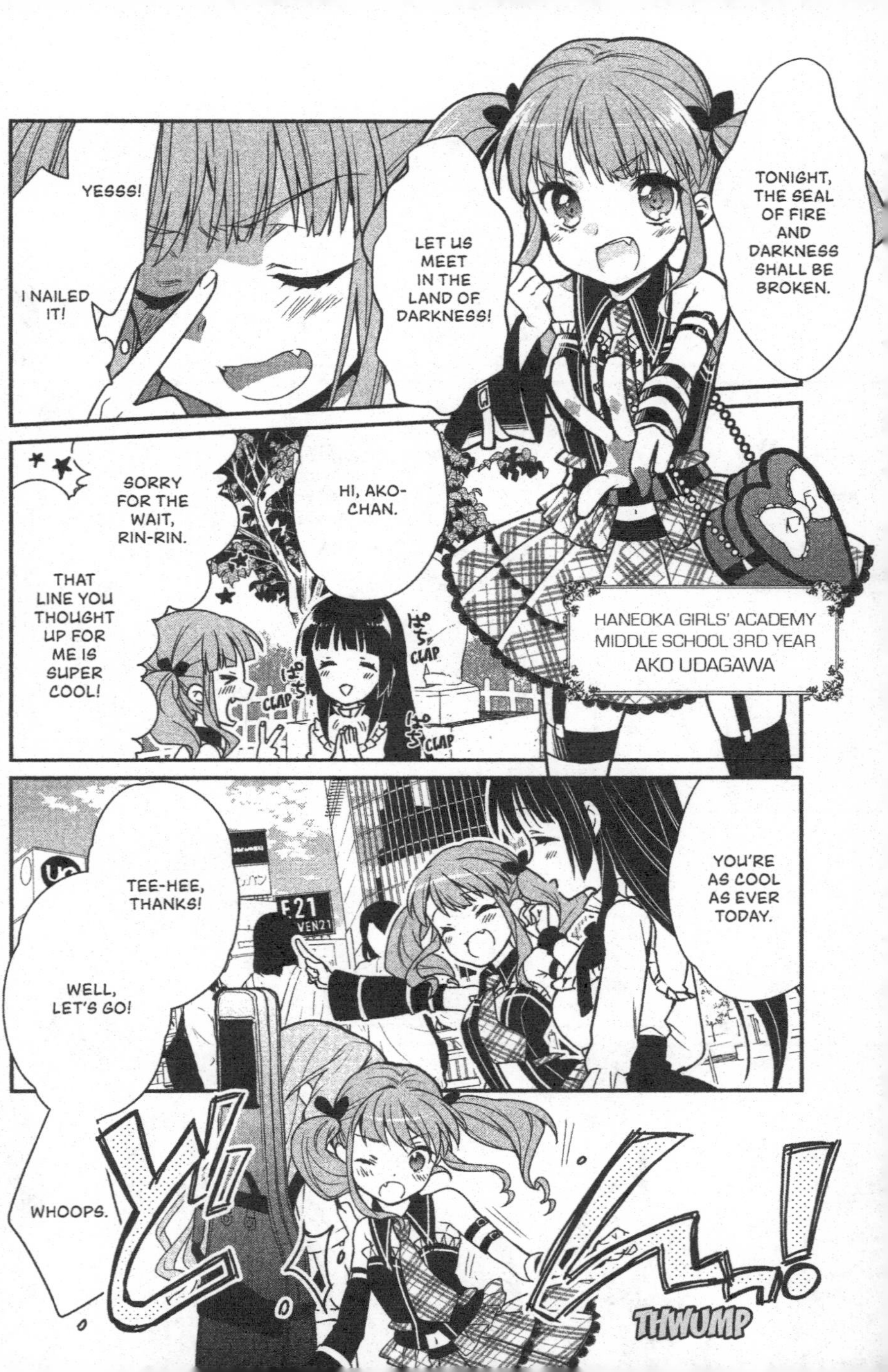
TONIGHT, THE SEAL OF FIRE AND DARKNESS SHALL BE BROKEN.
LET US MEET IN THE LAND OF DARKNESS!
YESSS!
I NAILED IT!
HANEOKA GIRLS' ACADEMY MIDDLE SCHOOL 3RD YEAR AKO UDAGAWA
HI, AKO-CHAN.
CLAP
CLAP
CLAP
SORRY FOR THE WAIT, RIN-RIN.
THAT LINE YOU THOUGHT UP FOR ME IS SUPER COOL!
YOU'RE AS COOL AS EVER TODAY.
TEE-HEE, THANKS!
F21
VEN21
WELL, LET'S GO!
WHOOPS.
THWUMP

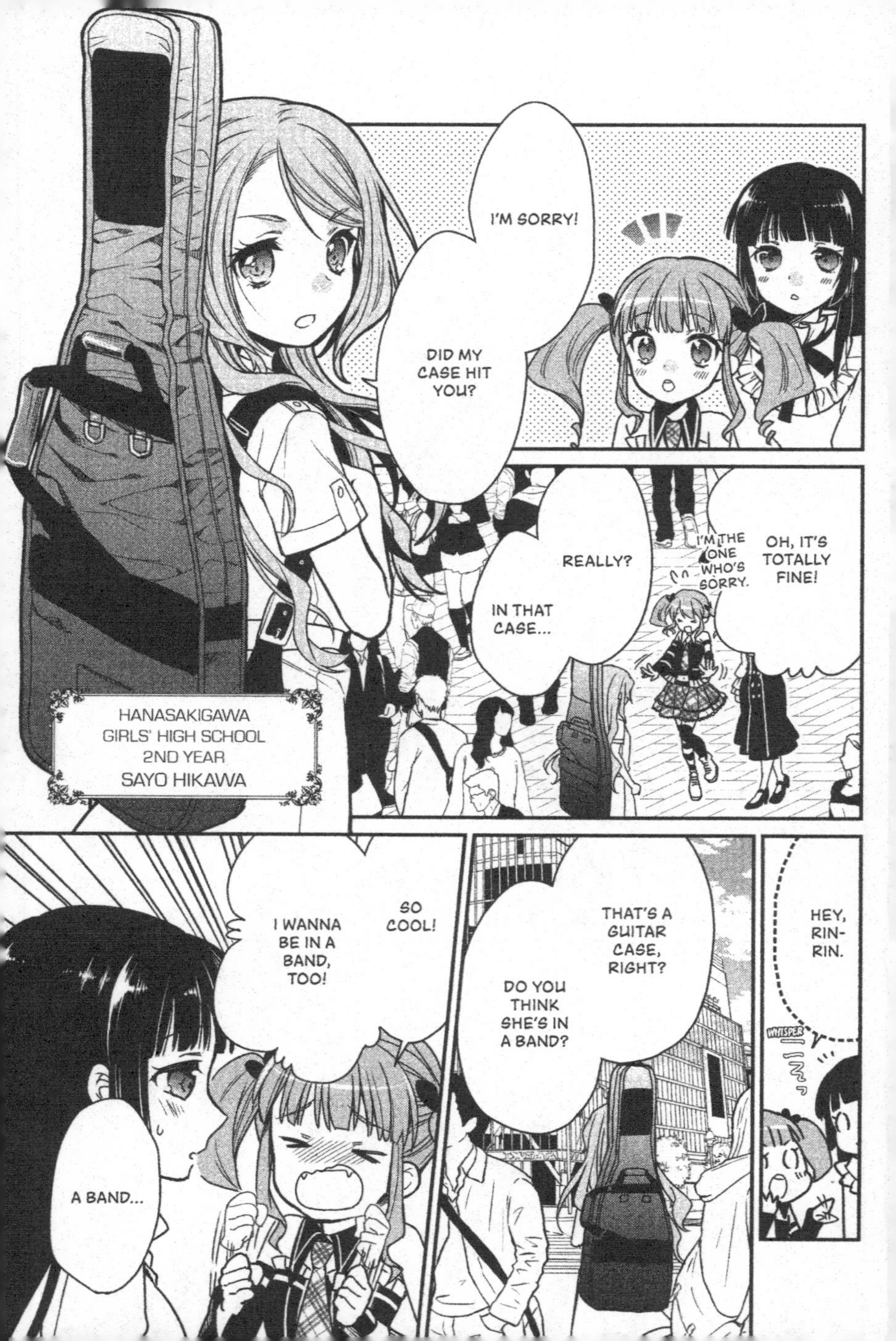
I'M SORRY!
DID MY CASE HIT YOU?
OH, IT'S TOTALLY FINE!
I'M THE ONE WHO'S SORRY.
REALLY?
IN THAT CASE...
HANASAKIGAWA GIRLS' HIGH SCHOOL 2ND YEAR SAYO HIKAWA
HEY, RIN-RIN.
WHISPER
THAT'S A GUITAR CASE, RIGHT?
DO YOU THINK SHE'S IN A BAND?
SO COOL!
I WANNA BE IN A BAND, TOO!
A BAND...

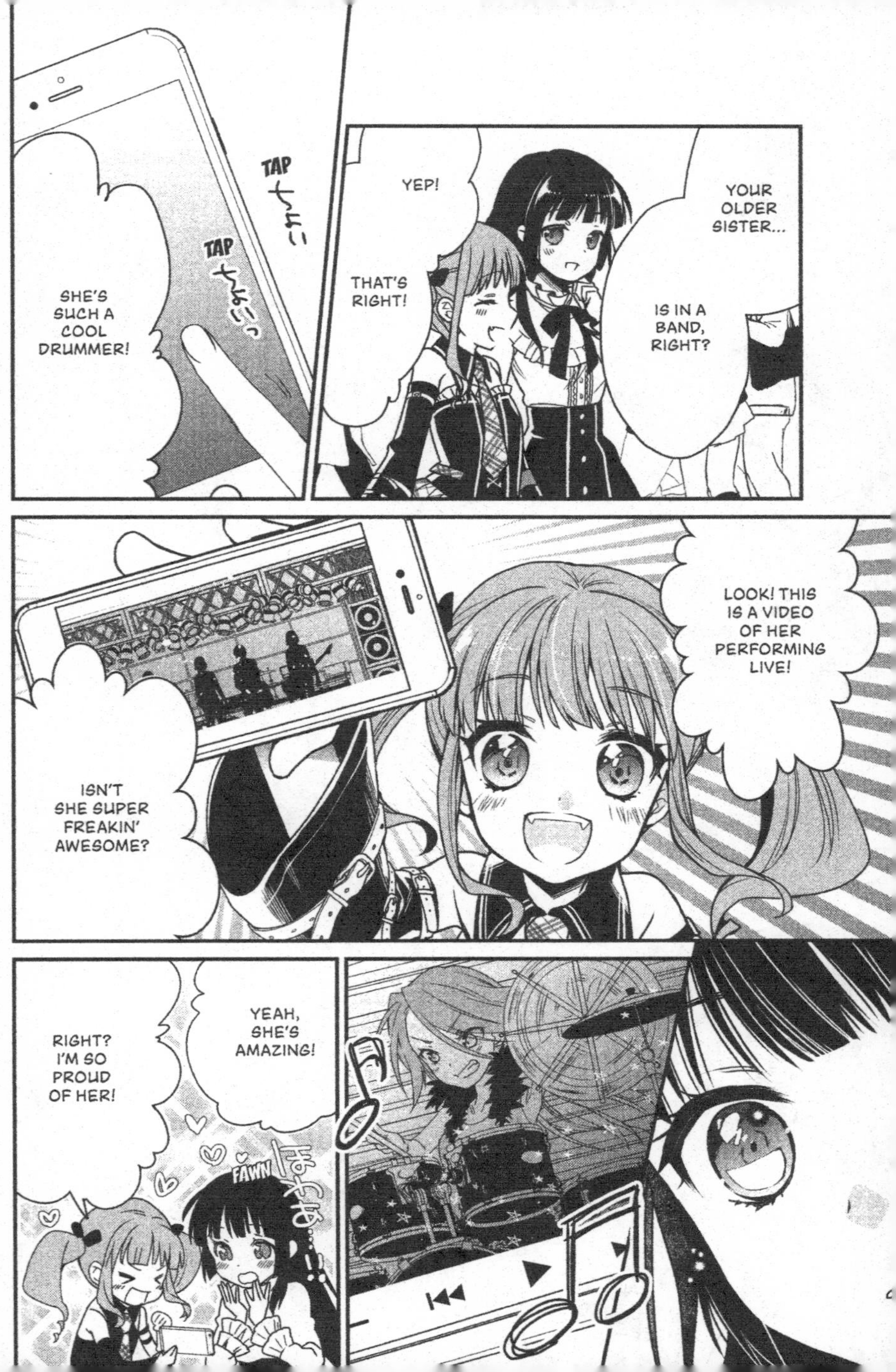
YOUR OLDER SISTER...
IS IN A BAND, RIGHT?
YEP!
THAT'S RIGHT!
TAP ちょい
TAP ちょいっ
SHE'S SUCH A COOL DRUMMER!
LOOK! THIS IS A VIDEO OF HER PERFORMING LIVE!
ISN'T SHE SUPER FREAKIN' AWESOME?
YEAH, SHE'S AMAZING!
RIGHT? I'M SO PROUD OF HER!
FAWN ほわぁ…

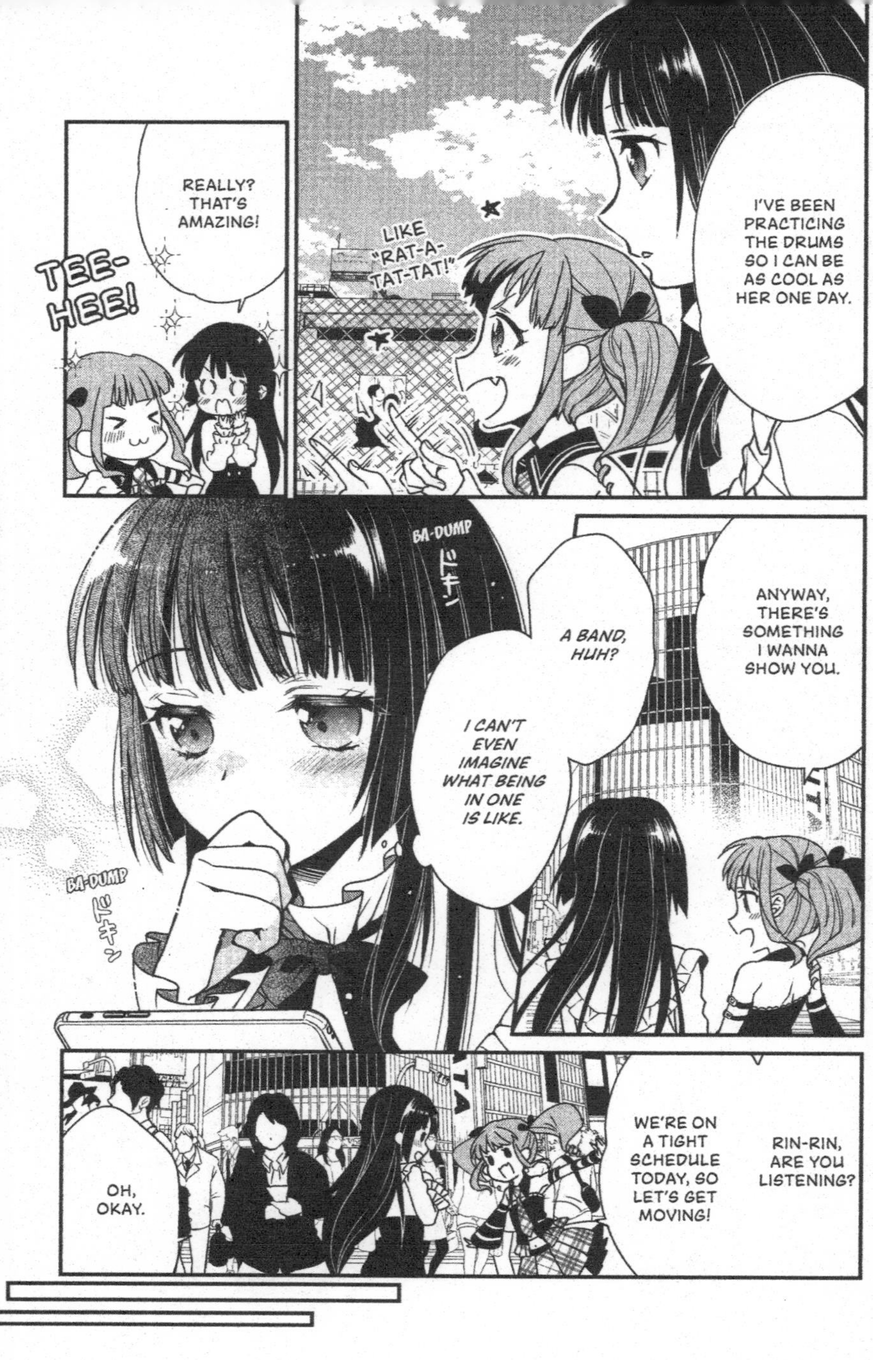
I'VE BEEN PRACTICING THE DRUMS SO I CAN BE AS COOL AS HER ONE DAY.
LIKE "RAT-A-TAT-TAT!"
REALLY? THAT'S AMAZING!
TEE-HEE!
ANYWAY, THERE'S SOMETHING I WANNA SHOW YOU.
BA-DUMP
ドキン
A BAND, HUH?
I CAN'T EVEN IMAGINE WHAT BEING IN ONE IS LIKE.
BA-DUMP
ドキン
RIN-RIN, ARE YOU LISTENING?
WE'RE ON A TIGHT SCHEDULE TODAY, SO LET'S GET MOVING!
OH, OKAY.

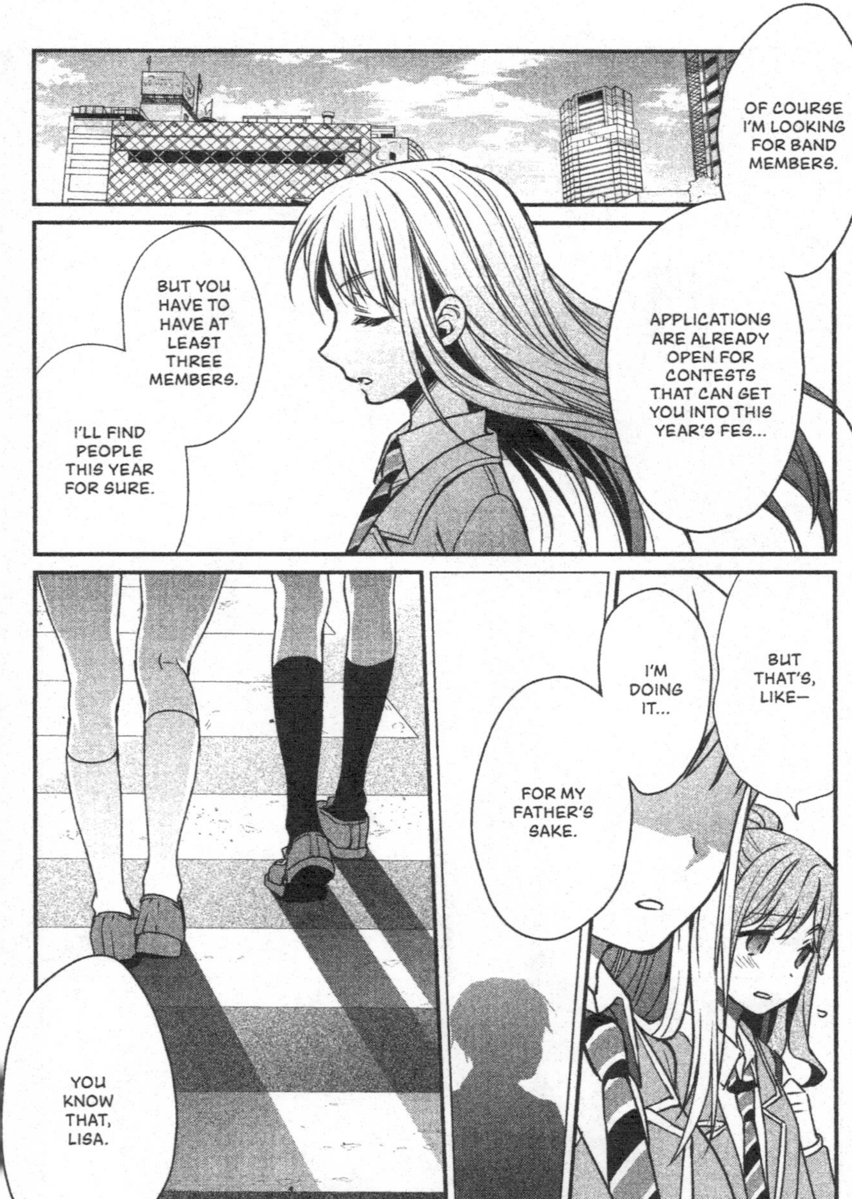
OF COURSE I'M LOOKING FOR BAND MEMBERS.
APPLICATIONS ARE ALREADY OPEN FOR CONTESTS THAT CAN GET YOU INTO THIS YEAR'S FES...
BUT YOU HAVE TO HAVE AT LEAST THREE MEMBERS.
I'LL FIND PEOPLE THIS YEAR FOR SURE.
BUT THAT'S, LIKE—
I'M DOING IT...
FOR MY FATHER'S SAKE.
YOU KNOW THAT, LISA.

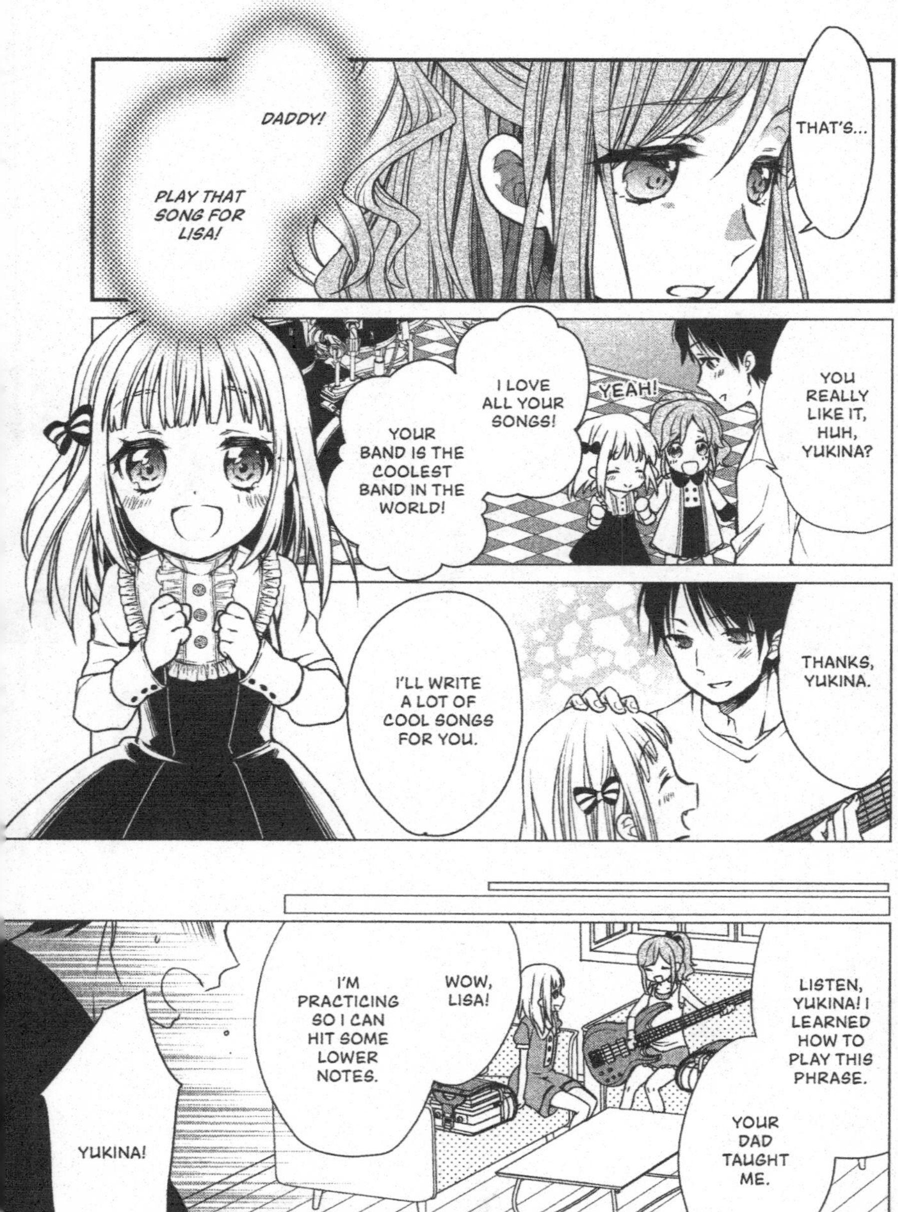
THAT'S...
DADDY!
PLAY THAT SONG FOR LISA!
YOU REALLY LIKE IT, HUH, YUKINA?
YEAH!
I LOVE ALL YOUR SONGS!
YOUR BAND IS THE COOLEST BAND IN THE WORLD!
THANKS, YUKINA.
I'LL WRITE A LOT OF COOL SONGS FOR YOU.
LISTEN, YUKINA! I LEARNED HOW TO PLAY THIS PHRASE.
YOUR DAD TAUGHT ME.
WOW, LISA!
I'M PRACTICING SO I CAN HIT SOME LOWER NOTES.
YUKINA!

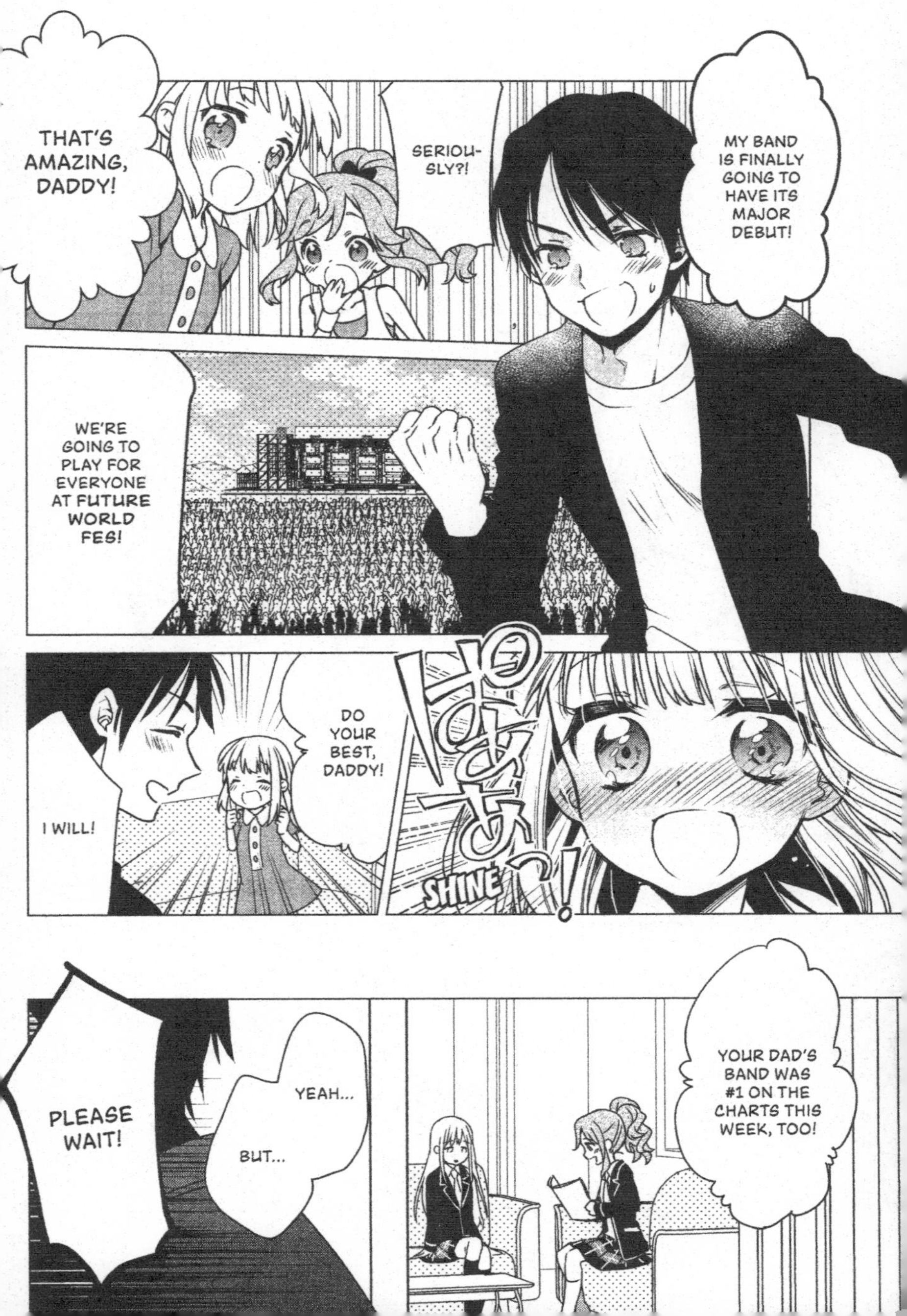
MY BAND IS FINALLY GOING TO HAVE ITS MAJOR DEBUT!
SERIOU-SLY?!
THAT'S AMAZING, DADDY!
WE'RE GOING TO PLAY FOR EVERYONE AT FUTURE WORLD FES!
SHINE
DO YOUR BEST, DADDY!
I WILL!
YOUR DAD'S BAND WAS #1 ON THE CHARTS THIS WEEK, TOO!
YEAH...
BUT...
PLEASE WAIT!

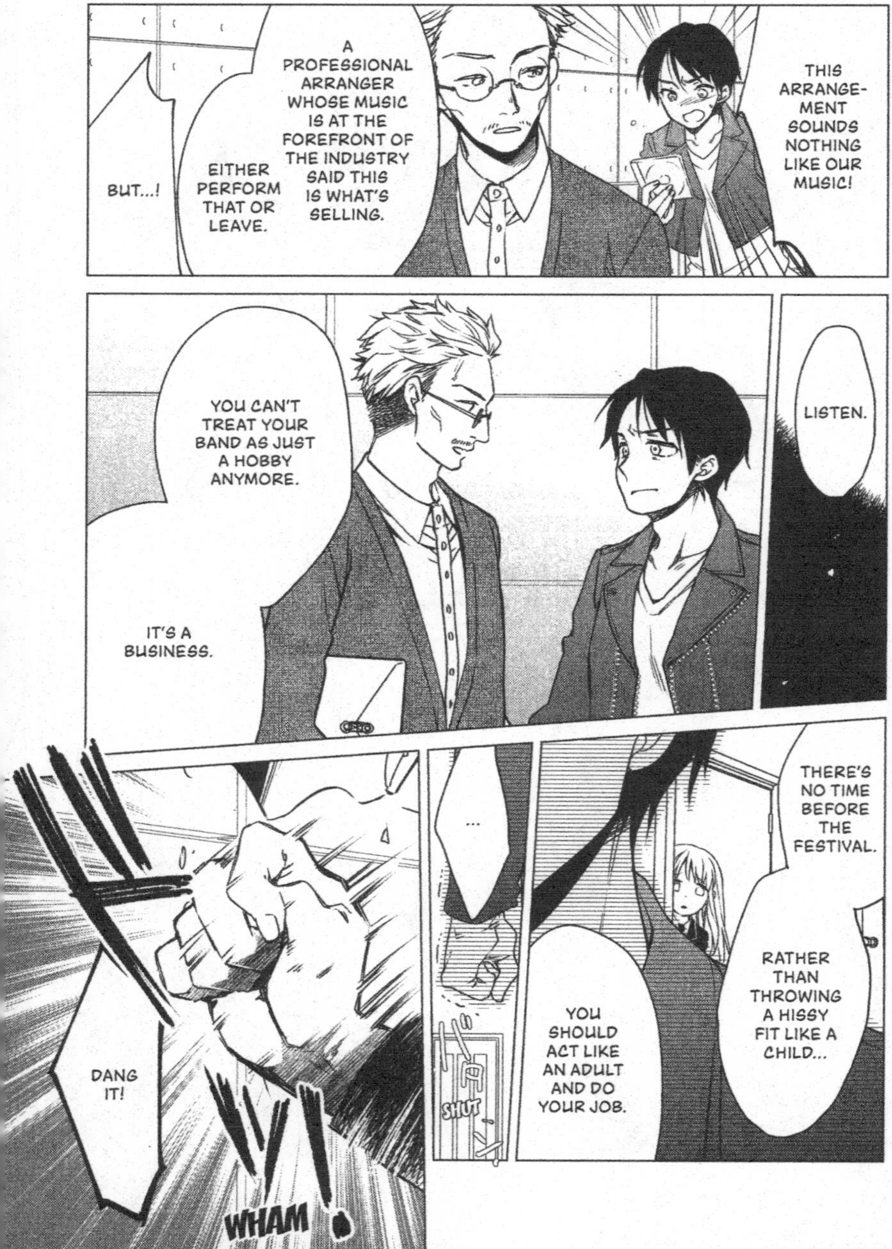
THIS ARRANGE-MENT SOUNDS NOTHING LIKE OUR MUSIC!
A PROFESSIONAL ARRANGER WHOSE MUSIC IS AT THE FOREFRONT OF THE INDUSTRY SAID THIS IS WHAT'S SELLING.
EITHER PERFORM THAT OR LEAVE.
BUT...!
LISTEN.
YOU CAN'T TREAT YOUR BAND AS JUST A HOBBY ANYMORE.
IT'S A BUSINESS.
THERE'S NO TIME BEFORE THE FESTIVAL.
RATHER THAN THROWING A HISSY FIT LIKE A CHILD...
YOU SHOULD ACT LIKE AN ADULT AND DO YOUR JOB.
...
SHUT
DANG IT!
WHAM!

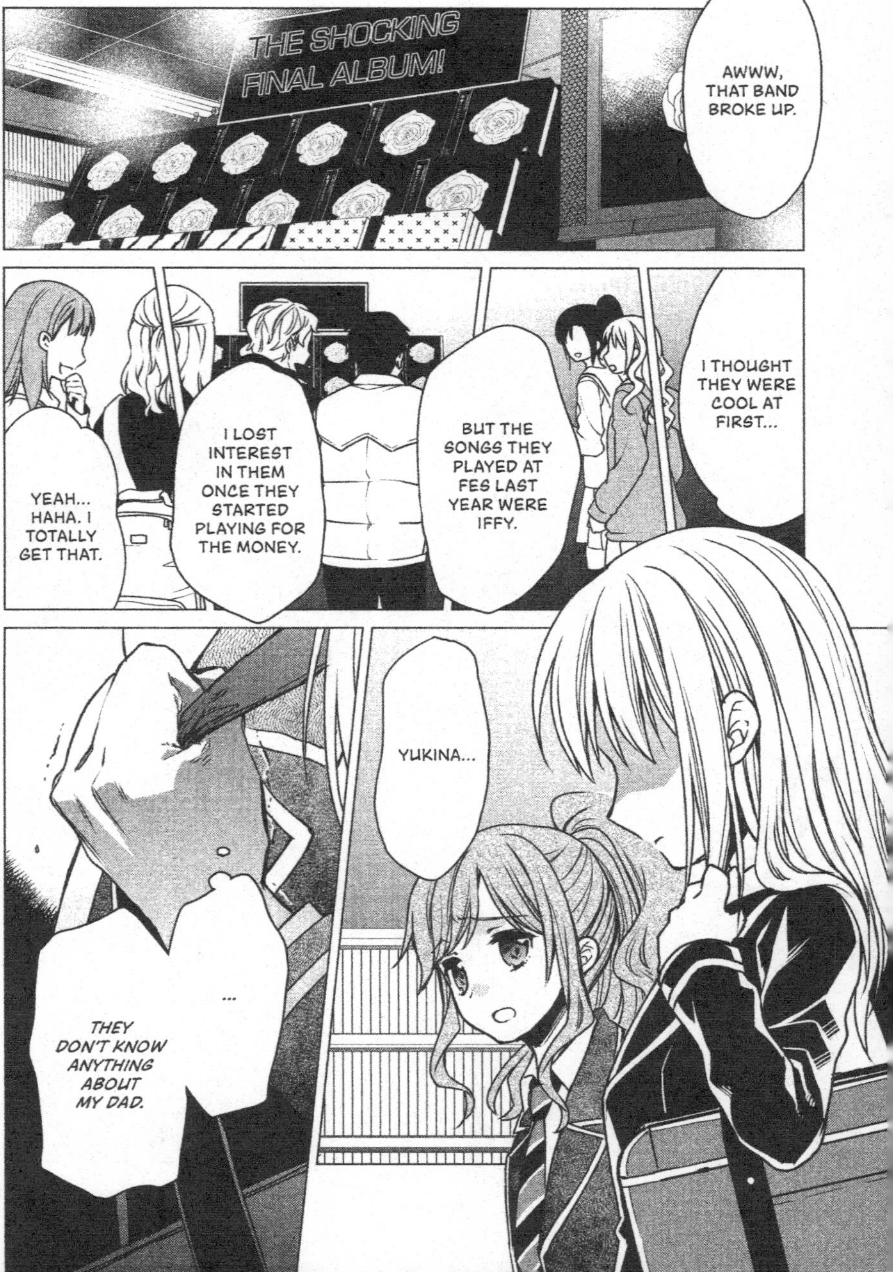
AWWW, THAT BAND BROKE UP.
THE SHOCKING FINAL ALBUM!
I THOUGHT THEY WERE COOL AT FIRST...
BUT THE SONGS THEY PLAYED AT FES LAST YEAR WERE IFFY.
I LOST INTEREST IN THEM ONCE THEY STARTED PLAYING FOR THE MONEY.
YEAH... HAHA. I TOTALLY GET THAT.
YUKINA...
...
THEY DON'T KNOW ANYTHING ABOUT MY DAD.

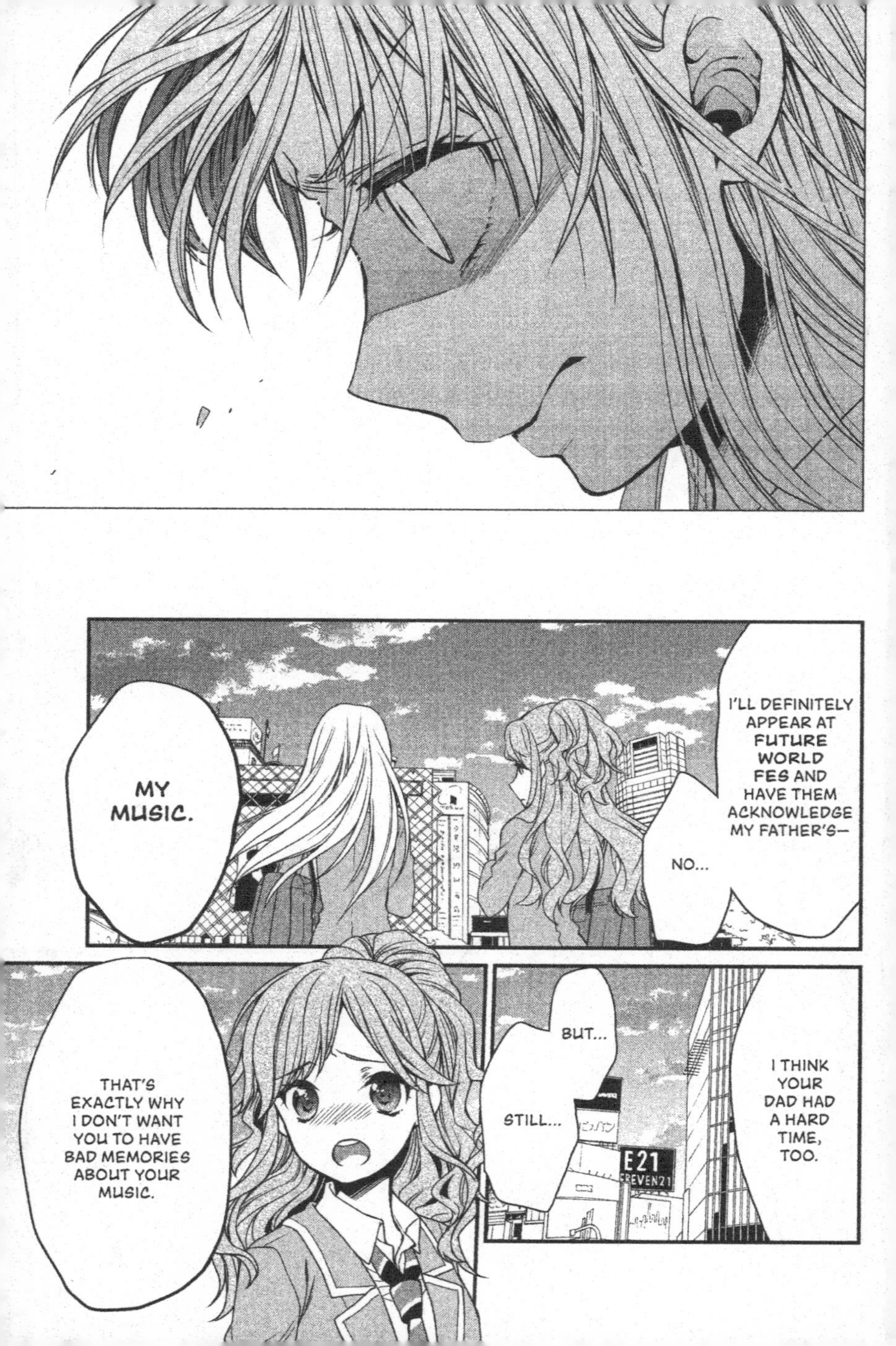
I'LL DEFINITELY APPEAR AT FUTURE WORLD FES AND HAVE THEM ACKNOWLEDGE MY FATHER'S—
NO...
MY MUSIC.
I THINK YOUR DAD HAD A HARD TIME, TOO.
BUT...
STILL...
THAT'S EXACTLY WHY I DON'T WANT YOU TO HAVE BAD MEMORIES ABOUT YOUR MUSIC.

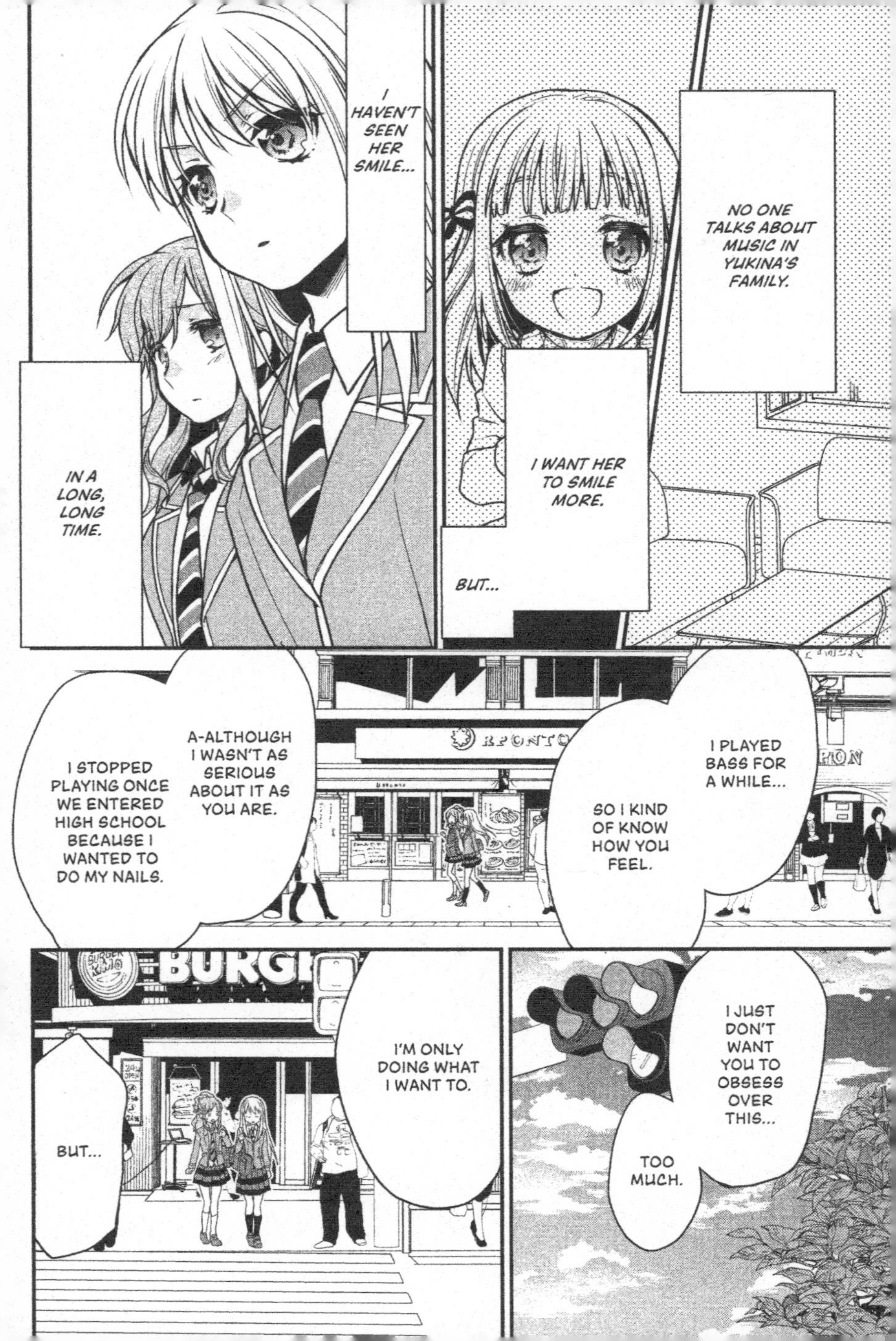
NO ONE TALKS ABOUT MUSIC IN YUKINA'S FAMILY.
I WANT HER TO SMILE MORE.
BUT...
I HAVEN'T SEEN HER SMILE...
IN A LONG, LONG TIME.
I PLAYED BASS FOR A WHILE...
SO I KIND OF KNOW HOW YOU FEEL.
A-ALTHOUGH I WASN'T AS SERIOUS ABOUT IT AS YOU ARE.
I STOPPED PLAYING ONCE WE ENTERED HIGH SCHOOL BECAUSE I WANTED TO DO MY NAILS.
I JUST DON'T WANT YOU TO OBSESS OVER THIS...
TOO MUCH.
I'M ONLY DOING WHAT I WANT TO.
BUT...

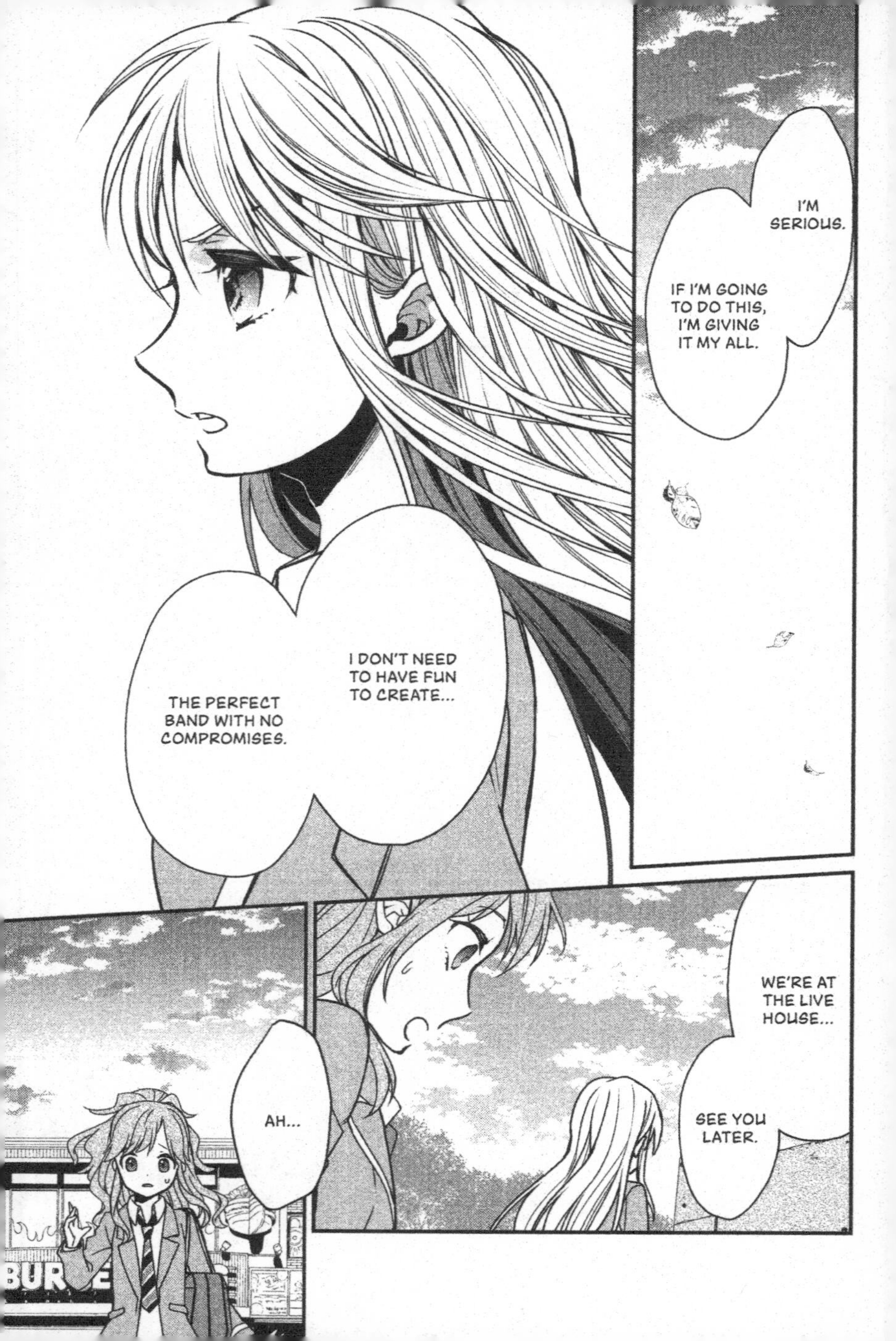
I'M SERIOUS.
IF I'M GOING TO DO THIS, I'M GIVING IT MY ALL.
I DON'T NEED TO HAVE FUN TO CREATE...
THE PERFECT BAND WITH NO COMPROMISES.
WE'RE AT THE LIVE HOUSE...
SEE YOU LATER.
AH...

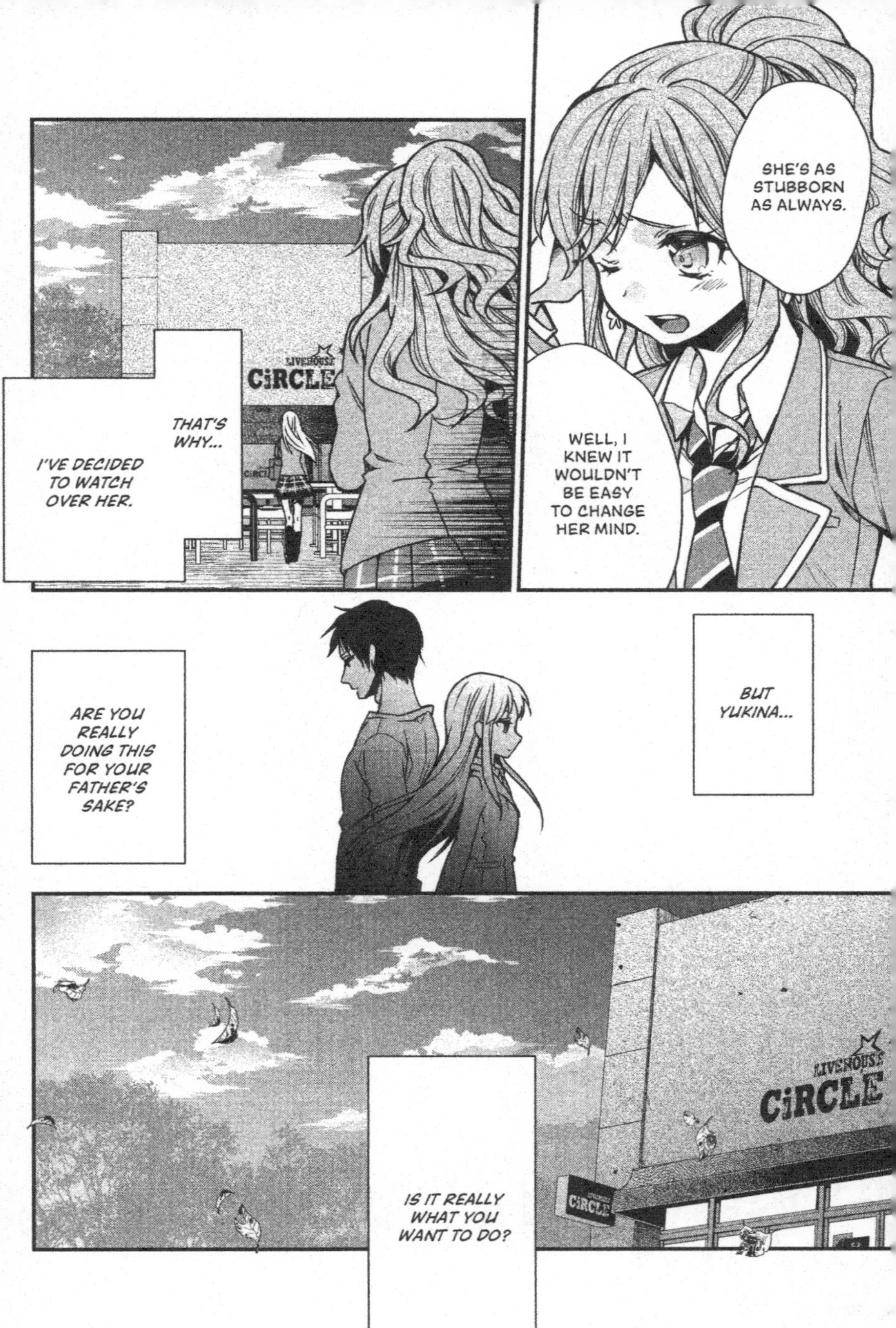
SHE'S AS STUBBORN AS ALWAYS.
WELL, I KNEW IT WOULDN'T BE EASY TO CHANGE HER MIND.
THAT'S WHY...
I'VE DECIDED TO WATCH OVER HER.
LIVEHOUSE CiRCLE
BUT YUKINA...
ARE YOU REALLY DOING THIS FOR YOUR FATHER'S SAKE?
LIVEHOUSE CiRCLE
CiRCLE
IS IT REALLY WHAT YOU WANT TO DO?

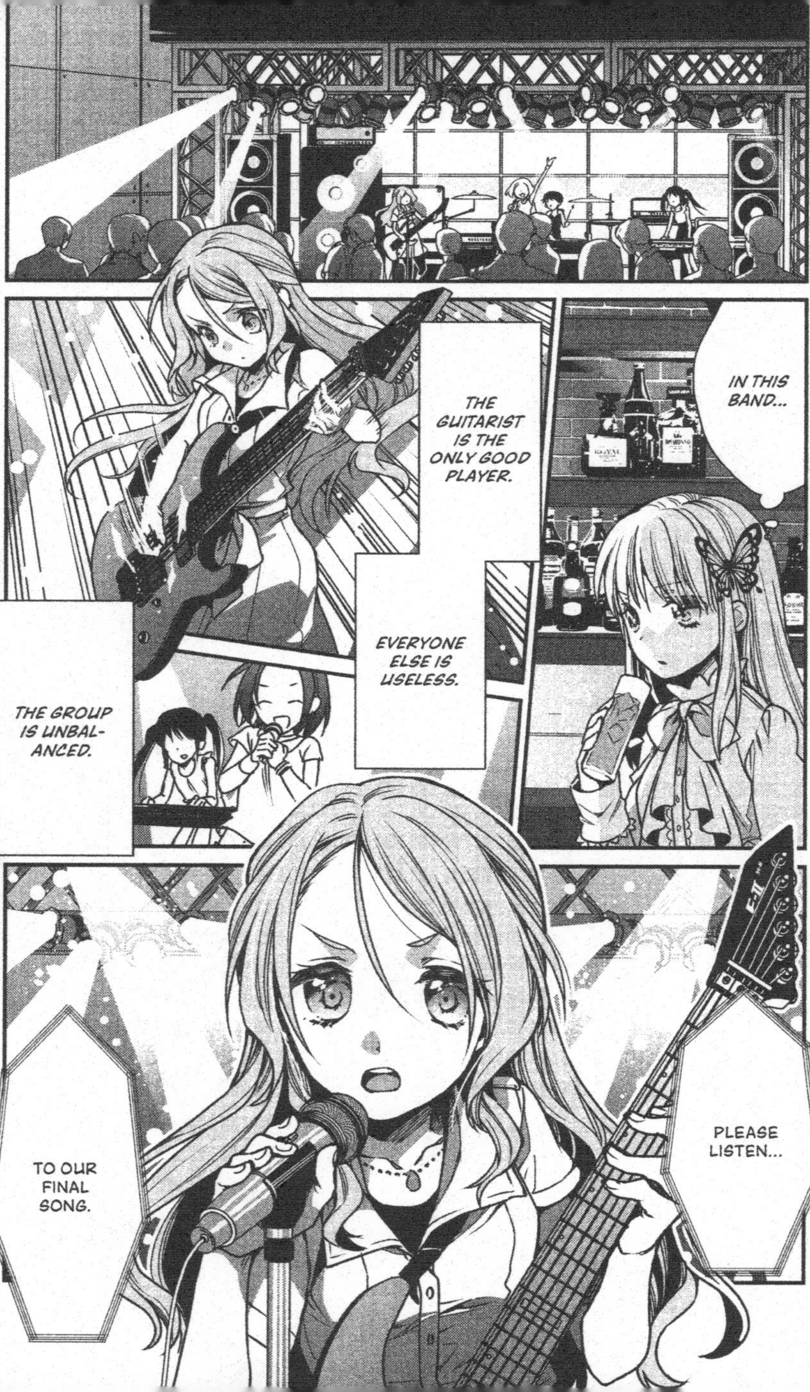
IN THIS BAND...
THE GUITARIST IS THE ONLY GOOD PLAYER.
EVERYONE ELSE IS USELESS.
THE GROUP IS UNBAL-ANCED.
PLEASE LISTEN...
TO OUR FINAL SONG.

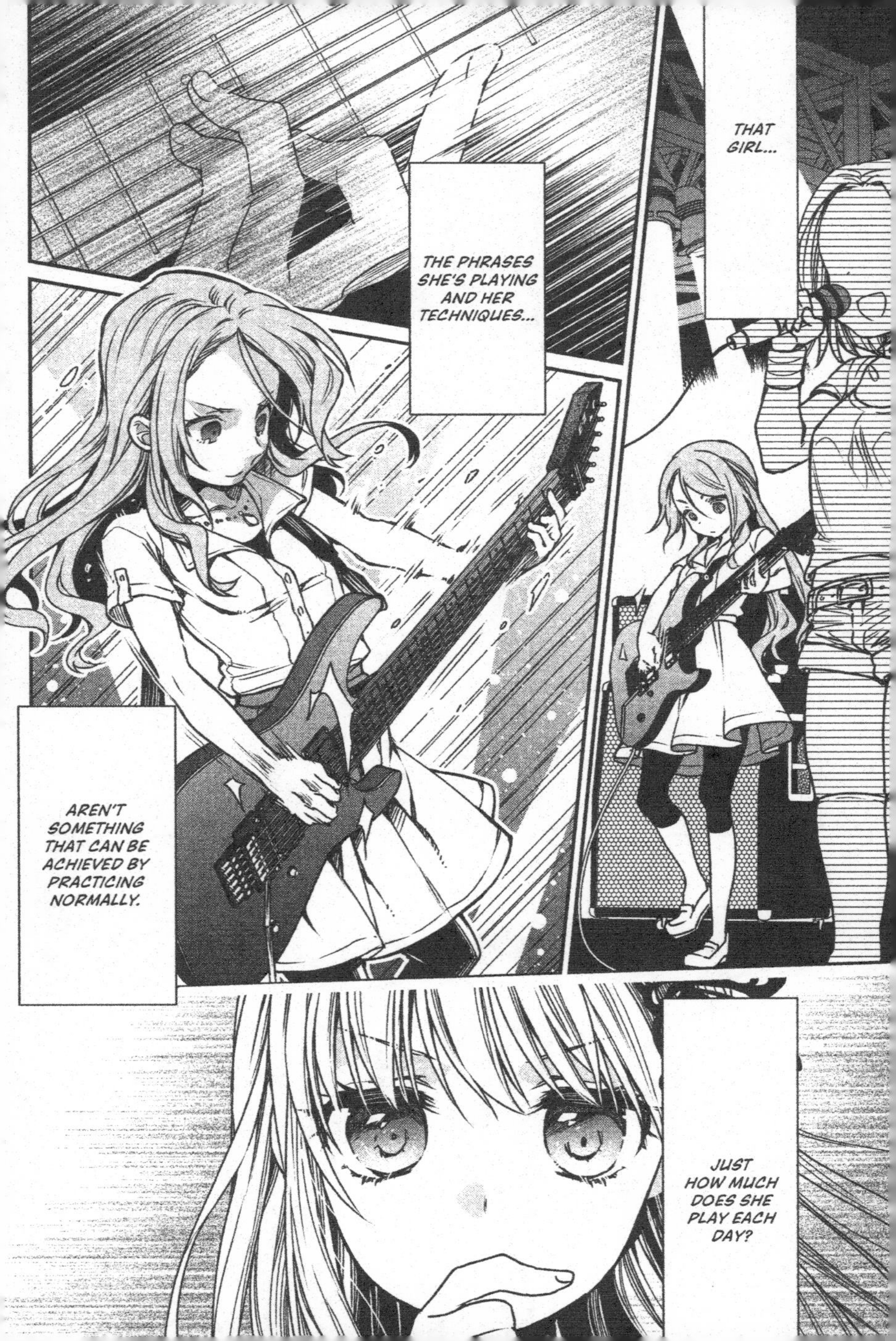
THAT GIRL...
THE PHRASES SHE'S PLAYING AND HER TECHNIQUES...
AREN'T SOMETHING THAT CAN BE ACHIEVED BY PRACTICING NORMALLY.
JUST HOW MUCH DOES SHE PLAY EACH DAY?

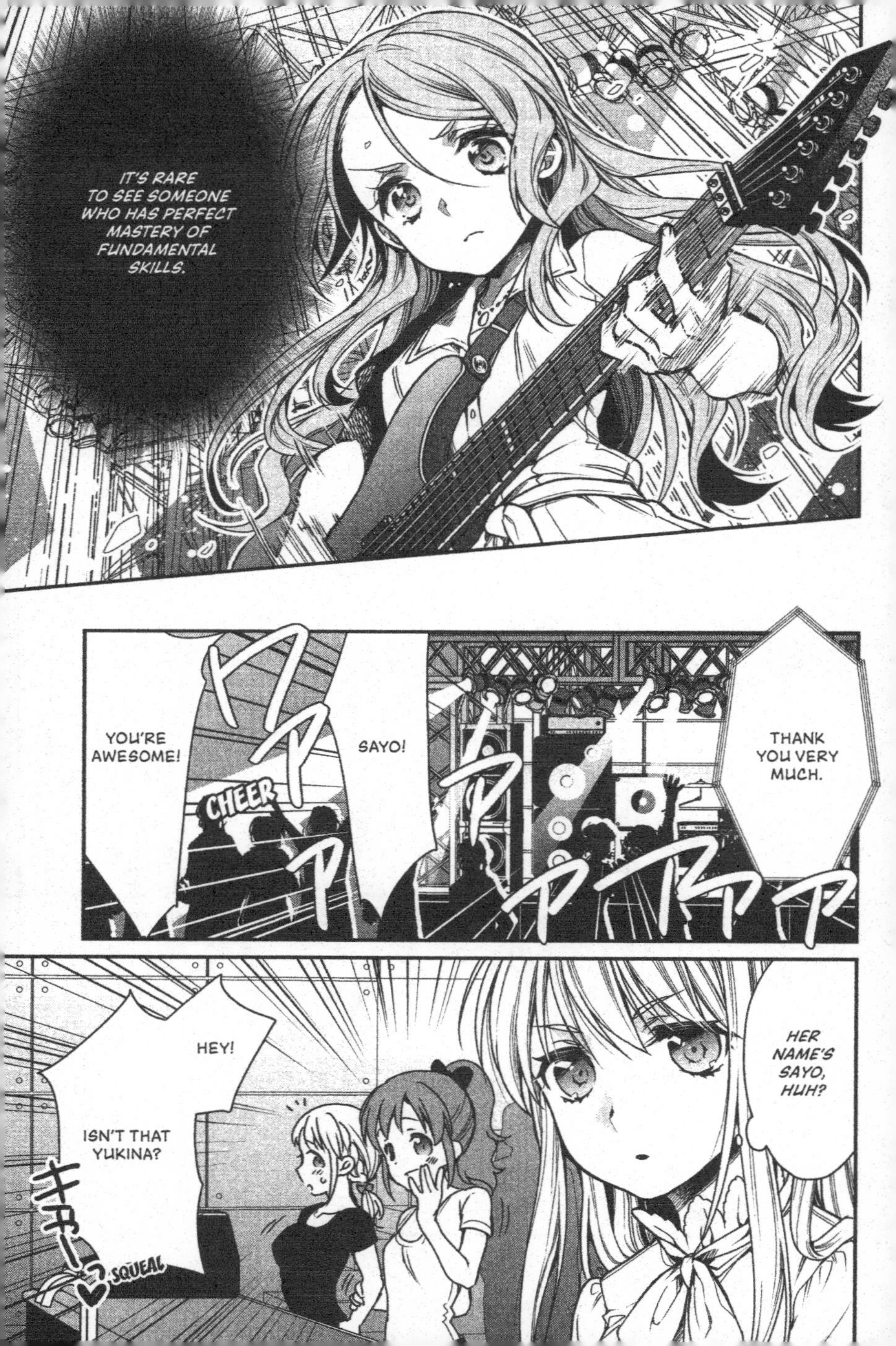
IT'S RARE TO SEE SOMEONE WHO HAS PERFECT MASTERY OF FUNDAMENTAL SKILLS.
THANK YOU VERY MUCH.
SAYO!
YOU'RE AWESOME!
CHEER
HER NAME'S SAYO, HUH?
HEY!
ISN'T THAT YUKINA?
SQUEAL

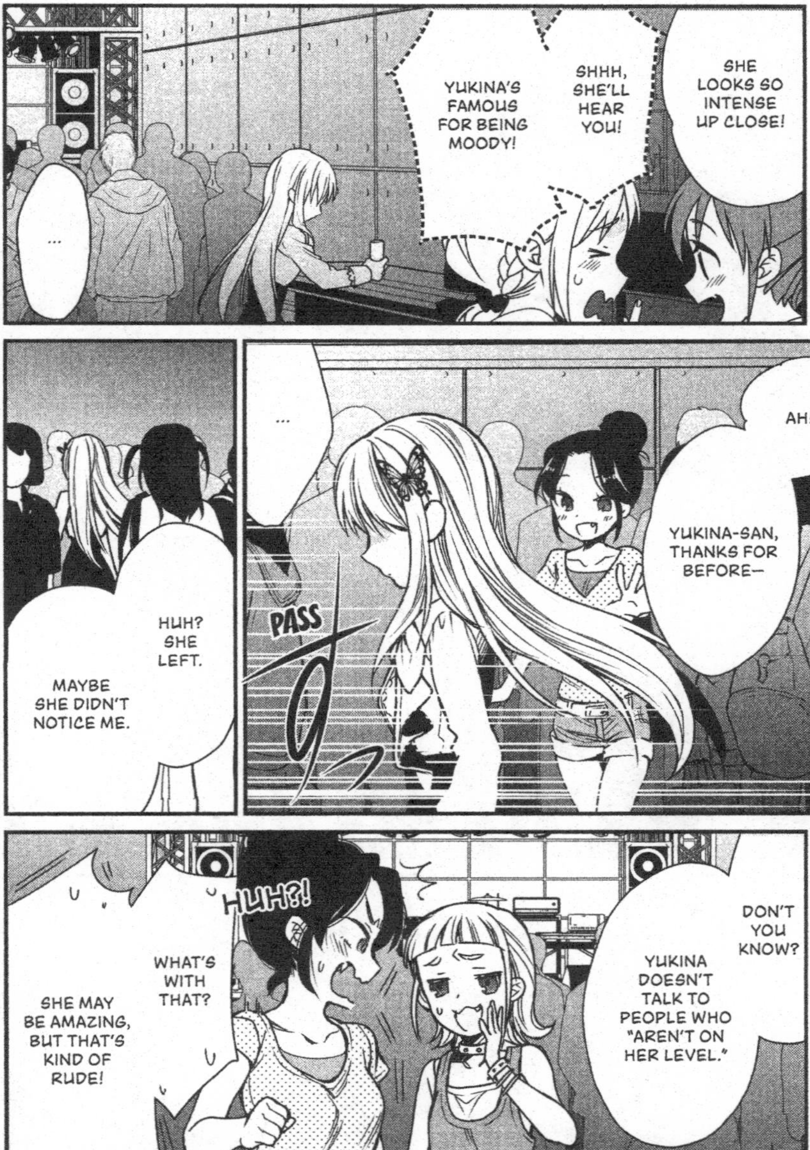

SHE LOOKS SO INTENSE UP CLOSE!
SHHH, SHE'LL HEAR YOU!
YUKINA'S FAMOUS FOR BEING MOODY!
...
AH!
YUKINA-SAN, THANKS FOR BEFORE—
...
PASS
HUH? SHE LEFT.
MAYBE SHE DIDN'T NOTICE ME.
DON'T YOU KNOW?
YUKINA DOESN'T TALK TO PEOPLE WHO "AREN'T ON HER LEVEL."
HUH?!
WHAT'S WITH THAT?
SHE MAY BE AMAZING, BUT THAT'S KIND OF RUDE!

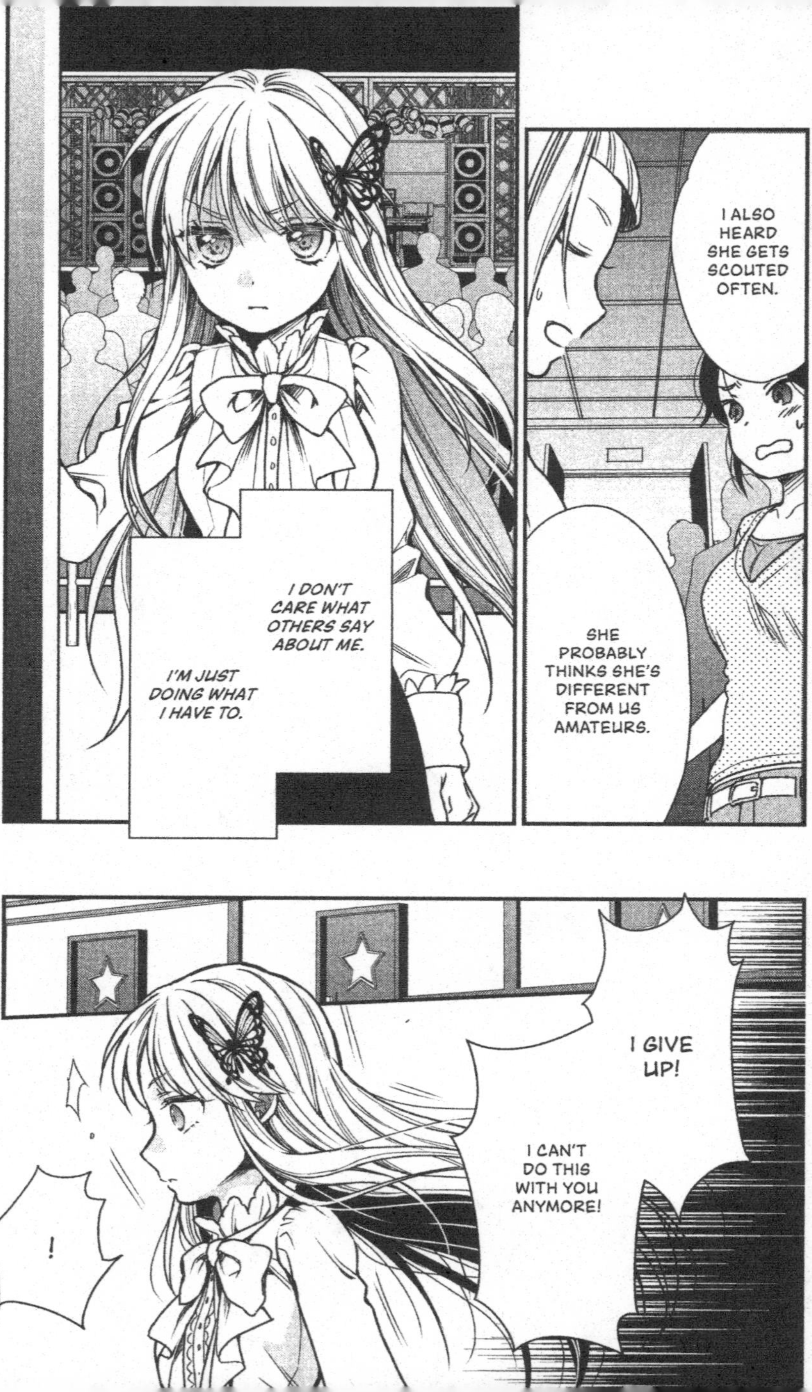
I ALSO HEARD SHE GETS SCOUTED OFTEN.
SHE PROBABLY THINKS SHE'S DIFFERENT FROM US AMATEURS.
I DON'T CARE WHAT OTHERS SAY ABOUT ME.
I'M JUST DOING WHAT I HAVE TO.
I GIVE UP!
I CAN'T DO THIS WITH YOU ANYMORE!
!

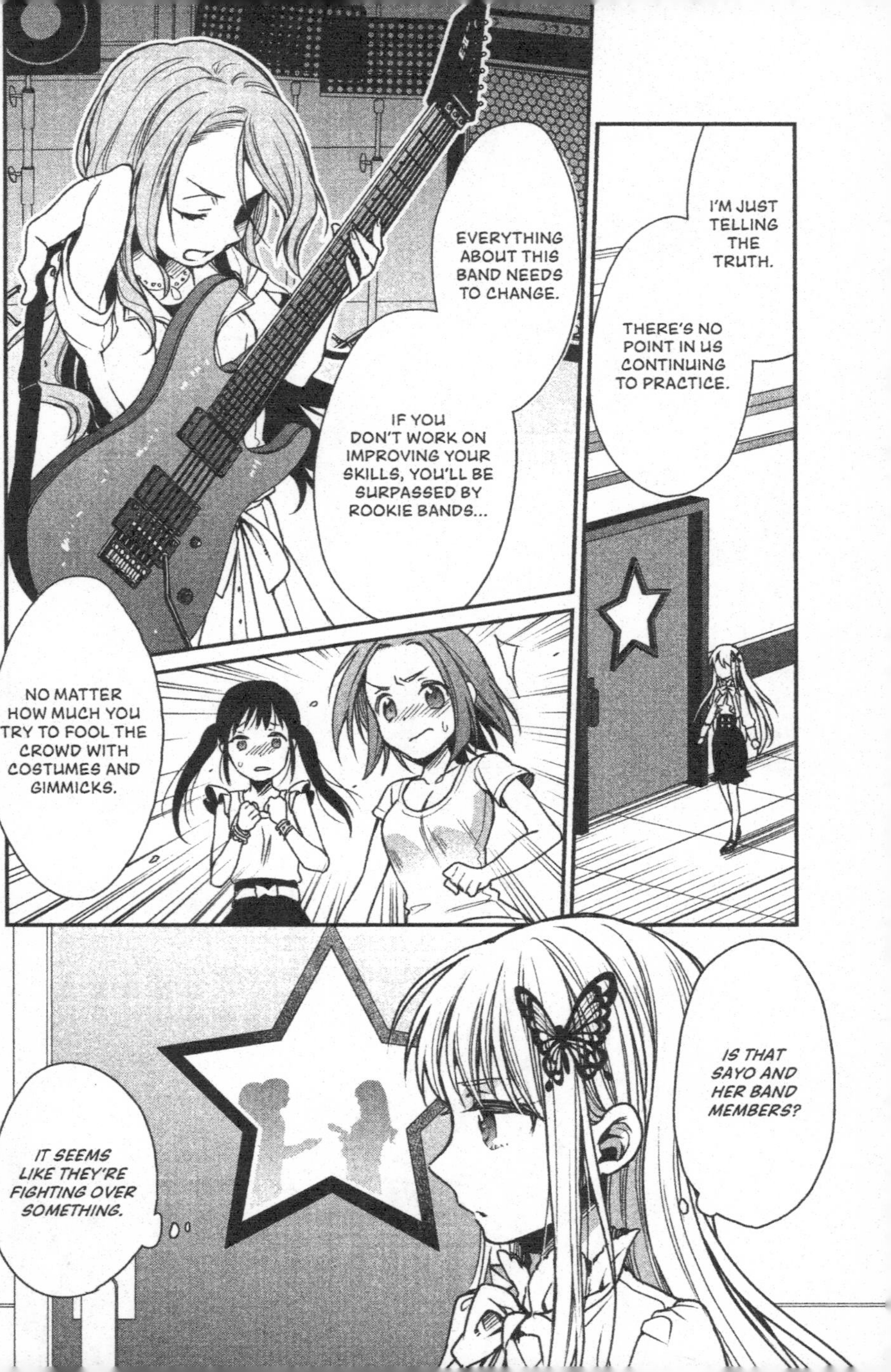
I'M JUST TELLING THE TRUTH.
THERE'S NO POINT IN US CONTINUING TO PRACTICE.
EVERYTHING ABOUT THIS BAND NEEDS TO CHANGE.
IF YOU DON'T WORK ON IMPROVING YOUR SKILLS, YOU'LL BE SURPASSED BY ROOKIE BANDS...
NO MATTER HOW MUCH YOU TRY TO FOOL THE CROWD WITH COSTUMES AND GIMMICKS.
IS THAT SAYO AND HER BAND MEMBERS?
IT SEEMS LIKE THEY'RE FIGHTING OVER SOMETHING.

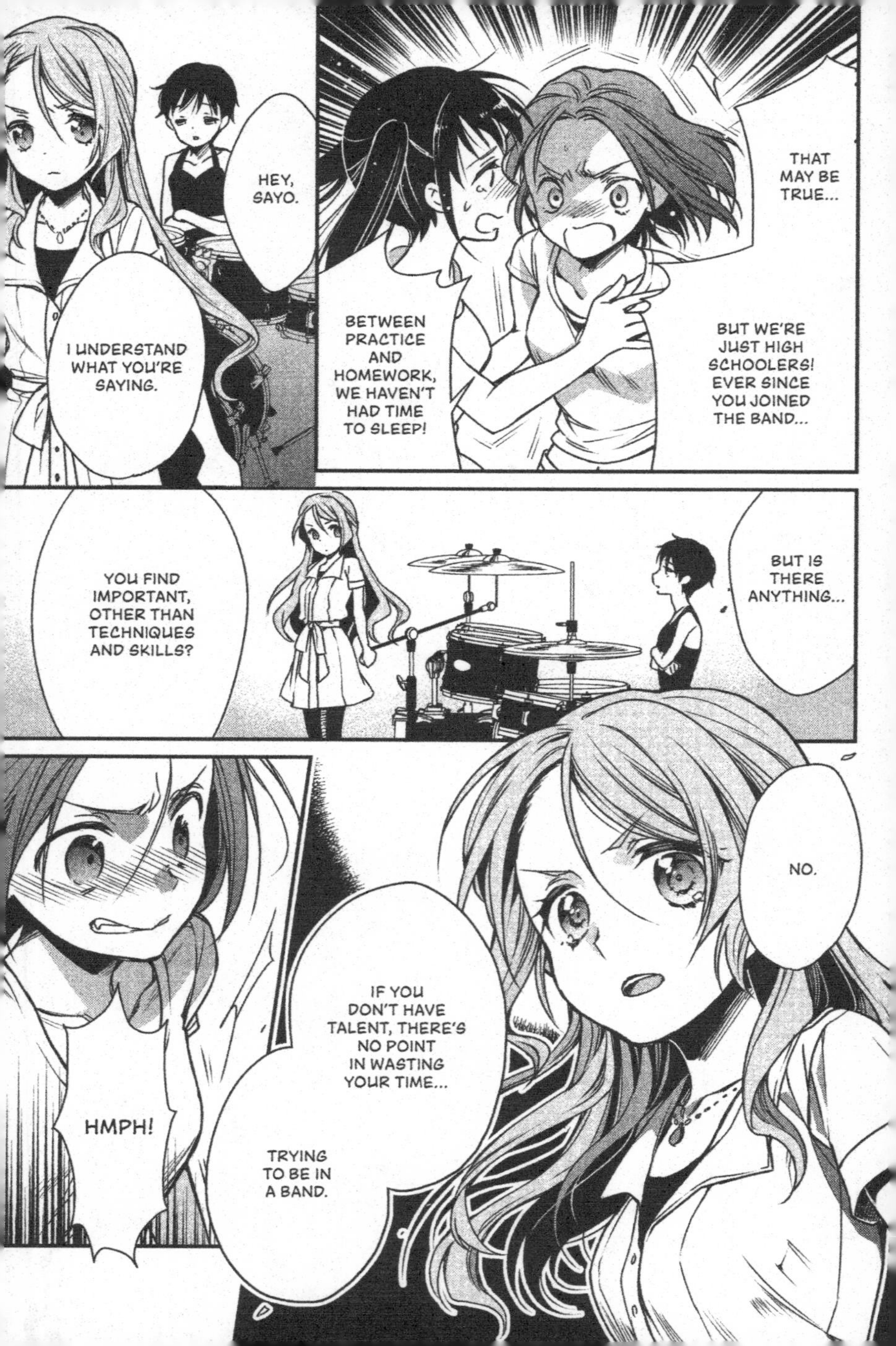
THAT MAY BE TRUE...
BUT WE'RE JUST HIGH SCHOOLERS! EVER SINCE YOU JOINED THE BAND...
BETWEEN PRACTICE AND HOMEWORK, WE HAVEN'T HAD TIME TO SLEEP!
HEY, SAYO.
I UNDERSTAND WHAT YOU'RE SAYING.
BUT IS THERE ANYTHING...
YOU FIND IMPORTANT, OTHER THAN TECHNIQUES AND SKILLS?
NO.
IF YOU DON'T HAVE TALENT, THERE'S NO POINT IN WASTING YOUR TIME...
TRYING TO BE IN A BAND.
HMPH!

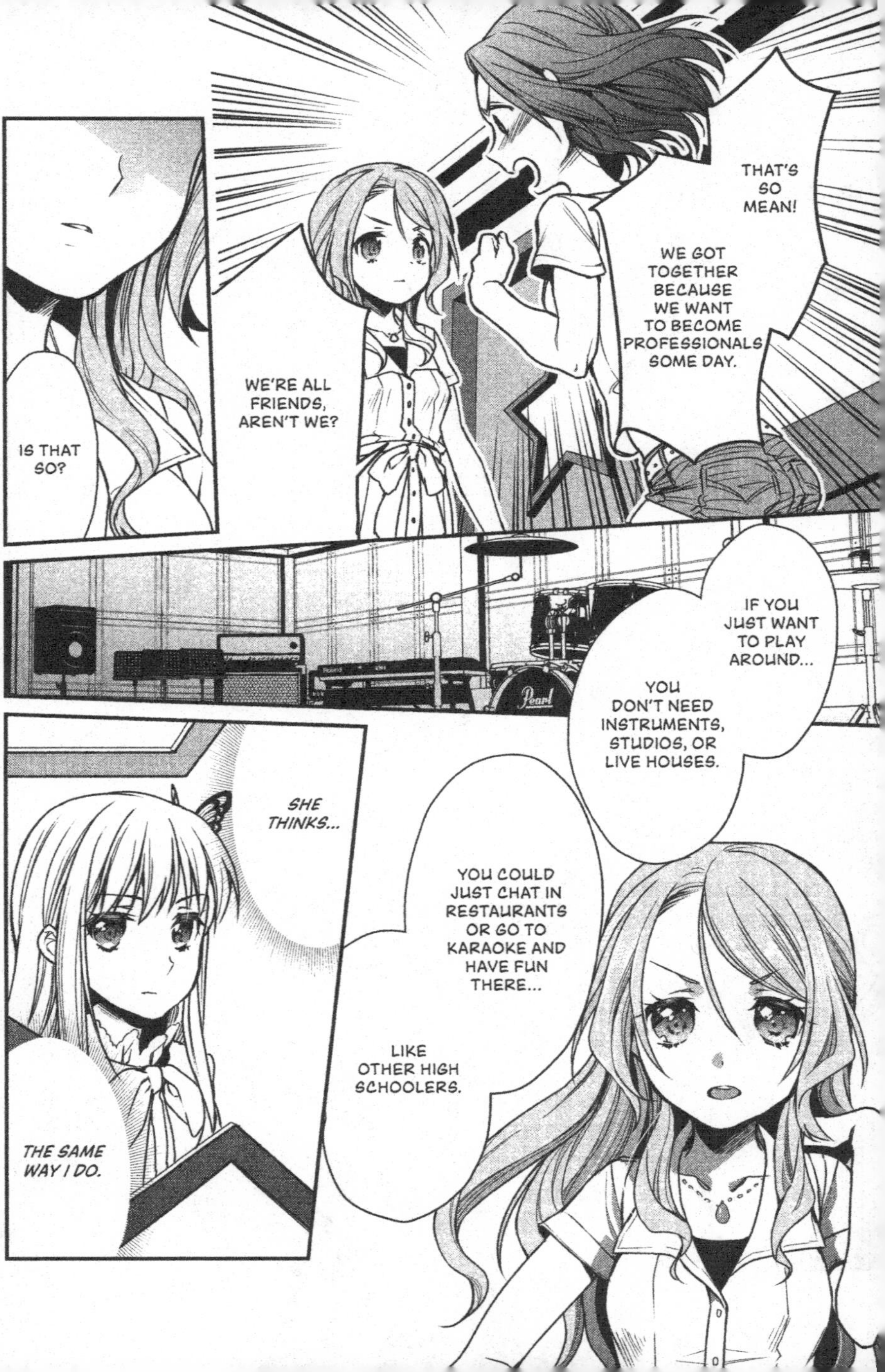
THAT'S SO MEAN!
WE GOT TOGETHER BECAUSE WE WANT TO BECOME PROFESSIONALS SOME DAY.
WE'RE ALL FRIENDS, AREN'T WE?
IS THAT SO?
IF YOU JUST WANT TO PLAY AROUND...
YOU DON'T NEED INSTRUMENTS, STUDIOS, OR LIVE HOUSES.
YOU COULD JUST CHAT IN RESTAURANTS OR GO TO KARAOKE AND HAVE FUN THERE...
LIKE OTHER HIGH SCHOOLERS.
SHE THINKS...
THE SAME WAY I DO.

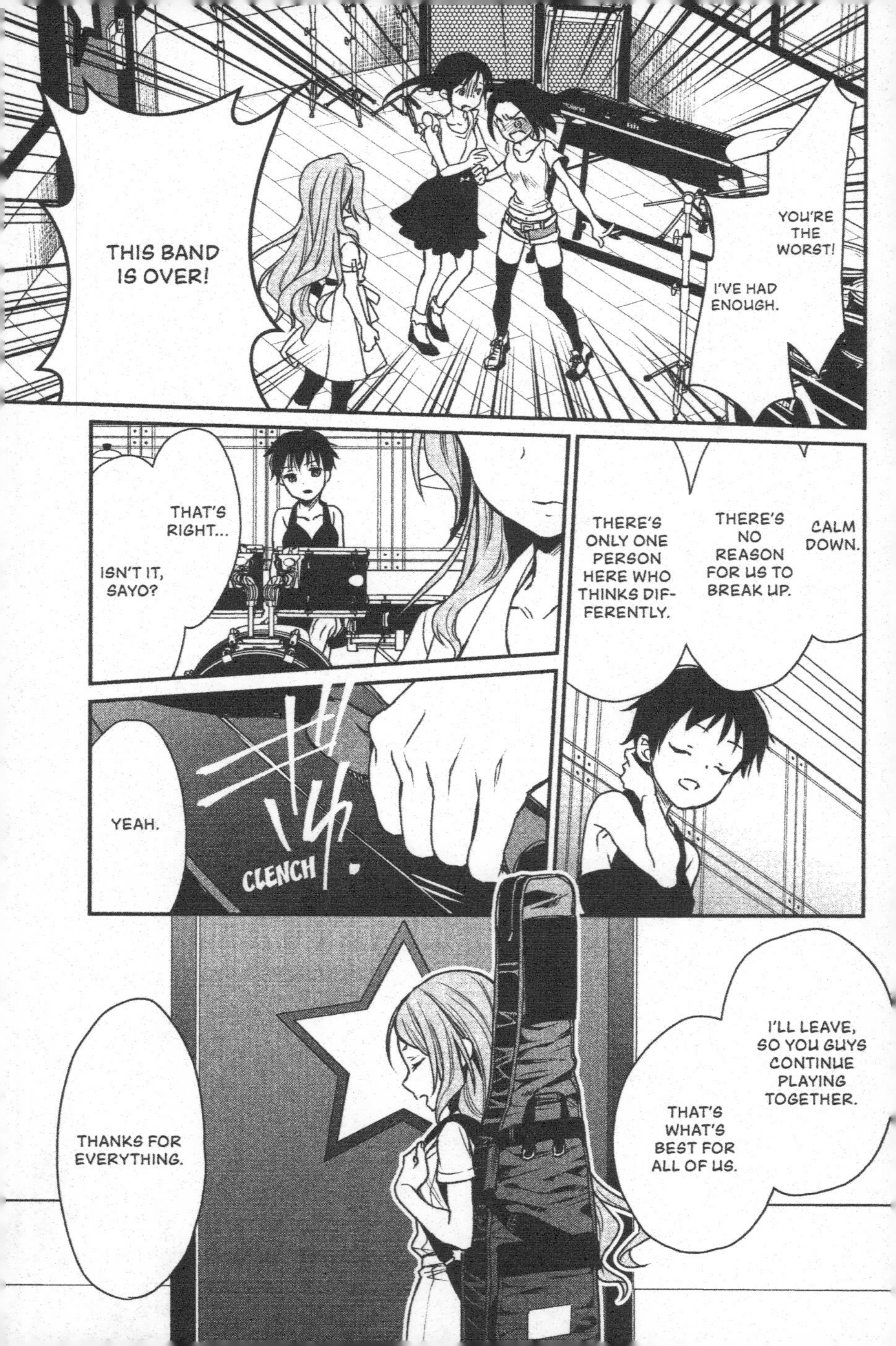
YOU'RE THE WORST!
I'VE HAD ENOUGH.
THIS BAND IS OVER!
CALM DOWN.
THERE'S NO REASON FOR US TO BREAK UP.
THERE'S ONLY ONE PERSON HERE WHO THINKS DIF-FERENTLY.
THAT'S RIGHT...
ISN'T IT, SAYO?
YEAH.
CLENCH
I'LL LEAVE, SO YOU GUYS CONTINUE PLAYING TOGETHER.
THAT'S WHAT'S BEST FOR ALL OF US.
THANKS FOR EVERYTHING.

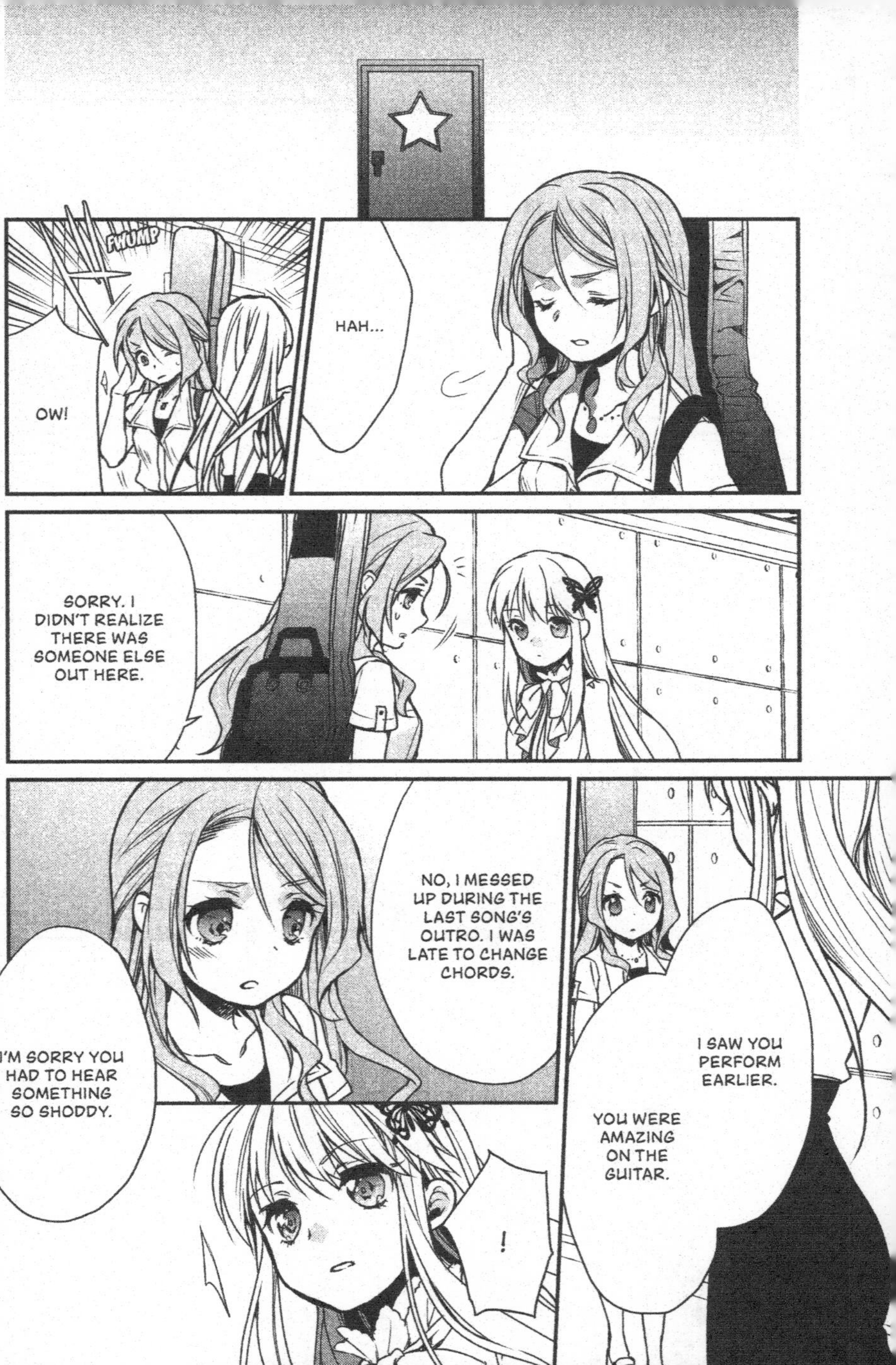
HAH...
FWUMP
OW!
SORRY. I DIDN'T REALIZE THERE WAS SOMEONE ELSE OUT HERE.
I SAW YOU PERFORM EARLIER.
YOU WERE AMAZING ON THE GUITAR.
NO, I MESSED UP DURING THE LAST SONG'S OUTRO. I WAS LATE TO CHANGE CHORDS.
I'M SORRY YOU HAD TO HEAR SOMETHING SO SHODDY.
!

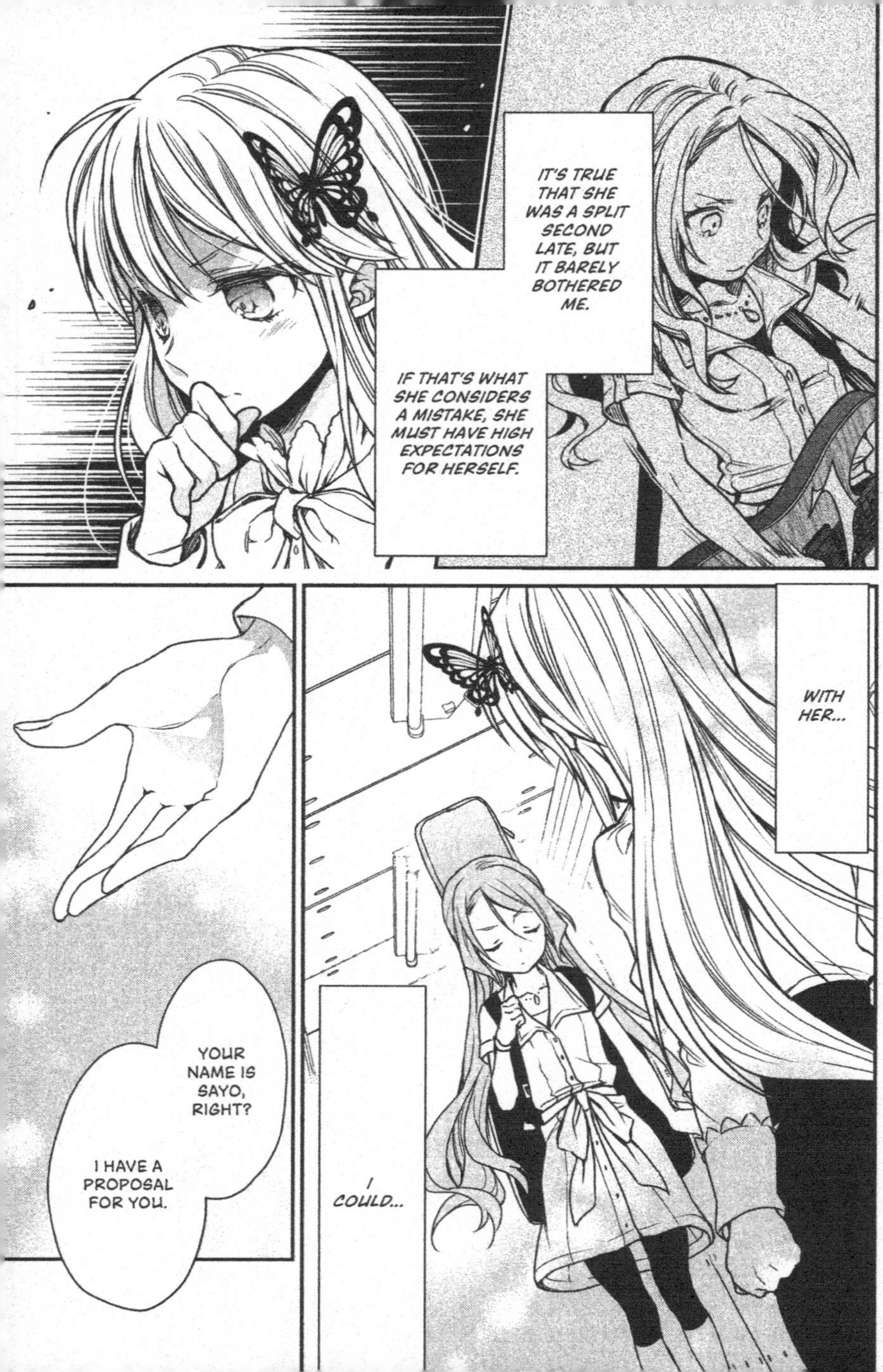
IT'S TRUE THAT SHE WAS A SPLIT SECOND LATE, BUT IT BARELY BOTHERED ME.
IF THAT'S WHAT SHE CONSIDERS A MISTAKE, SHE MUST HAVE HIGH EXPECTATIONS FOR HERSELF.
WITH HER...
I COULD...
YOUR NAME IS SAYO, RIGHT?
I HAVE A PROPOSAL FOR YOU.

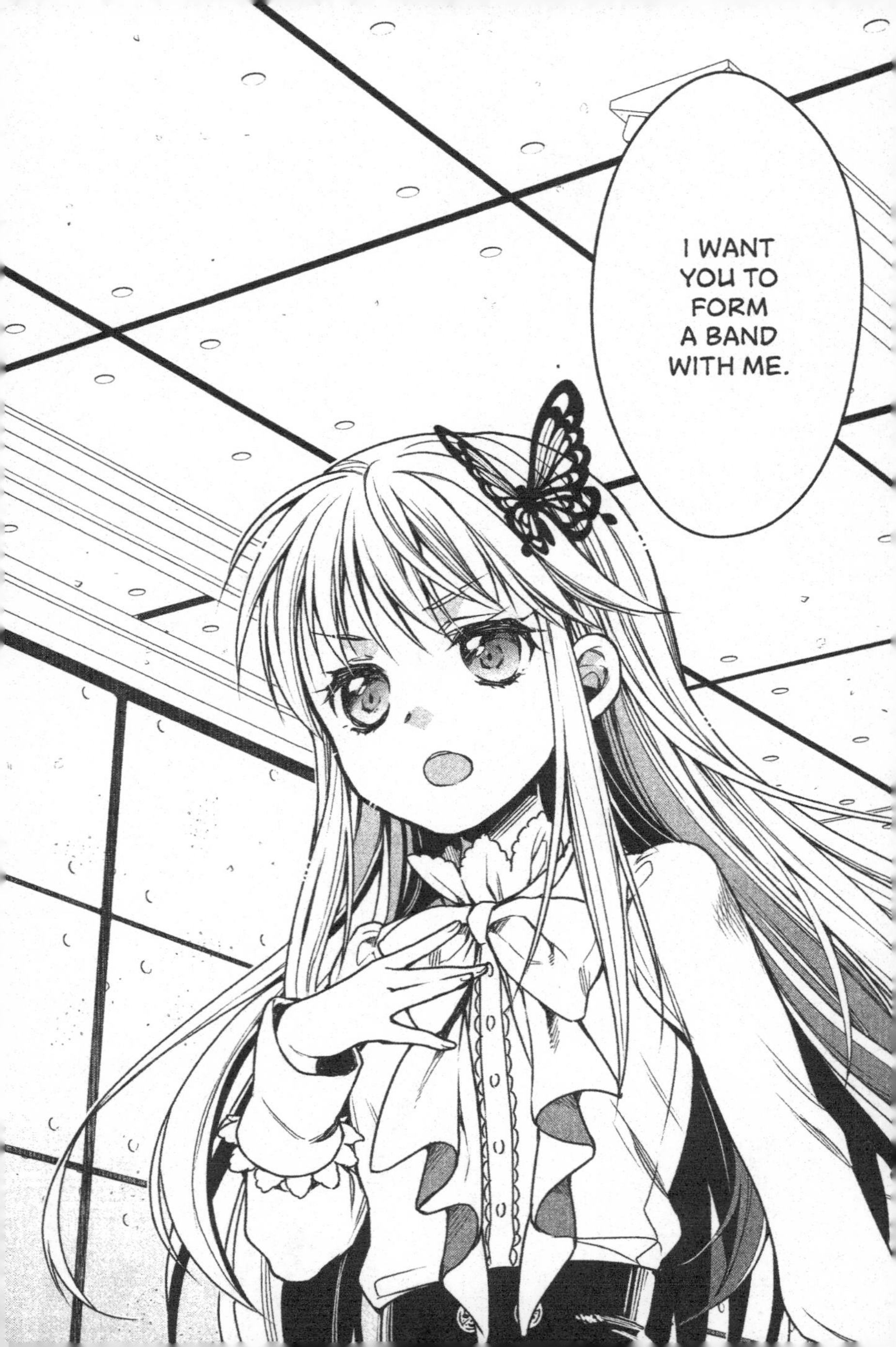
I WANT YOU TO FORM A BAND WITH ME.

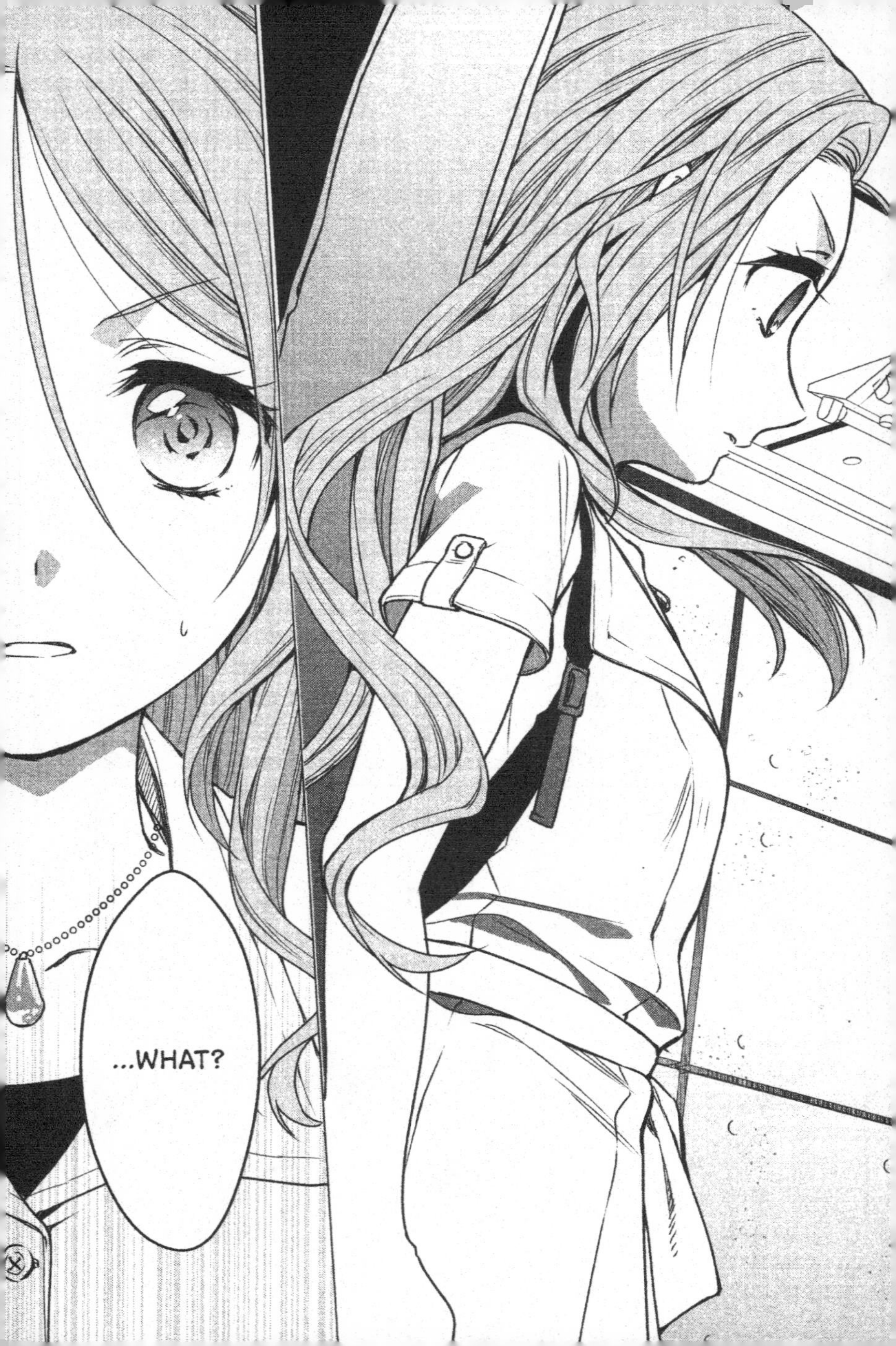
...WHAT?

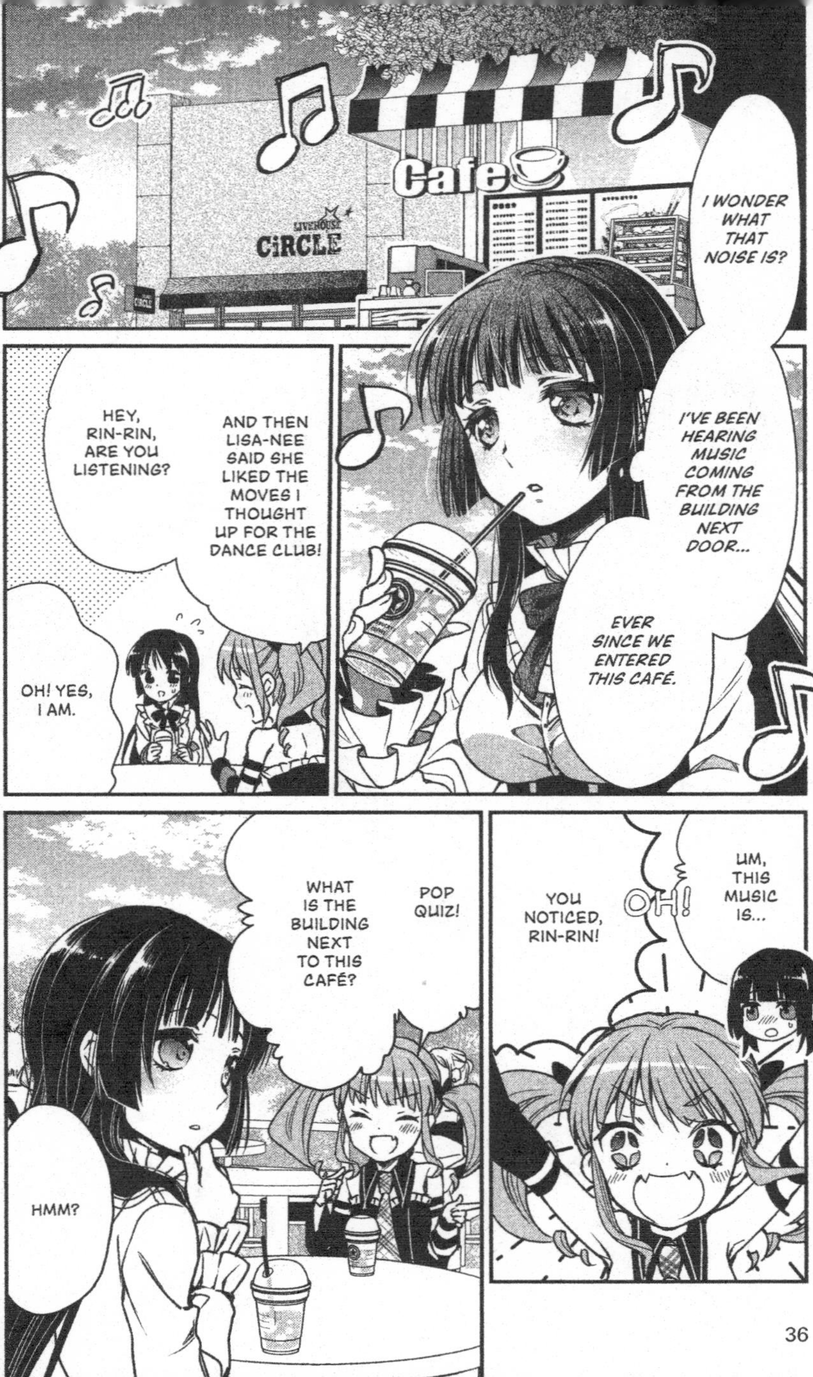
Cafe
LIVEHOUSE
CiRCLE
CiRCLE
I WONDER WHAT THAT NOISE IS?
I'VE BEEN HEARING MUSIC COMING FROM THE BUILDING NEXT DOOR...
EVER SINCE WE ENTERED THIS CAFÉ.
AND THEN LISA-NEE SAID SHE LIKED THE MOVES I THOUGHT UP FOR THE DANCE CLUB!
HEY, RIN-RIN, ARE YOU LISTENING?
OH! YES, I AM.
UM, THIS MUSIC IS...
OH!
YOU NOTICED, RIN-RIN!
POP QUIZ!
WHAT IS THE BUILDING NEXT TO THIS CAFÉ?
HMM?

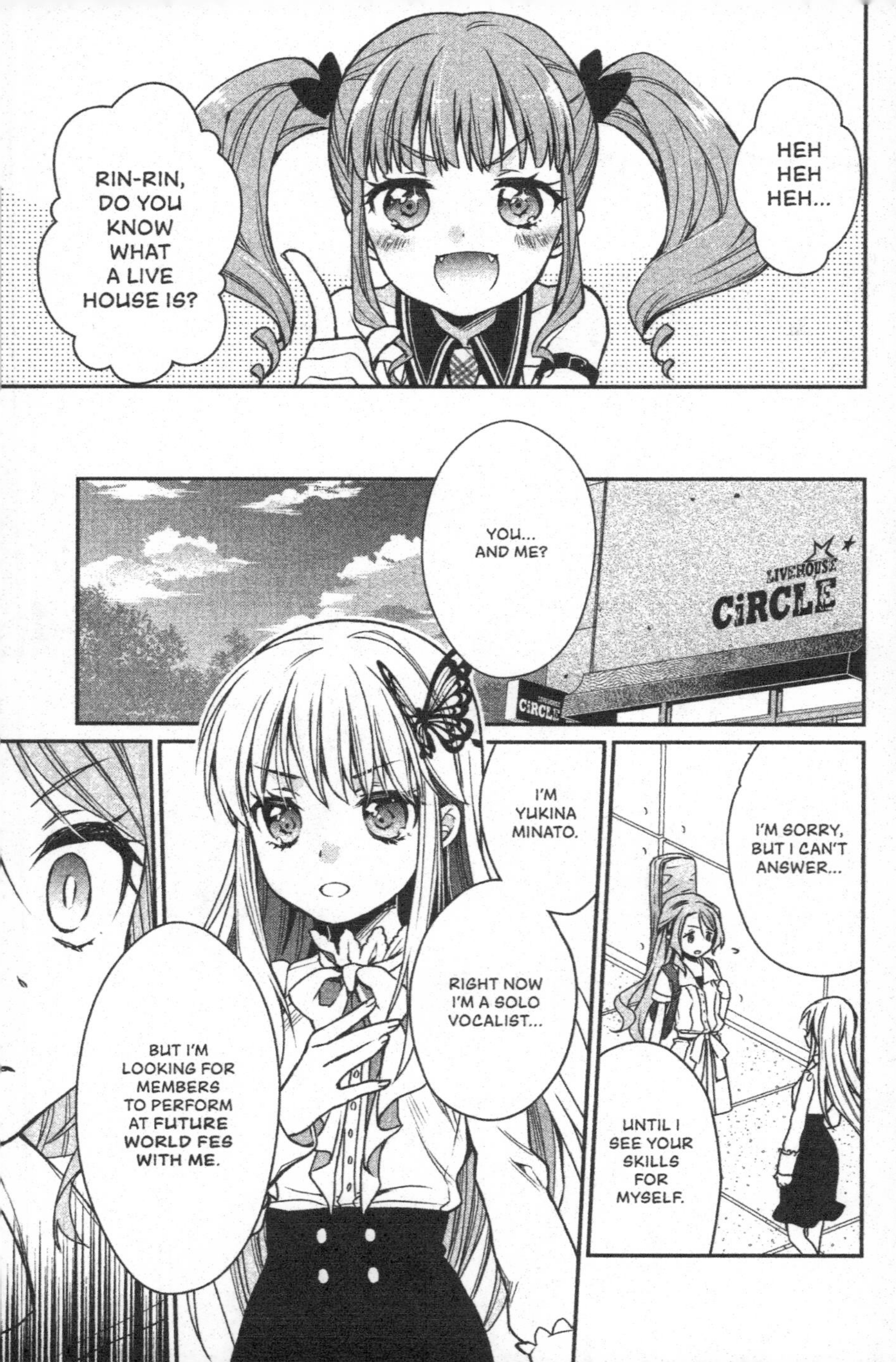
HEH HEH HEH...
RIN-RIN, DO YOU KNOW WHAT A LIVE HOUSE IS?
YOU... AND ME?
LIVEHOUSE CiRCLE
CiRCLE
I'M SORRY, BUT I CAN'T ANSWER...
UNTIL I SEE YOUR SKILLS FOR MYSELF.
I'M YUKINA MINATO.
RIGHT NOW I'M A SOLO VOCALIST...
BUT I'M LOOKING FOR MEMBERS TO PERFORM AT FUTURE WORLD FES WITH ME.

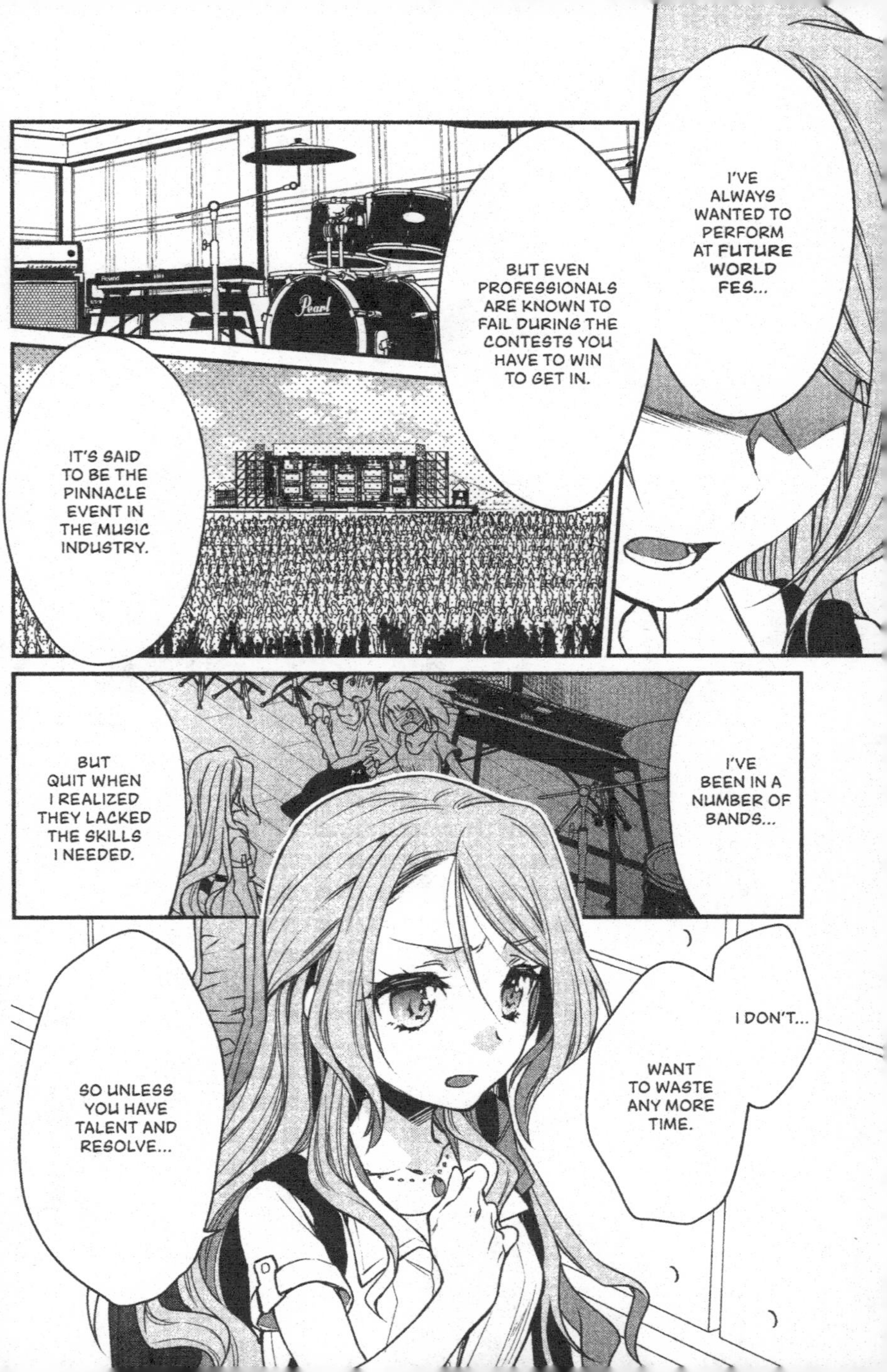
I'VE ALWAYS WANTED TO PERFORM AT FUTURE WORLD FES...
BUT EVEN PROFESSIONALS ARE KNOWN TO FAIL DURING THE CONTESTS YOU HAVE TO WIN TO GET IN.
IT'S SAID TO BE THE PINNACLE EVENT IN THE MUSIC INDUSTRY.
I'VE BEEN IN A NUMBER OF BANDS...
BUT QUIT WHEN I REALIZED THEY LACKED THE SKILLS I NEEDED.
I DON'T...
WANT TO WASTE ANY MORE TIME.
SO UNLESS YOU HAVE TALENT AND RESOLVE...

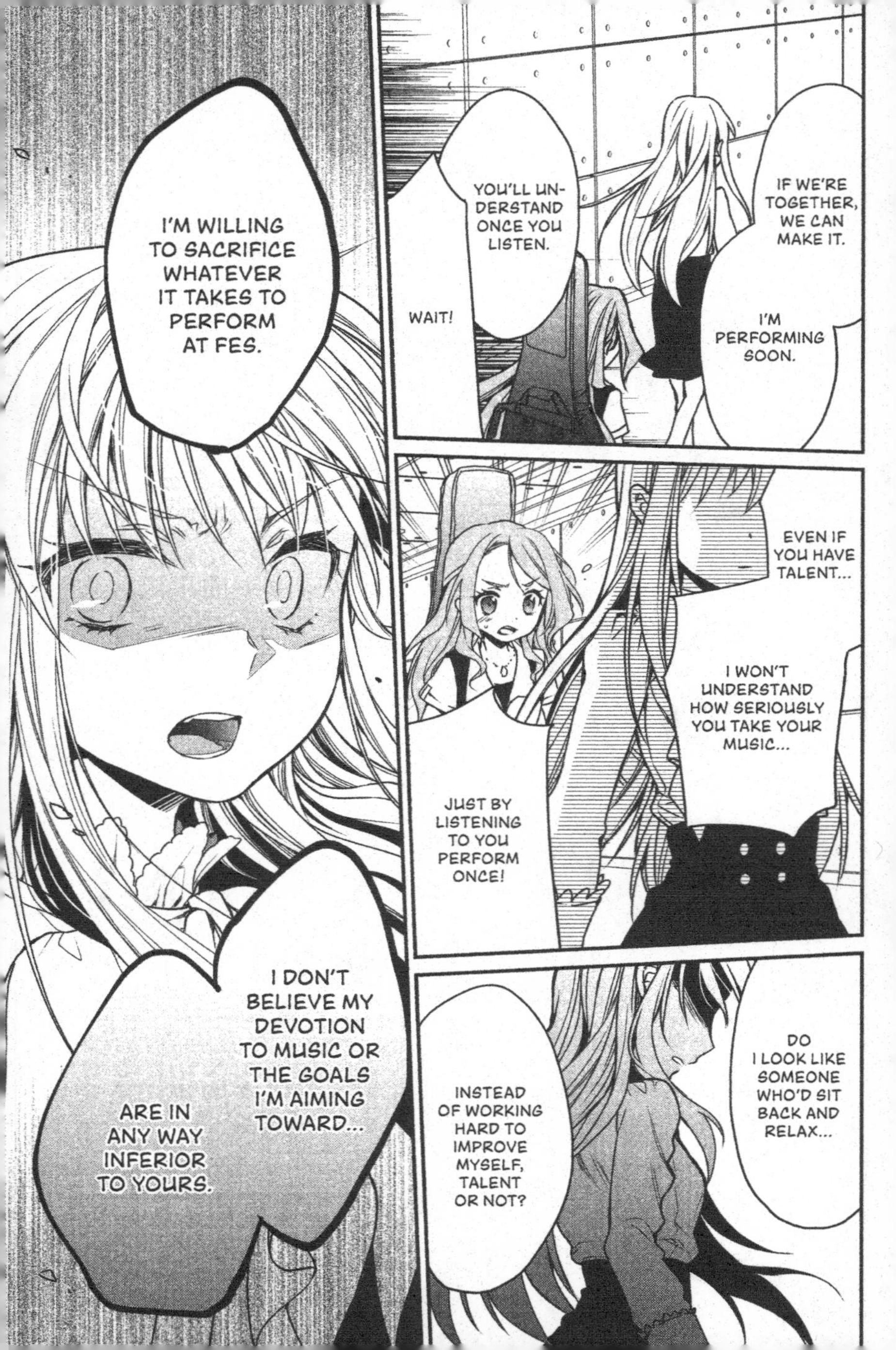
IF WE'RE TOGETHER, WE CAN MAKE IT.
I'M PERFORMING SOON.
YOU'LL UN-DERSTAND ONCE YOU LISTEN.
WAIT!
EVEN IF YOU HAVE TALENT...
I WON'T UNDERSTAND HOW SERIOUSLY YOU TAKE YOUR MUSIC...
JUST BY LISTENING TO YOU PERFORM ONCE!
DO I LOOK LIKE SOMEONE WHO'D SIT BACK AND RELAX...
INSTEAD OF WORKING HARD TO IMPROVE MYSELF, TALENT OR NOT?
I'M WILLING TO SACRIFICE WHATEVER IT TAKES TO PERFORM AT FES.
I DON'T BELIEVE MY DEVOTION TO MUSIC OR THE GOALS I'M AIMING TOWARD...
ARE IN ANY WAY INFERIOR TO YOURS.

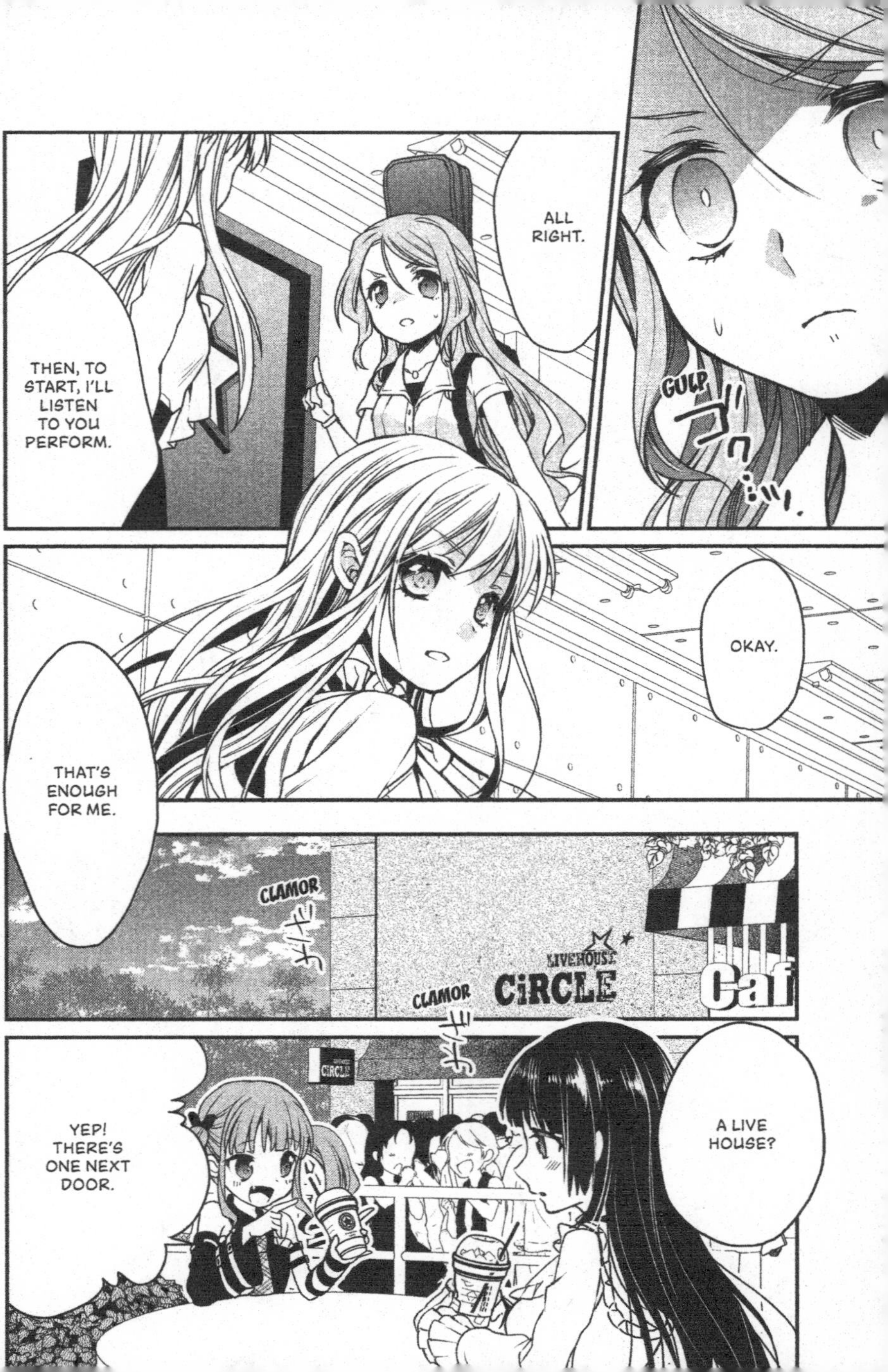
GULP
ALL RIGHT.
THEN, TO START, I'LL LISTEN TO YOU PERFORM.
OKAY.
THAT'S ENOUGH FOR ME.
Caf
LIVEHOUSE CiRCLE
CLAMOR
CLAMOR
A LIVE HOUSE?
YEP! THERE'S ONE NEXT DOOR.

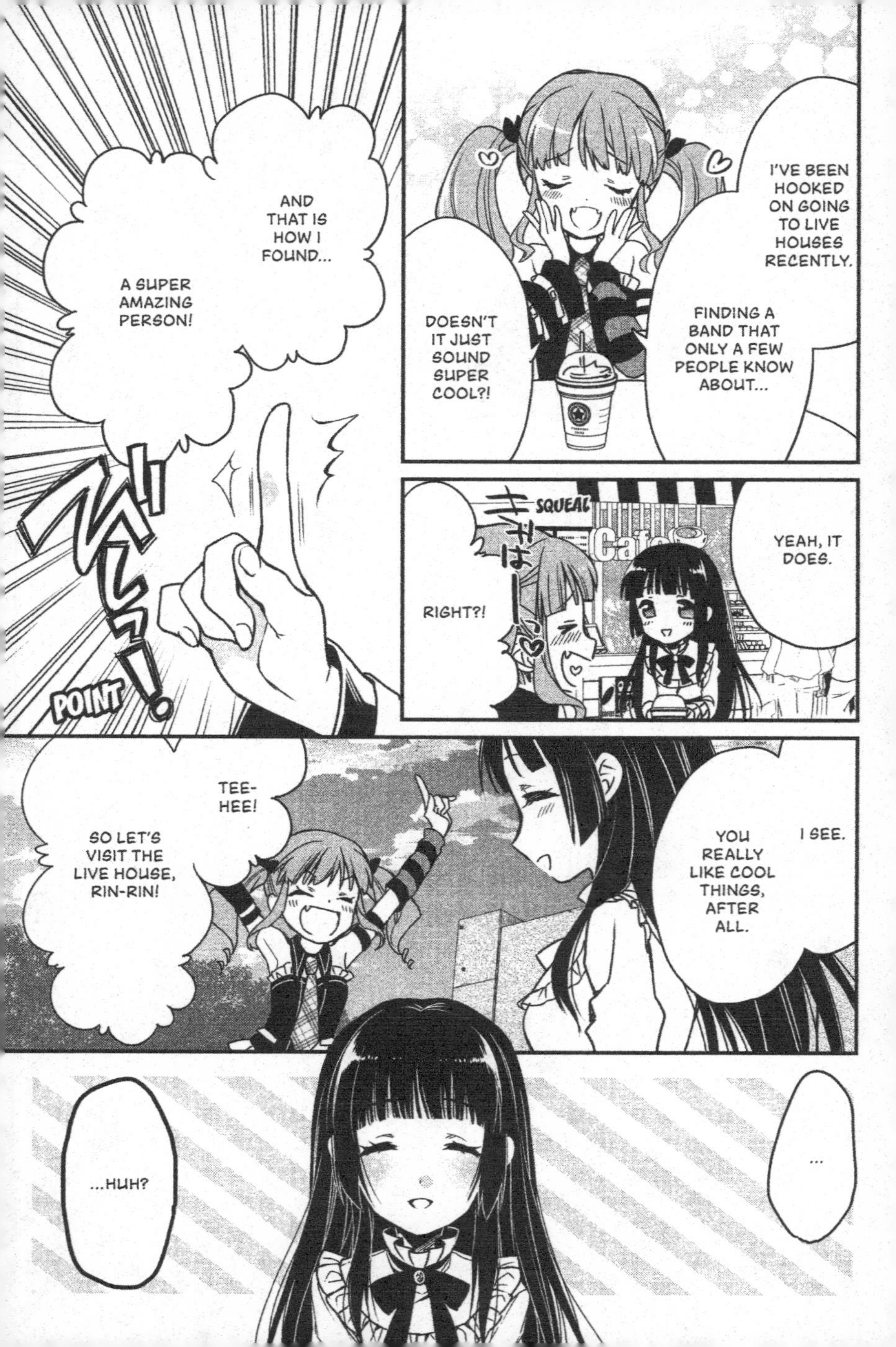
I'VE BEEN HOOKED ON GOING TO LIVE HOUSES RECENTLY.
FINDING A BAND THAT ONLY A FEW PEOPLE KNOW ABOUT...
DOESN'T IT JUST SOUND SUPER COOL?!
YEAH, IT DOES.
SQUEAL
RIGHT?!
AND THAT IS HOW I FOUND...
A SUPER AMAZING PERSON!
POINT
I SEE.
YOU REALLY LIKE COOL THINGS, AFTER ALL.
TEE-HEE!
SO LET'S VISIT THE LIVE HOUSE, RIN-RIN!
...
...HUH?

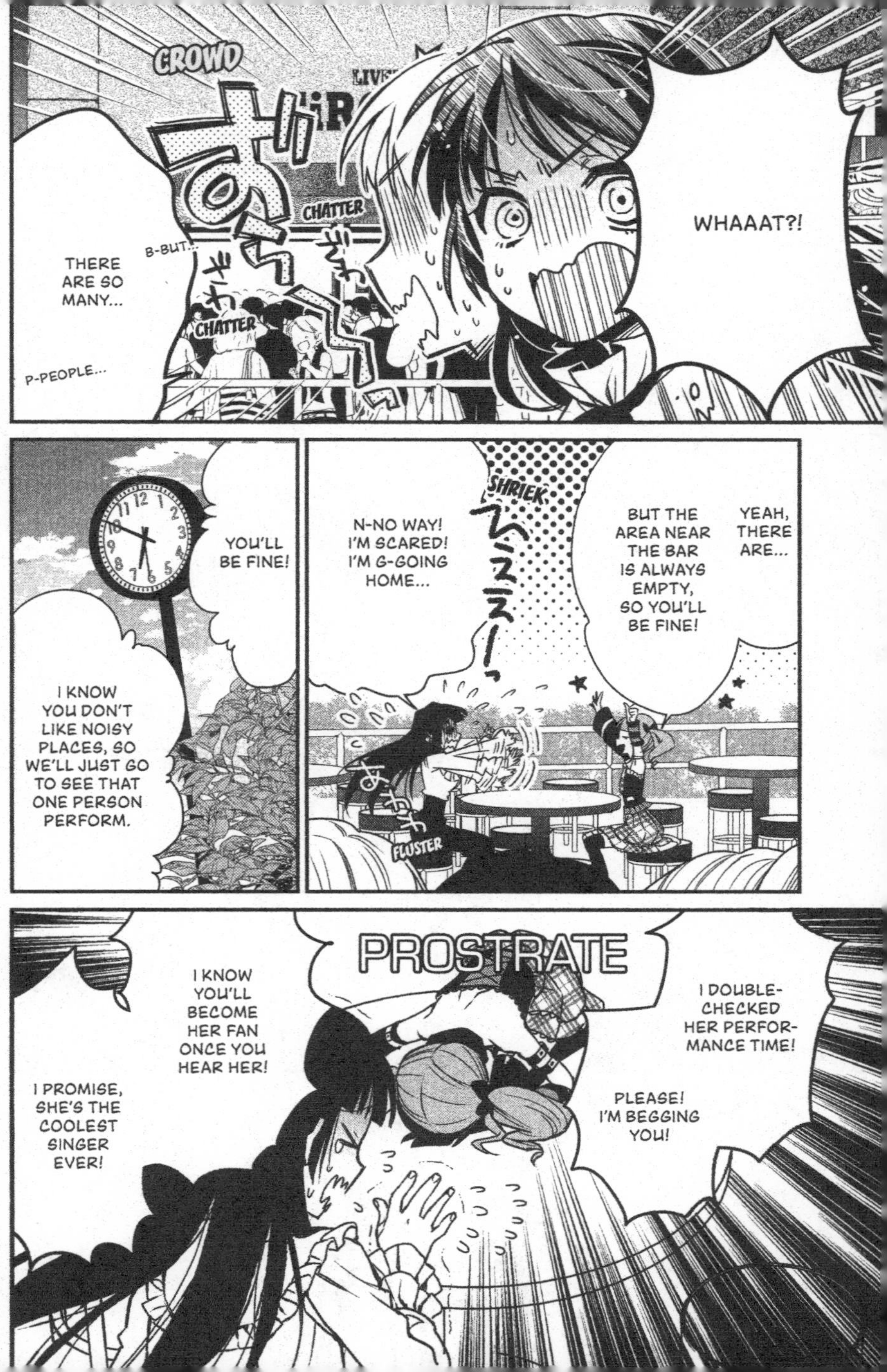
WHAAAT?!
CROWD
CHATTER
B-BUT...
THERE ARE SO MANY...
CHATTER
P-PEOPLE...
YEAH, THERE ARE...
BUT THE AREA NEAR THE BAR IS ALWAYS EMPTY, SO YOU'LL BE FINE!
SHRIEK
N-NO WAY! I'M SCARED! I'M G-GOING HOME...
FLUSTER
YOU'LL BE FINE!
I KNOW YOU DON'T LIKE NOISY PLACES, SO WE'LL JUST GO TO SEE THAT ONE PERSON PERFORM.
PROSTRATE
I DOUBLE-CHECKED HER PERFORMANCE TIME!
PLEASE! I'M BEGGING YOU!
I KNOW YOU'LL BECOME HER FAN ONCE YOU HEAR HER!
I PROMISE, SHE'S THE COOLEST SINGER EVER!

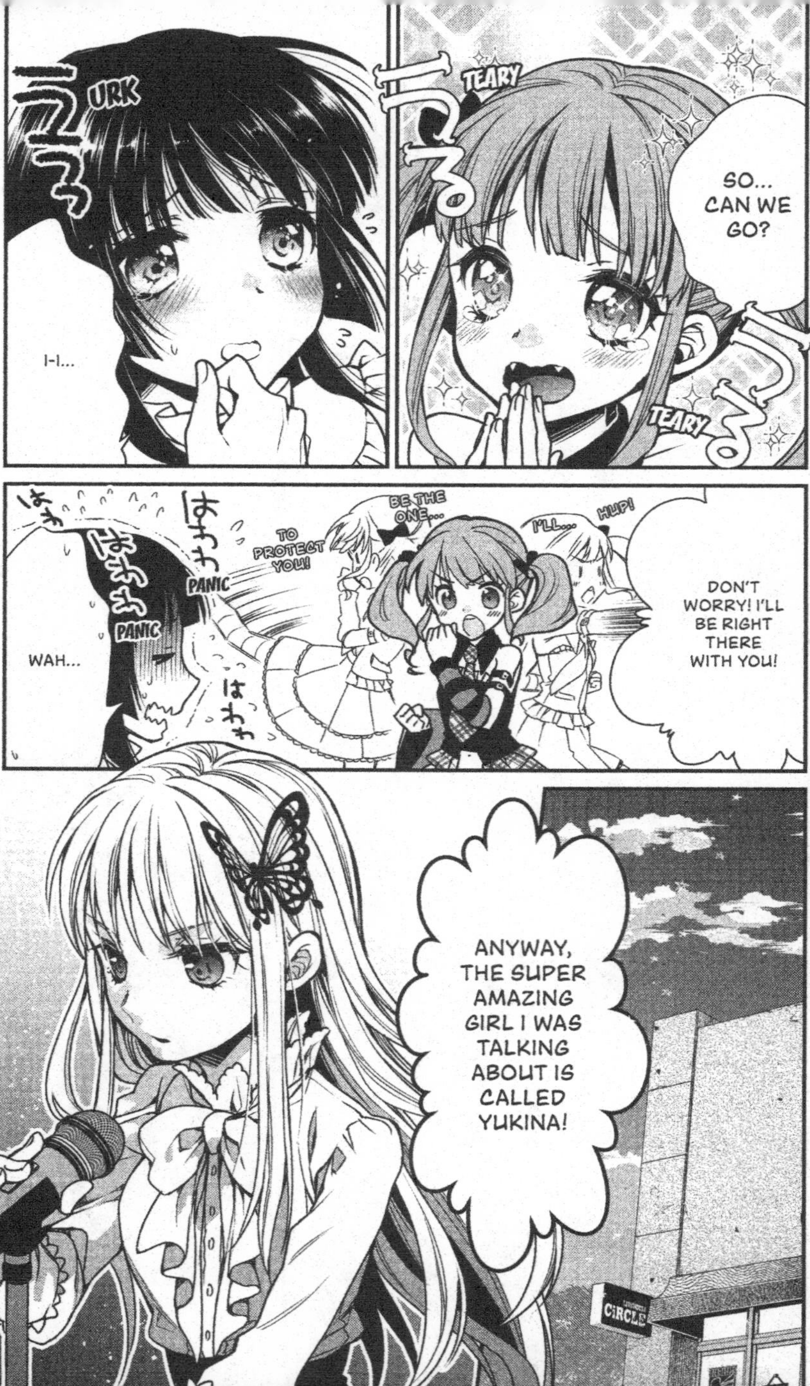
SO... CAN WE GO?
TEARY
TEARY
URK
I-I...
DON'T WORRY! I'LL BE RIGHT THERE WITH YOU!
HUP!
I'LL...
BE THE ONE...
TO PROTECT YOU!
PANIC
PANIC
WAH...
ANYWAY, THE SUPER AMAZING GIRL I WAS TALKING ABOUT IS CALLED YUKINA!
CiRCLE

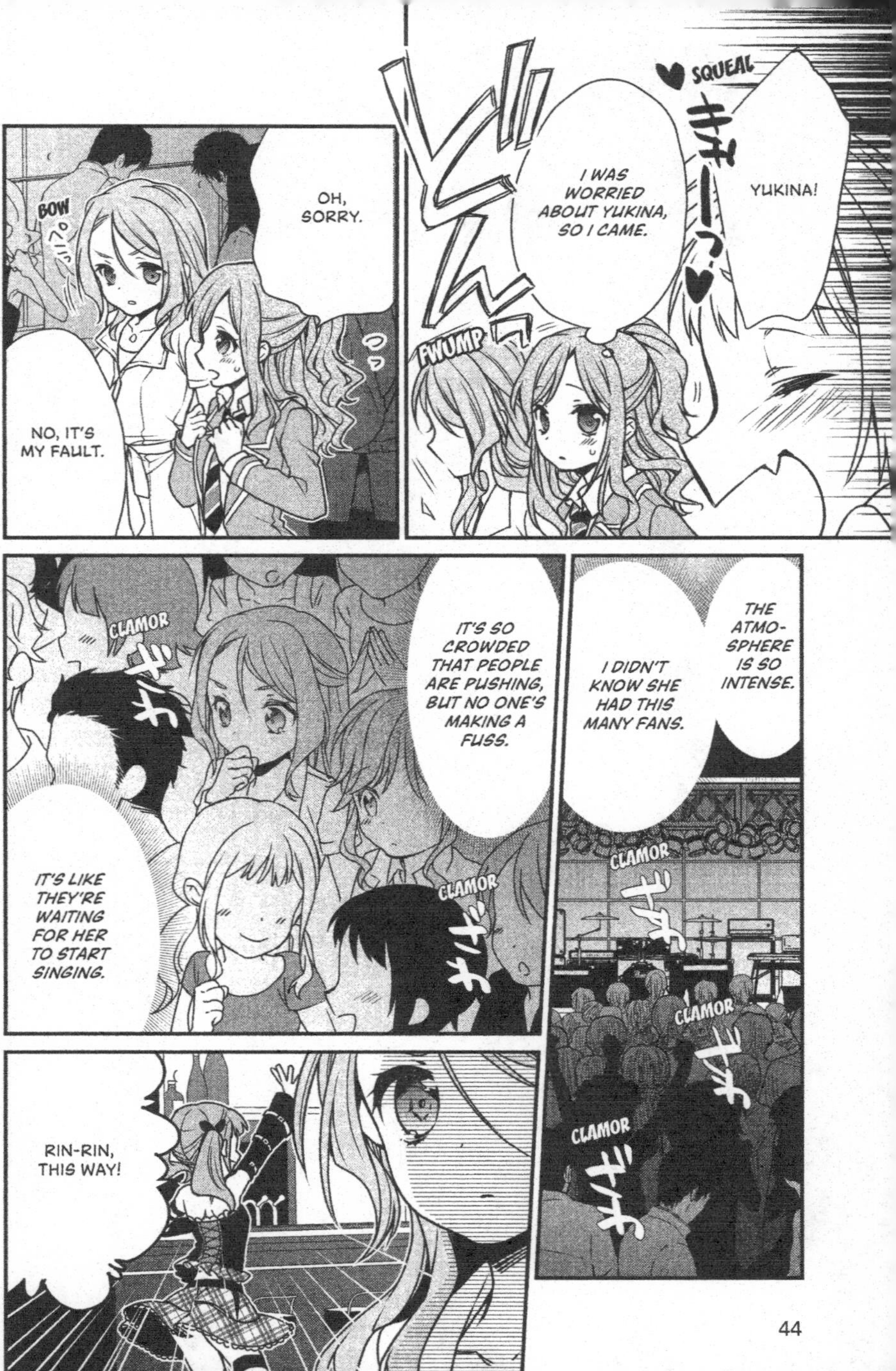

SQUEAL
YUKINA!
I WAS WORRIED ABOUT YUKINA, SO I CAME.
FWUMP
OH, SORRY.
BOW
NO, IT'S MY FAULT.
THE ATMOSPHERE IS SO INTENSE.
I DIDN'T KNOW SHE HAD THIS MANY FANS.
CLAMOR
CLAMOR
CLAMOR
IT'S SO CROWDED THAT PEOPLE ARE PUSHING, BUT NO ONE'S MAKING A FUSS.
CLAMOR
CLAMOR
IT'S LIKE THEY'RE WAITING FOR HER TO START SINGING.
RIN-RIN, THIS WAY!

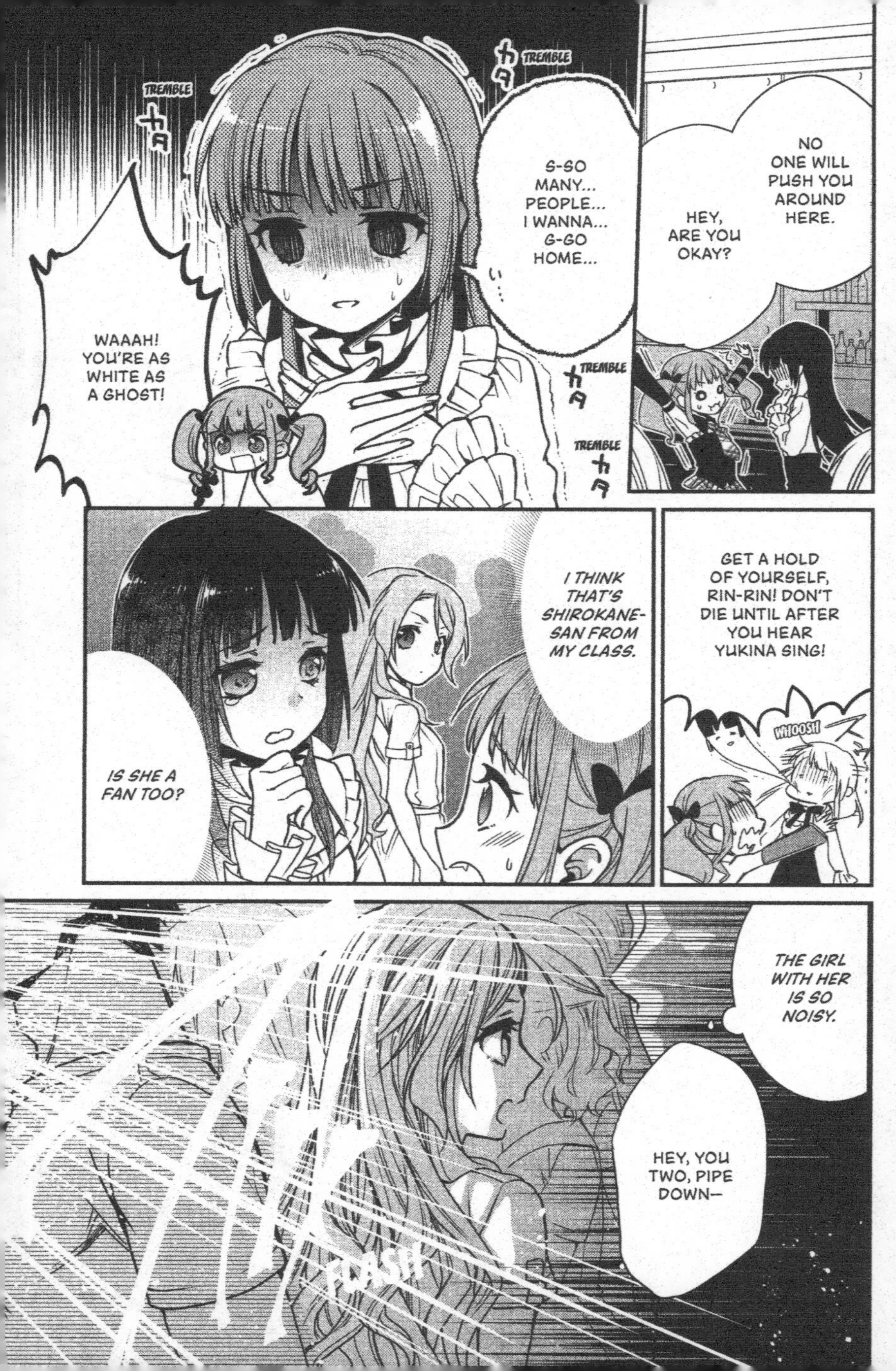
NO ONE WILL PUSH YOU AROUND HERE.
HEY, ARE YOU OKAY?
TREMBLE
S-SO MANY... PEOPLE... I WANNA... G-GO HOME...
TREMBLE
WAAAH! YOU'RE AS WHITE AS A GHOST!
TREMBLE
TREMBLE
GET A HOLD OF YOURSELF, RIN-RIN! DON'T DIE UNTIL AFTER YOU HEAR YUKINA SING!
WHOOSH
I THINK THAT'S SHIROKANE-SAN FROM MY CLASS.
IS SHE A FAN TOO?
THE GIRL WITH HER IS SO NOISY.
HEY, YOU TWO, PIPE DOWN—
FLASH!

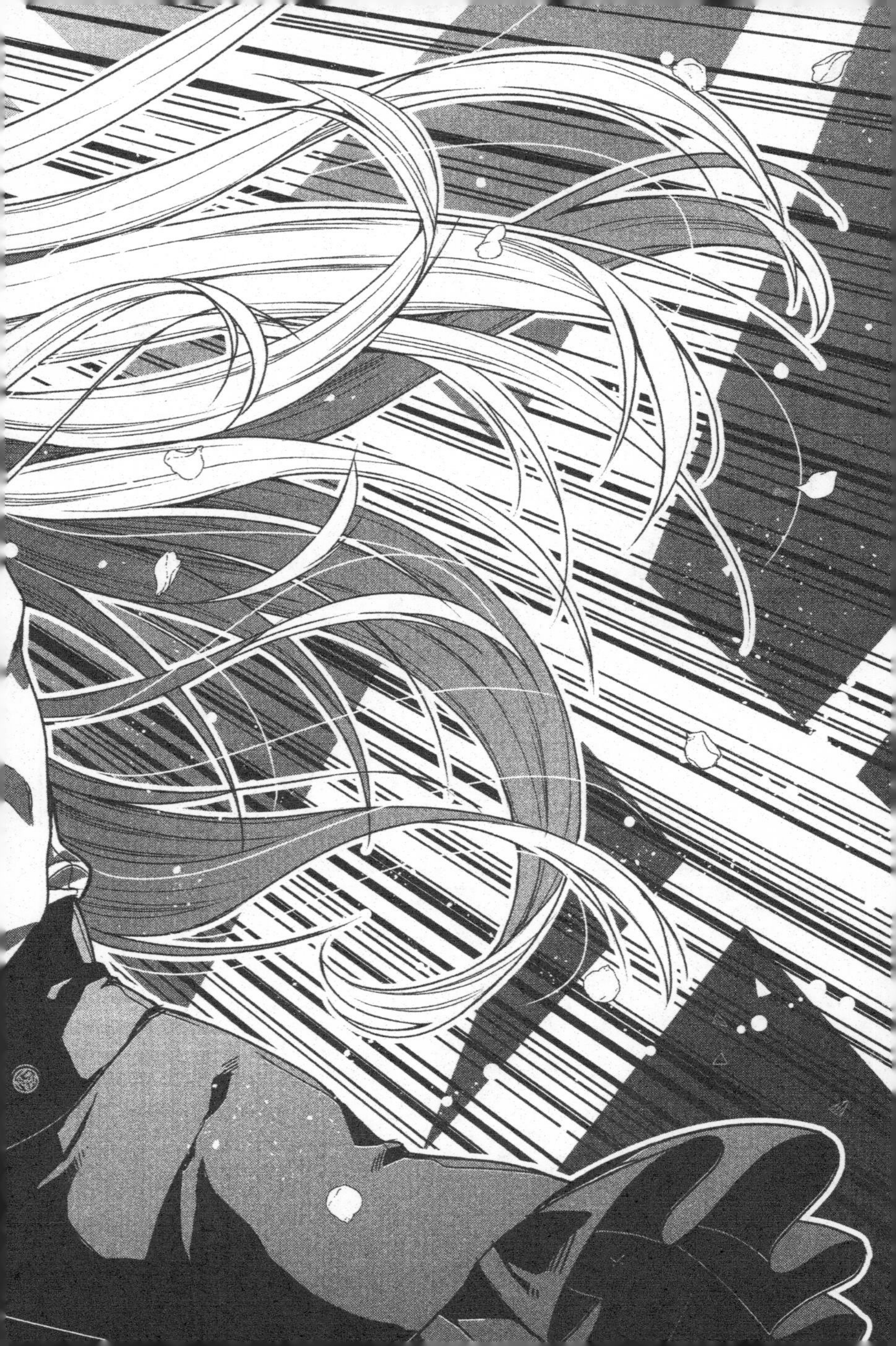

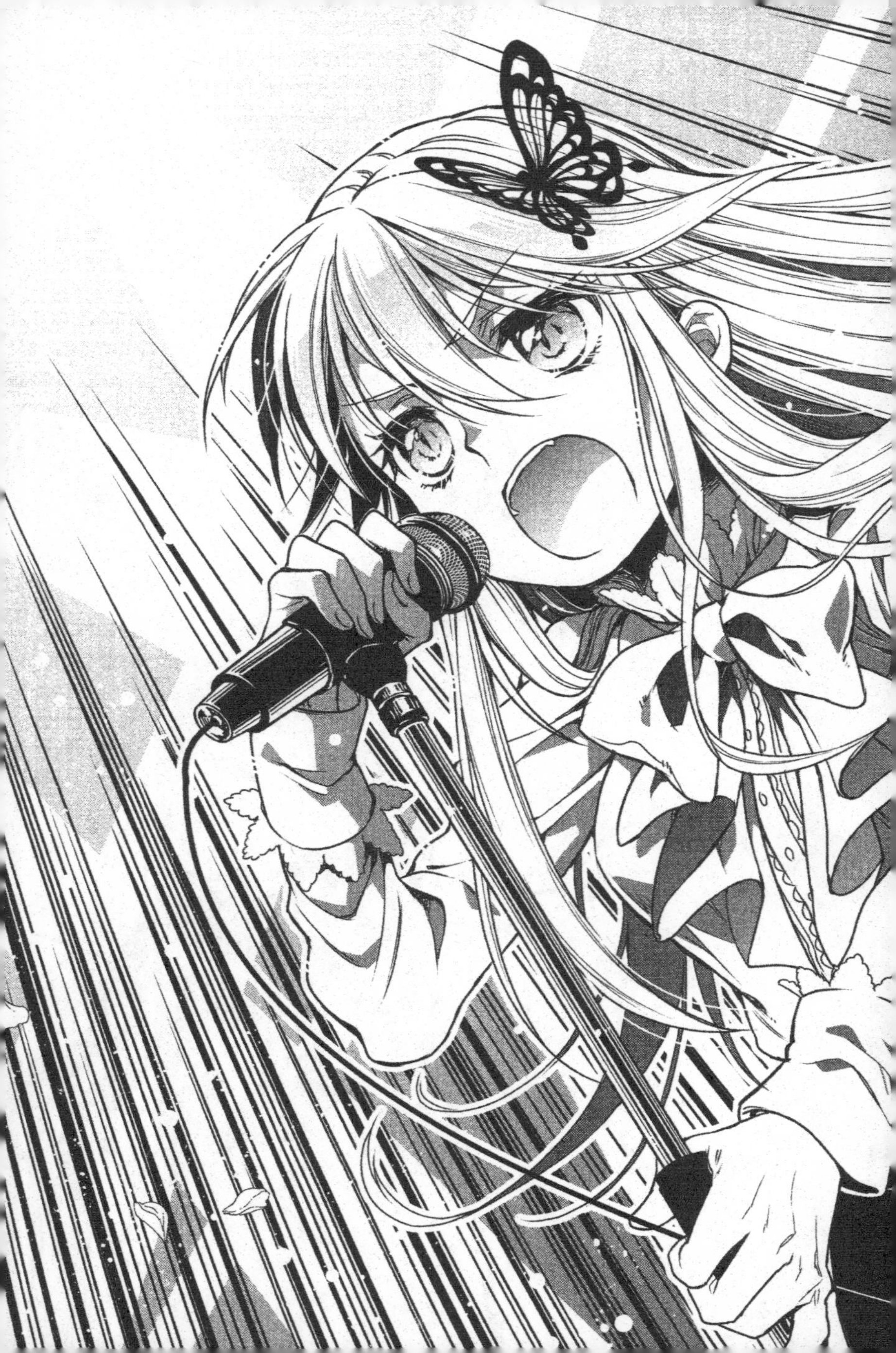

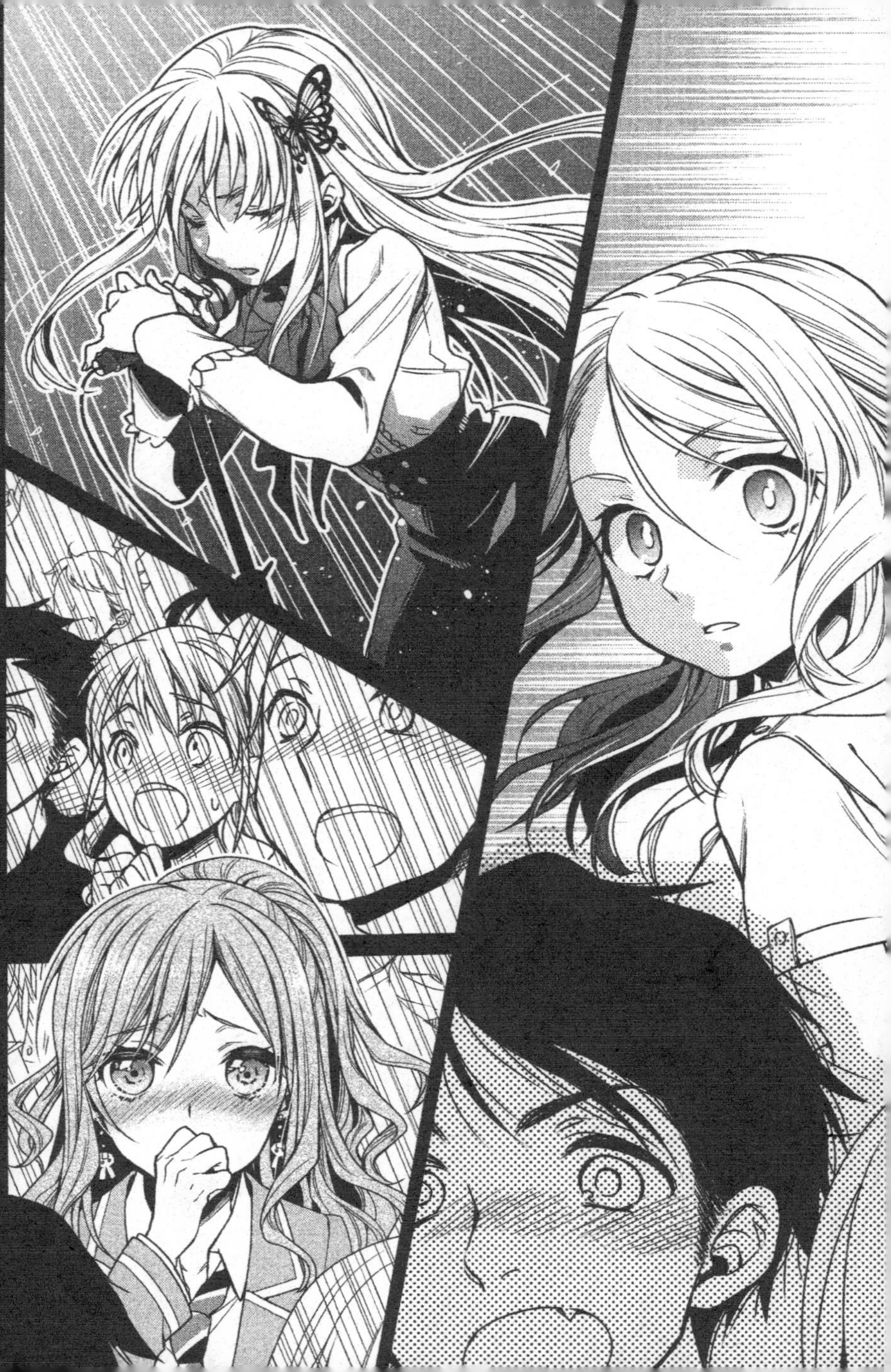

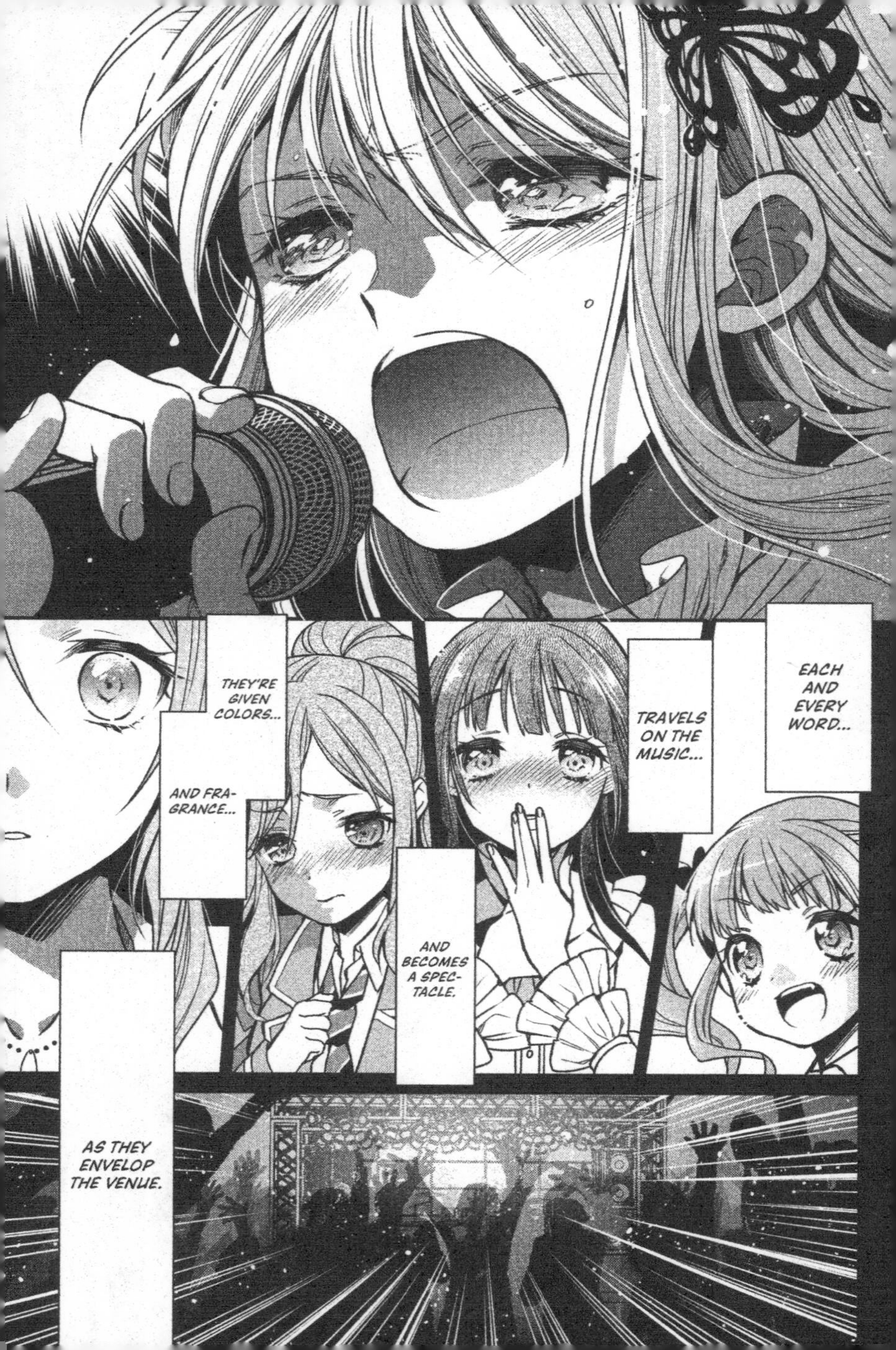
EACH AND EVERY WORD...
TRAVELS ON THE MUSIC...
AND BECOMES A SPEC-TACLE.
THEY'RE GIVEN COLORS...
AND FRA-GRANCE...
AS THEY ENVELOP THE VENUE.

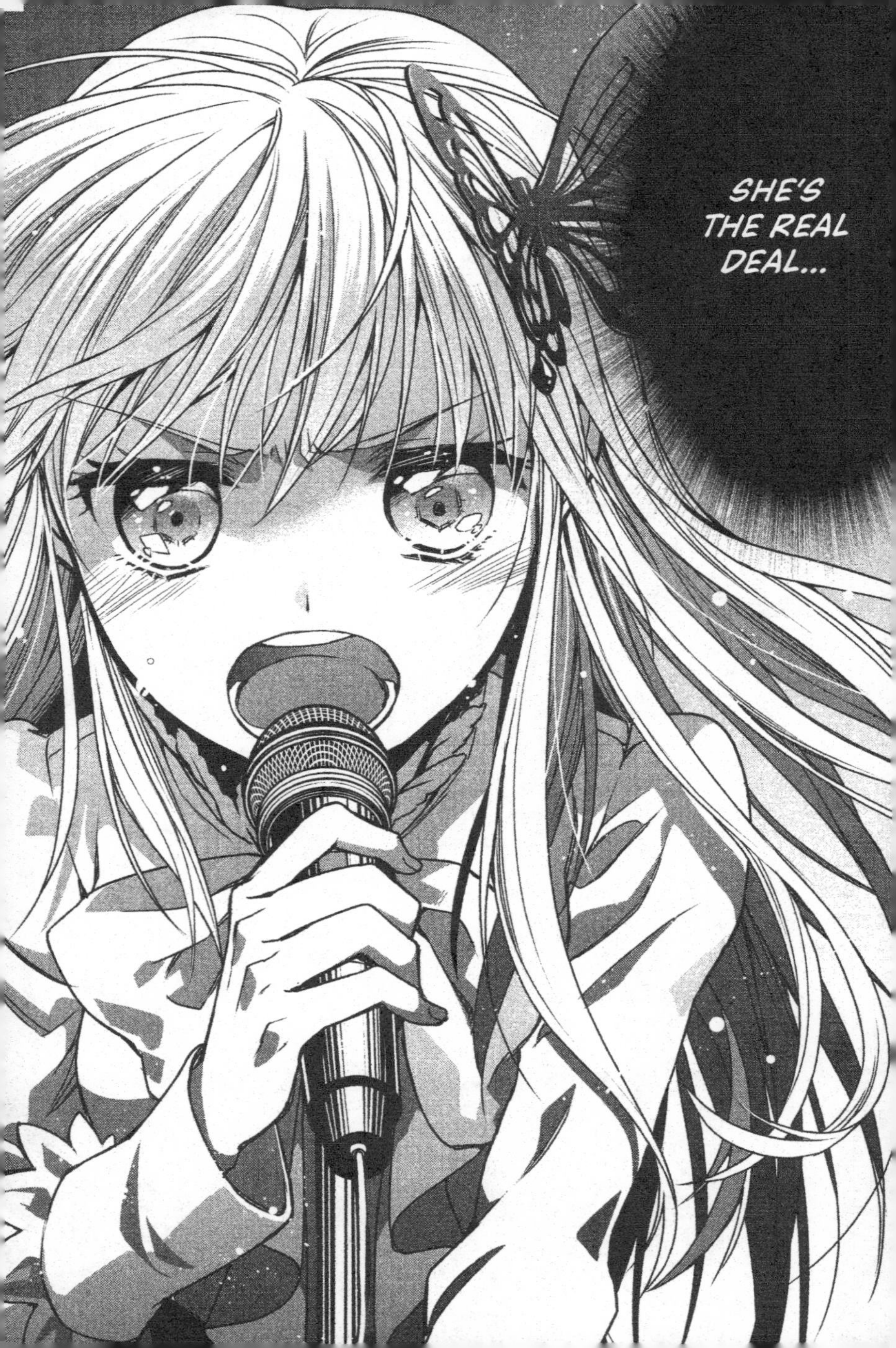
SHE'S THE REAL DEAL...

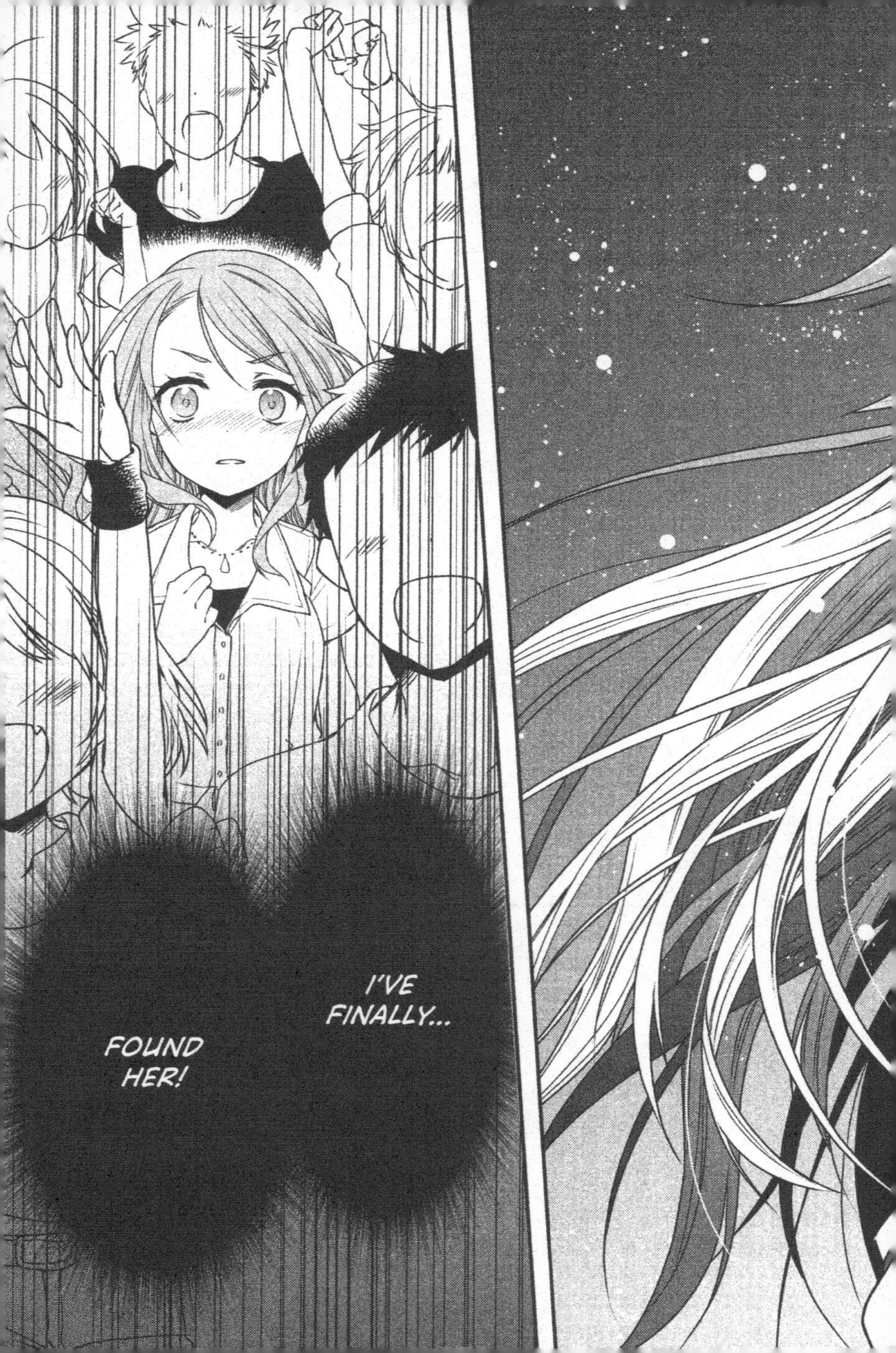
I'VE FINALLY...
FOUND HER!

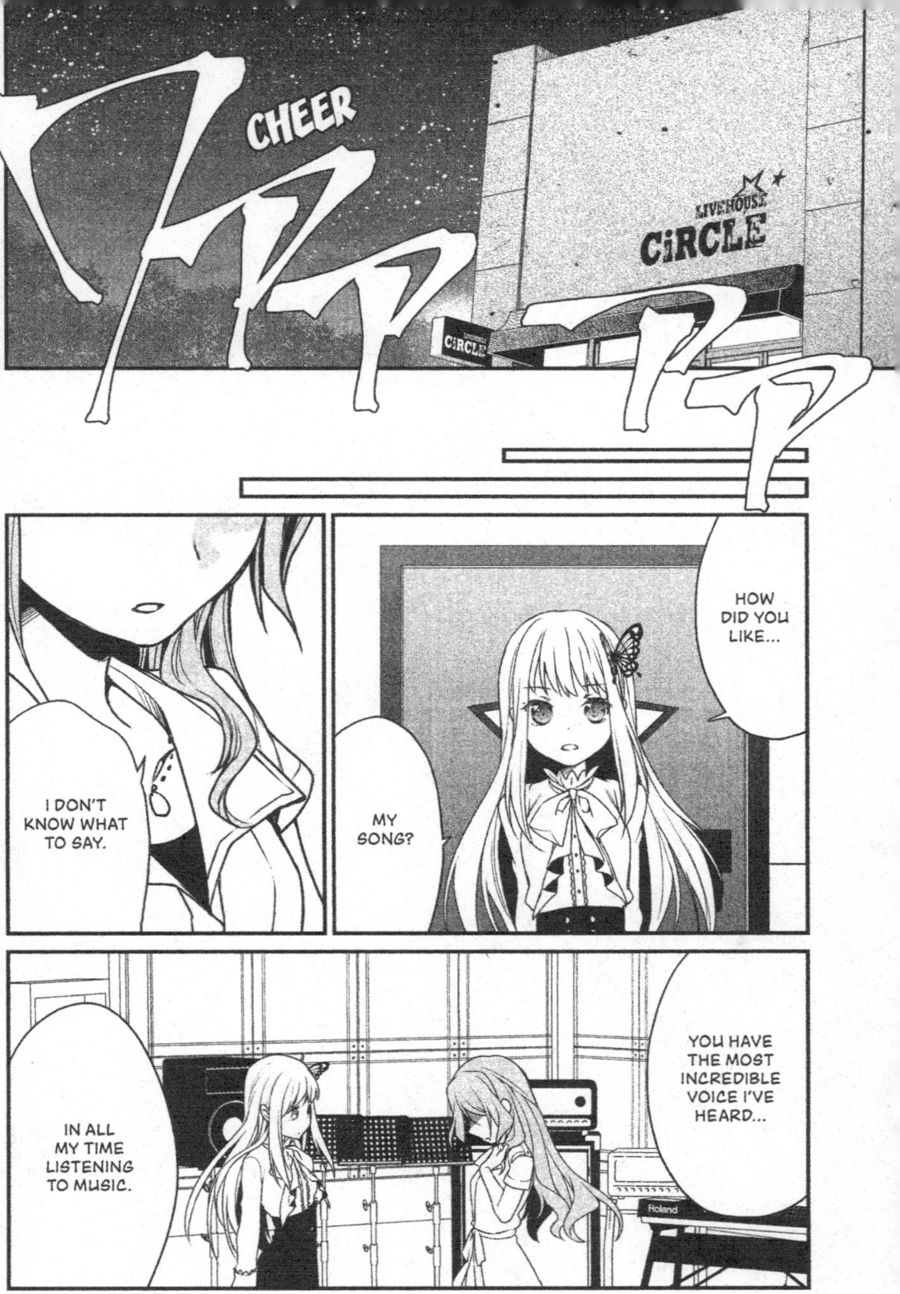
CHEER
LIVEHOUSE
CiRCLE
CiRCLE
HOW DID YOU LIKE...
MY SONG?
I DON'T KNOW WHAT TO SAY.
YOU HAVE THE MOST INCREDIBLE VOICE I'VE HEARD...
IN ALL MY TIME LISTENING TO MUSIC.
Roland

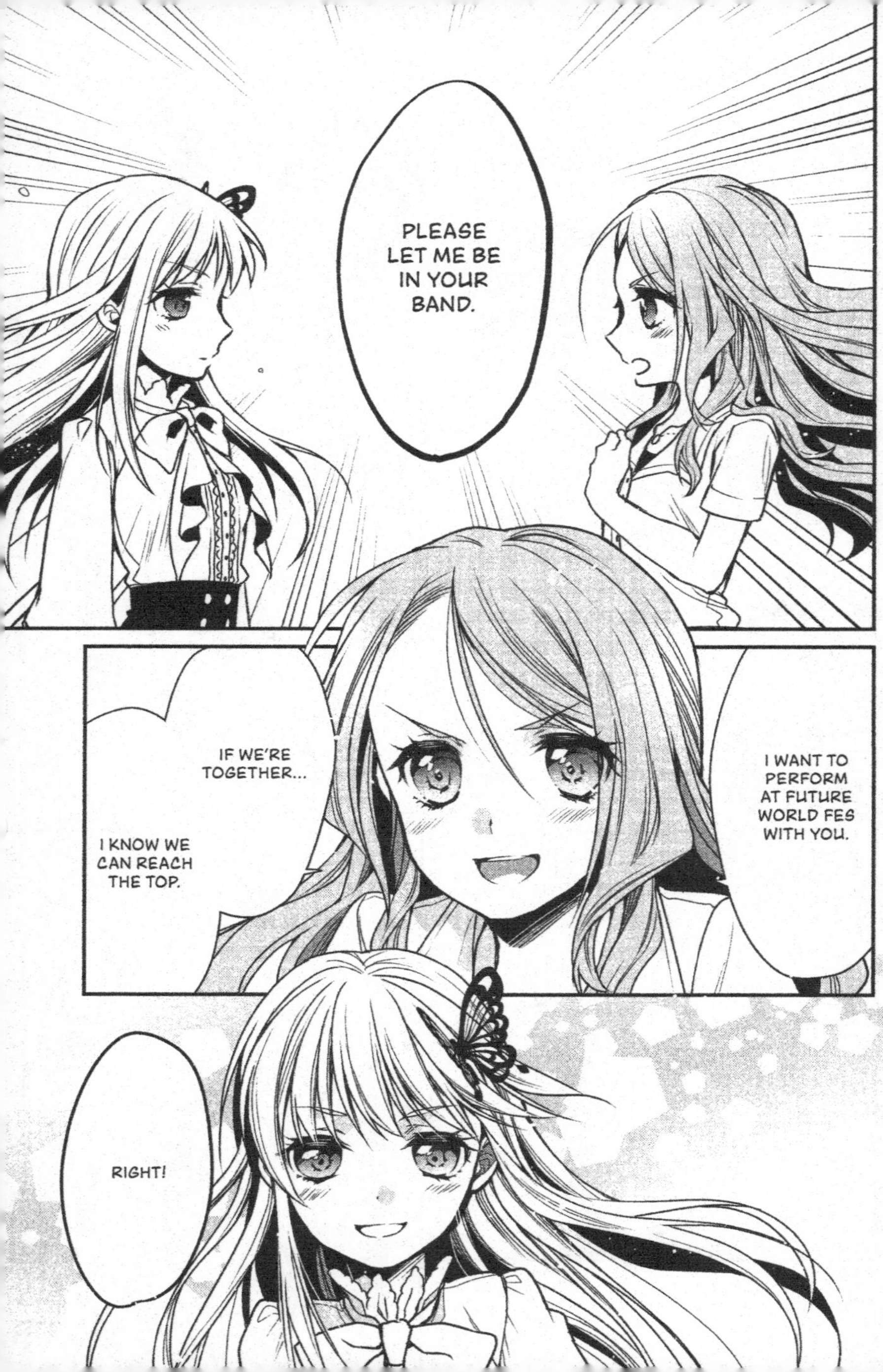
PLEASE LET ME BE IN YOUR BAND.
I WANT TO PERFORM AT FUTURE WORLD FES WITH YOU.
IF WE'RE TOGETHER...
I KNOW WE CAN REACH THE TOP.
RIGHT!

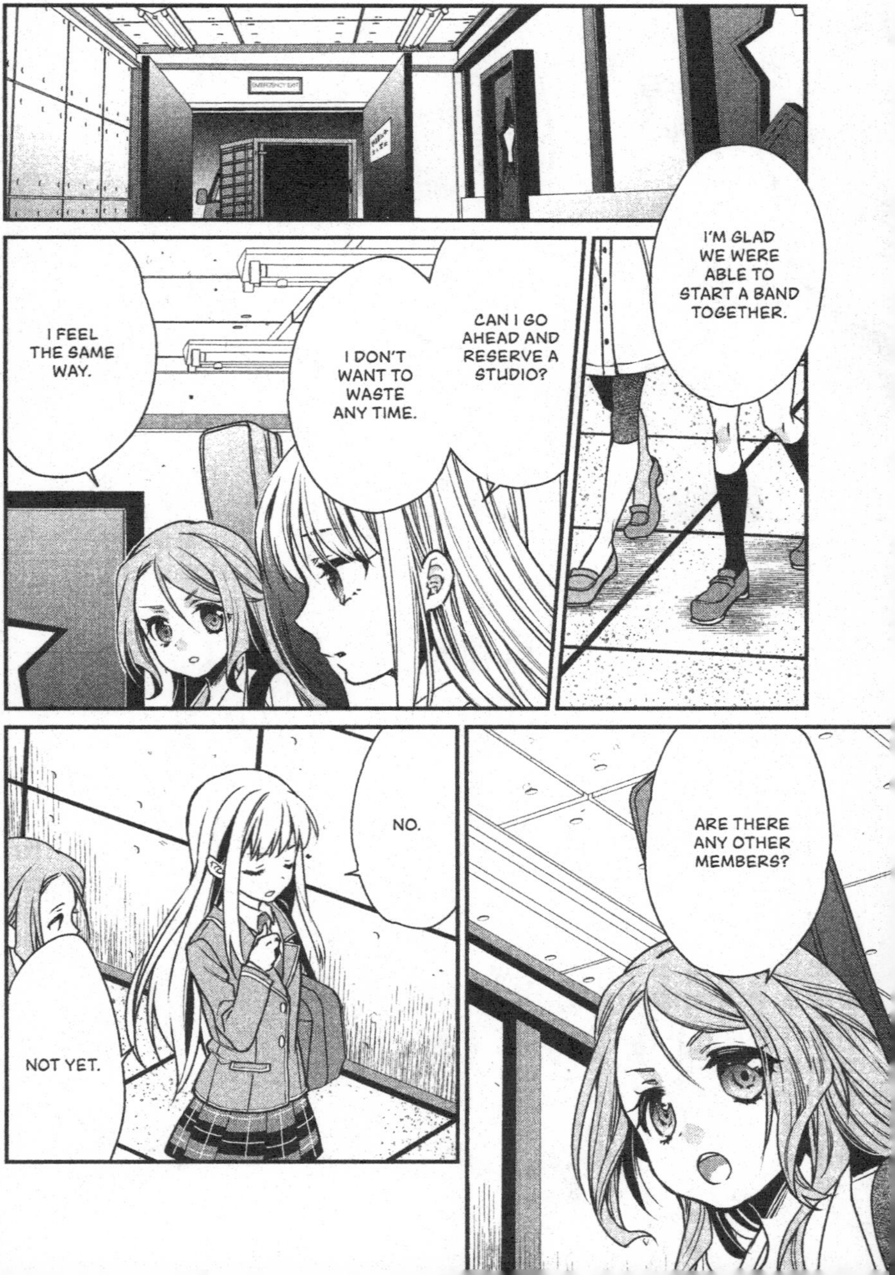
I'M GLAD WE WERE ABLE TO START A BAND TOGETHER.
CAN I GO AHEAD AND RESERVE A STUDIO?
I DON'T WANT TO WASTE ANY TIME.
I FEEL THE SAME WAY.
ARE THERE ANY OTHER MEMBERS?
NO.
NOT YET.

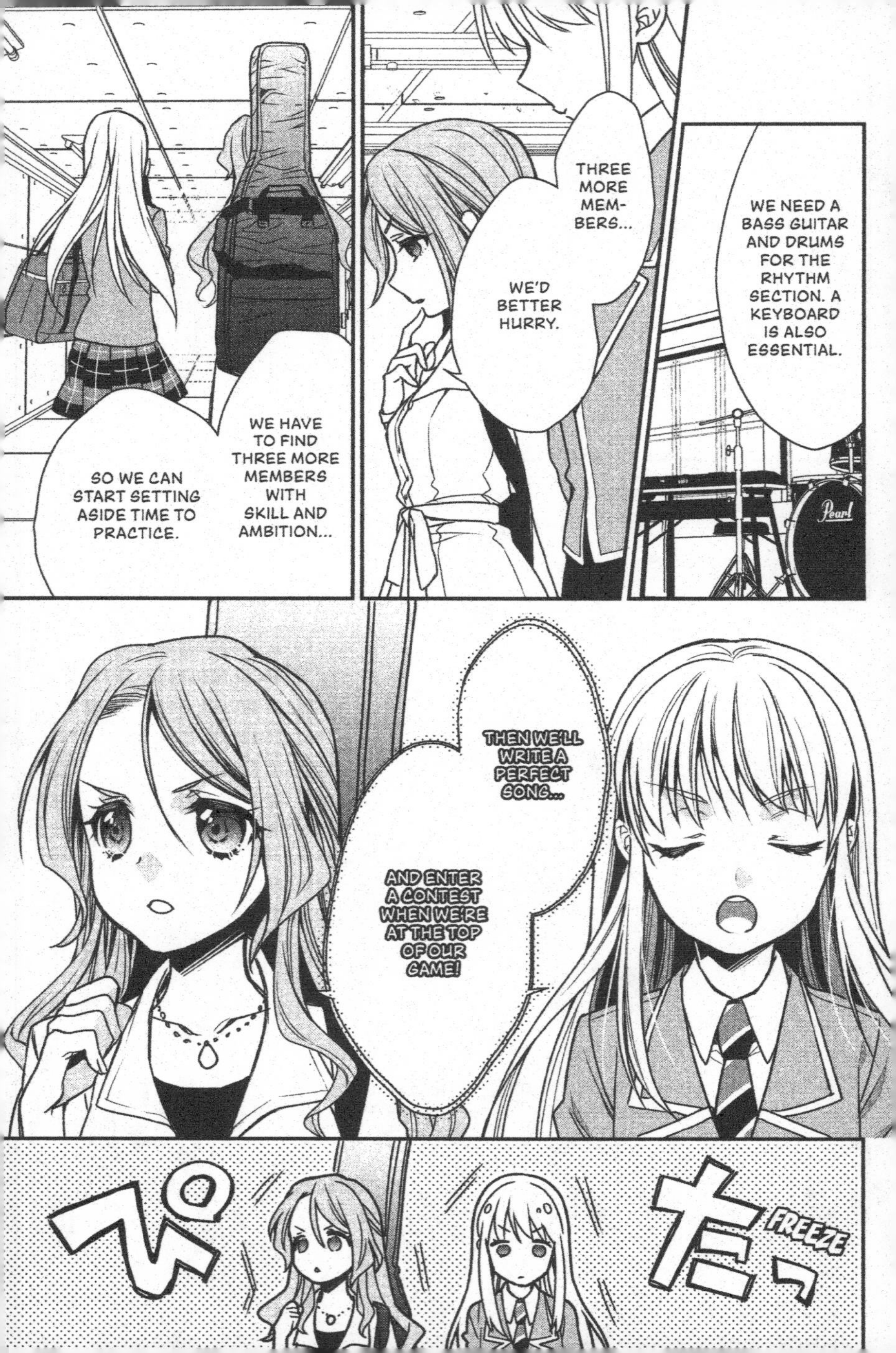

WE NEED A BASS GUITAR AND DRUMS FOR THE RHYTHM SECTION. A KEYBOARD IS ALSO ESSENTIAL.
THREE MORE MEM-BERS...
WE'D BETTER HURRY.
WE HAVE TO FIND THREE MORE MEMBERS WITH SKILL AND AMBITION...
SO WE CAN START SETTING ASIDE TIME TO PRACTICE.
THEN WE'LL WRITE A PERFECT SONG...
AND ENTER A CONTEST WHEN WE'RE AT THE TOP OF OUR GAME!
ぴたっ
FREEZE

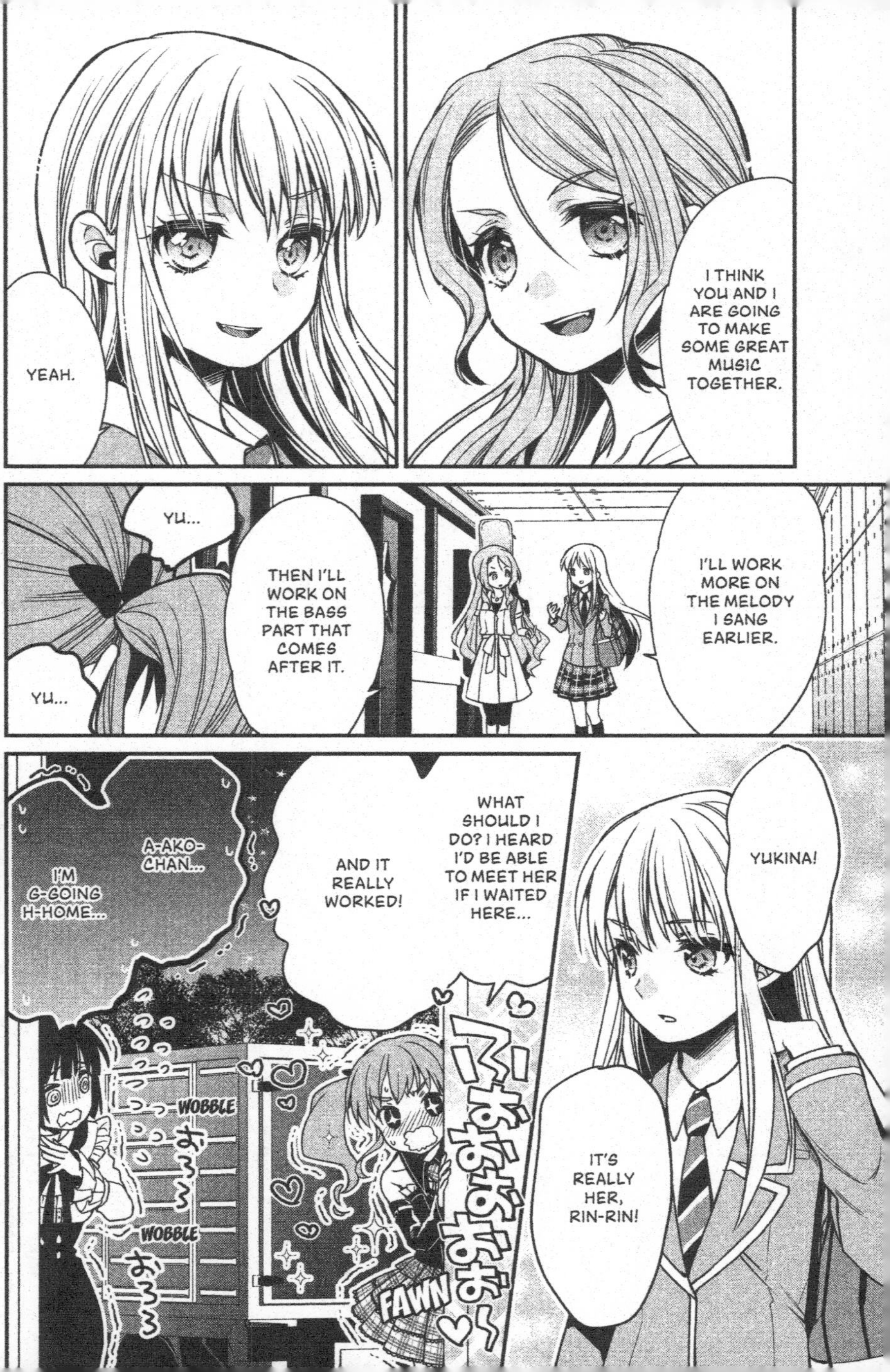
I THINK YOU AND I ARE GOING TO MAKE SOME GREAT MUSIC TOGETHER.
YEAH.
I'LL WORK MORE ON THE MELODY I SANG EARLIER.
THEN I'LL WORK ON THE BASS PART THAT COMES AFTER IT.
YU...
YU...
YUKINA!
IT'S REALLY HER, RIN-RIN!
WHAT SHOULD I DO? I HEARD I'D BE ABLE TO MEET HER IF I WAITED HERE...
AND IT REALLY WORKED!
FAWN
A-AKO-CHAN...
I'M G-GOING H-HOME...
WOBBLE
WOBBLE

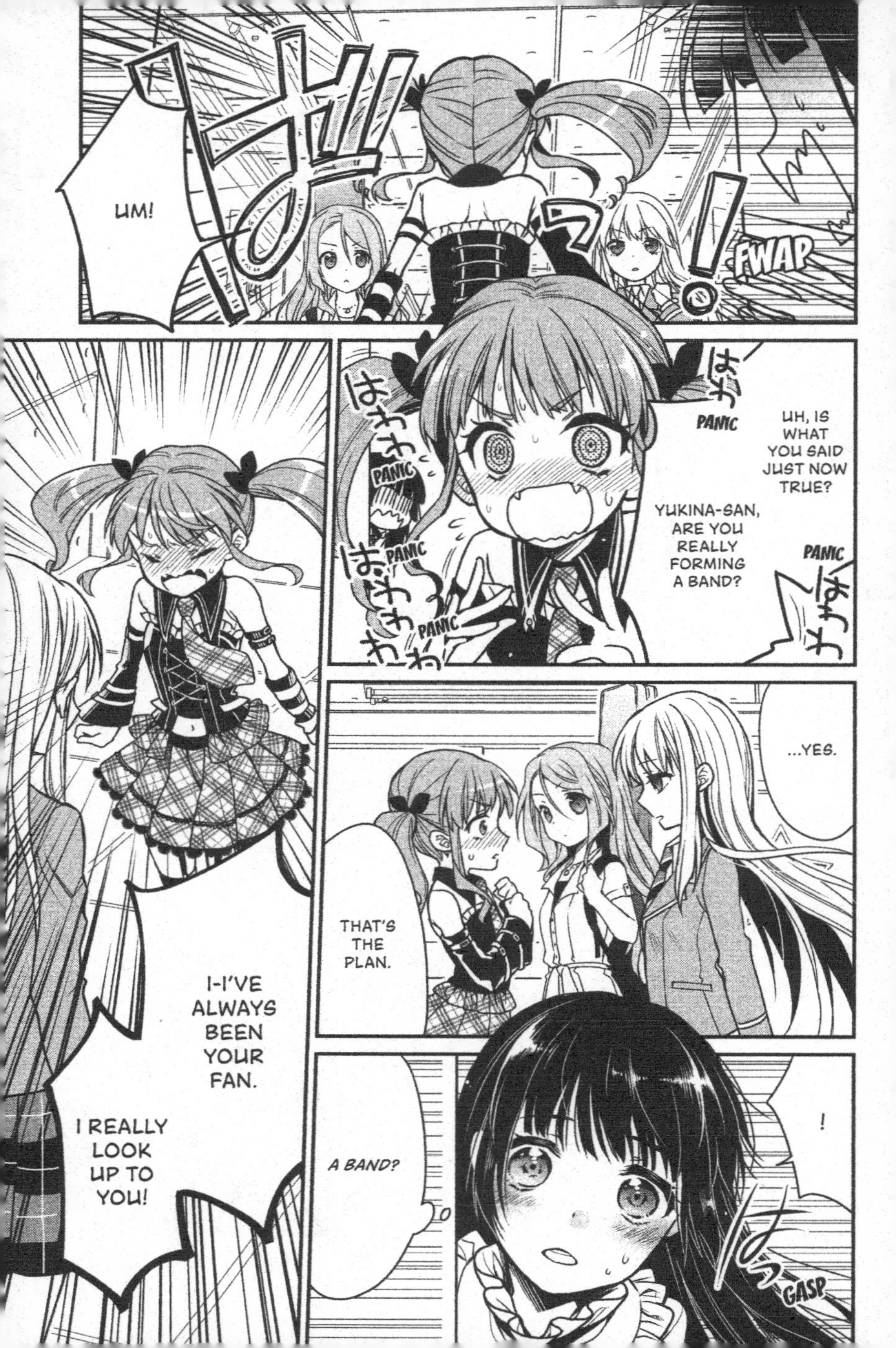
FWAP
UM!
PANIC
UH, IS WHAT YOU SAID JUST NOW TRUE?
YUKINA-SAN, ARE YOU REALLY FORMING A BAND?
PANIC
PANIC
PANIC
PANIC
...YES.
THAT'S THE PLAN.
!
A BAND?
GASP
I-I'VE ALWAYS BEEN YOUR FAN.
I REALLY LOOK UP TO YOU!

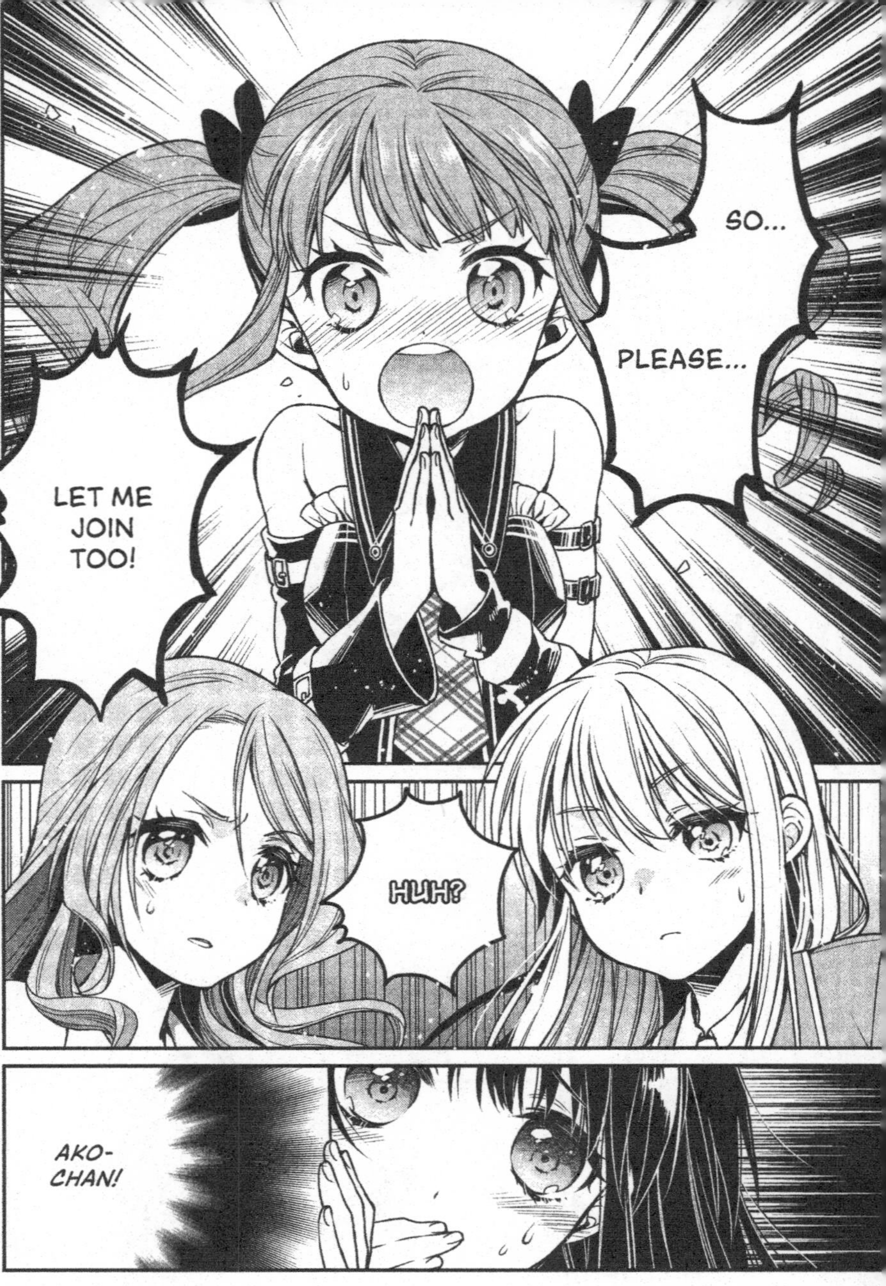
SO...
PLEASE...
LET ME JOIN TOO!
HUH?
AKO-CHAN!

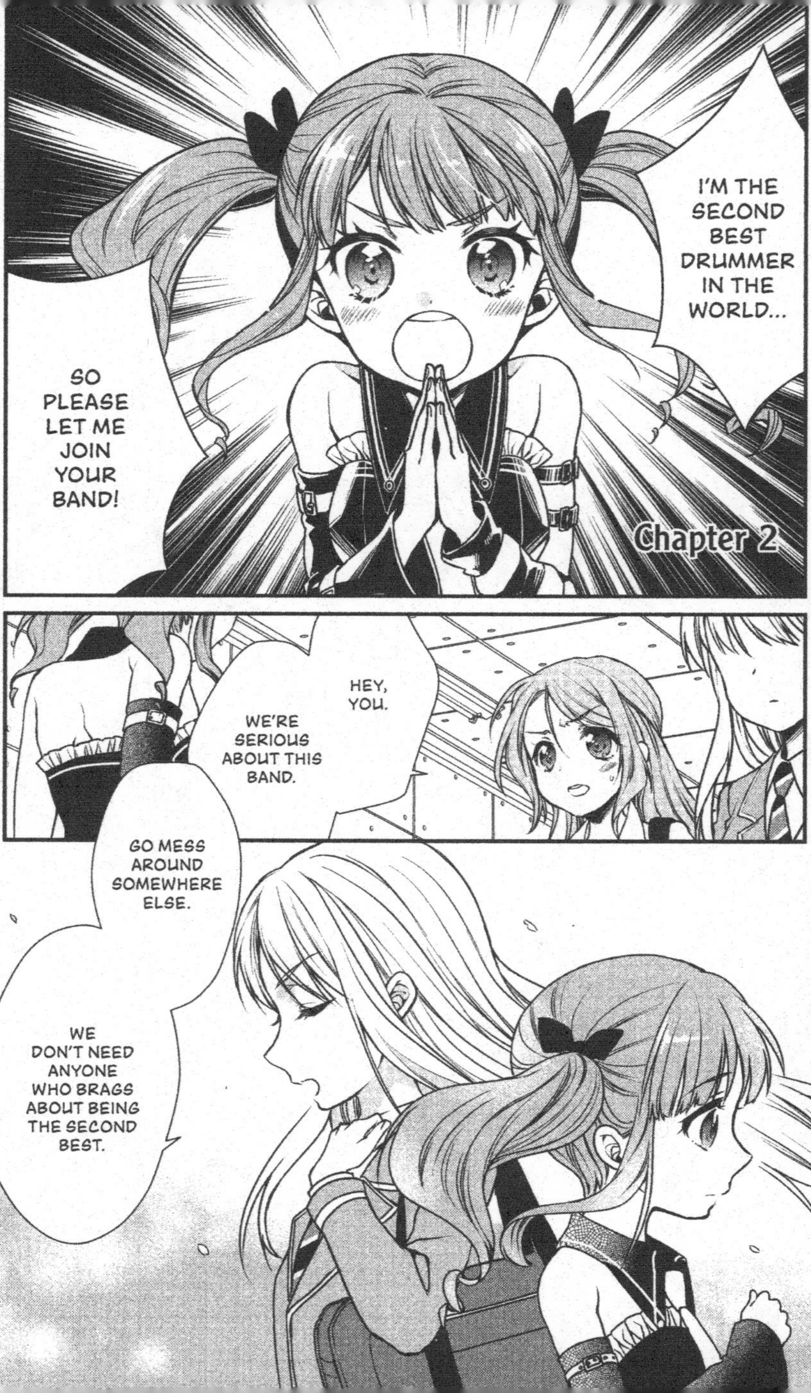
I'M THE SECOND BEST DRUMMER IN THE WORLD...
SO PLEASE LET ME JOIN YOUR BAND!
Chapter 2
HEY, YOU.
WE'RE SERIOUS ABOUT THIS BAND.
GO MESS AROUND SOMEWHERE ELSE.
WE DON'T NEED ANYONE WHO BRAGS ABOUT BEING THE SECOND BEST.

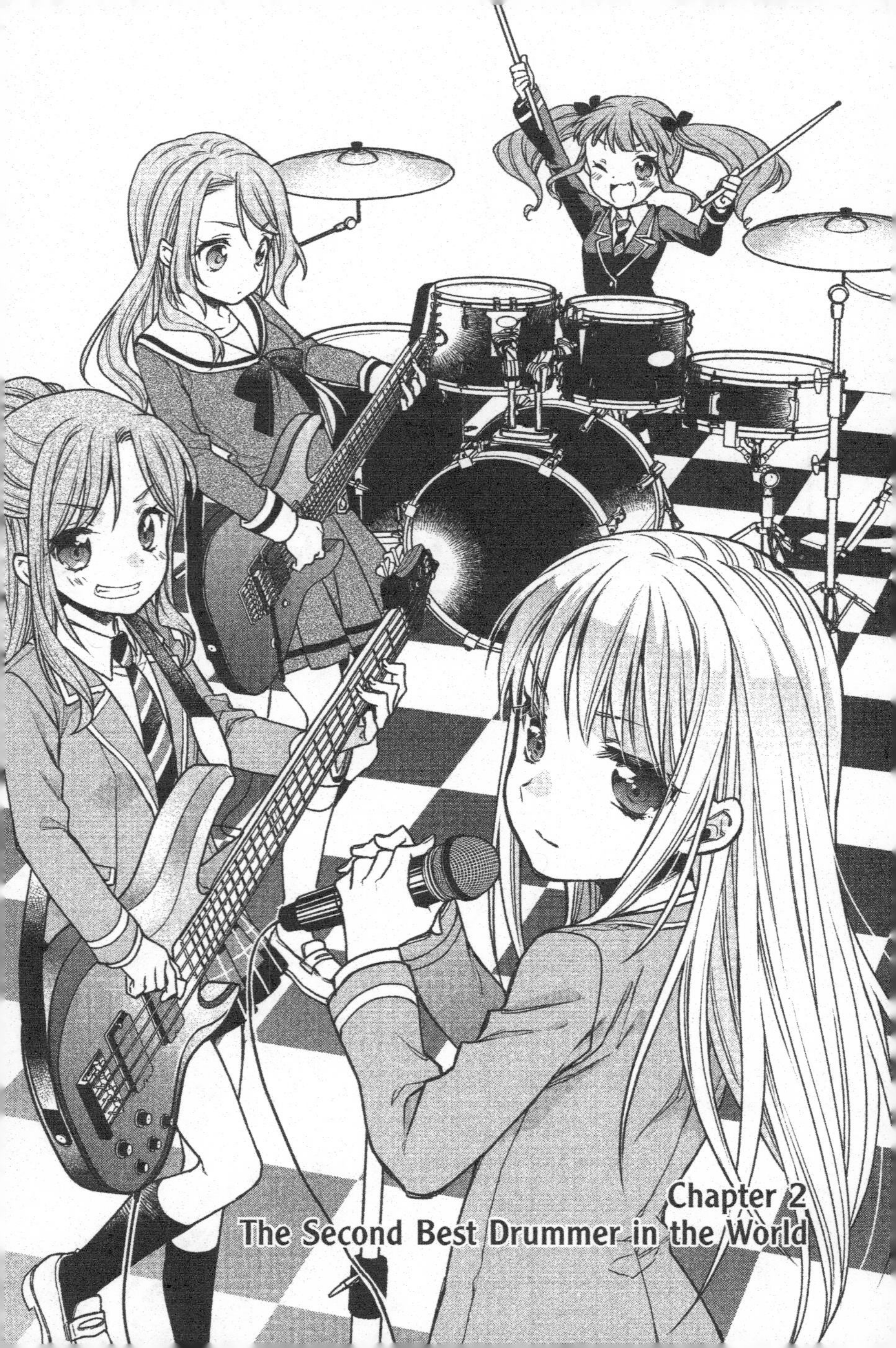

Chapter 2
The Second Best Drummer in the World

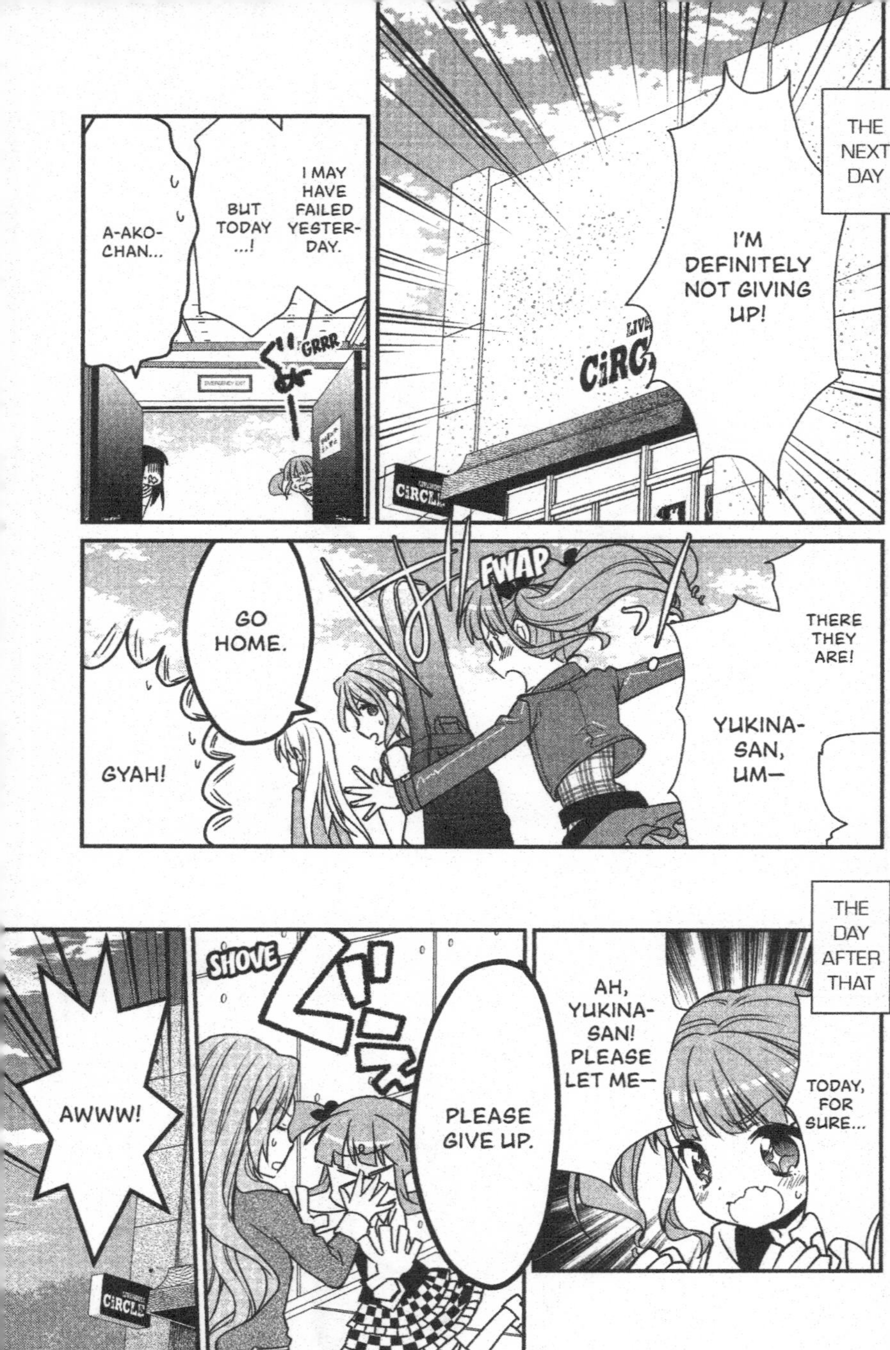
THE NEXT DAY
I'M DEFINITELY NOT GIVING UP!
I MAY HAVE FAILED YESTER-DAY.
BUT TODAY ...!
GRRR
A-AKO-CHAN...
THERE THEY ARE!
YUKINA-SAN, UM—
FWAP
GO HOME.
GYAH!
THE DAY AFTER THAT
TODAY, FOR SURE...
AH, YUKINA-SAN! PLEASE LET ME—
SHOVE
PLEASE GIVE UP.
AWWW!

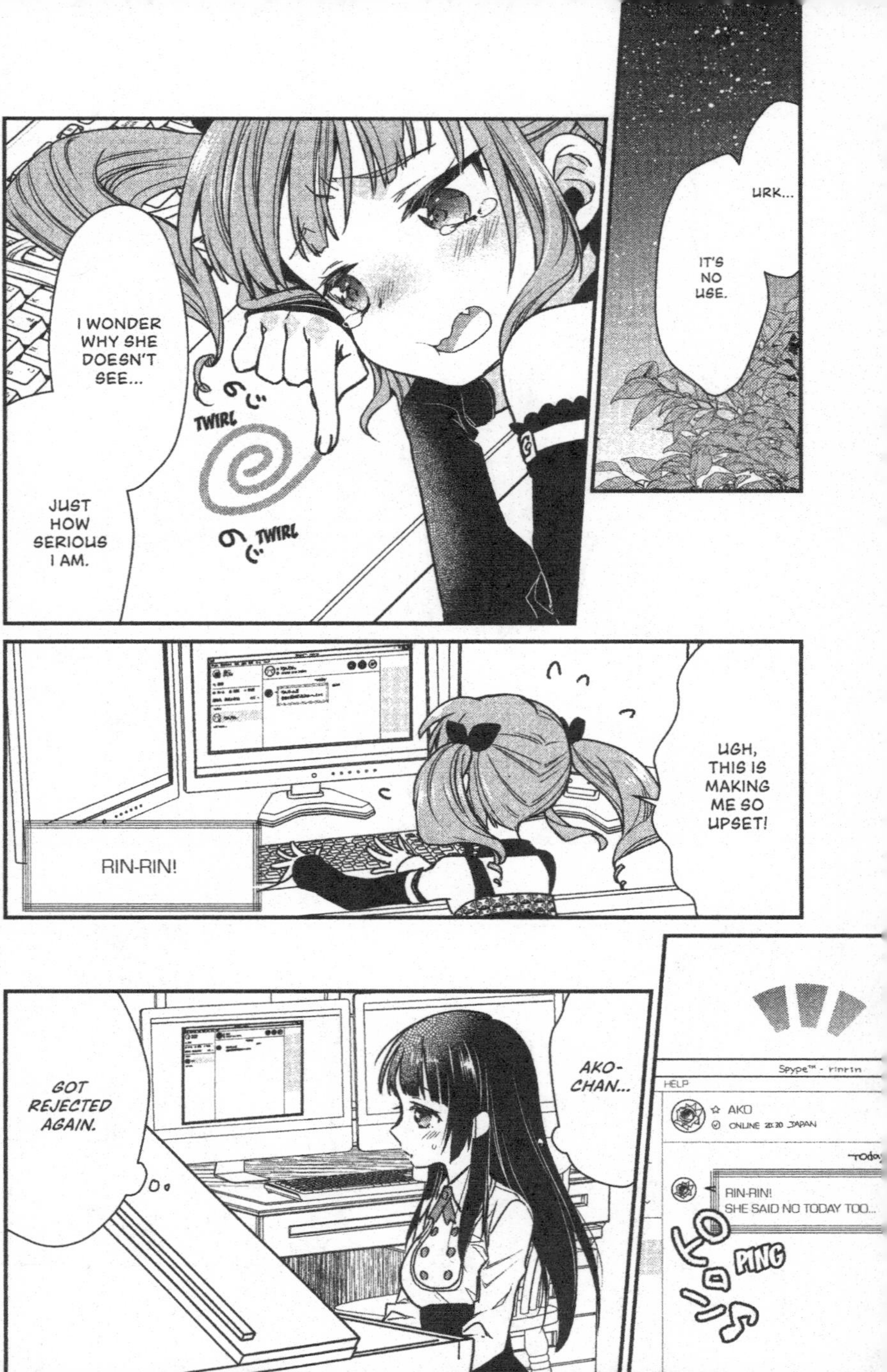
URK...
IT'S NO USE.
I WONDER WHY SHE DOESN'T SEE...
TWIRL
TWIRL
JUST HOW SERIOUS I AM.
UGH, THIS IS MAKING ME SO UPSET!
RIN-RIN!
Spype™ - rinrin
HELP
AKO
ONLINE 20:30 JAPAN
Today
RIN-RIN!
SHE SAID NO TODAY TOO...
PING
AKO-CHAN...
GOT REJECTED AGAIN.

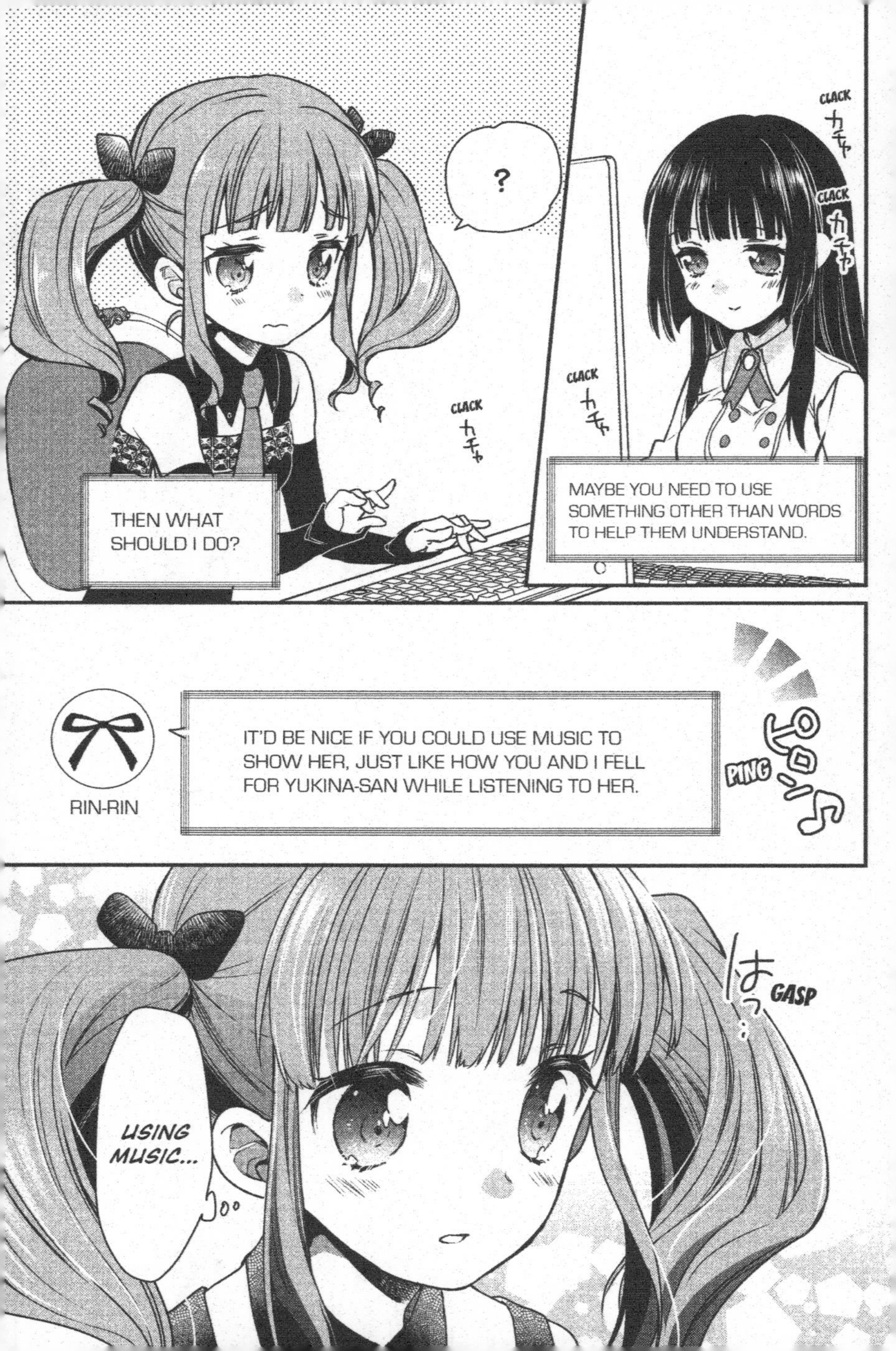

CLACK カチャ
CLACK カチャ
CLACK カチャ
MAYBE YOU NEED TO USE SOMETHING OTHER THAN WORDS TO HELP THEM UNDERSTAND.
?
CLACK カチャ
THEN WHAT SHOULD I DO?
PING ピローン♪
IT'D BE NICE IF YOU COULD USE MUSIC TO SHOW HER, JUST LIKE HOW YOU AND I FELL FOR YUKINA-SAN WHILE LISTENING TO HER.
RIN-RIN
GASP はっ
USING MUSIC...

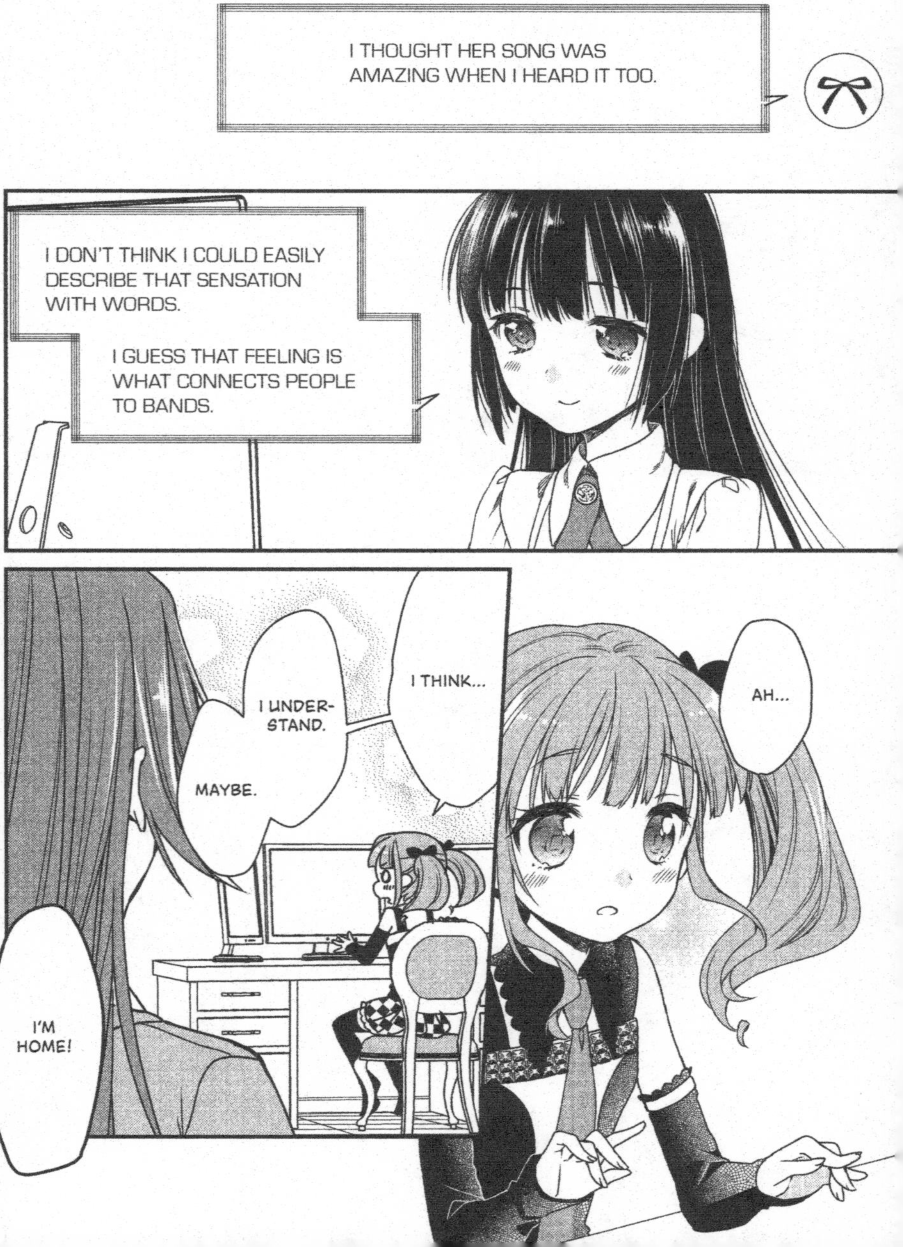
I THOUGHT HER SONG WAS AMAZING WHEN I HEARD IT TOO.
I DON'T THINK I COULD EASILY DESCRIBE THAT SENSATION WITH WORDS.
I GUESS THAT FEELING IS WHAT CONNECTS PEOPLE TO BANDS.
AH...
I THINK...
I UNDER-STAND.
MAYBE.
I'M HOME!

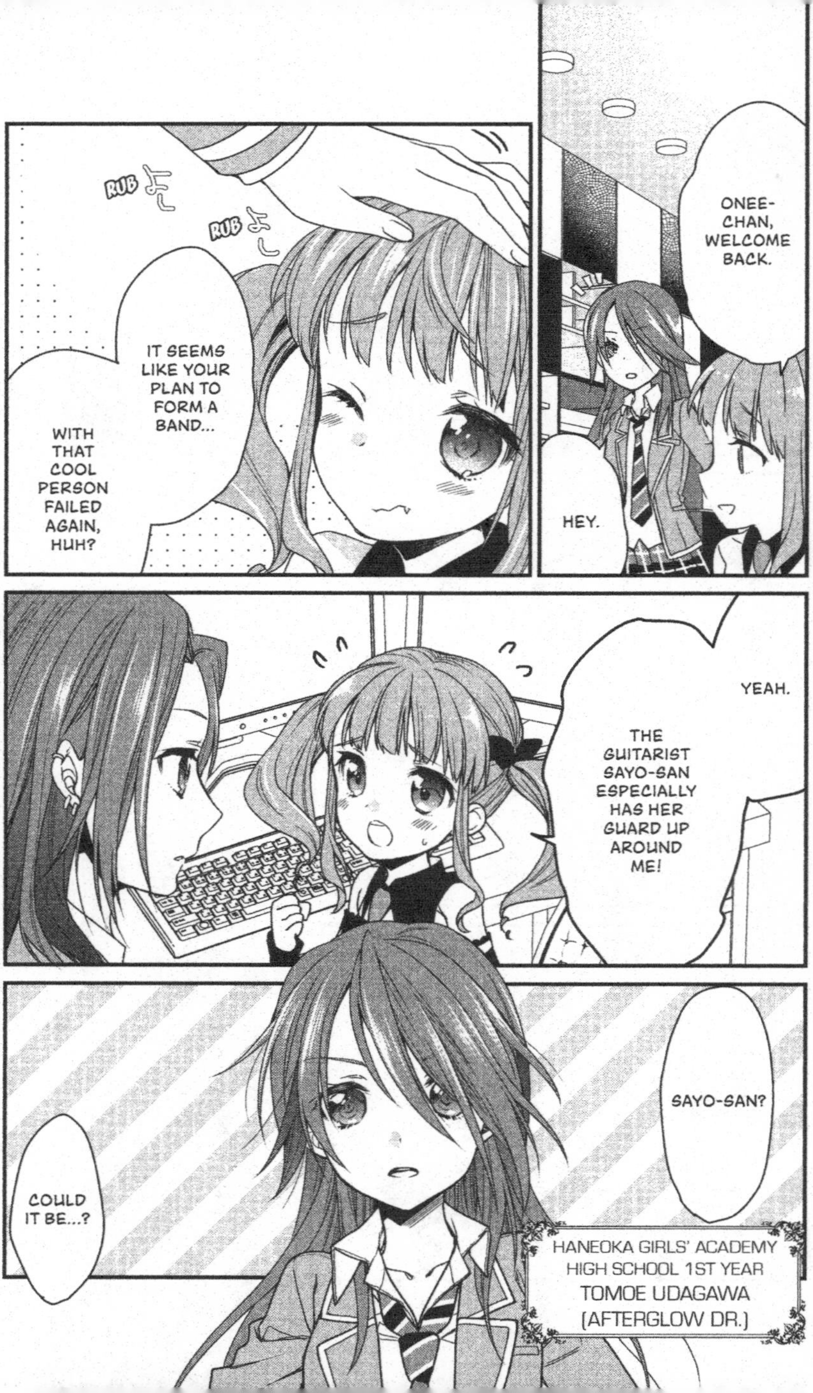
ONEE-CHAN, WELCOME BACK.
HEY.
RUB よし
RUB よし
IT SEEMS LIKE YOUR PLAN TO FORM A BAND...
WITH THAT COOL PERSON FAILED AGAIN, HUH?
YEAH.
THE GUITARIST SAYO-SAN ESPECIALLY HAS HER GUARD UP AROUND ME!
SAYO-SAN?
COULD IT BE...?
HANEOKA GIRLS' ACADEMY HIGH SCHOOL 1ST YEAR
TOMOE UDAGAWA
[AFTERGLOW DR.]

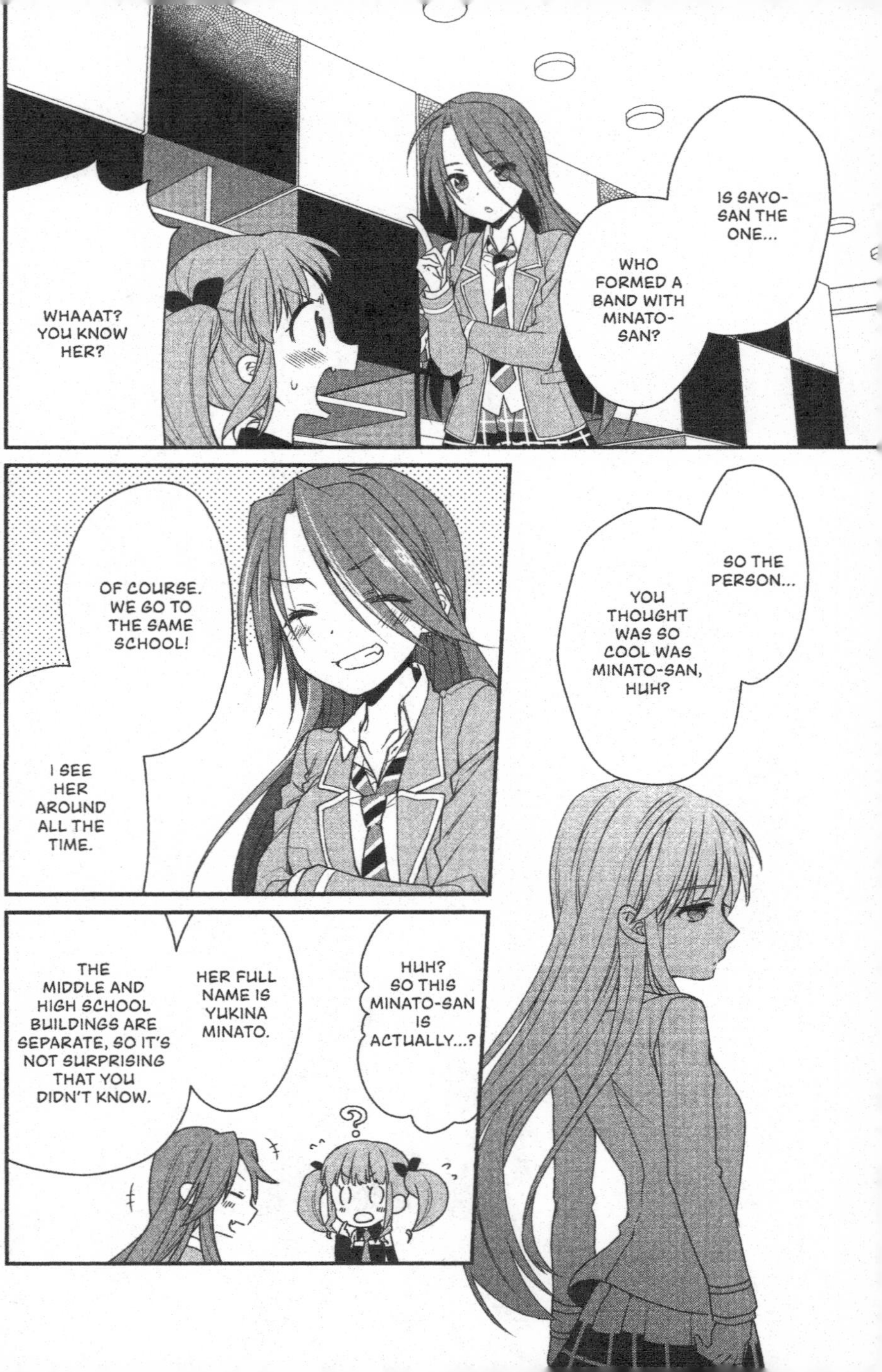
IS SAYO-SAN THE ONE...
WHO FORMED A BAND WITH MINATO-SAN?
WHAAAT? YOU KNOW HER?
SO THE PERSON...
YOU THOUGHT WAS SO COOL WAS MINATO-SAN, HUH?
OF COURSE. WE GO TO THE SAME SCHOOL!
I SEE HER AROUND ALL THE TIME.
HUH? SO THIS MINATO-SAN IS ACTUALLY...?
HER FULL NAME IS YUKINA MINATO.
THE MIDDLE AND HIGH SCHOOL BUILDINGS ARE SEPARATE, SO IT'S NOT SURPRISING THAT YOU DIDN'T KNOW.

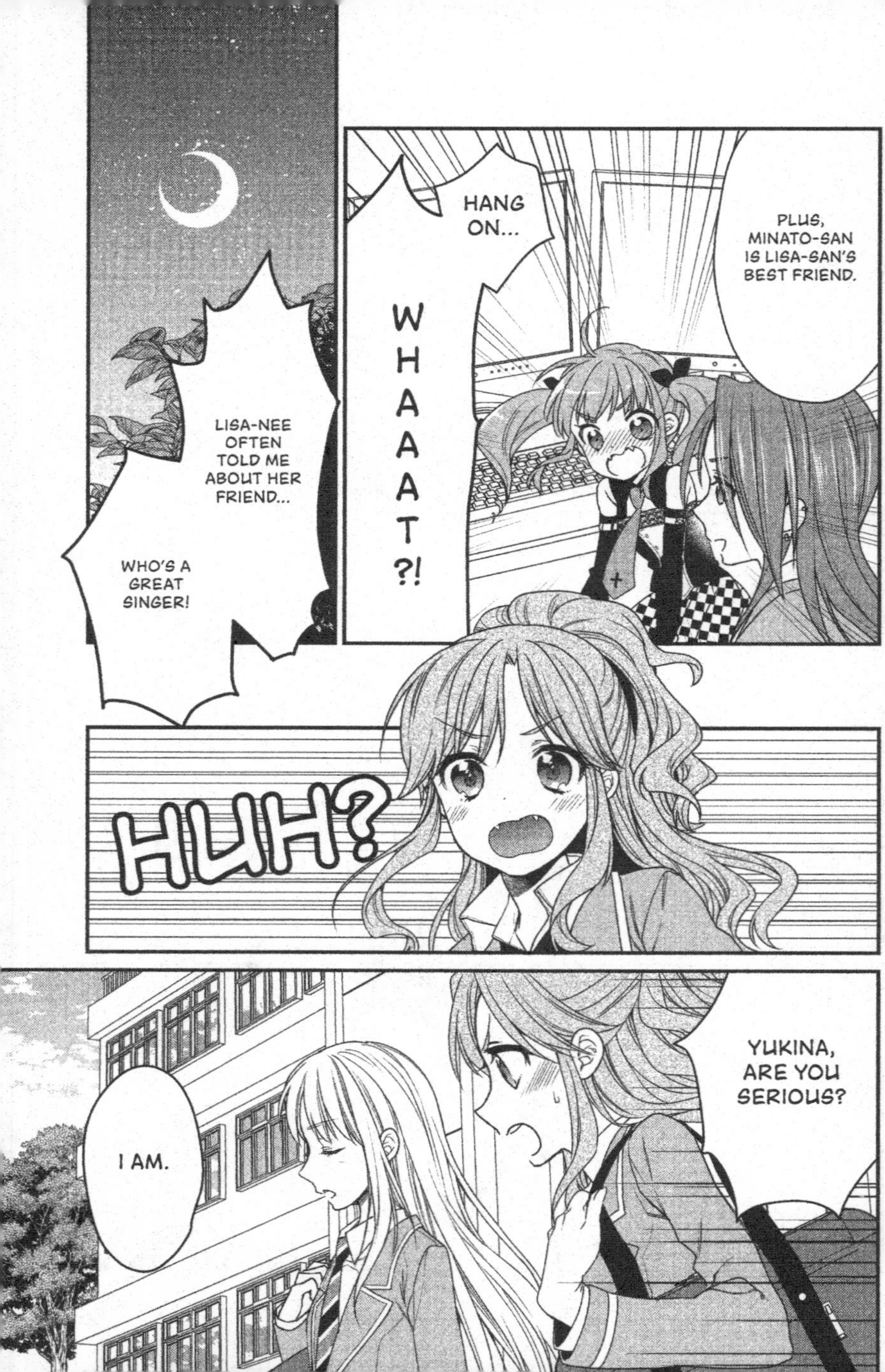
PLUS, MINATO-SAN IS LISA-SAN'S BEST FRIEND.
HANG ON...
WHAAAAT?!
LISA-NEE OFTEN TOLD ME ABOUT HER FRIEND...
WHO'S A GREAT SINGER!
HUH?
YUKINA, ARE YOU SERIOUS?
I AM.

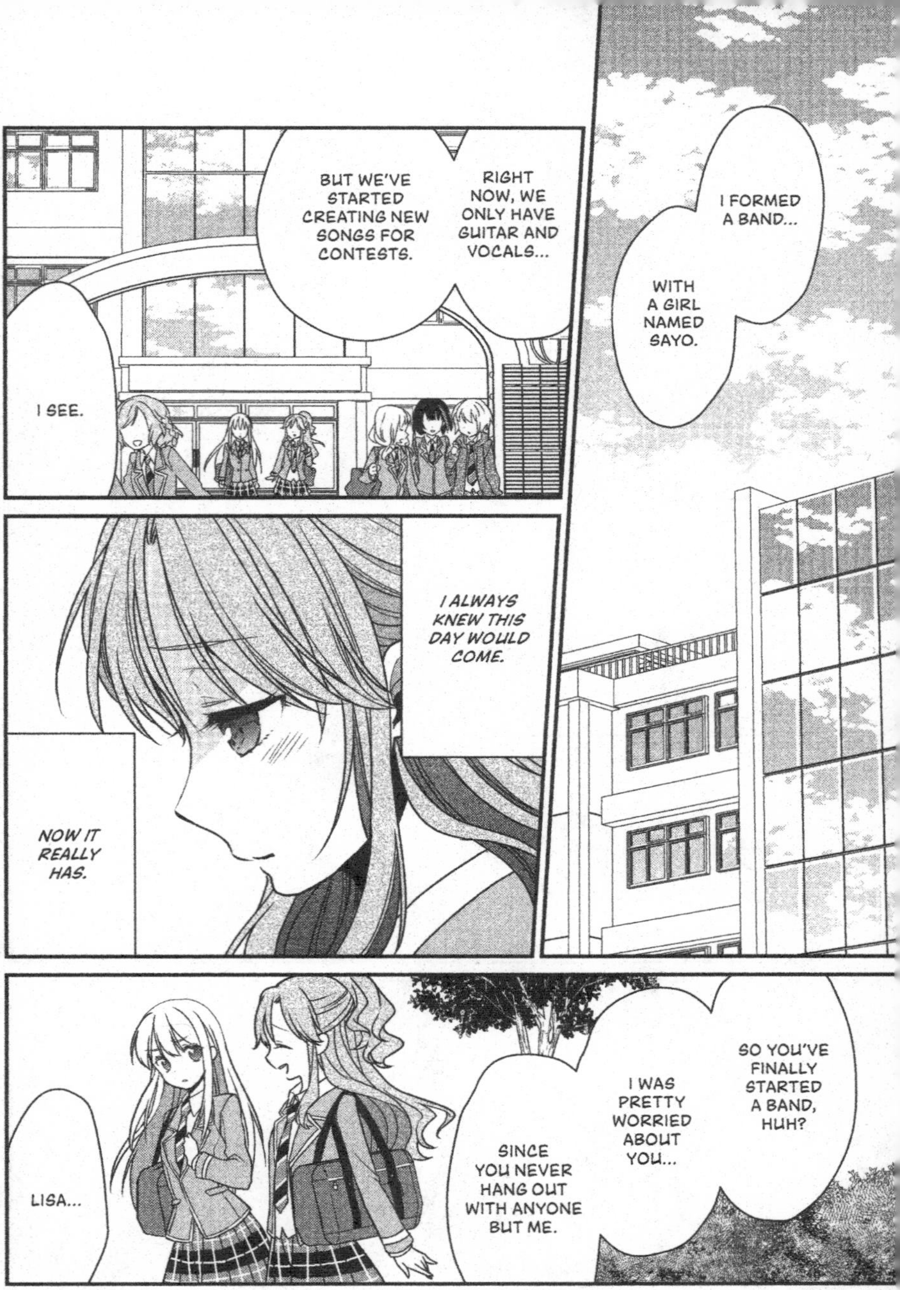
I FORMED A BAND...
WITH A GIRL NAMED SAYO.
RIGHT NOW, WE ONLY HAVE GUITAR AND VOCALS...
BUT WE'VE STARTED CREATING NEW SONGS FOR CONTESTS.
I SEE.
I ALWAYS KNEW THIS DAY WOULD COME.
NOW IT REALLY HAS.
SO YOU'VE FINALLY STARTED A BAND, HUH?
I WAS PRETTY WORRIED ABOUT YOU...
SINCE YOU NEVER HANG OUT WITH ANYONE BUT ME.
LISA...

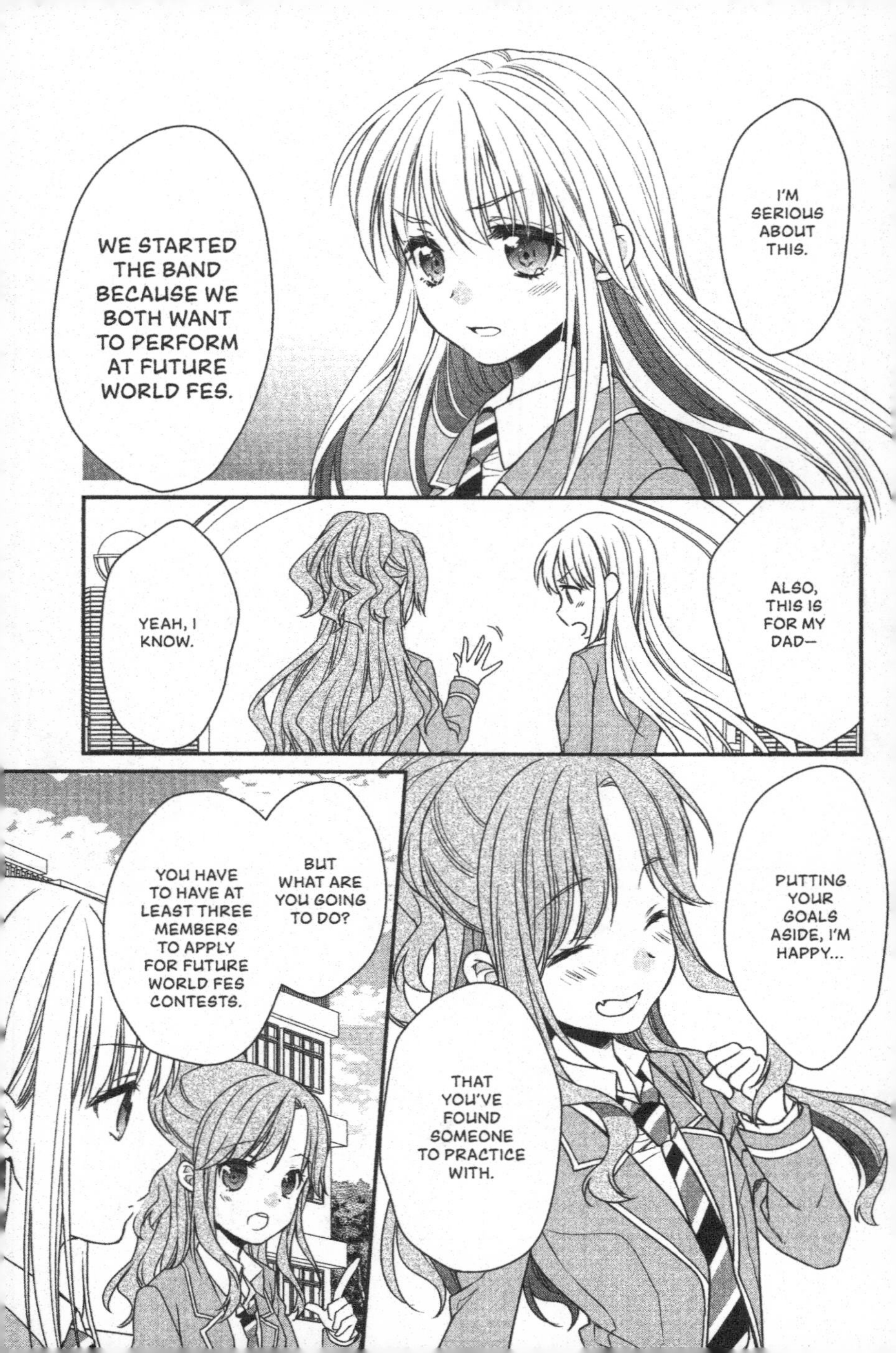
I'M SERIOUS ABOUT THIS.
WE STARTED THE BAND BECAUSE WE BOTH WANT TO PERFORM AT FUTURE WORLD FES.
ALSO, THIS IS FOR MY DAD—
YEAH, I KNOW.
PUTTING YOUR GOALS ASIDE, I'M HAPPY...
THAT YOU'VE FOUND SOMEONE TO PRACTICE WITH.
BUT WHAT ARE YOU GOING TO DO?
YOU HAVE TO HAVE AT LEAST THREE MEMBERS TO APPLY FOR FUTURE WORLD FES CONTESTS.

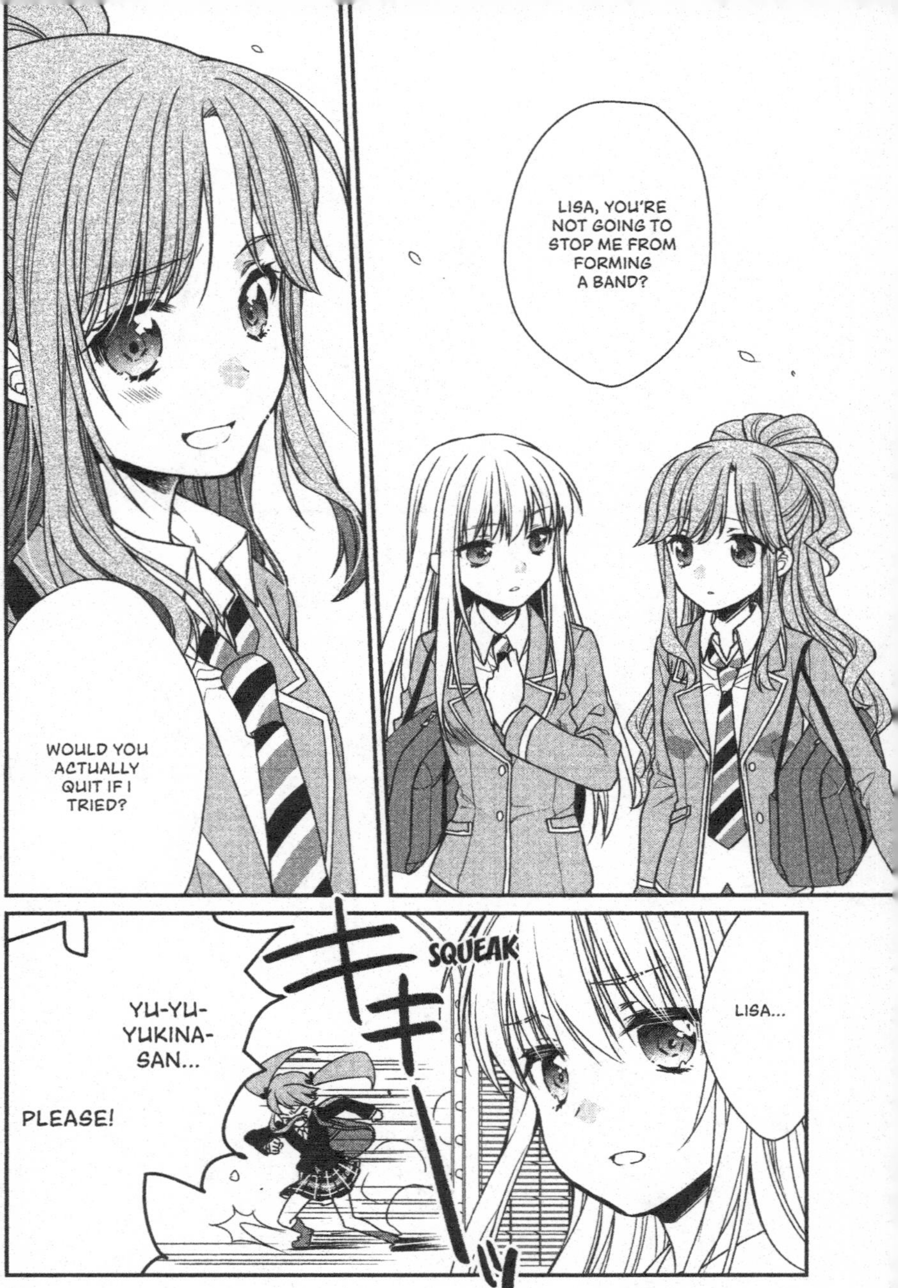
LISA, YOU'RE NOT GOING TO STOP ME FROM FORMING A BAND?
WOULD YOU ACTUALLY QUIT IF I TRIED?
LISA...
SQUEAK
YU-YU-YUKINA-SAN...
PLEASE!

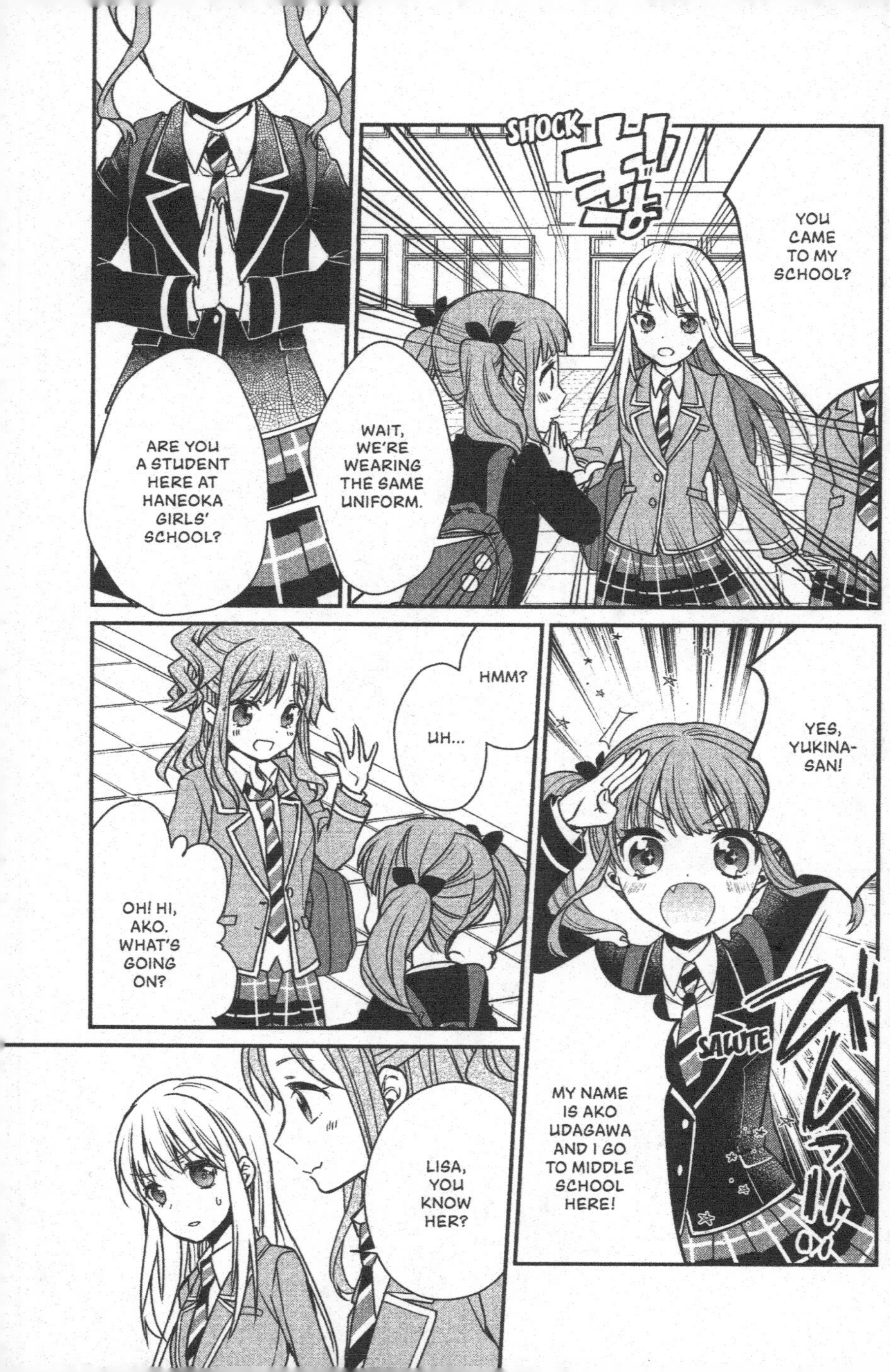
SHOCK
YOU CAME TO MY SCHOOL?
WAIT, WE'RE WEARING THE SAME UNIFORM.
ARE YOU A STUDENT HERE AT HANEOKA GIRLS' SCHOOL?
YES, YUKINA-SAN!
SALUTE
MY NAME IS AKO UDAGAWA AND I GO TO MIDDLE SCHOOL HERE!
HMM?
UH...
OH! HI, AKO. WHAT'S GOING ON?
LISA, YOU KNOW HER?

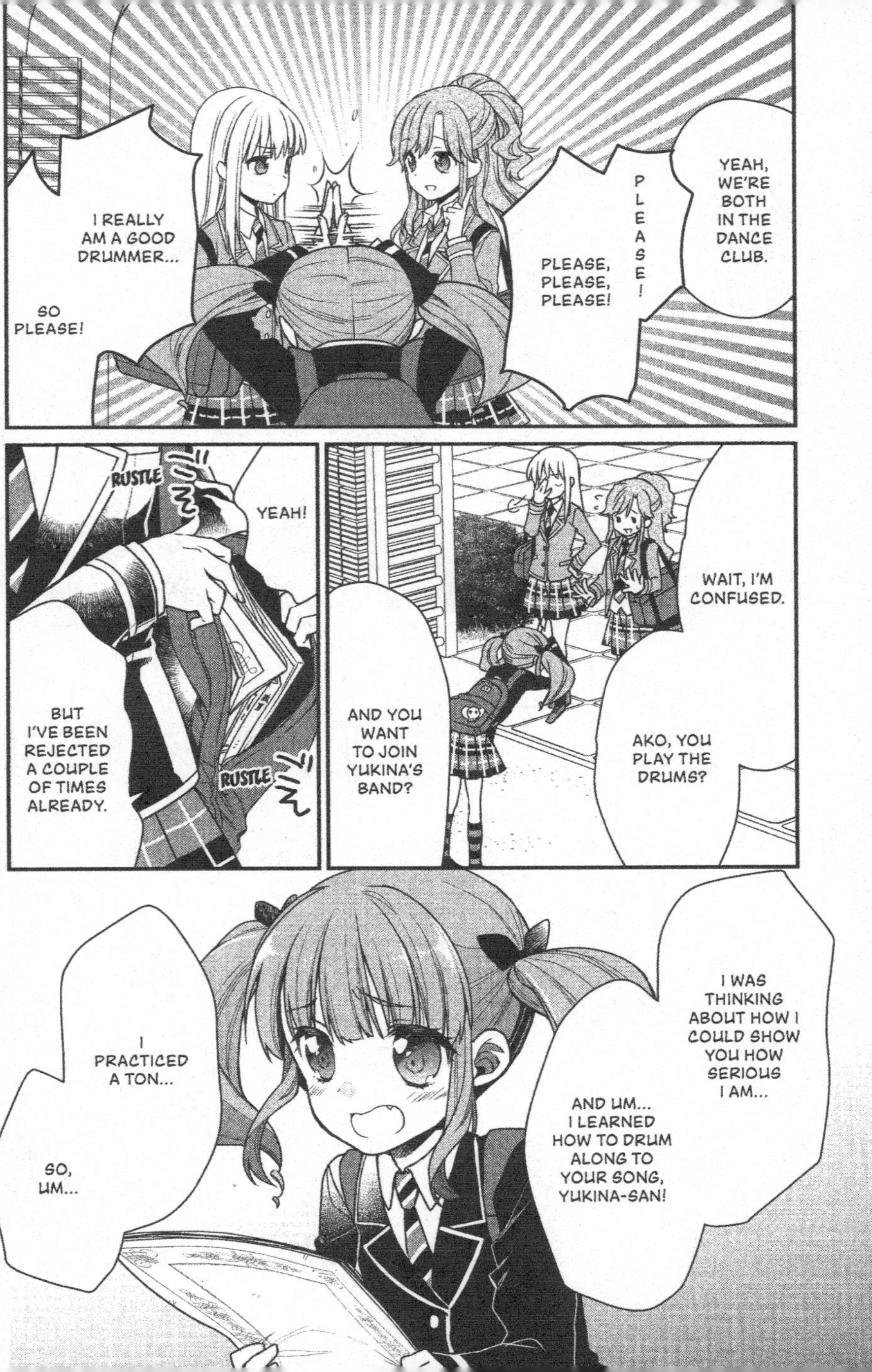
YEAH, WE'RE BOTH IN THE DANCE CLUB.
PLEASE!
PLEASE, PLEASE, PLEASE!
I REALLY AM A GOOD DRUMMER...
SO PLEASE!
WAIT, I'M CONFUSED.
AKO, YOU PLAY THE DRUMS?
AND YOU WANT TO JOIN YUKINA'S BAND?
RUSTLE
YEAH!
BUT I'VE BEEN REJECTED A COUPLE OF TIMES ALREADY.
RUSTLE
I WAS THINKING ABOUT HOW I COULD SHOW YOU HOW SERIOUS I AM...
AND UM... I LEARNED HOW TO DRUM ALONG TO YOUR SONG, YUKINA-SAN!
I PRACTICED A TON...
SO, UM...

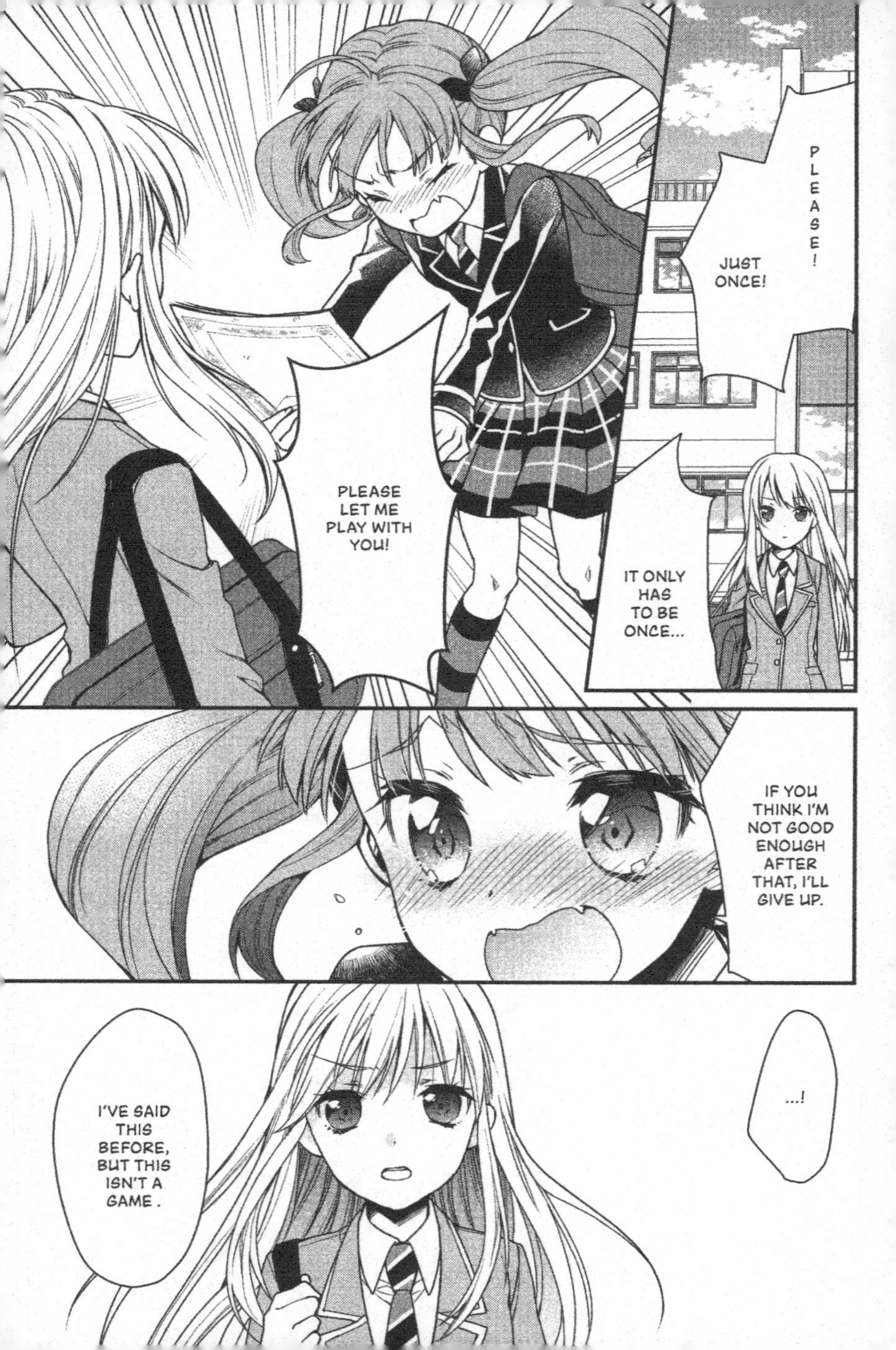
PLEASE!
JUST ONCE!
IT ONLY HAS TO BE ONCE...
PLEASE LET ME PLAY WITH YOU!
IF YOU THINK I'M NOT GOOD ENOUGH AFTER THAT, I'LL GIVE UP.
...!
I'VE SAID THIS BEFORE, BUT THIS ISN'T A GAME.

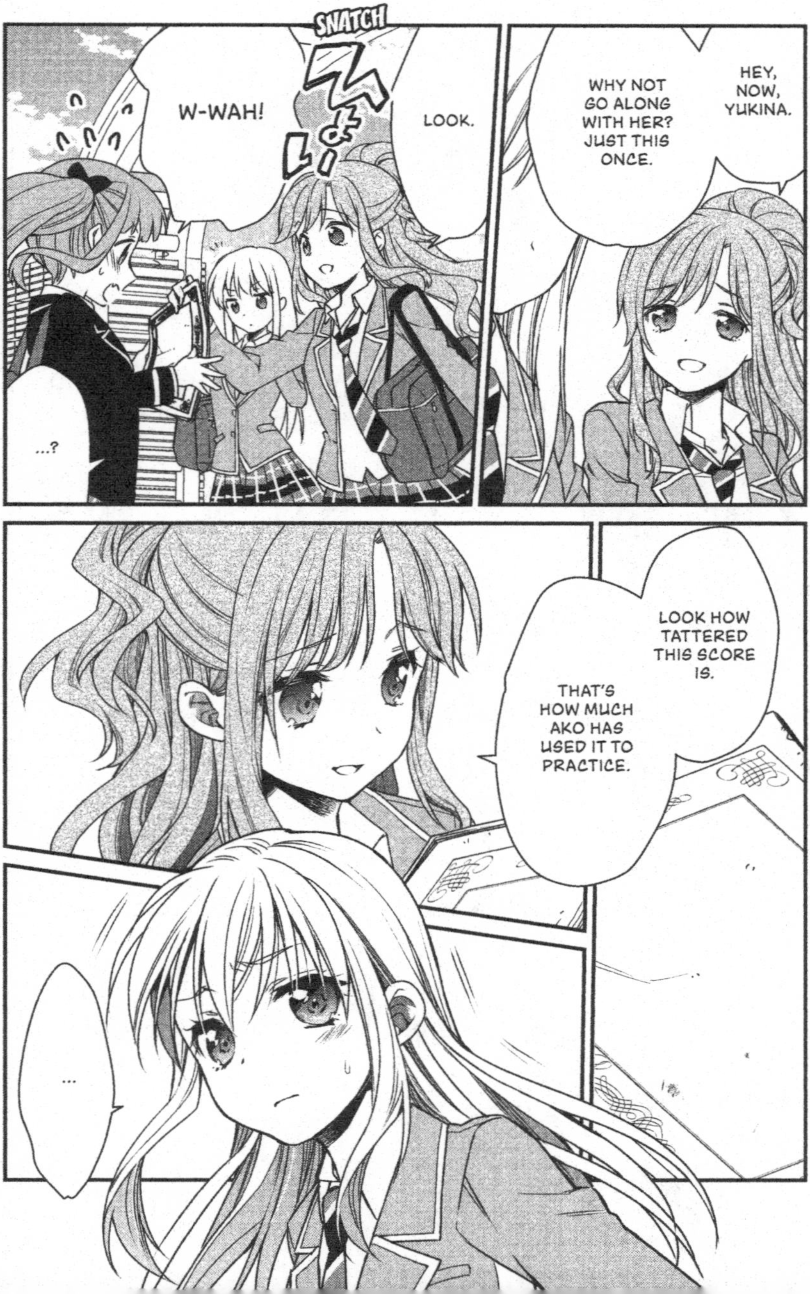
HEY, NOW, YUKINA.
WHY NOT GO ALONG WITH HER? JUST THIS ONCE.
SNATCH
LOOK.
W-WAH!
...?
LOOK HOW TATTERED THIS SCORE IS.
THAT'S HOW MUCH AKO HAS USED IT TO PRACTICE.
...

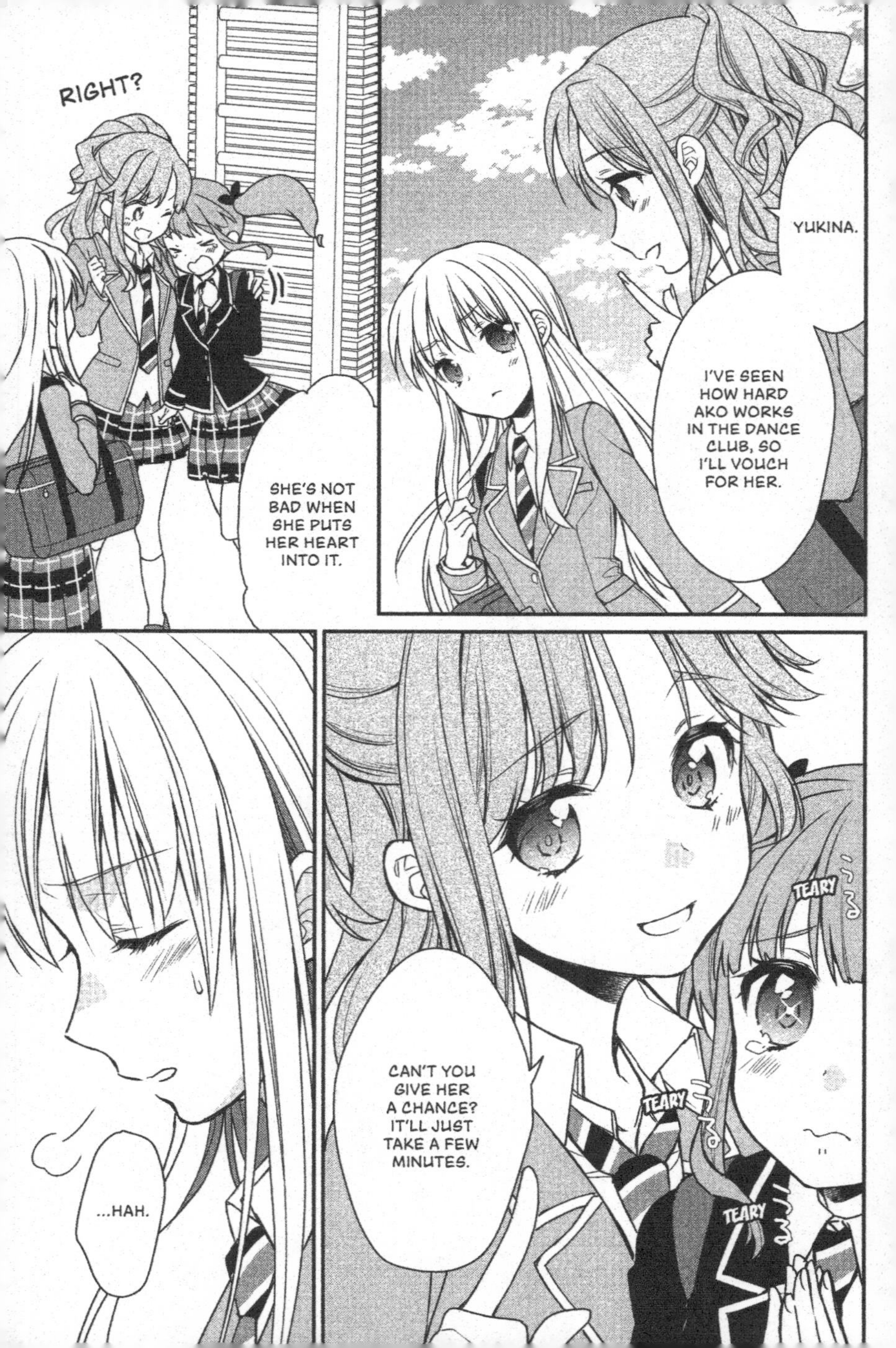
YUKINA.
I'VE SEEN HOW HARD AKO WORKS IN THE DANCE CLUB, SO I'LL VOUCH FOR HER.
RIGHT?
SHE'S NOT BAD WHEN SHE PUTS HER HEART INTO IT.
TEARY
CAN'T YOU GIVE HER A CHANCE? IT'LL JUST TAKE A FEW MINUTES.
TEARY
TEARY
...HAH.

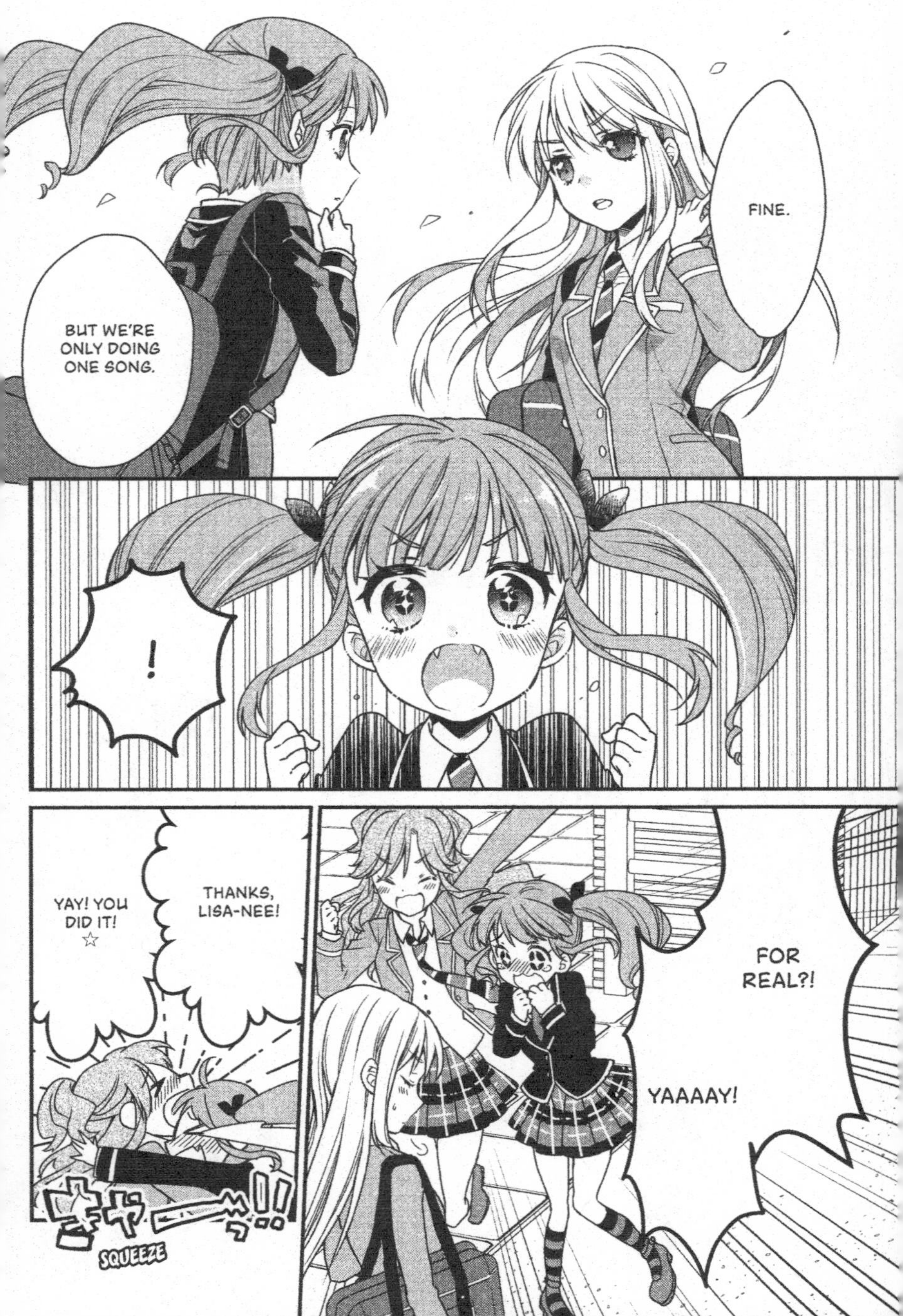
FINE.
BUT WE'RE ONLY DOING ONE SONG.
!
FOR REAL?!
YAAAAY!
THANKS, LISA-NEE!
YAY! YOU DID IT! ☆
SQUEEZE

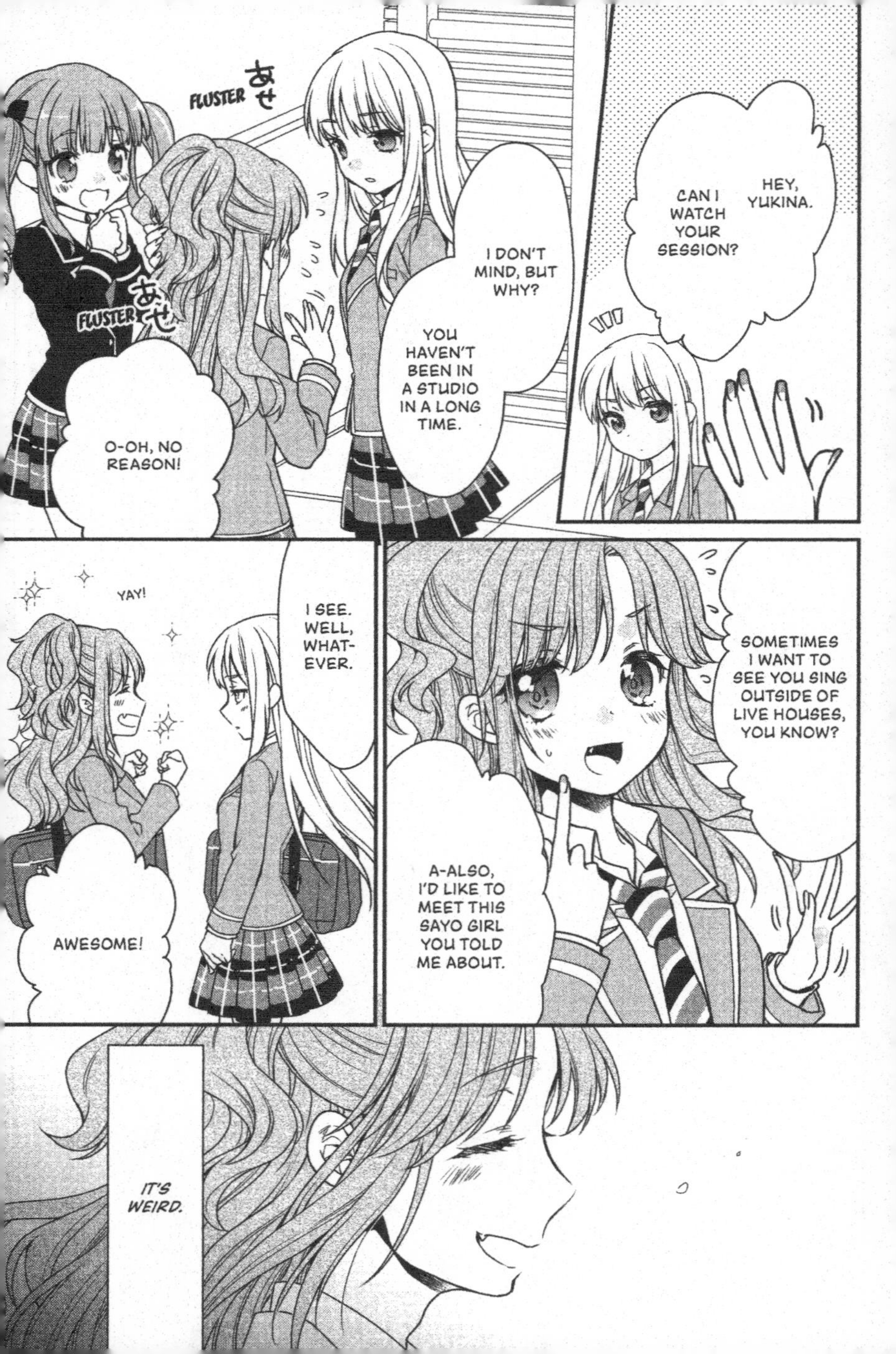
HEY, YUKINA.
CAN I WATCH YOUR SESSION?
I DON'T MIND, BUT WHY?
YOU HAVEN'T BEEN IN A STUDIO IN A LONG TIME.
FLUSTER あせ
FLUSTER あせ
O-OH, NO REASON!
SOMETIMES I WANT TO SEE YOU SING OUTSIDE OF LIVE HOUSES, YOU KNOW?
A-ALSO, I'D LIKE TO MEET THIS SAYO GIRL YOU TOLD ME ABOUT.
I SEE. WELL, WHAT-EVER.
YAY!
AWESOME!
IT'S WEIRD.

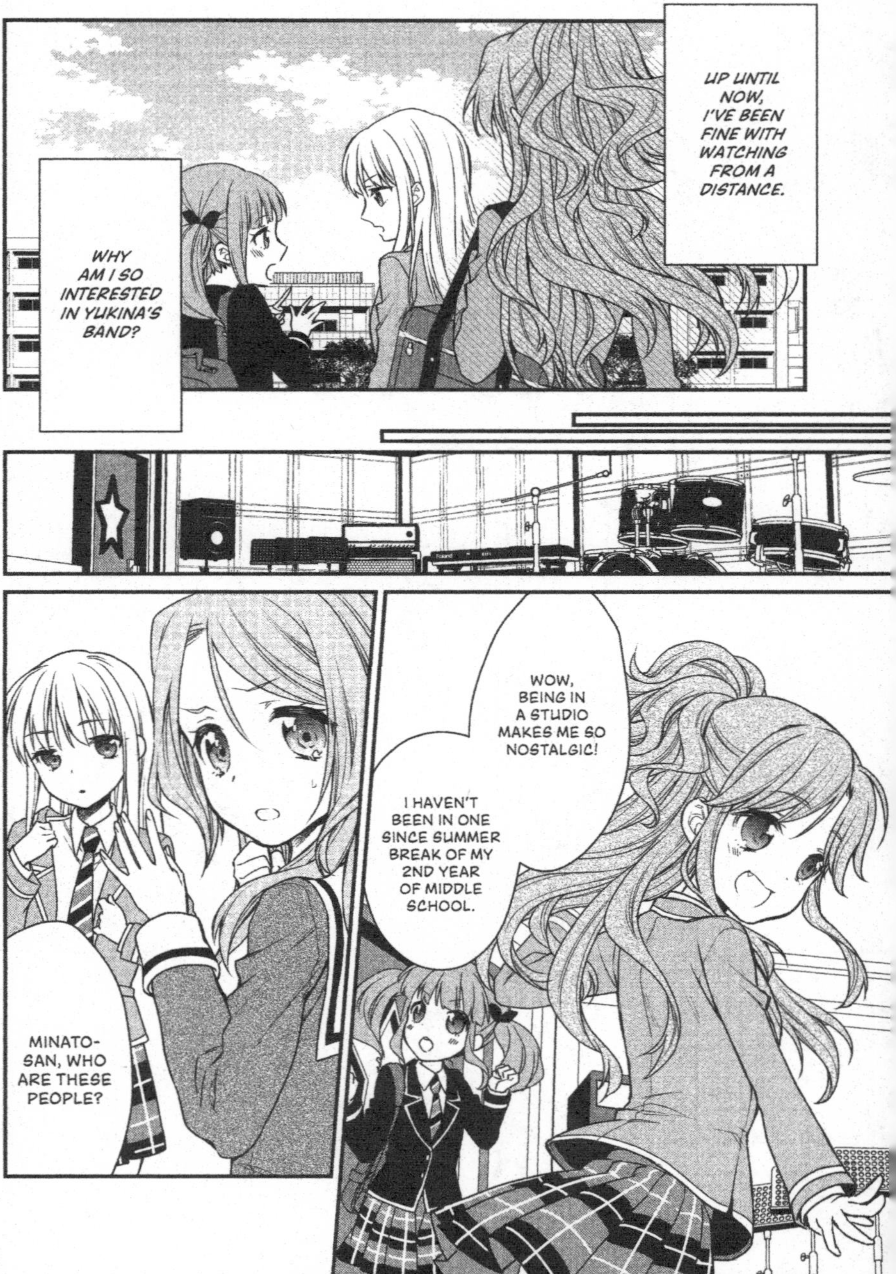
UP UNTIL NOW, I'VE BEEN FINE WITH WATCHING FROM A DISTANCE.
WHY AM I SO INTERESTED IN YUKINA'S BAND?
WOW, BEING IN A STUDIO MAKES ME SO NOSTALGIC!
I HAVEN'T BEEN IN ONE SINCE SUMMER BREAK OF MY 2ND YEAR OF MIDDLE SCHOOL.
MINATO-SAN, WHO ARE THESE PEOPLE?

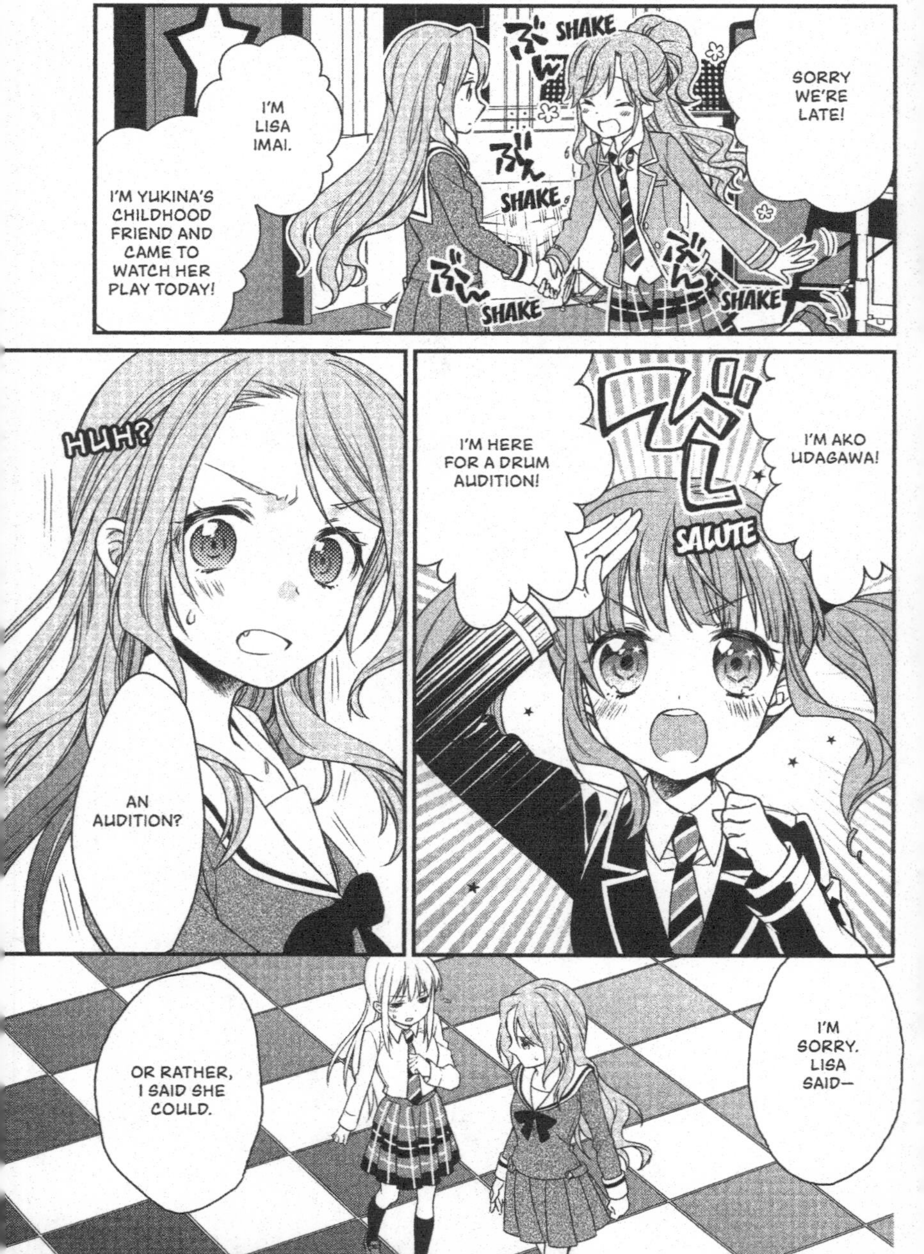

SORRY WE'RE LATE!
ぶん
SHAKE
ぶん
SHAKE
ぶん
SHAKE
ぶん
SHAKE
I'M LISA IMAI.
I'M YUKINA'S CHILDHOOD FRIEND AND CAME TO WATCH HER PLAY TODAY!
I'M AKO UDAGAWA!
びし
SALUTE
I'M HERE FOR A DRUM AUDITION!
HUH?
AN AUDITION?
I'M SORRY. LISA SAID—
OR RATHER, I SAID SHE COULD.

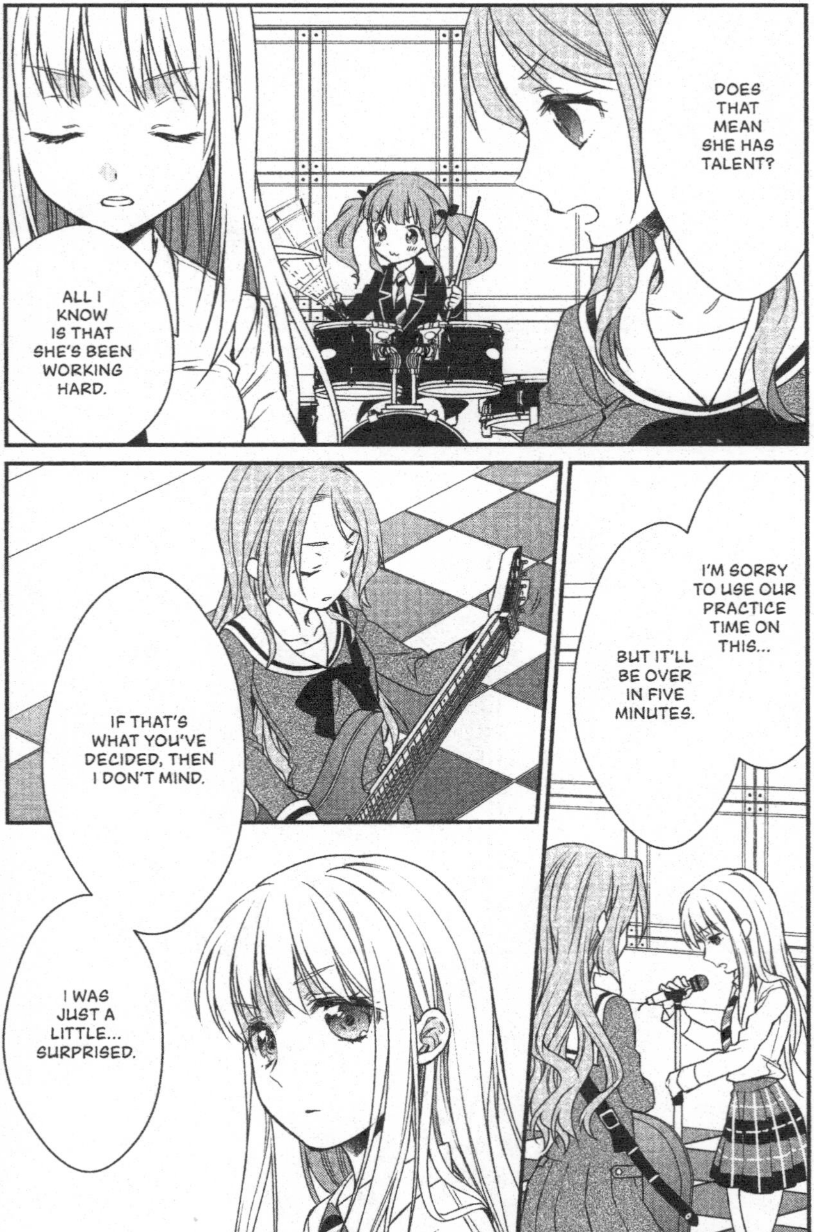
DOES THAT MEAN SHE HAS TALENT?
ALL I KNOW IS THAT SHE'S BEEN WORKING HARD.
I'M SORRY TO USE OUR PRACTICE TIME ON THIS...
BUT IT'LL BE OVER IN FIVE MINUTES.
IF THAT'S WHAT YOU'VE DECIDED, THEN I DON'T MIND.
I WAS JUST A LITTLE... SURPRISED.

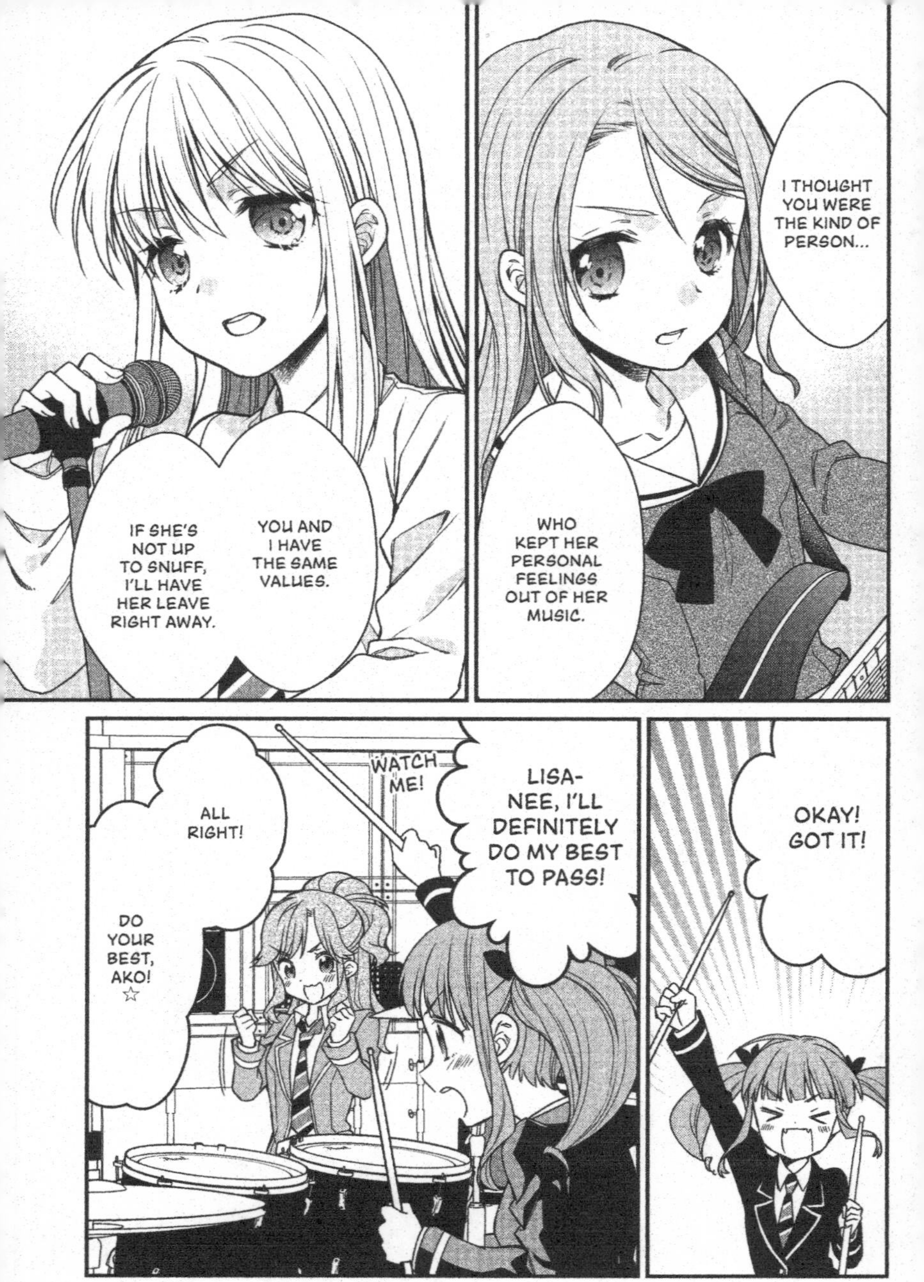
I THOUGHT YOU WERE THE KIND OF PERSON...
WHO KEPT HER PERSONAL FEELINGS OUT OF HER MUSIC.
YOU AND I HAVE THE SAME VALUES.
IF SHE'S NOT UP TO SNUFF, I'LL HAVE HER LEAVE RIGHT AWAY.
OKAY! GOT IT!
LISA-NEE, I'LL DEFINITELY DO MY BEST TO PASS!
WATCH ME!
ALL RIGHT!
DO YOUR BEST, AKO! ☆

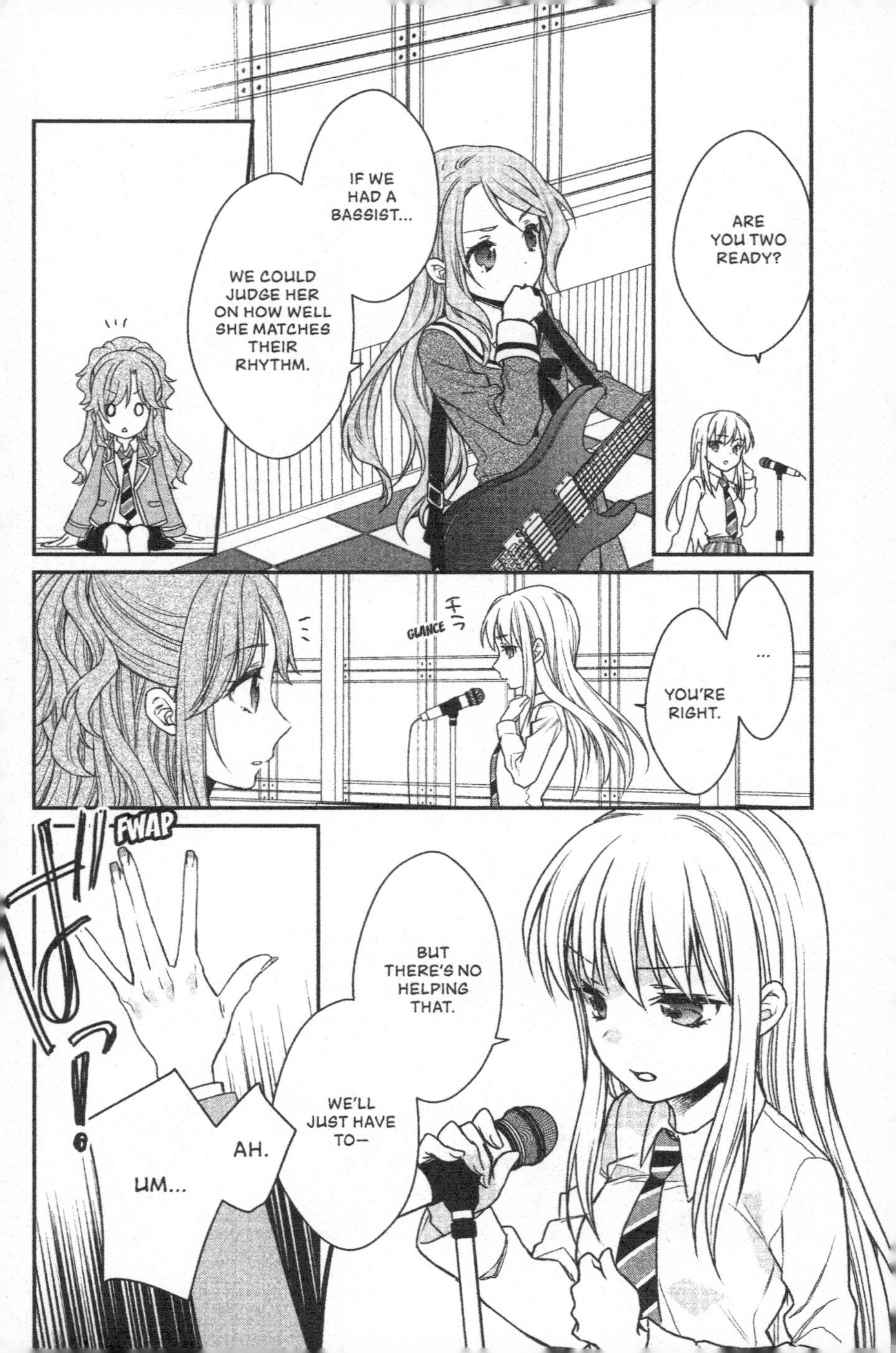
ARE YOU TWO READY?
IF WE HAD A BASSIST...
WE COULD JUDGE HER ON HOW WELL SHE MATCHES THEIR RHYTHM.
GLANCE
... YOU'RE RIGHT.
FWAP
BUT THERE'S NO HELPING THAT.
WE'LL JUST HAVE TO—
AH.
UM...

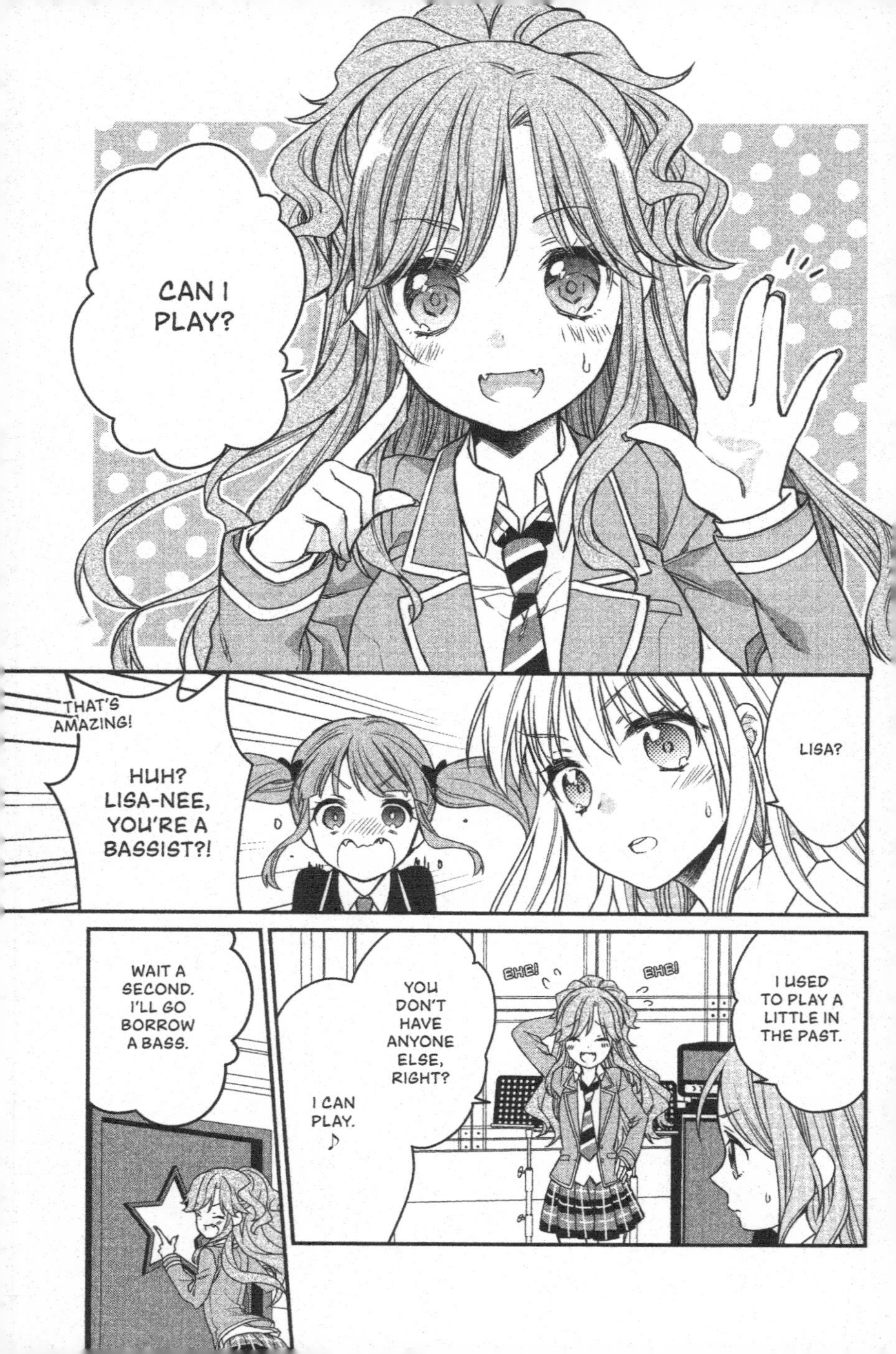
CAN I PLAY?
LISA?
HUH? LISA-NEE, YOU'RE A BASSIST?!
THAT'S AMAZING!
I USED TO PLAY A LITTLE IN THE PAST.
EHE!
EHE!
YOU DON'T HAVE ANYONE ELSE, RIGHT?
I CAN PLAY. ♪
WAIT A SECOND. I'LL GO BORROW A BASS.

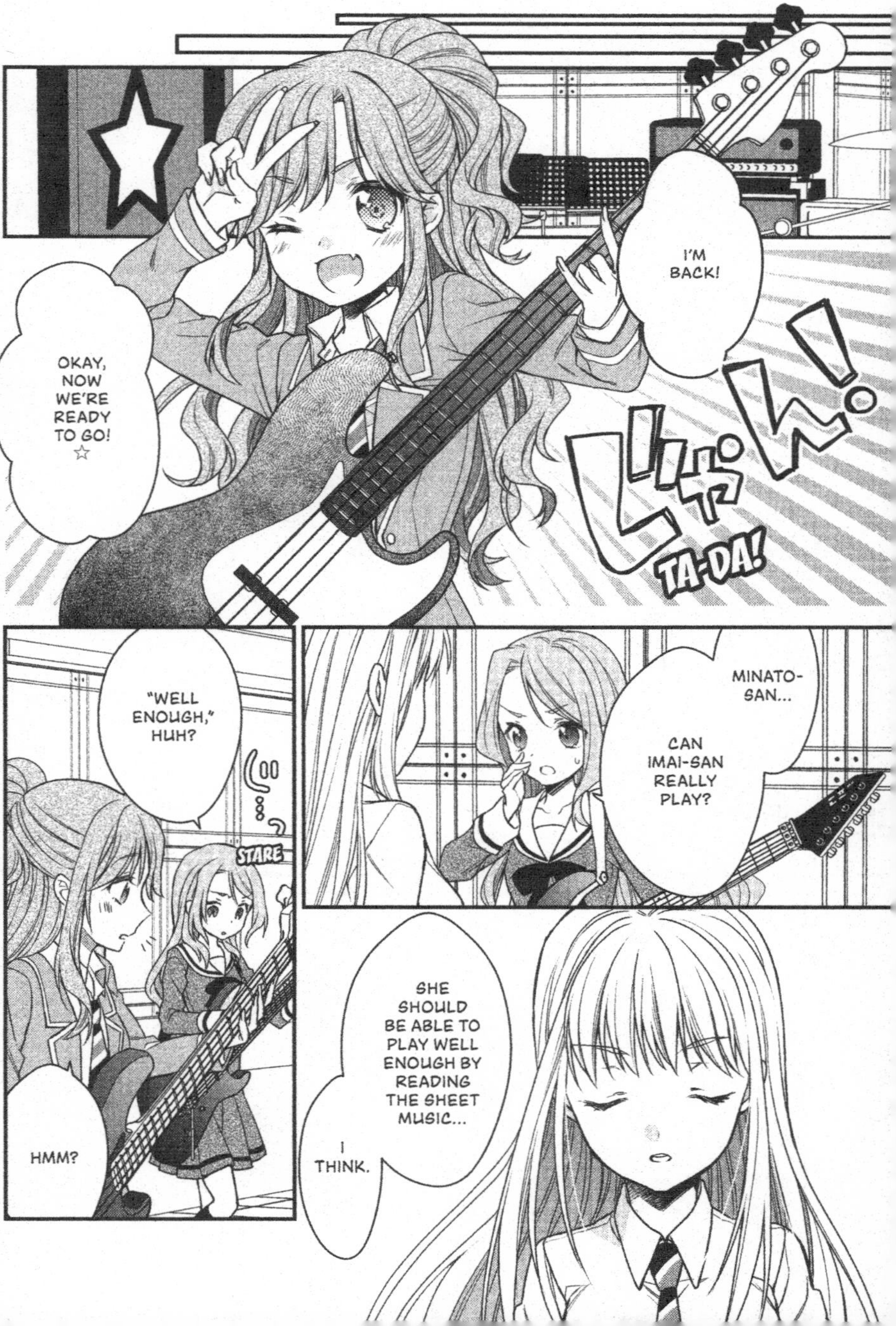
I'M BACK!
OKAY, NOW WE'RE READY TO GO! ☆
TA-DA!
MINATO-SAN...
CAN IMAI-SAN REALLY PLAY?
SHE SHOULD BE ABLE TO PLAY WELL ENOUGH BY READING THE SHEET MUSIC...
I THINK.
"WELL ENOUGH," HUH?
STARE
HMM?

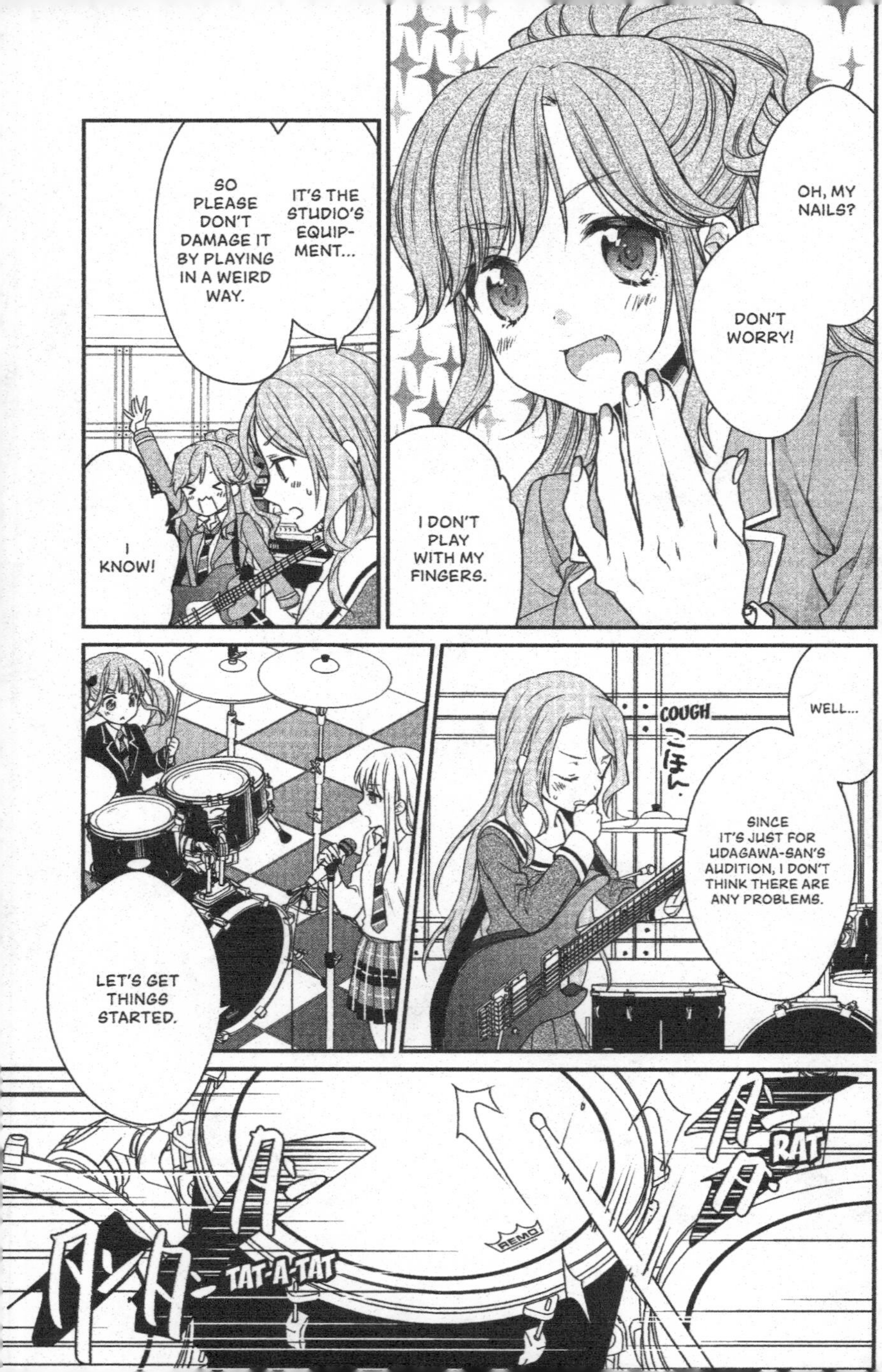
OH, MY NAILS?
DON'T WORRY!
I DON'T PLAY WITH MY FINGERS.
IT'S THE STUDIO'S EQUIPMENT...
SO PLEASE DON'T DAMAGE IT BY PLAYING IN A WEIRD WAY.
I KNOW!
WELL...
COUGH
こほん
SINCE IT'S JUST FOR UDAGAWA-SAN'S AUDITION, I DON'T THINK THERE ARE ANY PROBLEMS.
LET'S GET THINGS STARTED.
RAT
TAT-A-TAT
REMO

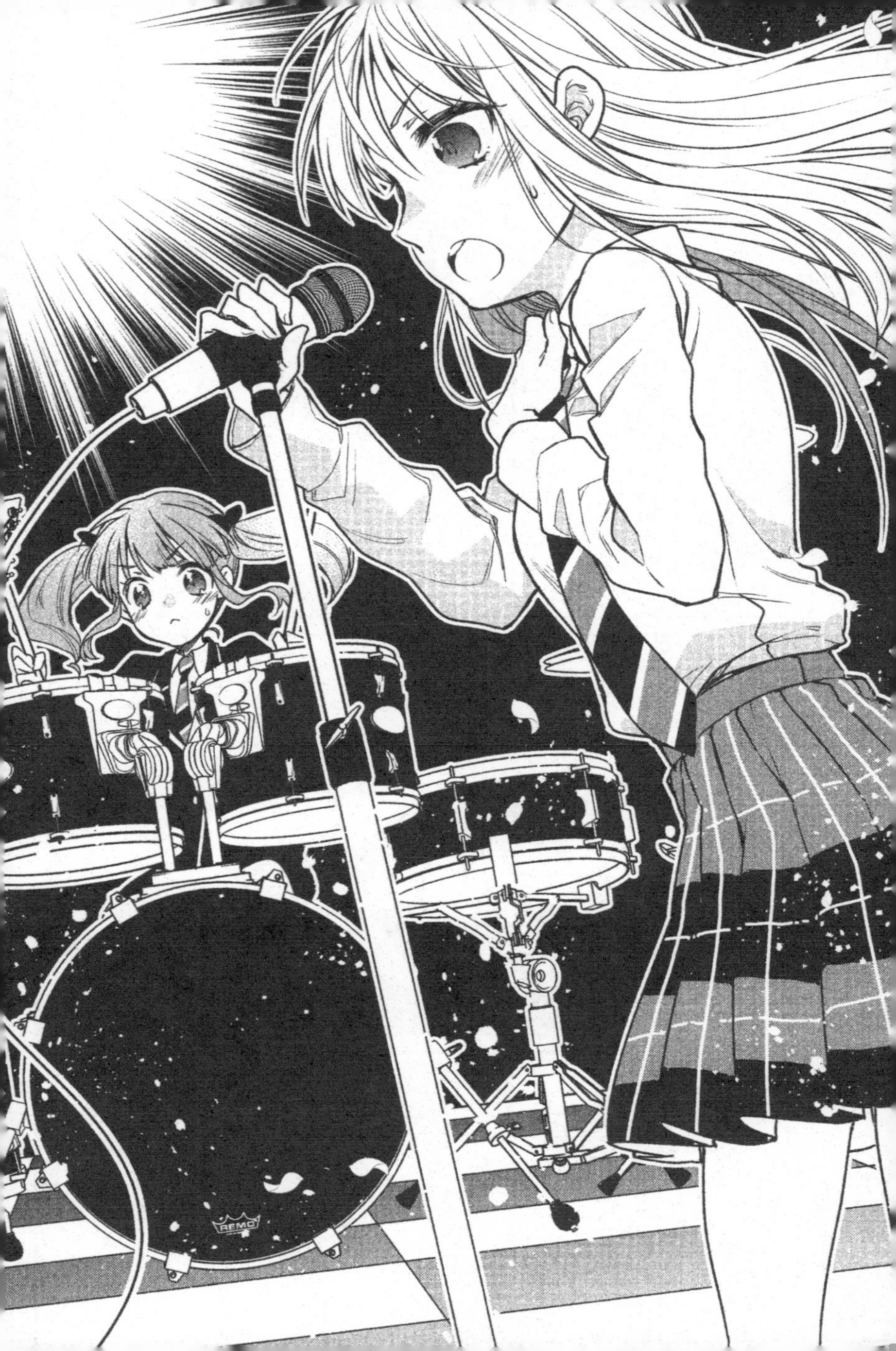
REMO

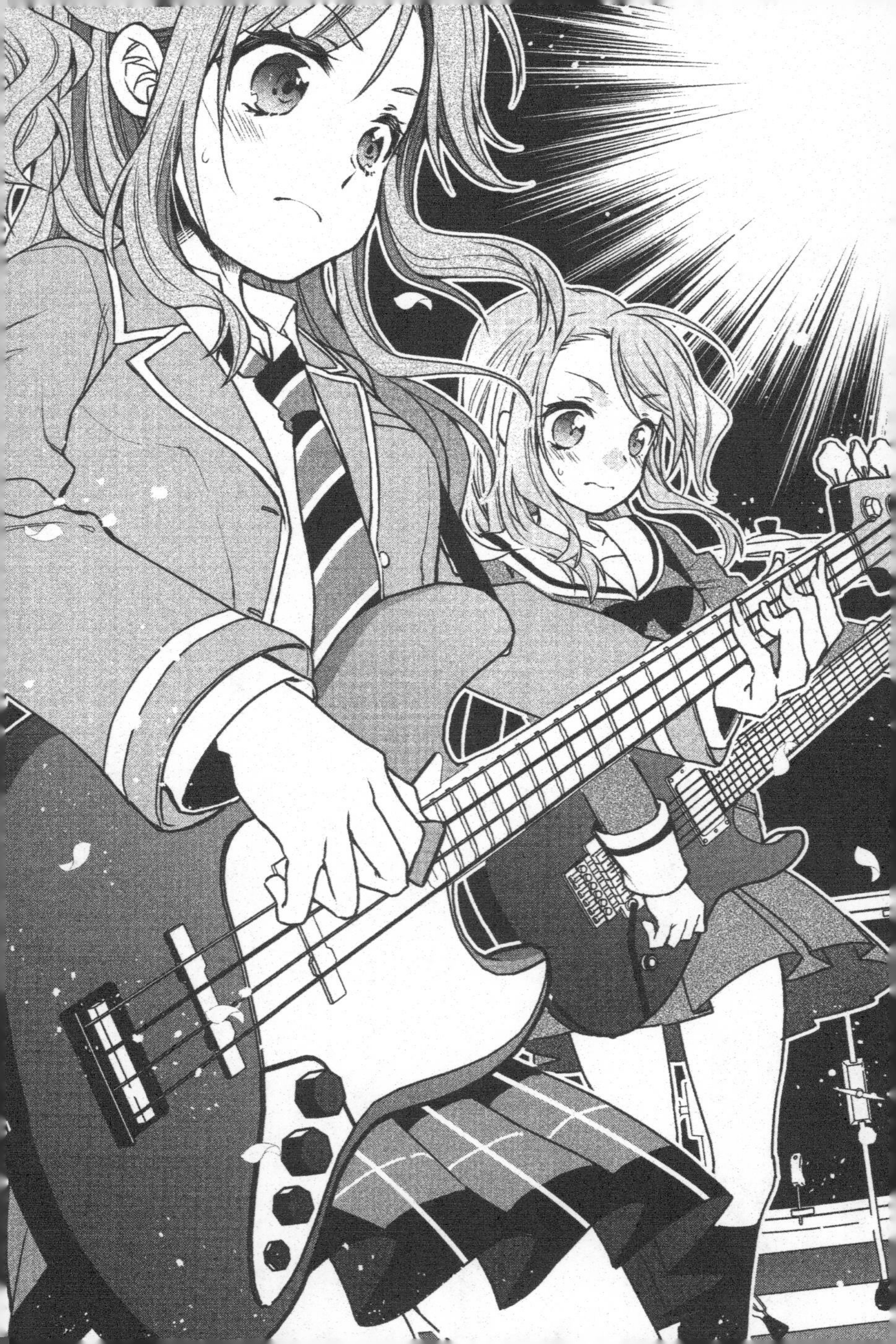

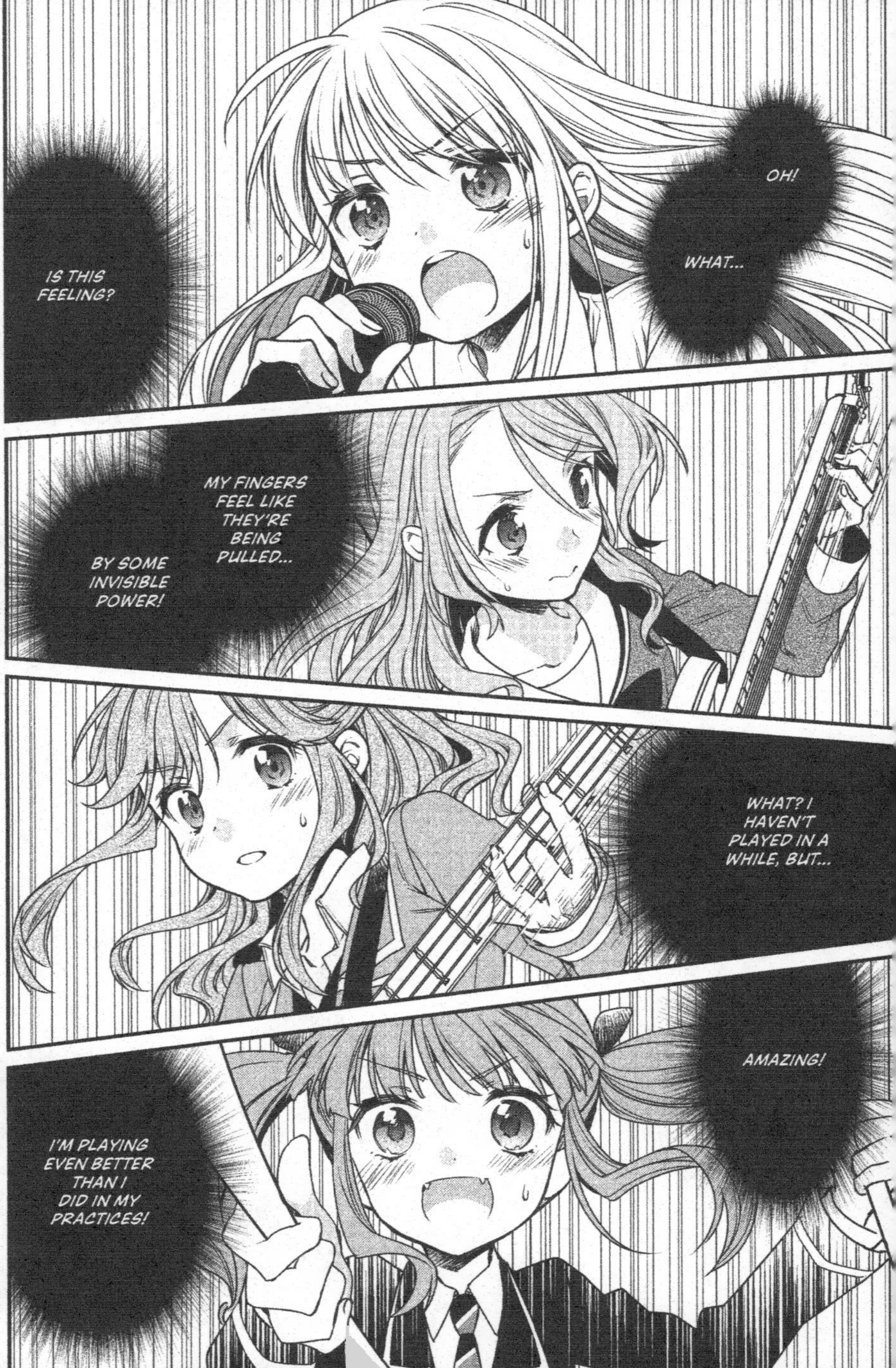
OH!
WHAT...
IS THIS FEELING?
MY FINGERS FEEL LIKE THEY'RE BEING PULLED...
BY SOME INVISIBLE POWER!
WHAT? I HAVEN'T PLAYED IN A WHILE, BUT...
AMAZING!
I'M PLAYING EVEN BETTER THAN I DID IN MY PRACTICES!

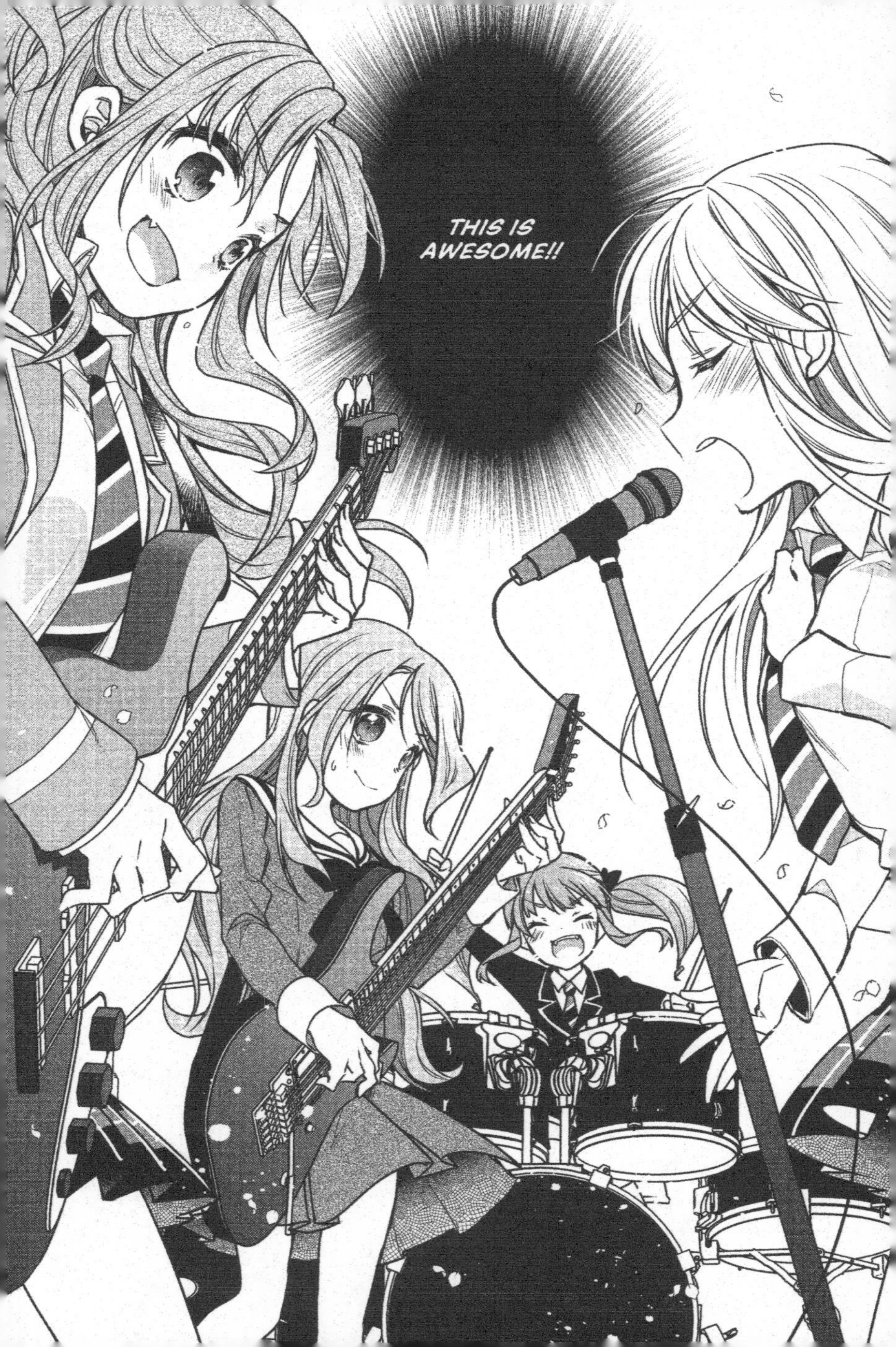
THIS IS AWESOME!!

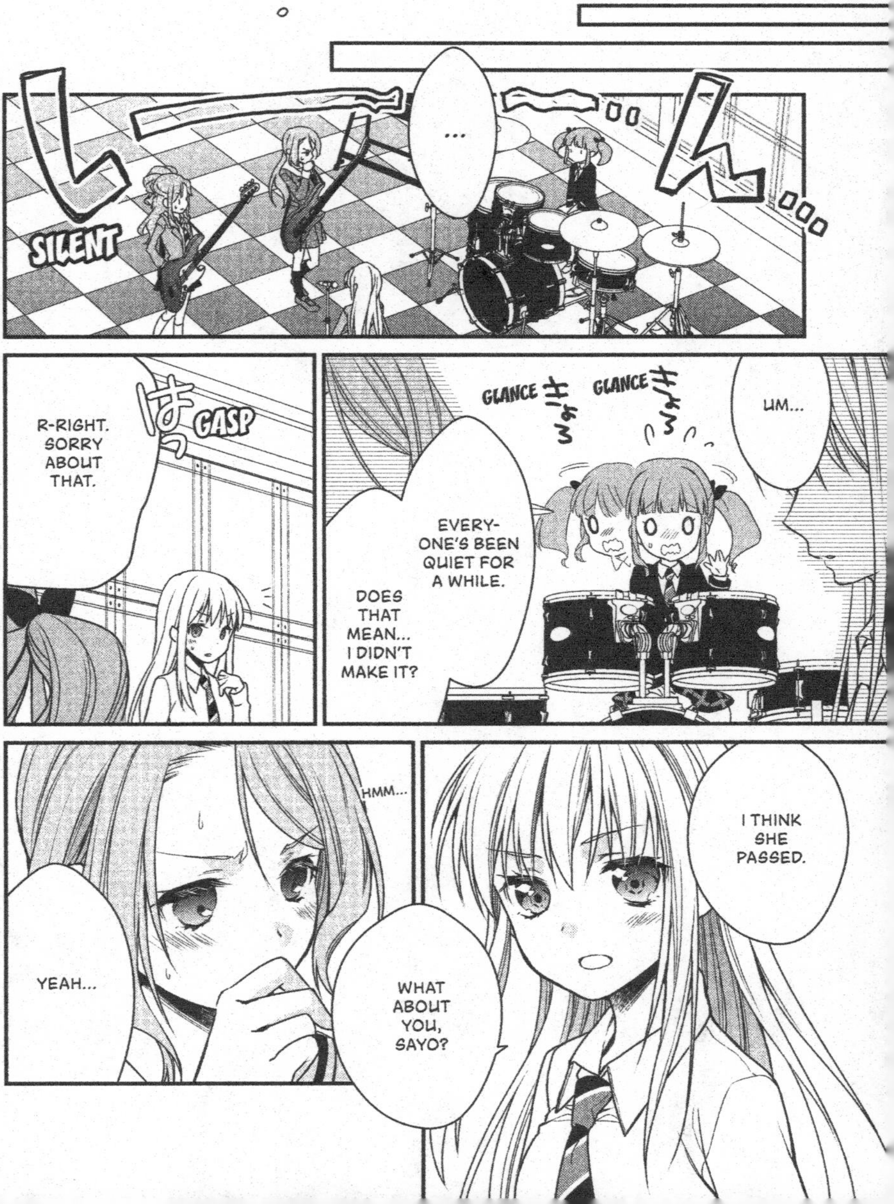
しーーーん
SILENT
...
UM...
GLANCE きょろ
GLANCE きょろ
EVERY-ONE'S BEEN QUIET FOR A WHILE.
DOES THAT MEAN... I DIDN'T MAKE IT?
はっ GASP
R-RIGHT. SORRY ABOUT THAT.
I THINK SHE PASSED.
WHAT ABOUT YOU, SAYO?
HMM...
YEAH...

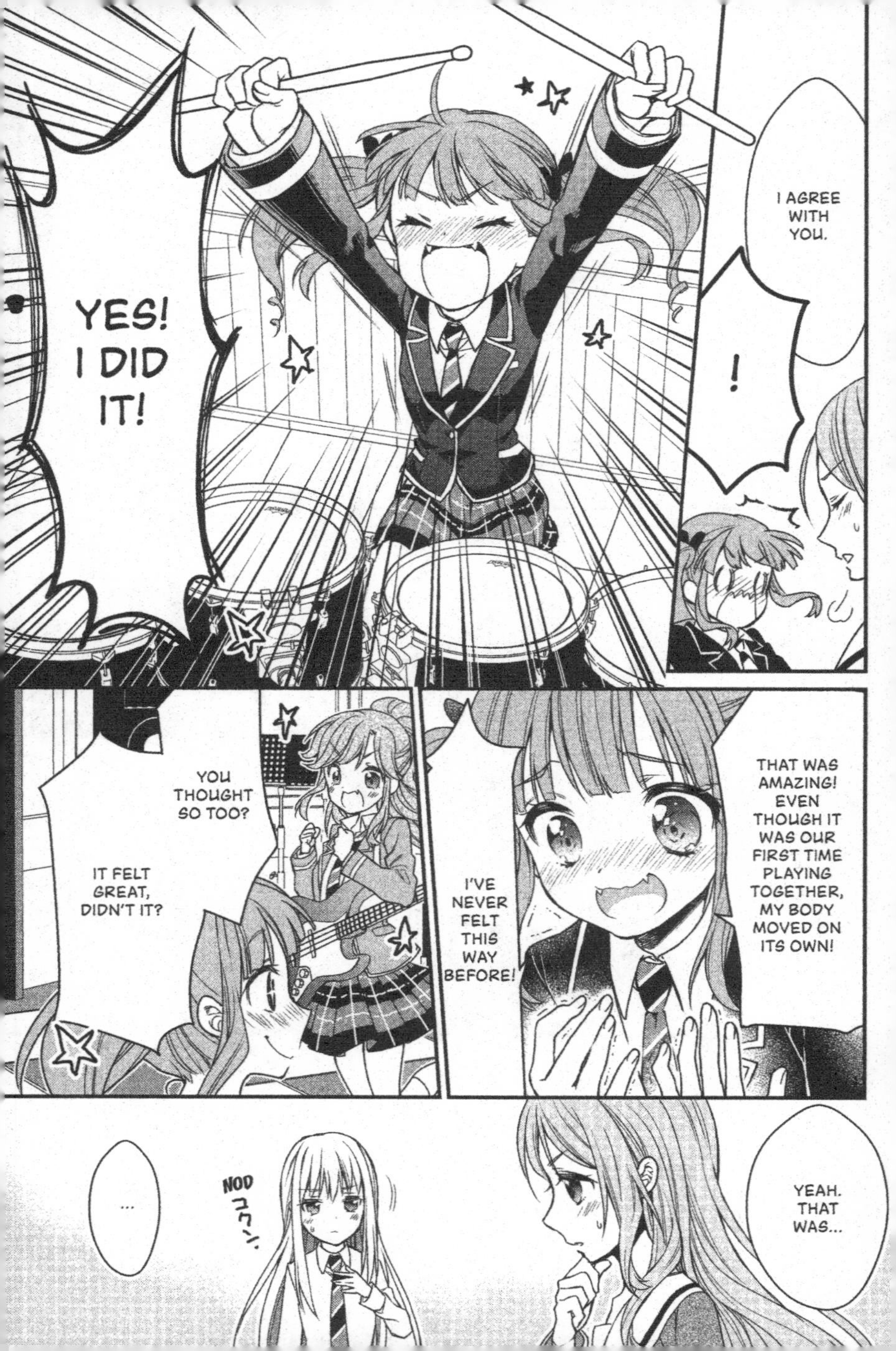
I AGREE WITH YOU.
!
YES! I DID IT!
THAT WAS AMAZING! EVEN THOUGH IT WAS OUR FIRST TIME PLAYING TOGETHER, MY BODY MOVED ON ITS OWN!
I'VE NEVER FELT THIS WAY BEFORE!
YOU THOUGHT SO TOO?
IT FELT GREAT, DIDN'T IT?
YEAH. THAT WAS...
NOD
コクン
...

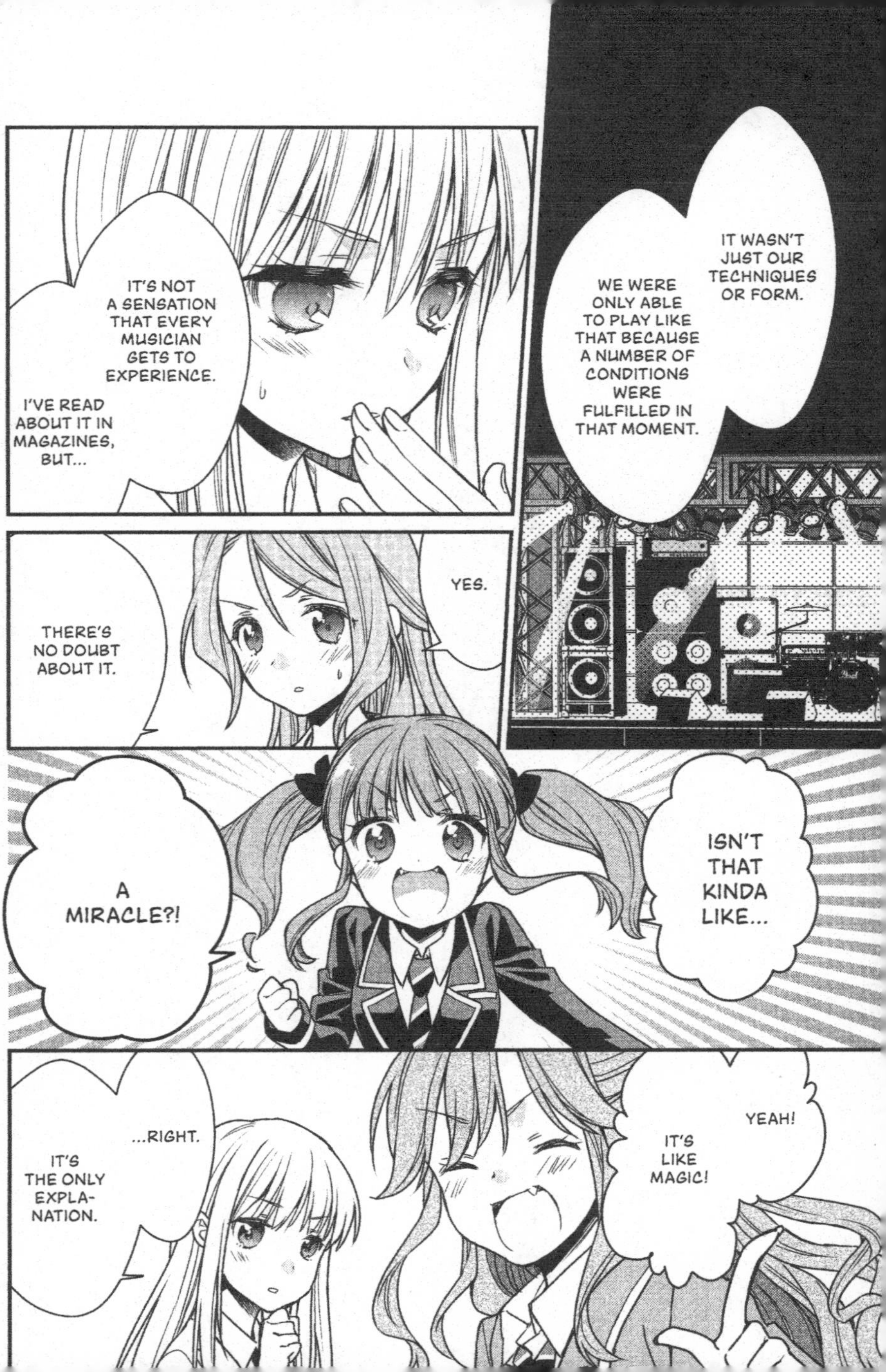
IT WASN'T JUST OUR TECHNIQUES OR FORM.
WE WERE ONLY ABLE TO PLAY LIKE THAT BECAUSE A NUMBER OF CONDITIONS WERE FULFILLED IN THAT MOMENT.
IT'S NOT A SENSATION THAT EVERY MUSICIAN GETS TO EXPERIENCE.
I'VE READ ABOUT IT IN MAGAZINES, BUT...
YES.
THERE'S NO DOUBT ABOUT IT.
ISN'T THAT KINDA LIKE...
A MIRACLE?!
YEAH!
IT'S LIKE MAGIC!
...RIGHT.
IT'S THE ONLY EXPLANATION.

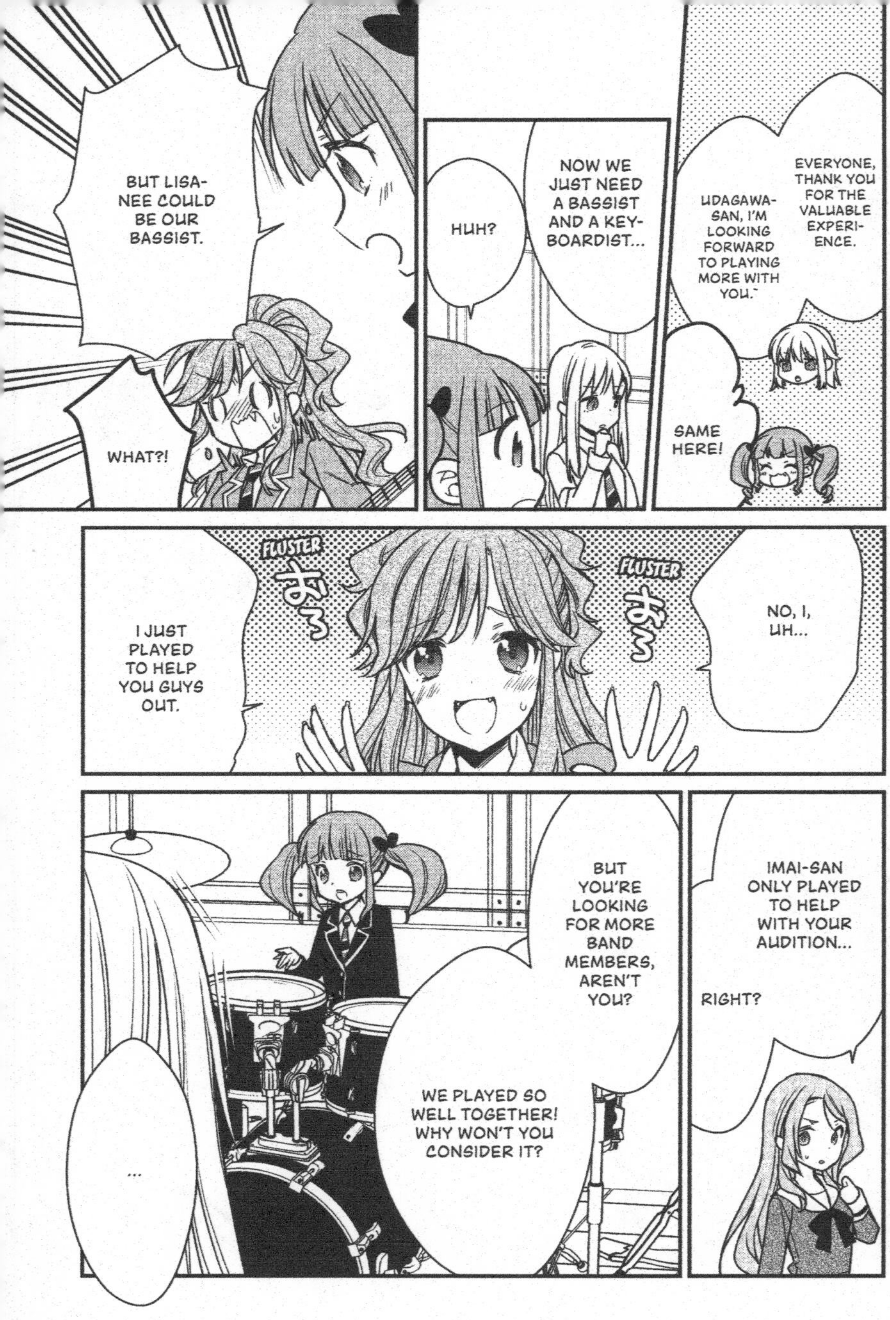
EVERYONE, THANK YOU FOR THE VALUABLE EXPERIENCE.
UDAGAWA-SAN, I'M LOOKING FORWARD TO PLAYING MORE WITH YOU.~
SAME HERE!
NOW WE JUST NEED A BASSIST AND A KEY-BOARDIST...
HUH?
BUT LISA-NEE COULD BE OUR BASSIST.
WHAT?!
NO, I, UH...
FLUSTER
おろ
FLUSTER
おろ
I JUST PLAYED TO HELP YOU GUYS OUT.
IMAI-SAN ONLY PLAYED TO HELP WITH YOUR AUDITION...
RIGHT?
BUT YOU'RE LOOKING FOR MORE BAND MEMBERS, AREN'T YOU?
WE PLAYED SO WELL TOGETHER! WHY WON'T YOU CONSIDER IT?
...

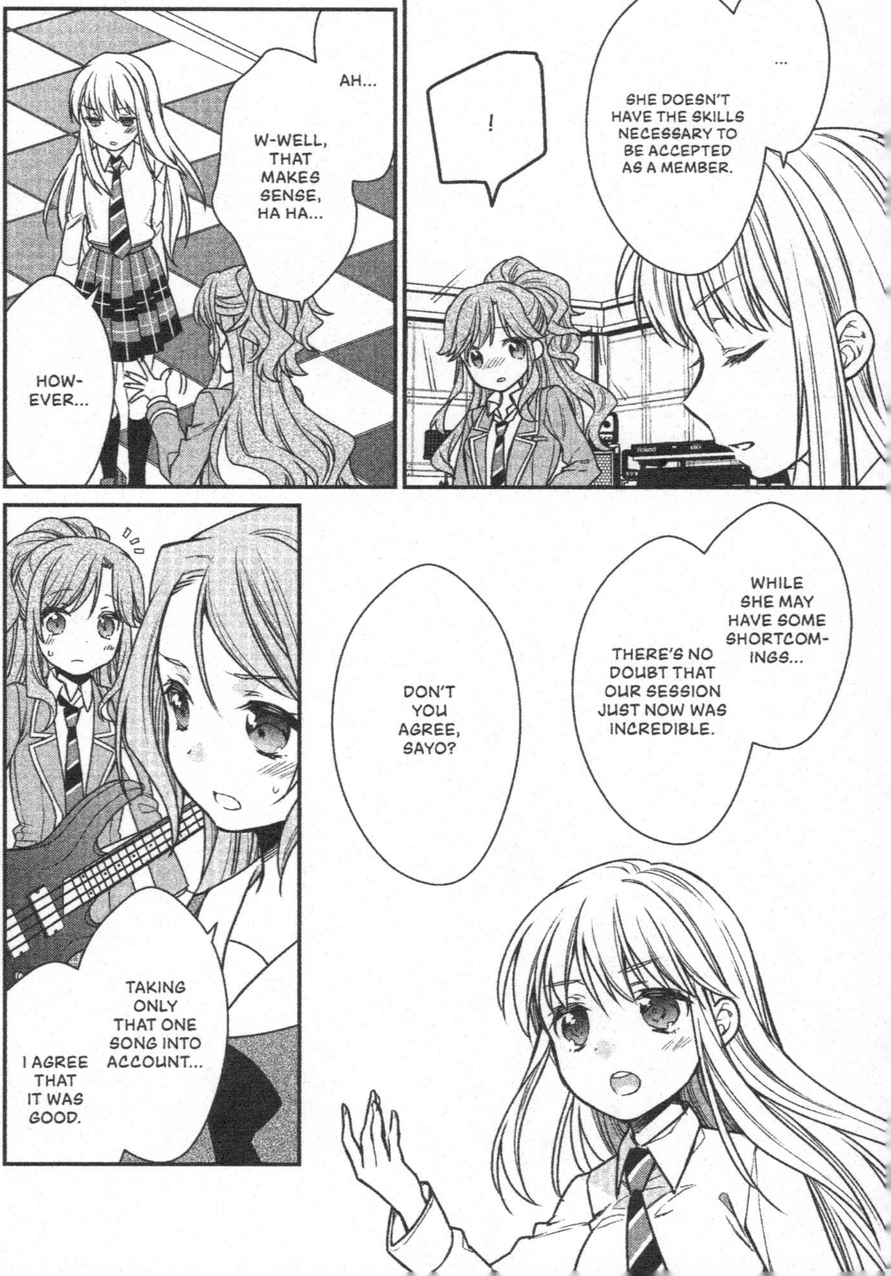
...
SHE DOESN'T HAVE THE SKILLS NECESSARY TO BE ACCEPTED AS A MEMBER.
!
AH...
W-WELL, THAT MAKES SENSE, HA HA...
HOW-EVER...
WHILE SHE MAY HAVE SOME SHORTCOM-INGS...
THERE'S NO DOUBT THAT OUR SESSION JUST NOW WAS INCREDIBLE.
DON'T YOU AGREE, SAYO?
TAKING ONLY THAT ONE SONG INTO ACCOUNT...
I AGREE THAT IT WAS GOOD.

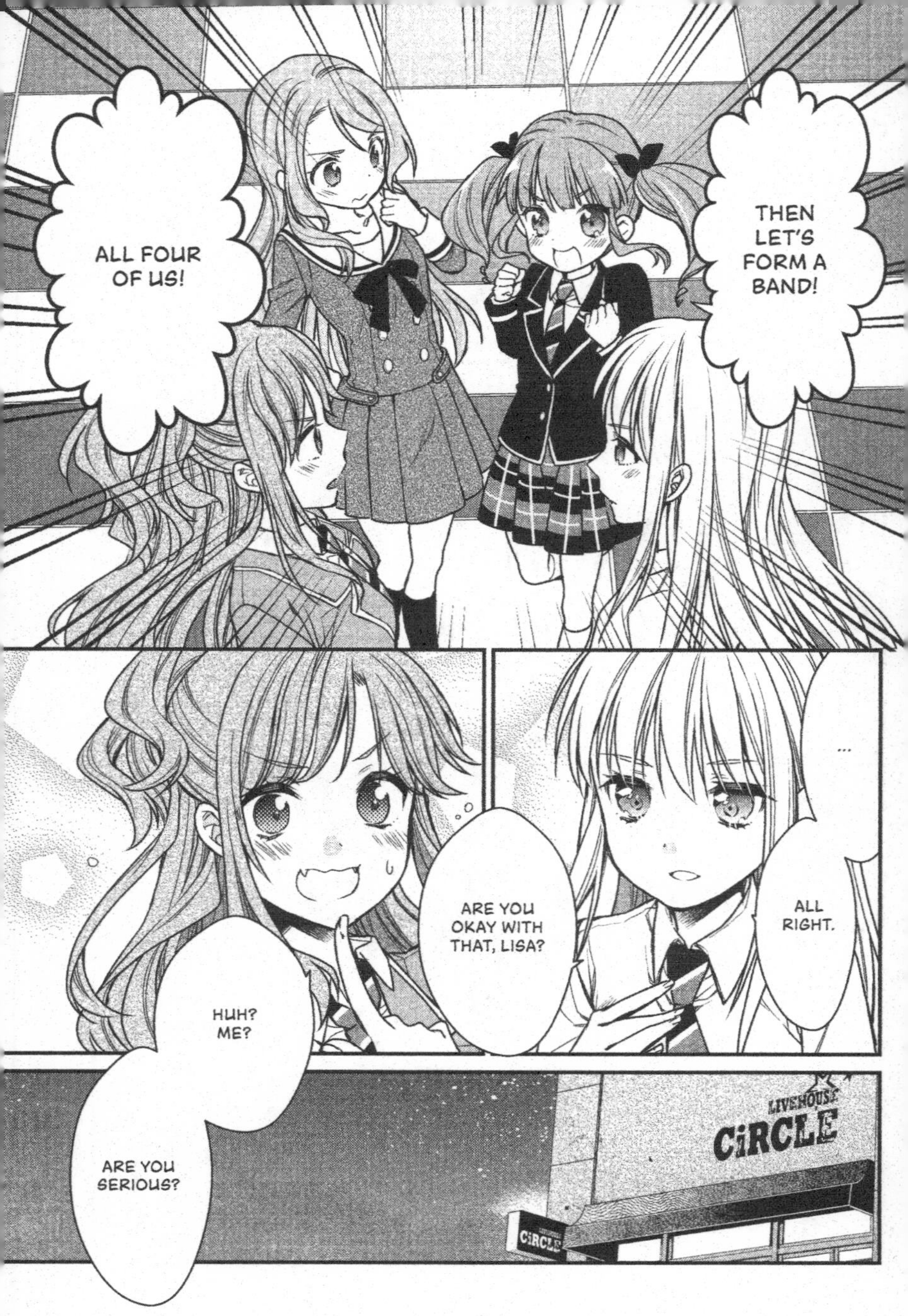
THEN LET'S FORM A BAND!
ALL FOUR OF US!
...
ALL RIGHT.
ARE YOU OKAY WITH THAT, LISA?
HUH? ME?
LIVEHOUSE CiRCLE
CiRCLE
ARE YOU SERIOUS?

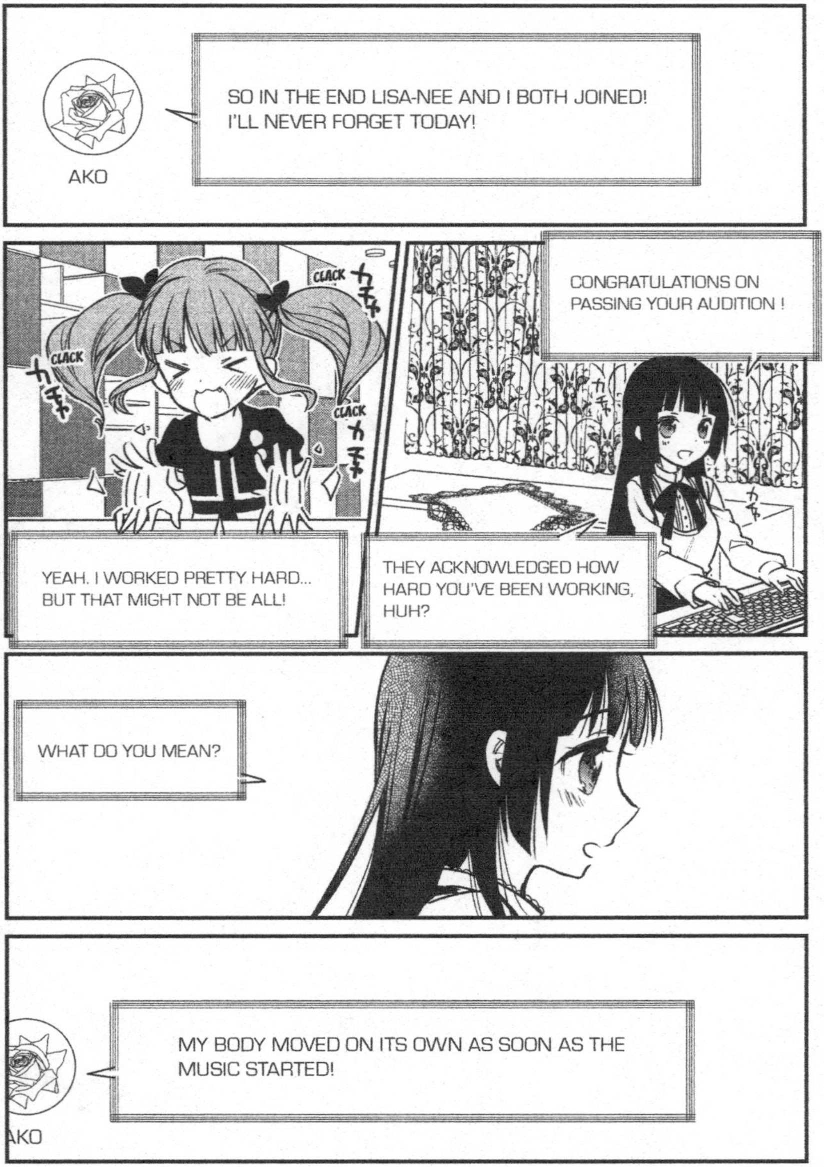
AKO
SO IN THE END LISA-NEE AND I BOTH JOINED! I'LL NEVER FORGET TODAY!
CONGRATULATIONS ON PASSING YOUR AUDITION !
THEY ACKNOWLEDGED HOW HARD YOU'VE BEEN WORKING, HUH?
CLACK カチャ
CLACK カチャ
CLACK カチャ
YEAH. I WORKED PRETTY HARD... BUT THAT MIGHT NOT BE ALL!
WHAT DO YOU MEAN?
AKO
MY BODY MOVED ON ITS OWN AS SOON AS THE MUSIC STARTED!

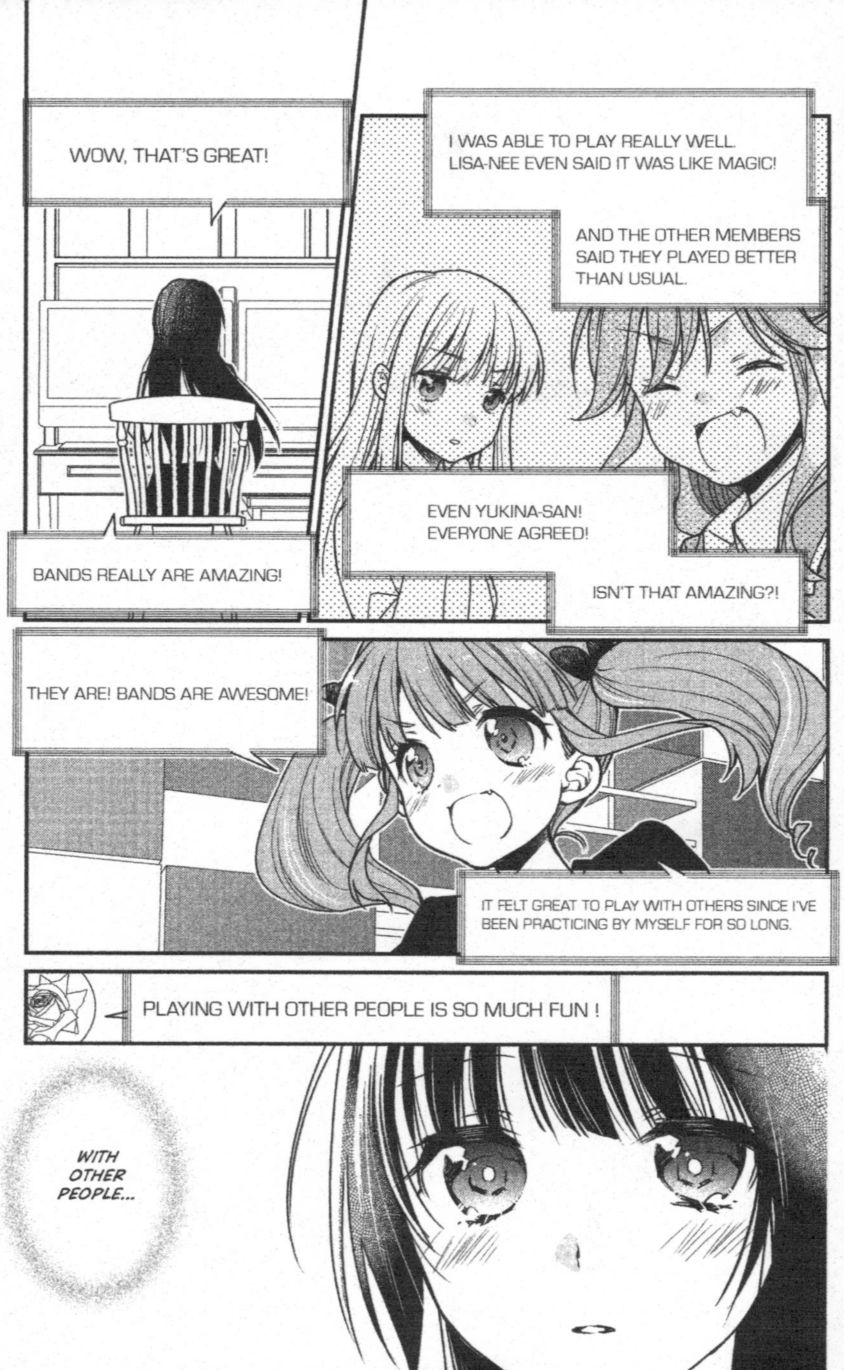
I WAS ABLE TO PLAY REALLY WELL. LISA-NEE EVEN SAID IT WAS LIKE MAGIC!
AND THE OTHER MEMBERS SAID THEY PLAYED BETTER THAN USUAL.
EVEN YUKINA-SAN! EVERYONE AGREED!
ISN'T THAT AMAZING?!
WOW, THAT'S GREAT!
BANDS REALLY ARE AMAZING!
THEY ARE! BANDS ARE AWESOME!
IT FELT GREAT TO PLAY WITH OTHERS SINCE I'VE BEEN PRACTICING BY MYSELF FOR SO LONG.
PLAYING WITH OTHER PEOPLE IS SO MUCH FUN !
WITH OTHER PEOPLE...

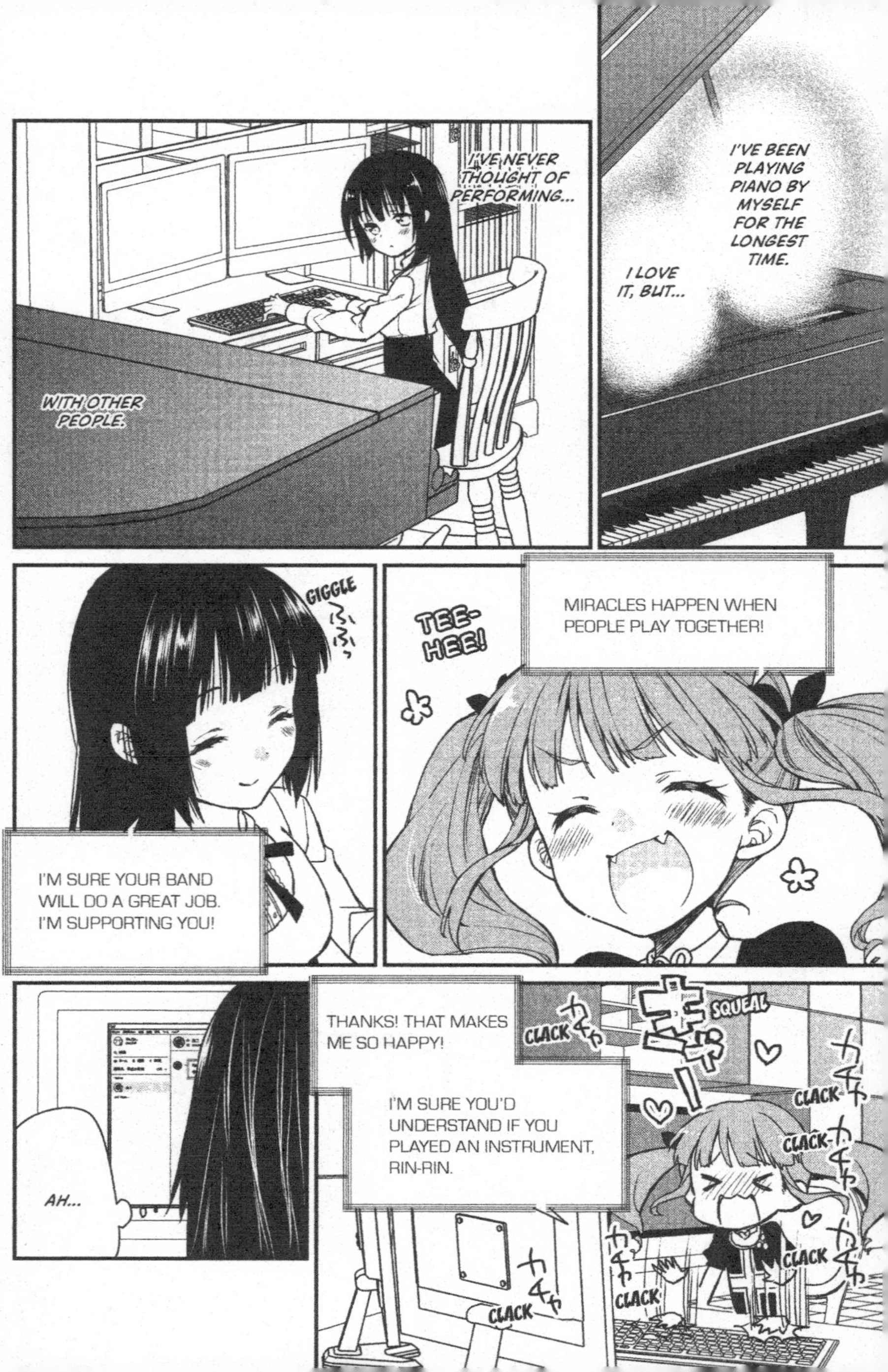
I'VE BEEN PLAYING PIANO BY MYSELF FOR THE LONGEST TIME.
I LOVE IT, BUT...
I'VE NEVER THOUGHT OF PERFORMING...
WITH OTHER PEOPLE.
MIRACLES HAPPEN WHEN PEOPLE PLAY TOGETHER!
TEE-HEE!
GIGGLE
I'M SURE YOUR BAND WILL DO A GREAT JOB. I'M SUPPORTING YOU!
SQUEAL
CLACK
CLACK
CLACK
CLACK
CLACK
THANKS! THAT MAKES ME SO HAPPY!
CLACK
I'M SURE YOU'D UNDERSTAND IF YOU PLAYED AN INSTRUMENT, RIN-RIN.
CLACK
AH...

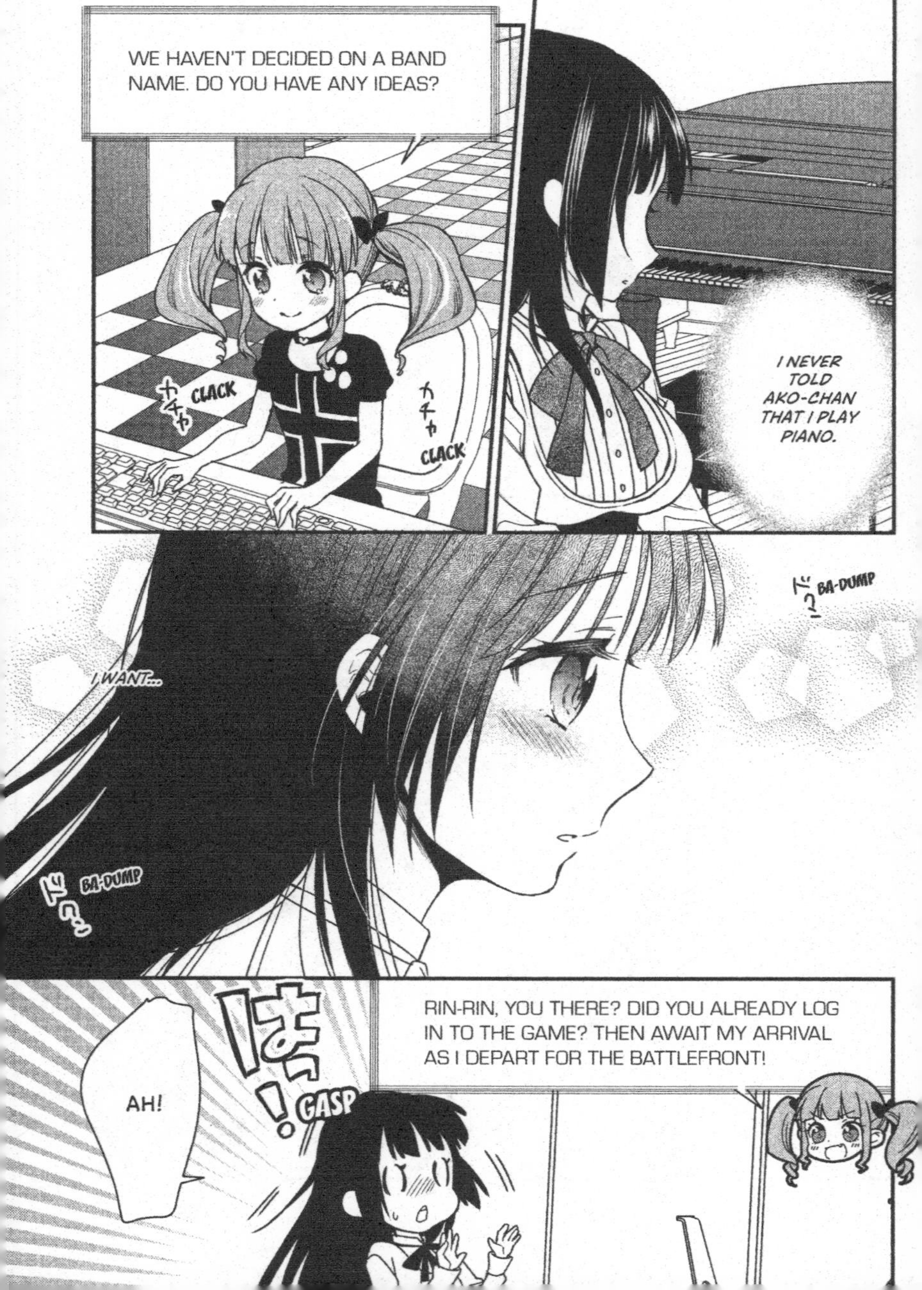
I NEVER TOLD AKO-CHAN THAT I PLAY PIANO.
WE HAVEN'T DECIDED ON A BAND NAME. DO YOU HAVE ANY IDEAS?
CLACK
CLACK
BA-DUMP
I WANT...
BA-DUMP
RIN-RIN, YOU THERE? DID YOU ALREADY LOG IN TO THE GAME? THEN AWAIT MY ARRIVAL AS I DEPART FOR THE BATTLEFRONT!
はっ!
GASP
AH!

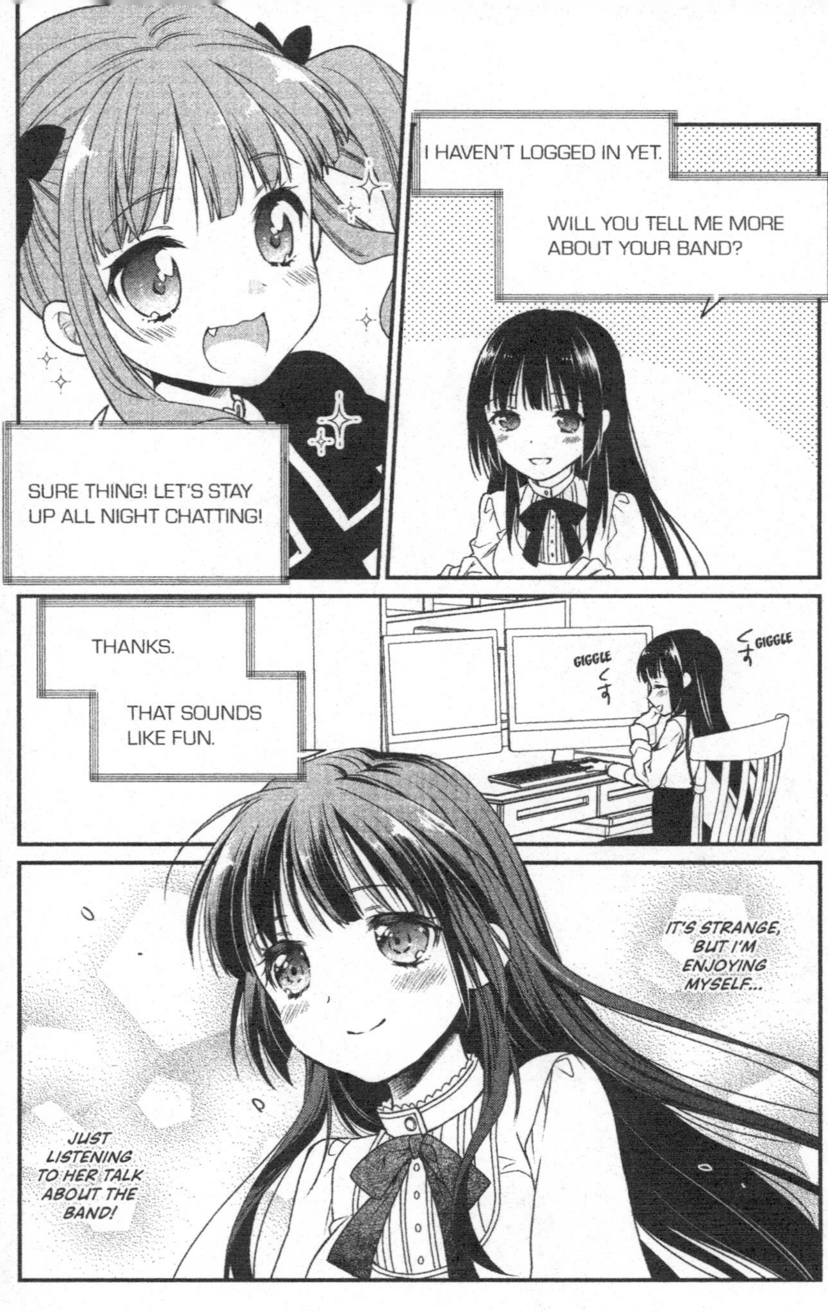
I HAVEN'T LOGGED IN YET.
WILL YOU TELL ME MORE ABOUT YOUR BAND?
SURE THING! LET'S STAY UP ALL NIGHT CHATTING!
THANKS.
THAT SOUNDS LIKE FUN.
くす GIGGLE
GIGGLE くす
IT'S STRANGE, BUT I'M ENJOYING MYSELF...
JUST LISTENING TO HER TALK ABOUT THE BAND!

Chapter 3
Each Other's Feelings

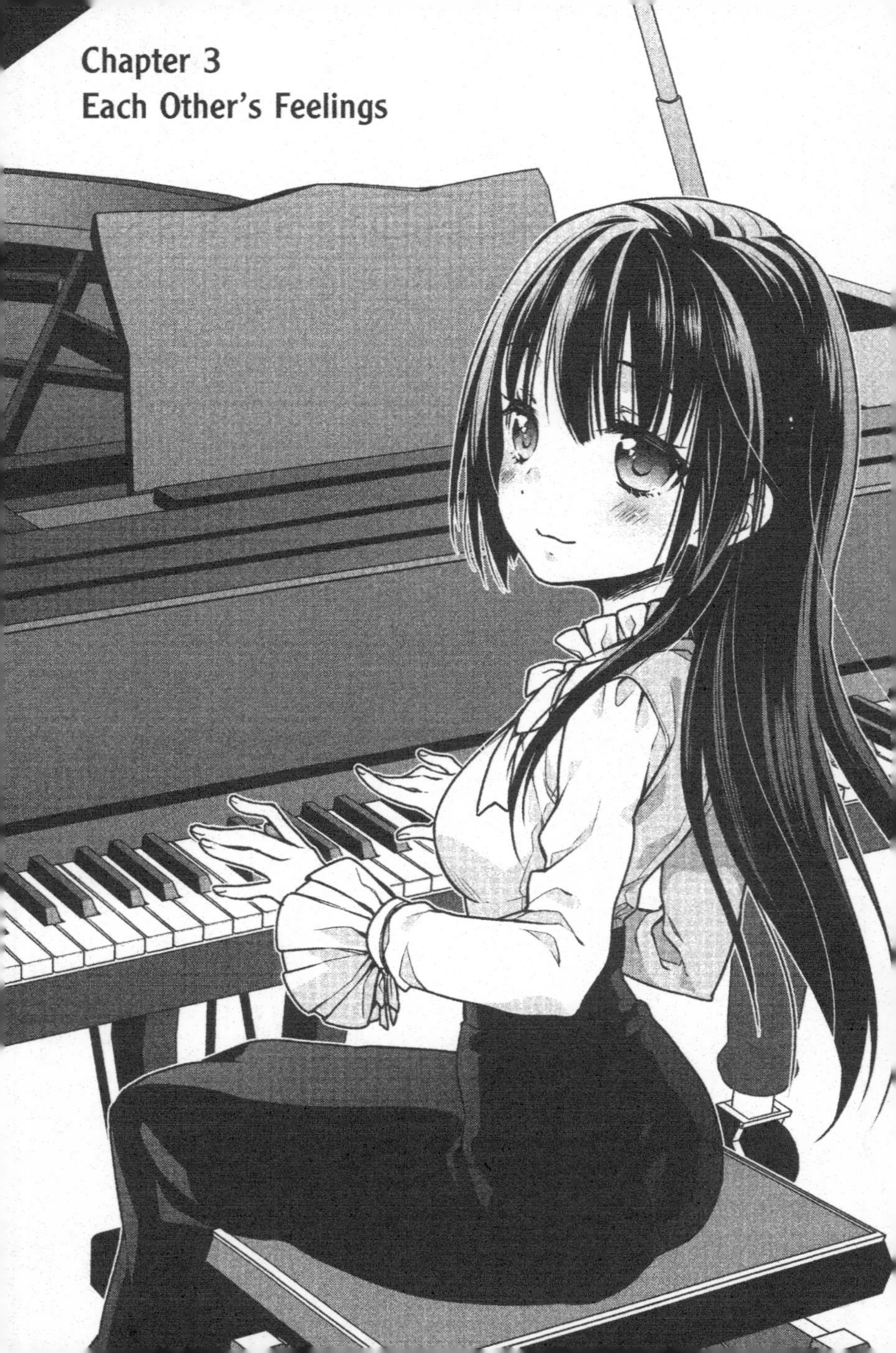

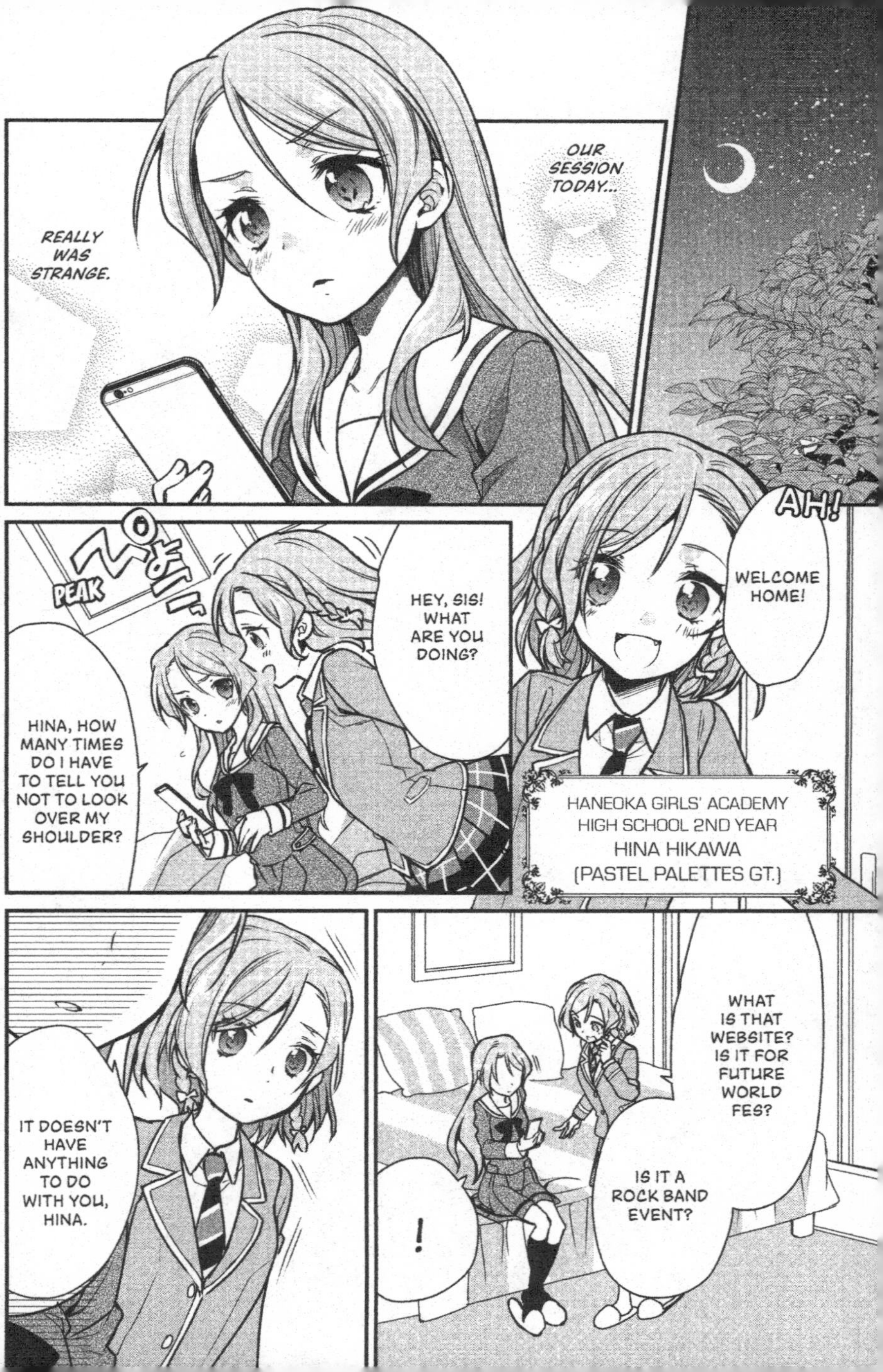

OUR SESSION TODAY...
REALLY WAS STRANGE.
AH!
WELCOME HOME!
HANEOKA GIRLS' ACADEMY HIGH SCHOOL 2ND YEAR
HINA HIKAWA
(PASTEL PALETTES GT.)
PEAK
HEY, SIS! WHAT ARE YOU DOING?
HINA, HOW MANY TIMES DO I HAVE TO TELL YOU NOT TO LOOK OVER MY SHOULDER?
WHAT IS THAT WEBSITE? IS IT FOR FUTURE WORLD FES?
IS IT A ROCK BAND EVENT?
!
IT DOESN'T HAVE ANYTHING TO DO WITH YOU, HINA.

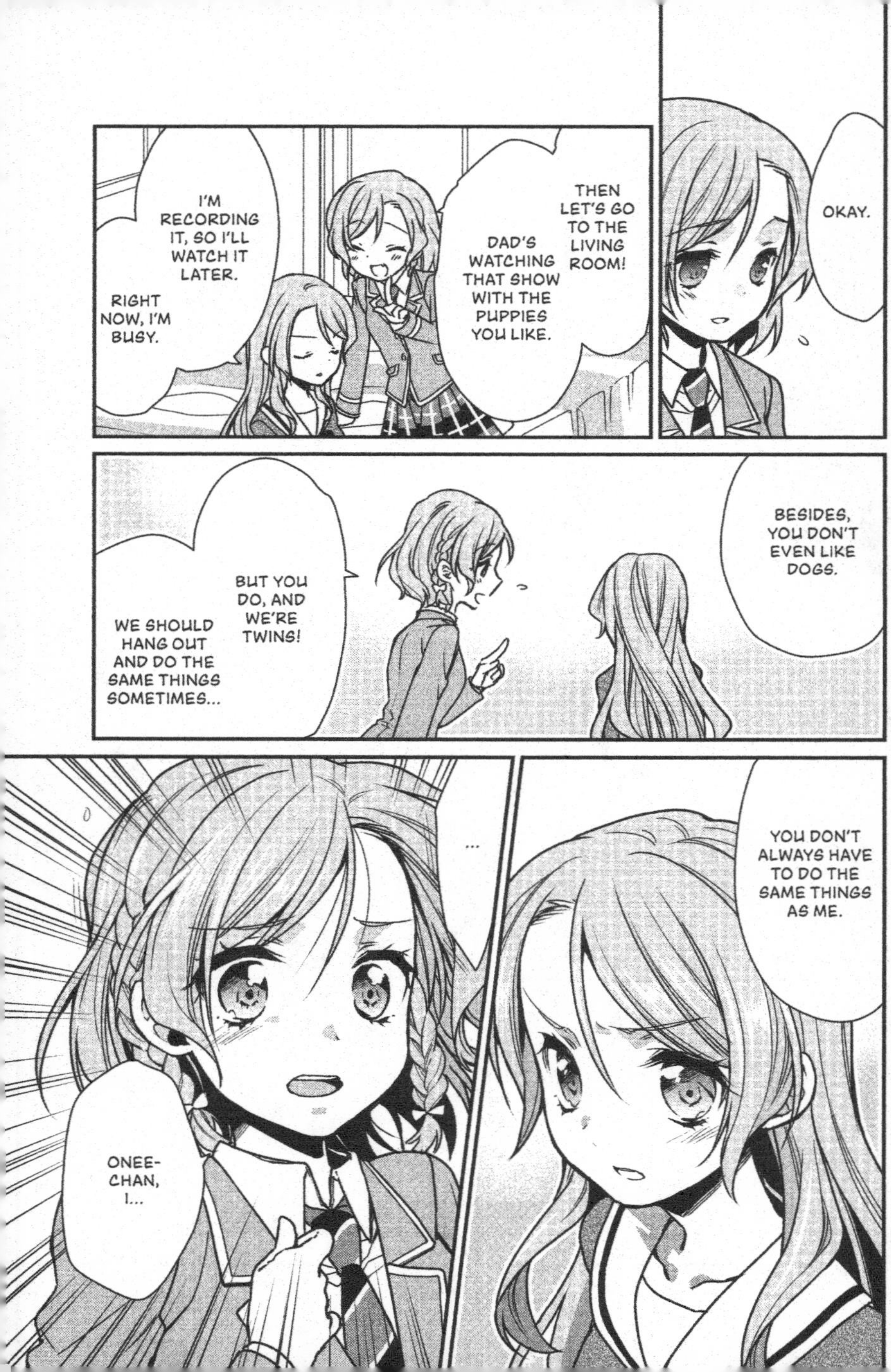
OKAY.
THEN LET'S GO TO THE LIVING ROOM!
DAD'S WATCHING THAT SHOW WITH THE PUPPIES YOU LIKE.
I'M RECORDING IT, SO I'LL WATCH IT LATER.
RIGHT NOW, I'M BUSY.
BESIDES, YOU DON'T EVEN LIKE DOGS.
BUT YOU DO, AND WE'RE TWINS!
WE SHOULD HANG OUT AND DO THE SAME THINGS SOMETIMES...
YOU DON'T ALWAYS HAVE TO DO THE SAME THINGS AS ME.
...
ONEE-CHAN, I...

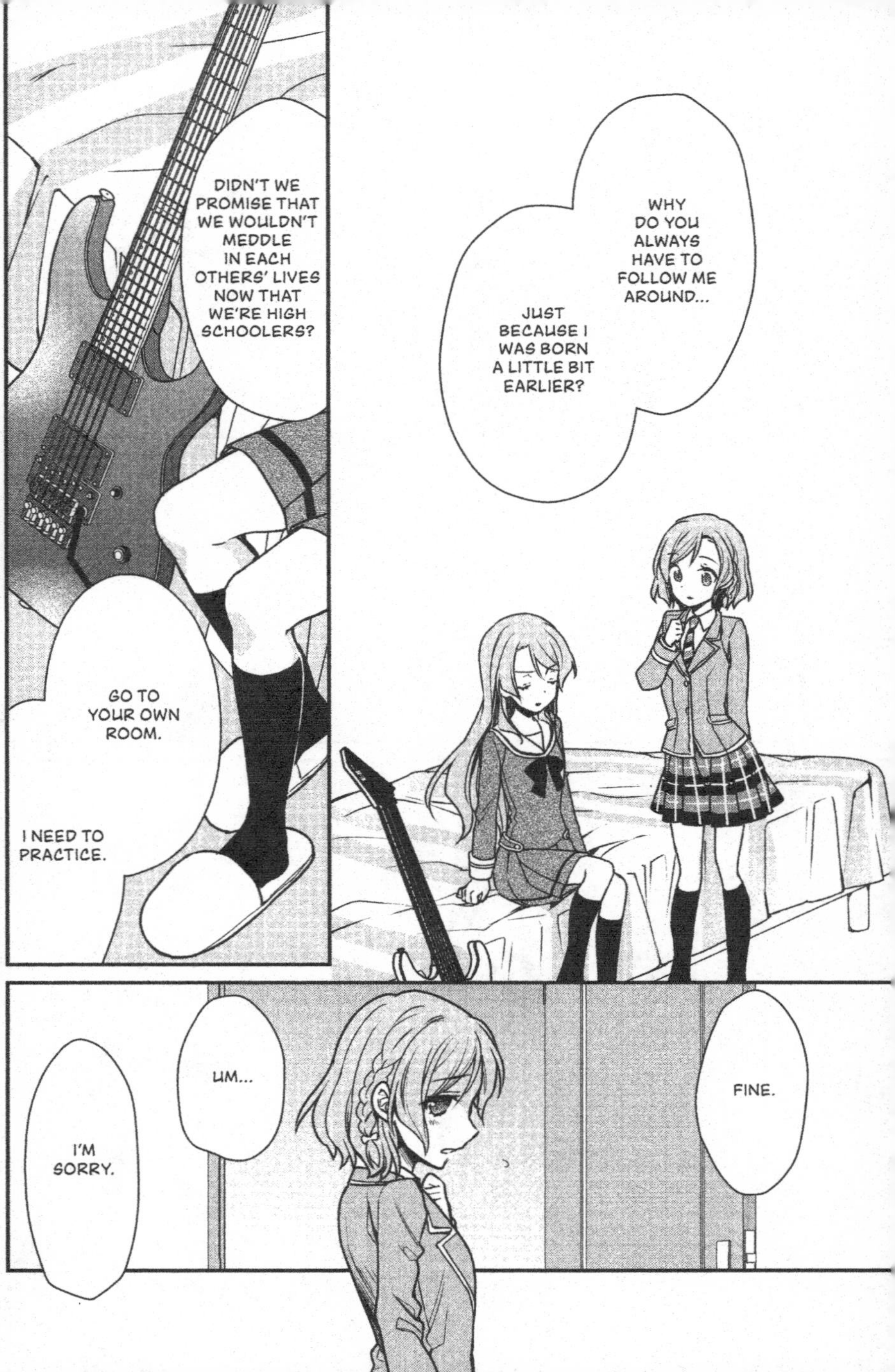
WHY DO YOU ALWAYS HAVE TO FOLLOW ME AROUND...
JUST BECAUSE I WAS BORN A LITTLE BIT EARLIER?
DIDN'T WE PROMISE THAT WE WOULDN'T MEDDLE IN EACH OTHERS' LIVES NOW THAT WE'RE HIGH SCHOOLERS?
GO TO YOUR OWN ROOM.
I NEED TO PRACTICE.
FINE.
UM...
I'M SORRY.

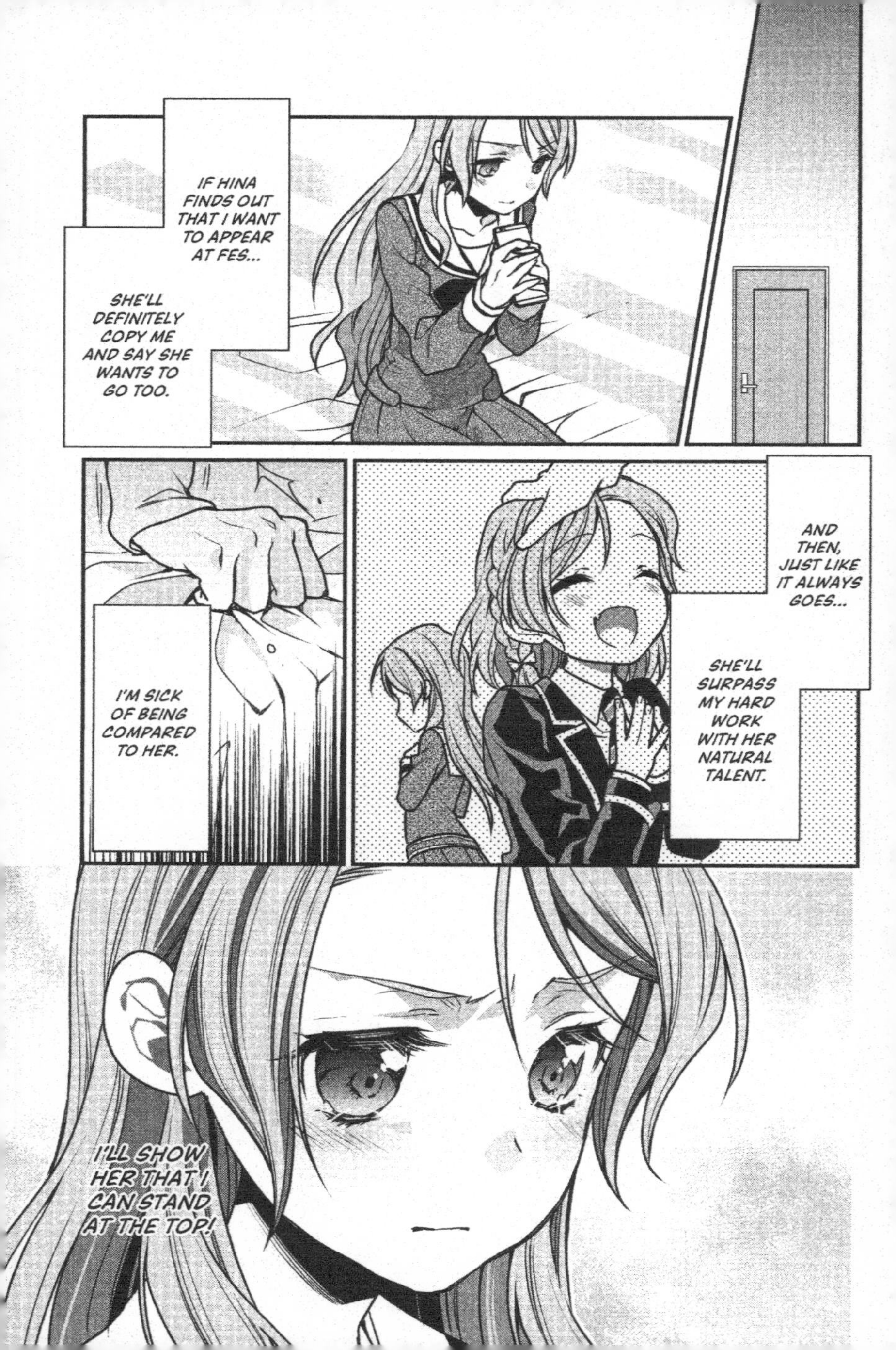
IF HINA FINDS OUT THAT I WANT TO APPEAR AT FES...
SHE'LL DEFINITELY COPY ME AND SAY SHE WANTS TO GO TOO.
AND THEN, JUST LIKE IT ALWAYS GOES...
SHE'LL SURPASS MY HARD WORK WITH HER NATURAL TALENT.
I'M SICK OF BEING COMPARED TO HER.
I'LL SHOW HER THAT I CAN STAND AT THE TOP!

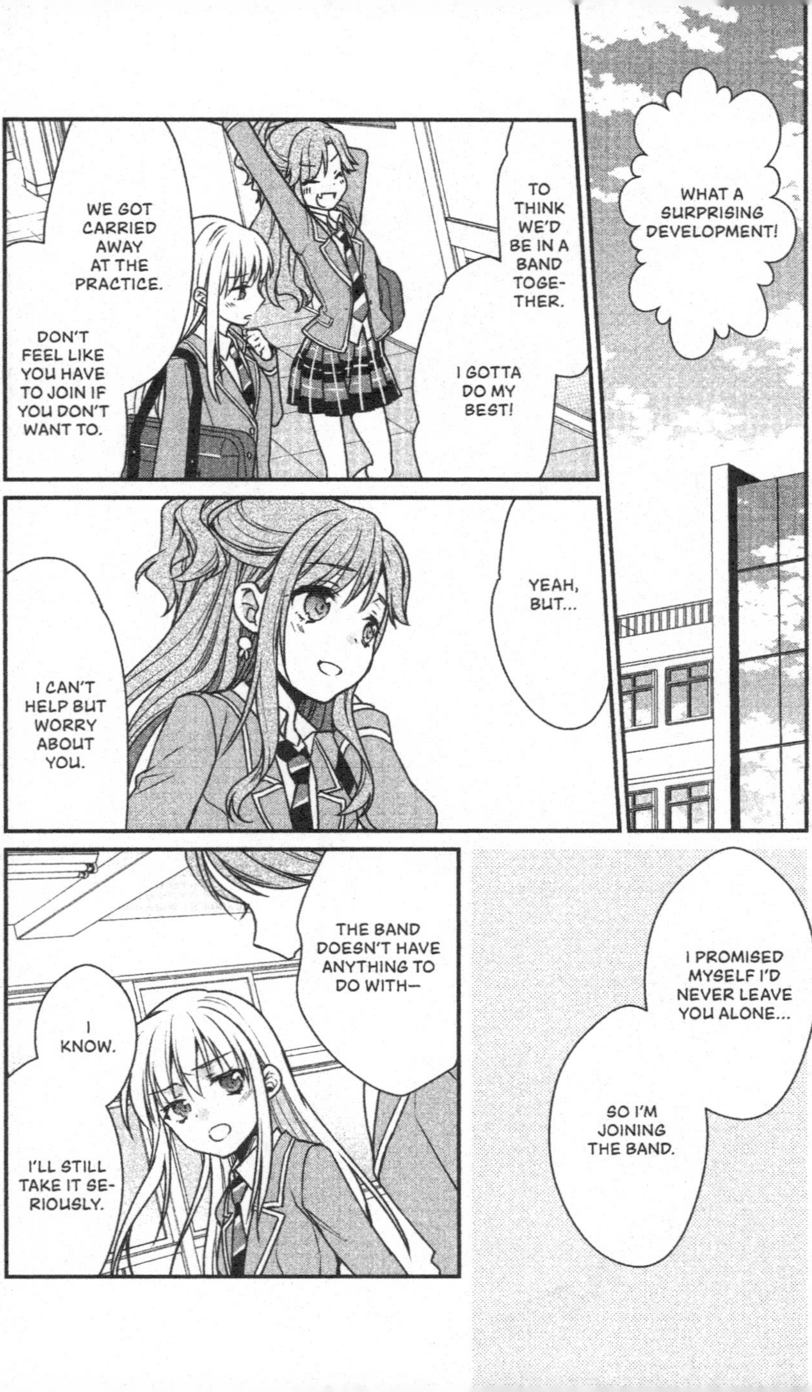
WHAT A SURPRISING DEVELOPMENT!
TO THINK WE'D BE IN A BAND TOGE-THER.
I GOTTA DO MY BEST!
WE GOT CARRIED AWAY AT THE PRACTICE.
DON'T FEEL LIKE YOU HAVE TO JOIN IF YOU DON'T WANT TO.
YEAH, BUT...
I CAN'T HELP BUT WORRY ABOUT YOU.
I PROMISED MYSELF I'D NEVER LEAVE YOU ALONE...
SO I'M JOINING THE BAND.
THE BAND DOESN'T HAVE ANYTHING TO DO WITH—
I KNOW.
I'LL STILL TAKE IT SE-RIOUSLY.

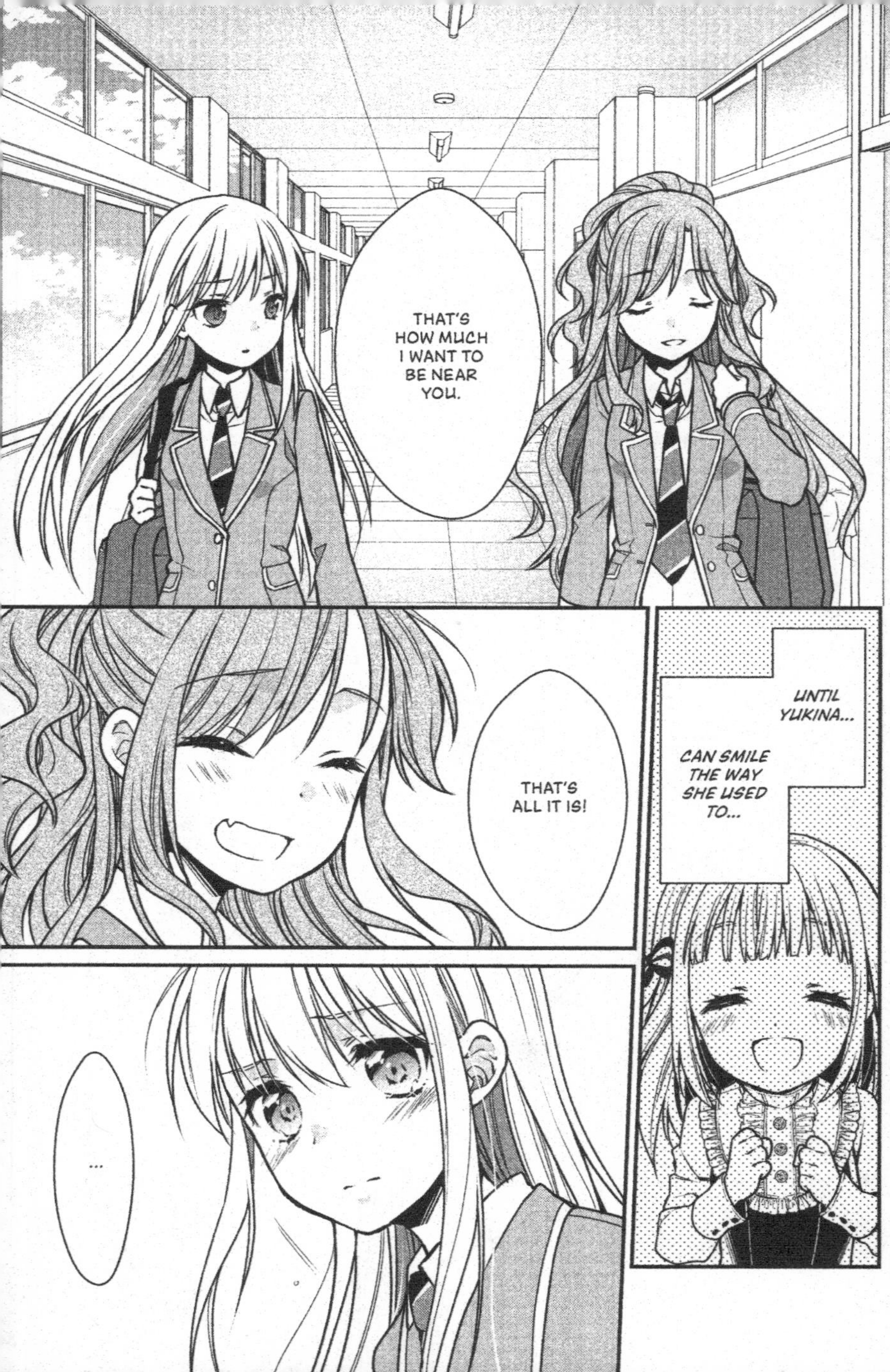
THAT'S HOW MUCH I WANT TO BE NEAR YOU.
UNTIL YUKINA...
CAN SMILE THE WAY SHE USED TO...
THAT'S ALL IT IS!
...

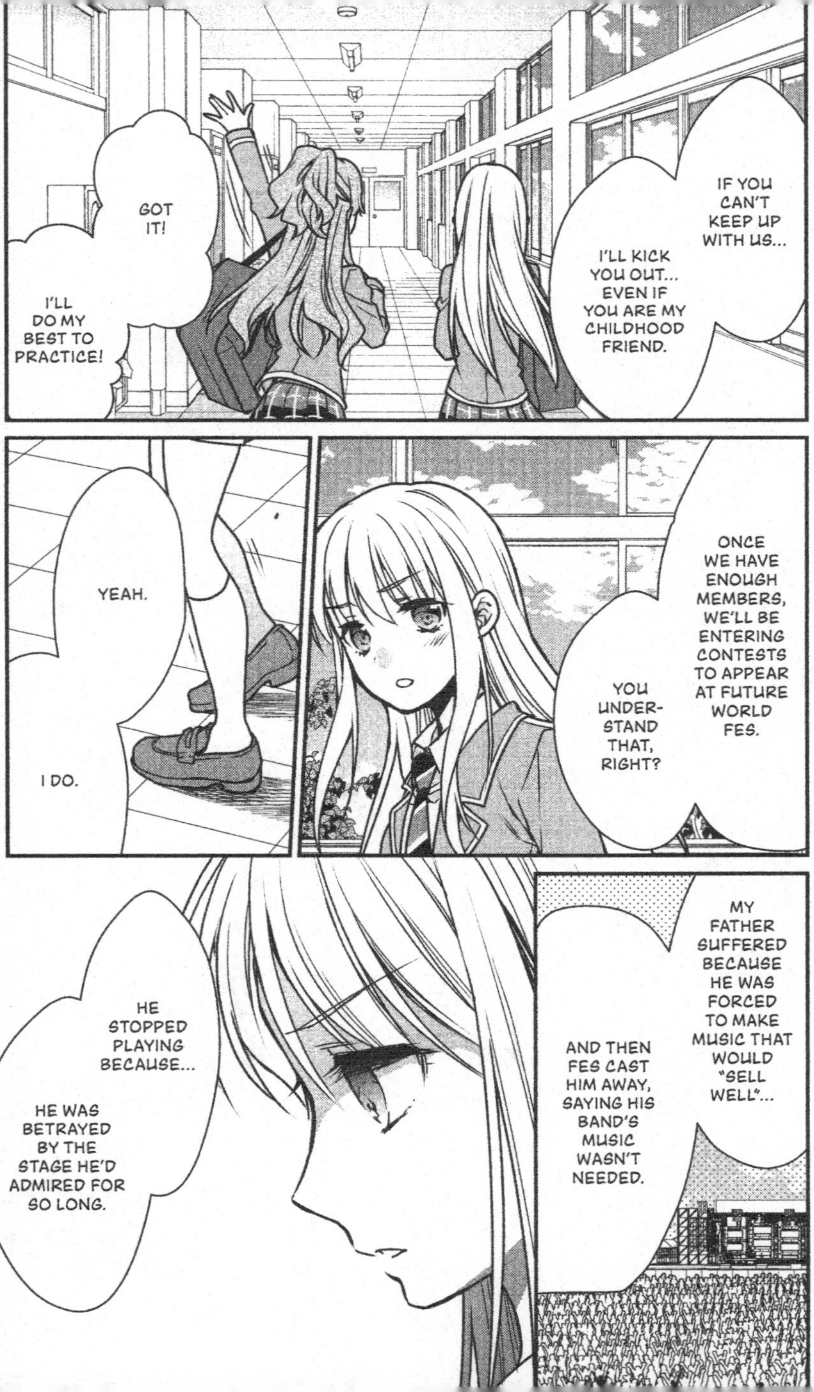
IF YOU CAN'T KEEP UP WITH US...
I'LL KICK YOU OUT... EVEN IF YOU ARE MY CHILDHOOD FRIEND.
GOT IT!
I'LL DO MY BEST TO PRACTICE!
ONCE WE HAVE ENOUGH MEMBERS, WE'LL BE ENTERING CONTESTS TO APPEAR AT FUTURE WORLD FES.
YOU UNDER-STAND THAT, RIGHT?
YEAH.
I DO.
MY FATHER SUFFERED BECAUSE HE WAS FORCED TO MAKE MUSIC THAT WOULD "SELL WELL"...
AND THEN FES CAST HIM AWAY, SAYING HIS BAND'S MUSIC WASN'T NEEDED.
HE STOPPED PLAYING BECAUSE...
HE WAS BETRAYED BY THE STAGE HE'D ADMIRED FOR SO LONG.

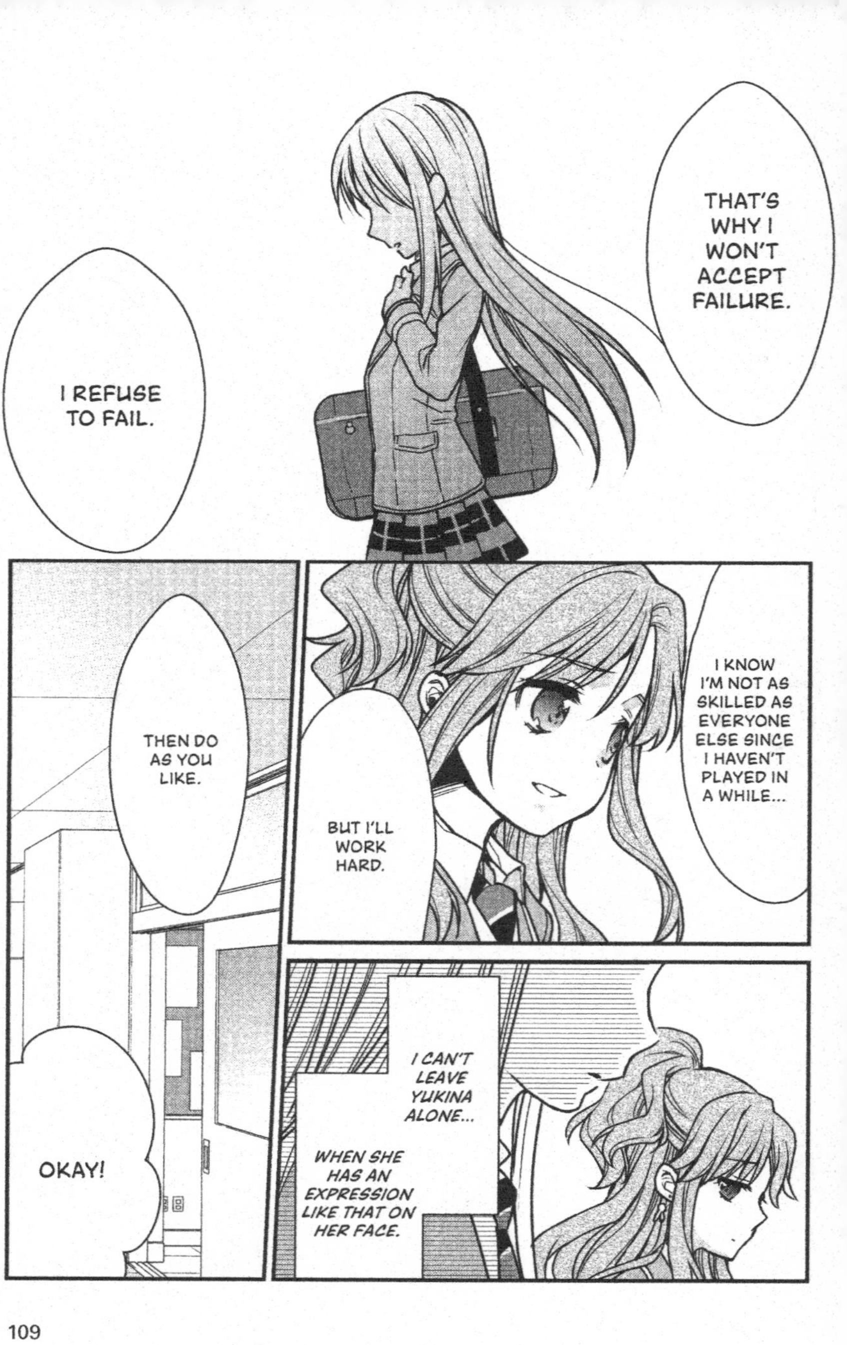
THAT'S WHY I WON'T ACCEPT FAILURE.
I REFUSE TO FAIL.
I KNOW I'M NOT AS SKILLED AS EVERYONE ELSE SINCE I HAVEN'T PLAYED IN A WHILE...
BUT I'LL WORK HARD.
I CAN'T LEAVE YUKINA ALONE...
WHEN SHE HAS AN EXPRESSION LIKE THAT ON HER FACE.
THEN DO AS YOU LIKE.
OKAY!

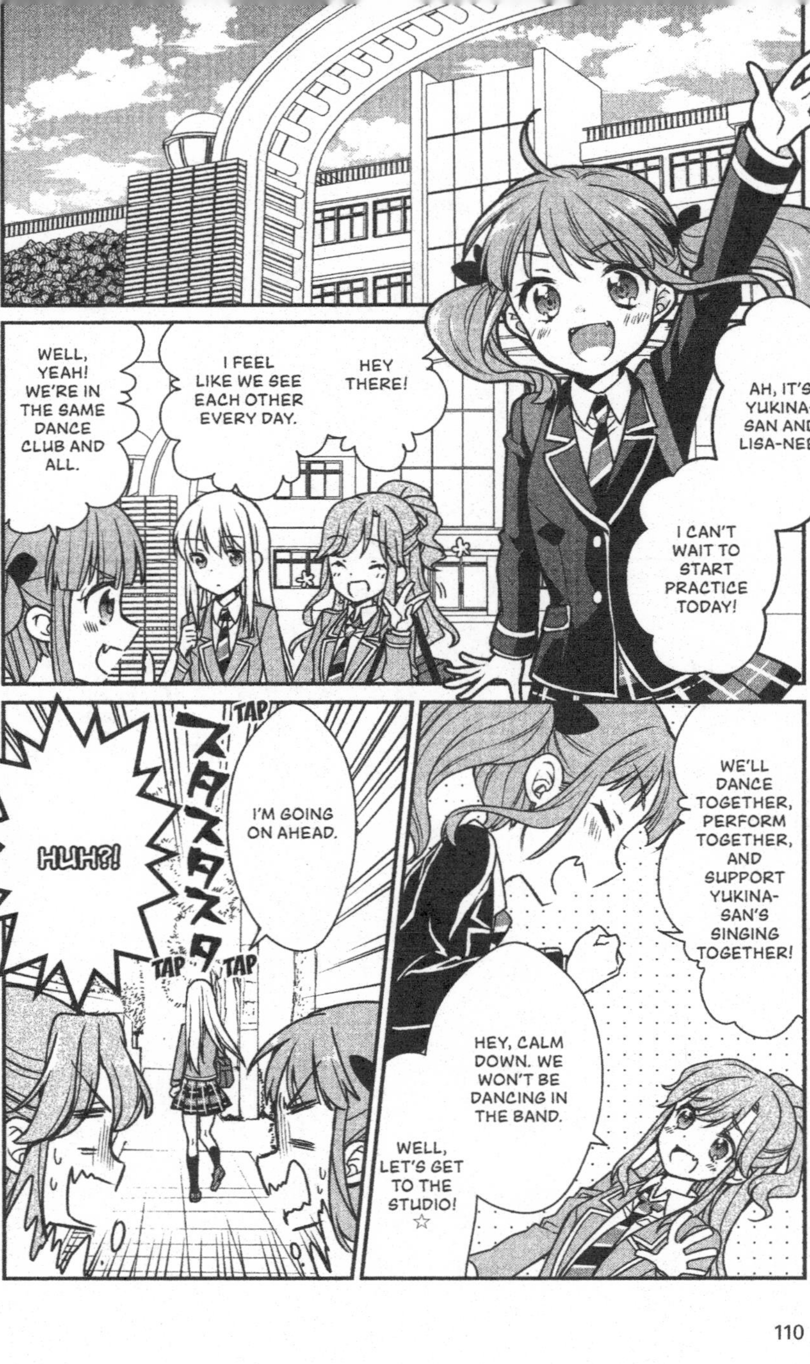
AH, IT'S YUKINA-SAN AND LISA-NEE!
I CAN'T WAIT TO START PRACTICE TODAY!
HEY THERE!
I FEEL LIKE WE SEE EACH OTHER EVERY DAY.
WELL, YEAH! WE'RE IN THE SAME DANCE CLUB AND ALL.
WE'LL DANCE TOGETHER, PERFORM TOGETHER, AND SUPPORT YUKINA-SAN'S SINGING TOGETHER!
HEY, CALM DOWN. WE WON'T BE DANCING IN THE BAND.
WELL, LET'S GET TO THE STUDIO! ☆
TAP
スタスタ
I'M GOING ON AHEAD.
TAP
TAP
HUH?!

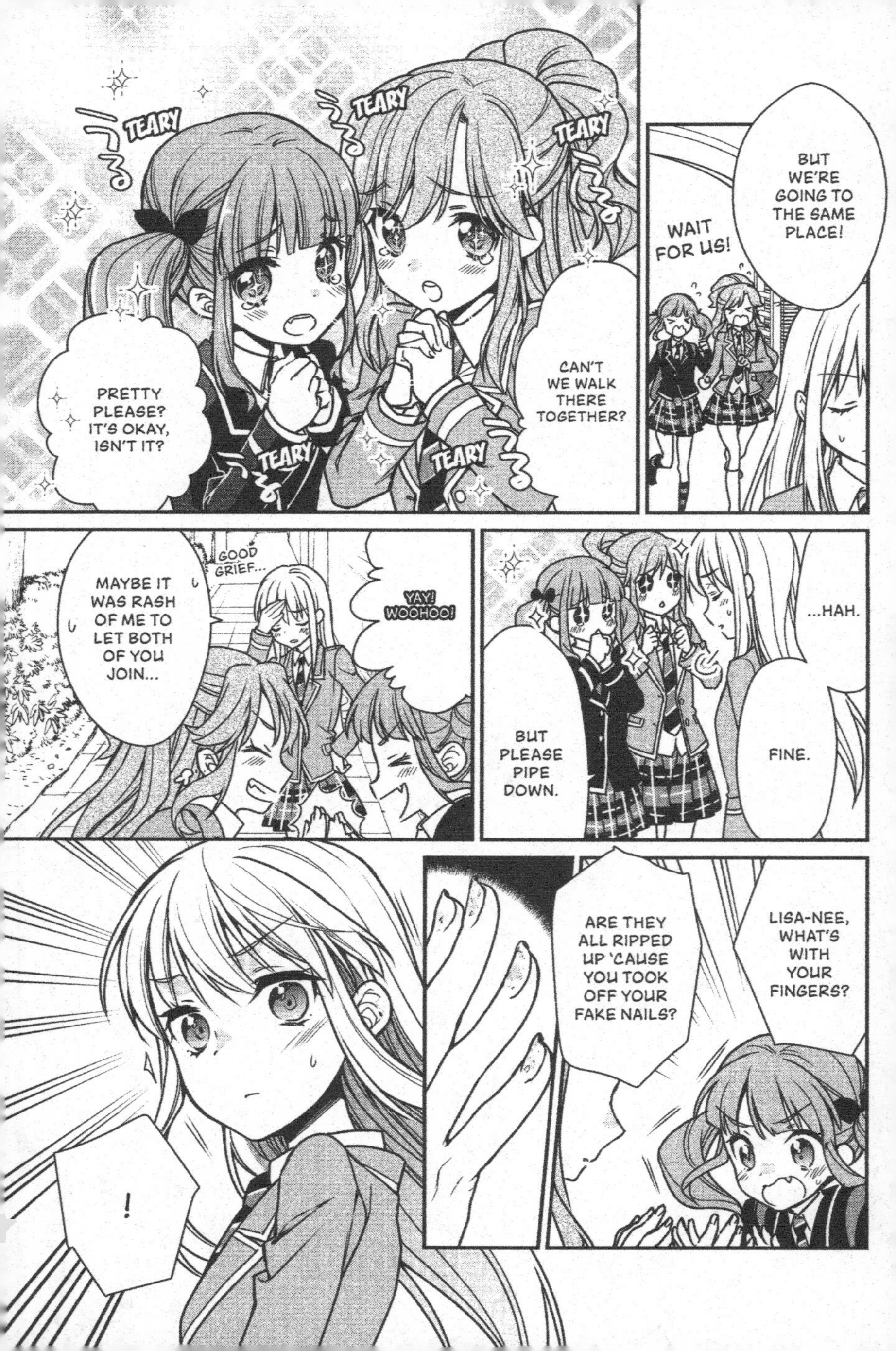
BUT WE'RE GOING TO THE SAME PLACE!
WAIT FOR US!
TEARY
TEARY
TEARY
CAN'T WE WALK THERE TOGETHER?
PRETTY PLEASE? IT'S OKAY, ISN'T IT?
TEARY
TEARY
...HAH.
FINE.
BUT PLEASE PIPE DOWN.
YAY! WOOHOO!
GOOD GRIEF...
MAYBE IT WAS RASH OF ME TO LET BOTH OF YOU JOIN...
LISA-NEE, WHAT'S WITH YOUR FINGERS?
ARE THEY ALL RIPPED UP 'CAUSE YOU TOOK OFF YOUR FAKE NAILS?
!

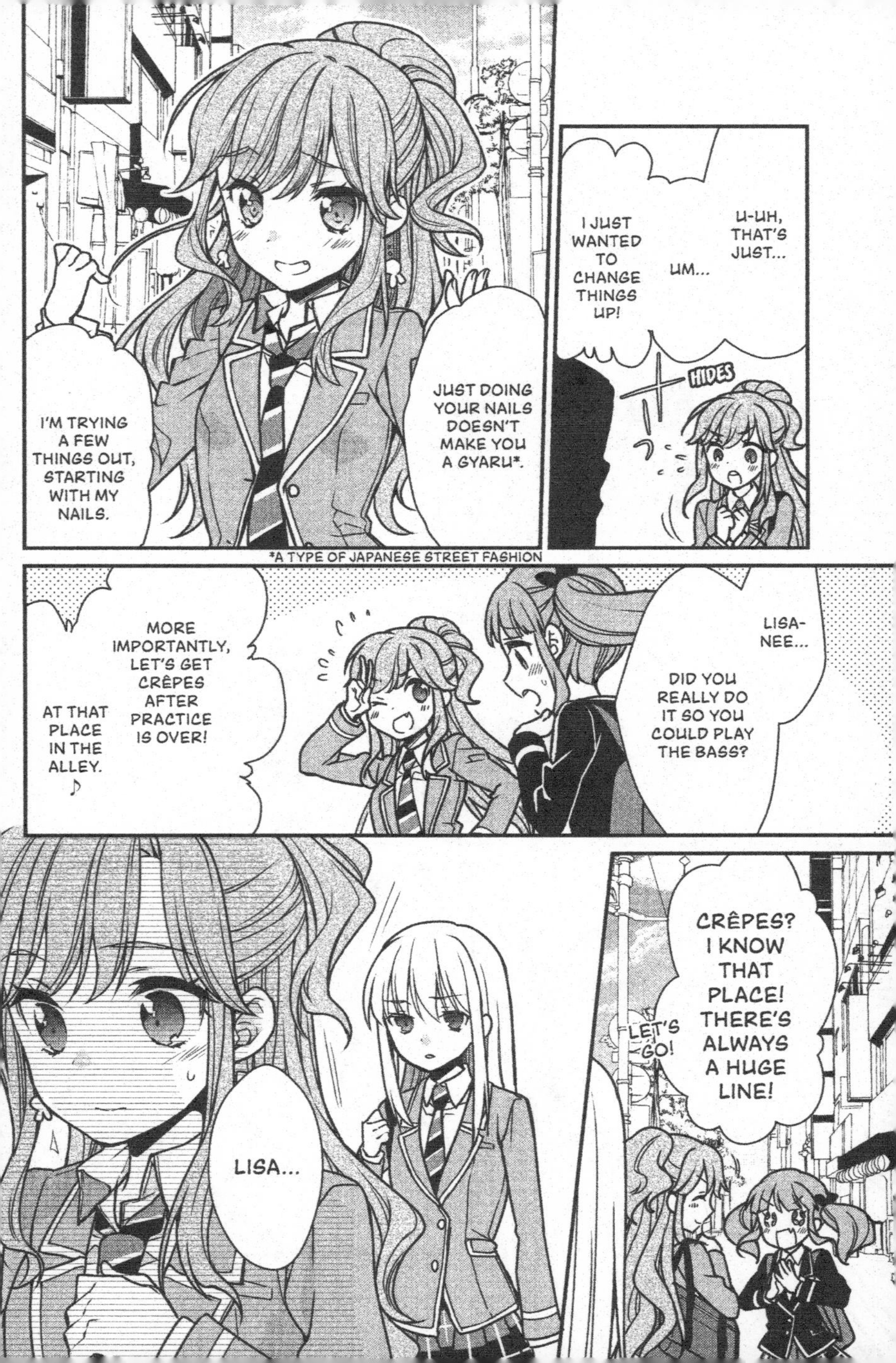
U-UH, THAT'S JUST...
UM...
I JUST WANTED TO CHANGE THINGS UP!
HIDES
JUST DOING YOUR NAILS DOESN'T MAKE YOU A GYARU*.
I'M TRYING A FEW THINGS OUT, STARTING WITH MY NAILS.
*A TYPE OF JAPANESE STREET FASHION
LISA-NEE...
DID YOU REALLY DO IT SO YOU COULD PLAY THE BASS?
MORE IMPORTANTLY, LET'S GET CRÊPES AFTER PRACTICE IS OVER!
AT THAT PLACE IN THE ALLEY. ♪
CRÊPES? I KNOW THAT PLACE! THERE'S ALWAYS A HUGE LINE!
LET'S GO!
LISA...

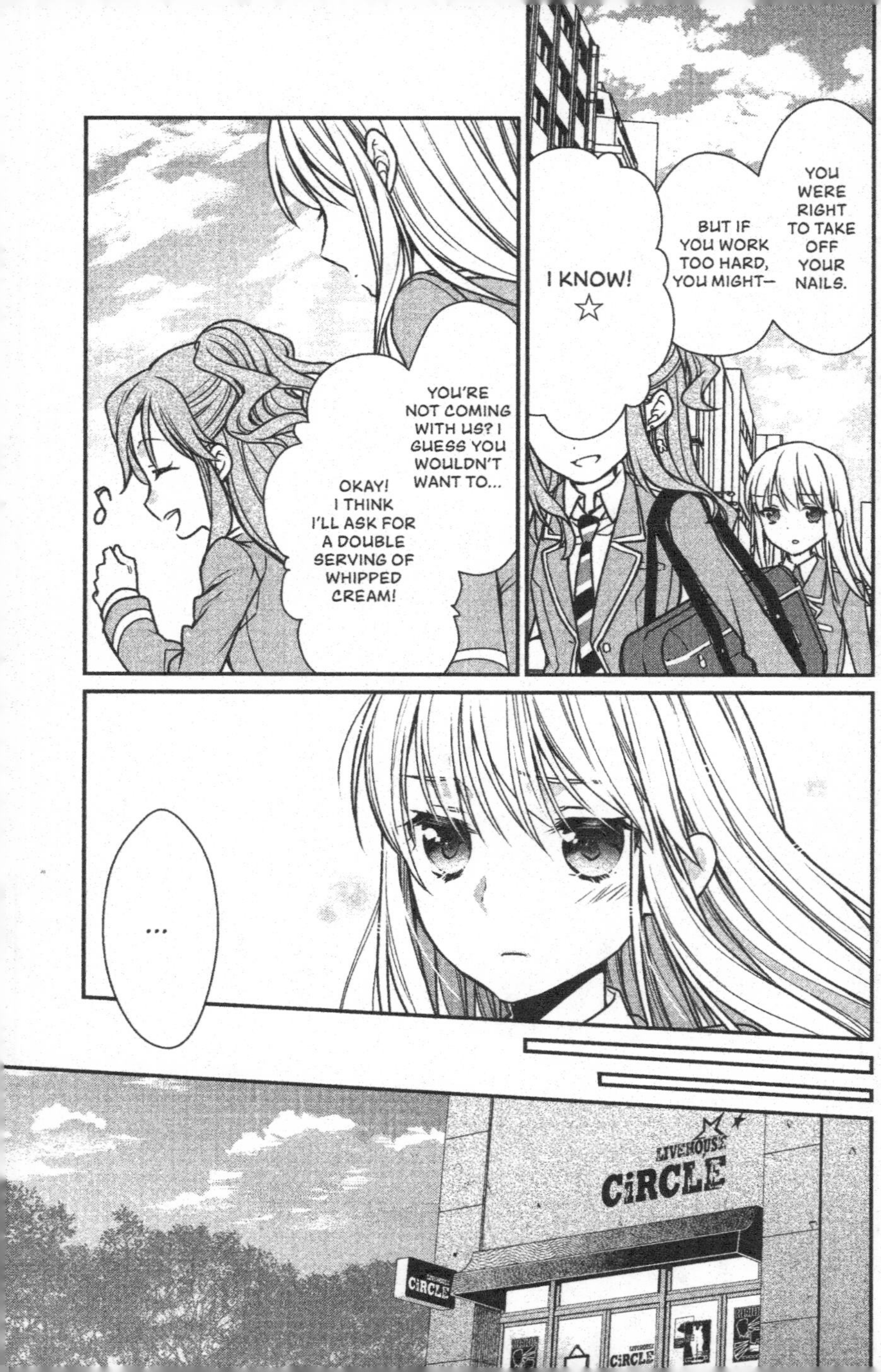
YOU WERE RIGHT TO TAKE OFF YOUR NAILS.
BUT IF YOU WORK TOO HARD, YOU MIGHT—
I KNOW! ☆
YOU'RE NOT COMING WITH US? I GUESS YOU WOULDN'T WANT TO...
OKAY! I THINK I'LL ASK FOR A DOUBLE SERVING OF WHIPPED CREAM!
...
LIVEHOUSE CiRCLE
CiRCLE

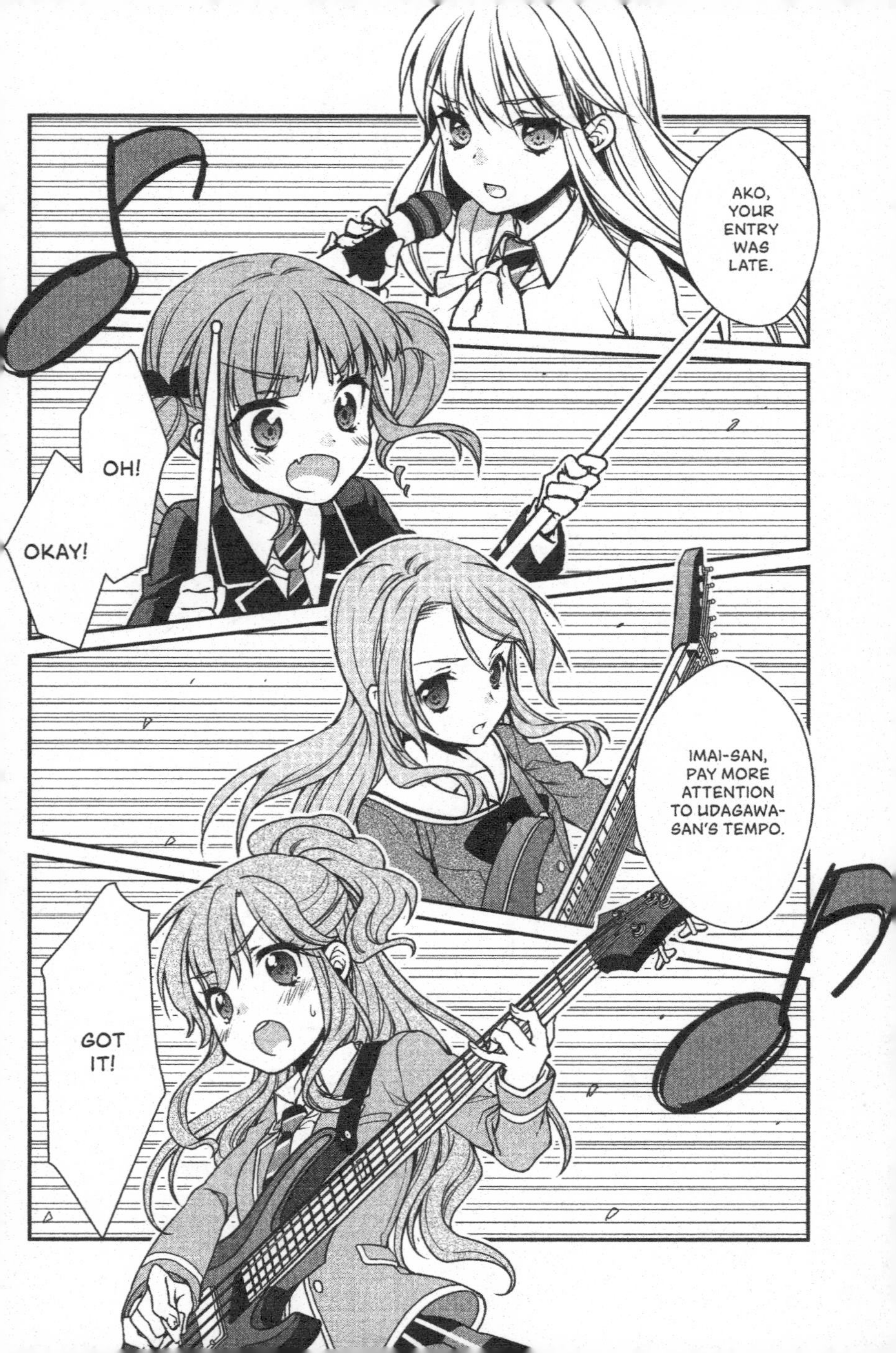
AKO, YOUR ENTRY WAS LATE.
OH!
OKAY!
IMAI-SAN, PAY MORE ATTENTION TO UDAGAWA-SAN'S TEMPO.
GOT IT!

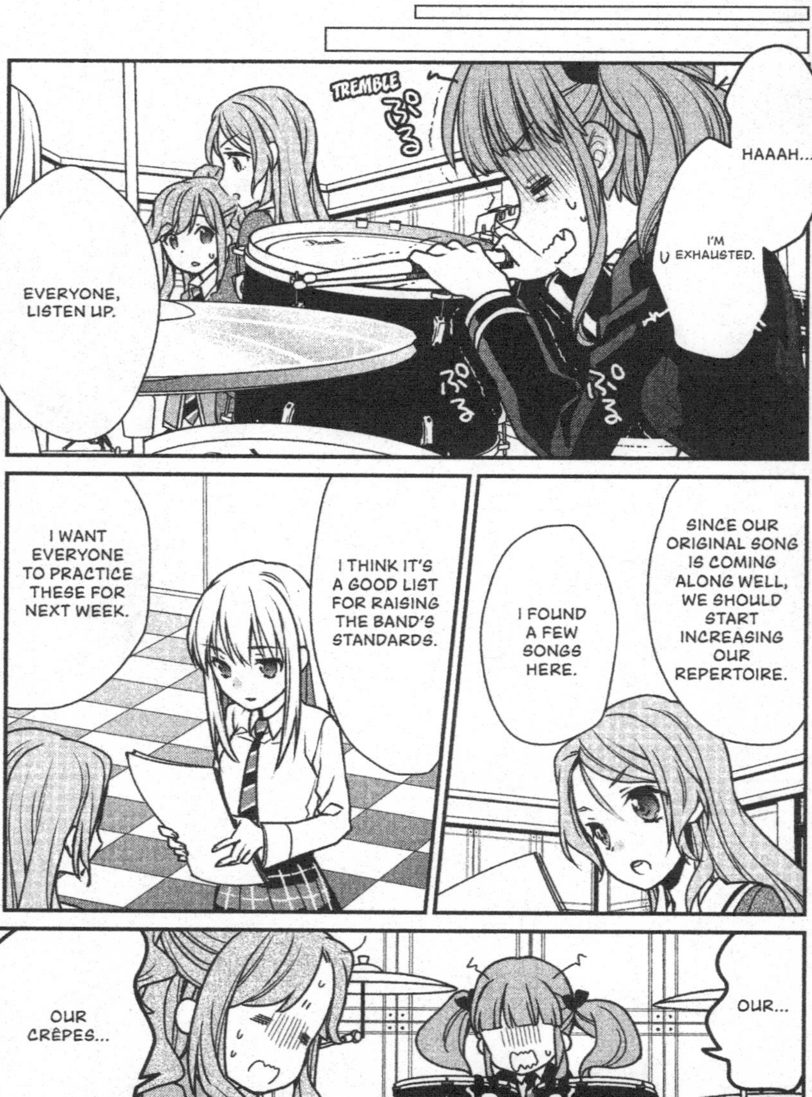
HAAAH...
I'M EXHAUSTED.
TREMBLE
ぷる
ぷる
ぷる
EVERYONE, LISTEN UP.
SINCE OUR ORIGINAL SONG IS COMING ALONG WELL, WE SHOULD START INCREASING OUR REPERTOIRE.
I FOUND A FEW SONGS HERE.
I THINK IT'S A GOOD LIST FOR RAISING THE BAND'S STANDARDS.
I WANT EVERYONE TO PRACTICE THESE FOR NEXT WEEK.
OUR...
OUR CRÊPES...

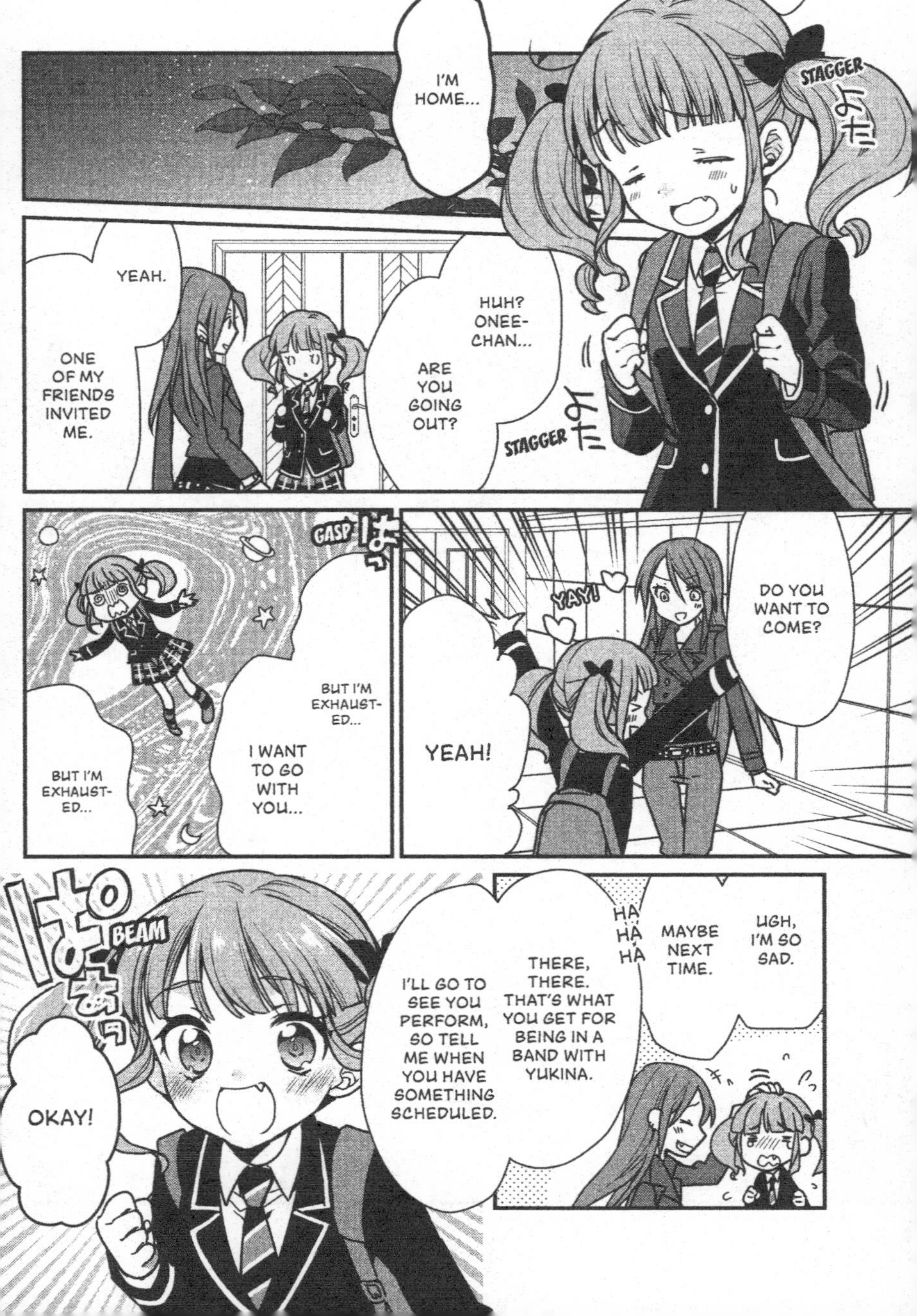
I'M HOME...
STAGGER
HUH? ONEE-CHAN...
ARE YOU GOING OUT?
STAGGER
YEAH.
ONE OF MY FRIENDS INVITED ME.
DO YOU WANT TO COME?
YAY!
YEAH!
GASP
BUT I'M EXHAUST-ED...
I WANT TO GO WITH YOU...
BUT I'M EXHAUST-ED...
UGH, I'M SO SAD.
MAYBE NEXT TIME.
HA HA HA
THERE, THERE. THAT'S WHAT YOU GET FOR BEING IN A BAND WITH YUKINA.
I'LL GO TO SEE YOU PERFORM, SO TELL ME WHEN YOU HAVE SOMETHING SCHEDULED.
BEAM
OKAY!

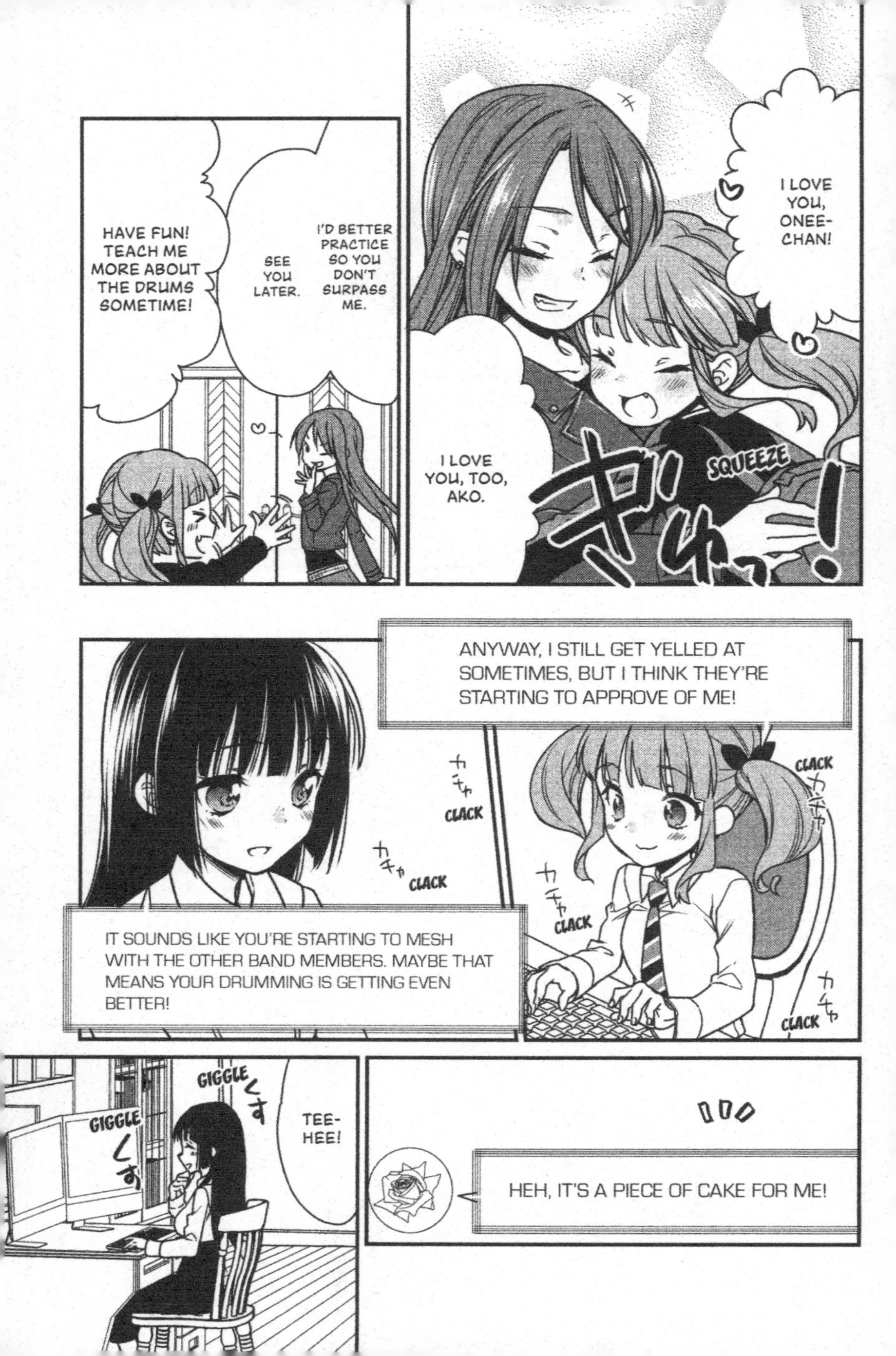
I LOVE YOU, ONEE-CHAN!
I LOVE YOU, TOO, AKO.
SQUEEZE
I'D BETTER PRACTICE SO YOU DON'T SURPASS ME.
SEE YOU LATER.
HAVE FUN! TEACH ME MORE ABOUT THE DRUMS SOMETIME!
ANYWAY, I STILL GET YELLED AT SOMETIMES, BUT I THINK THEY'RE STARTING TO APPROVE OF ME!
CLACK
CLACK
CLACK
CLACK
CLACK
IT SOUNDS LIKE YOU'RE STARTING TO MESH WITH THE OTHER BAND MEMBERS. MAYBE THAT MEANS YOUR DRUMMING IS GETTING EVEN BETTER!
HEH, IT'S A PIECE OF CAKE FOR ME!
TEE-HEE!
GIGGLE くす
GIGGLE くす

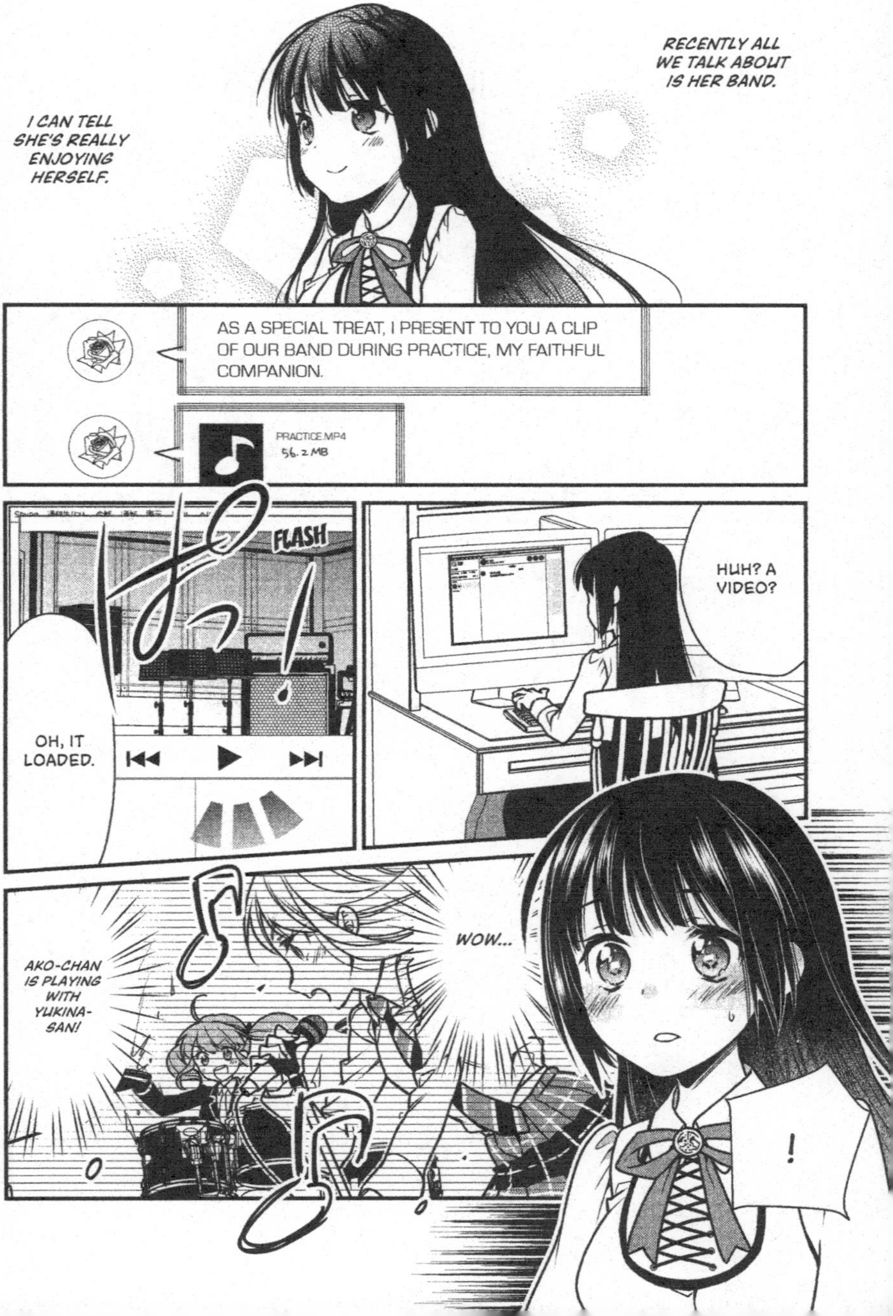
RECENTLY ALL WE TALK ABOUT IS HER BAND.
I CAN TELL SHE'S REALLY ENJOYING HERSELF.
AS A SPECIAL TREAT, I PRESENT TO YOU A CLIP OF OUR BAND DURING PRACTICE, MY FAITHFUL COMPANION.
PRACTICE.MP4
56.2 MB
HUH? A VIDEO?
FLASH
OH, IT LOADED.
!
WOW...
AKO-CHAN IS PLAYING WITH YUKINA-SAN!

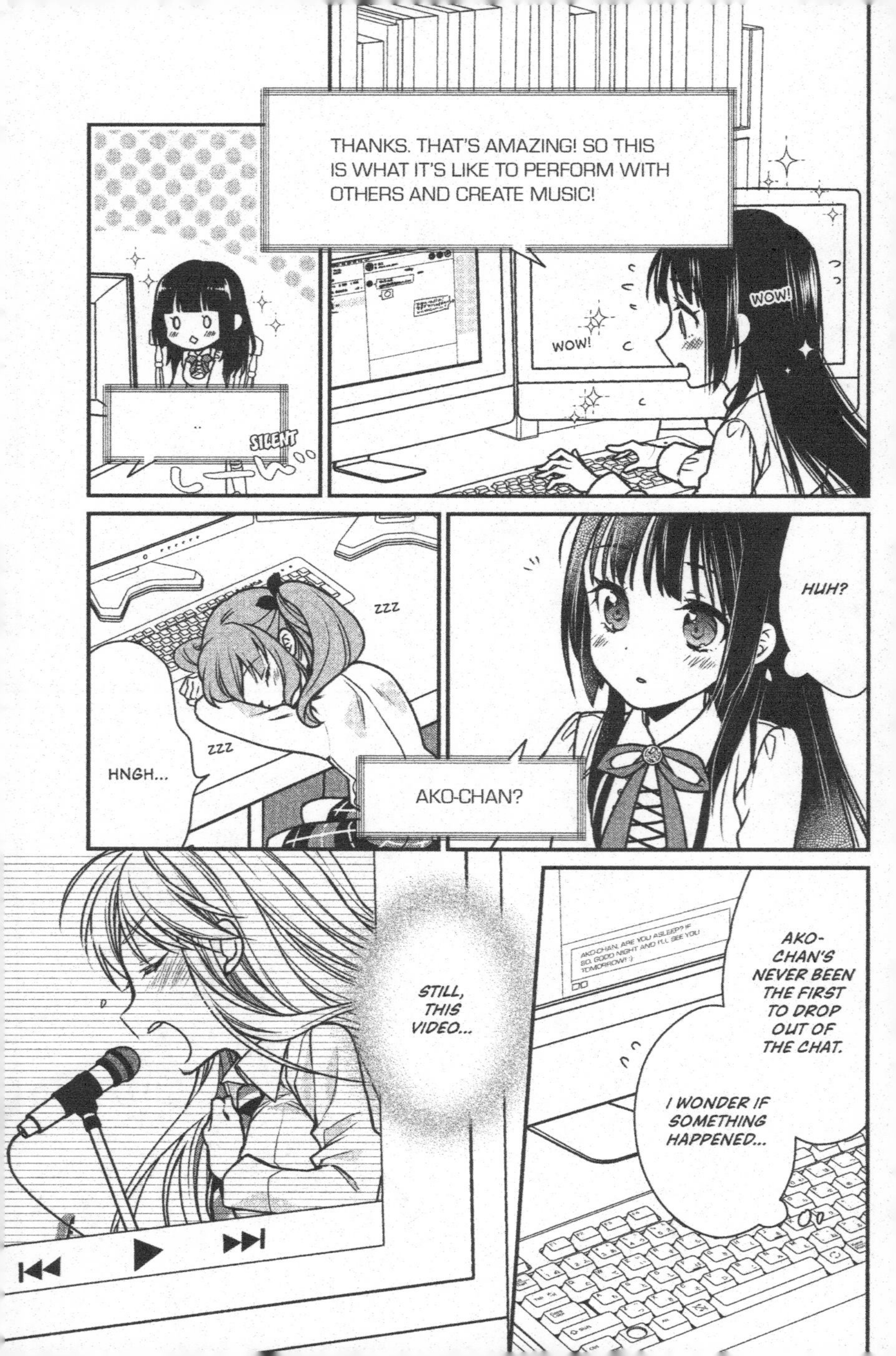
THANKS. THAT'S AMAZING! SO THIS IS WHAT IT'S LIKE TO PERFORM WITH OTHERS AND CREATE MUSIC!
WOW!
WOW!
..
SILENT
HUH?
AKO-CHAN?
ZZZ
ZZZ
HNGH...
AKO-CHAN, ARE YOU ASLEEP? IF SO, GOOD NIGHT AND I'LL SEE YOU TOMORROW! :)
AKO-CHAN'S NEVER BEEN THE FIRST TO DROP OUT OF THE CHAT.
I WONDER IF SOMETHING HAPPENED...
STILL, THIS VIDEO...

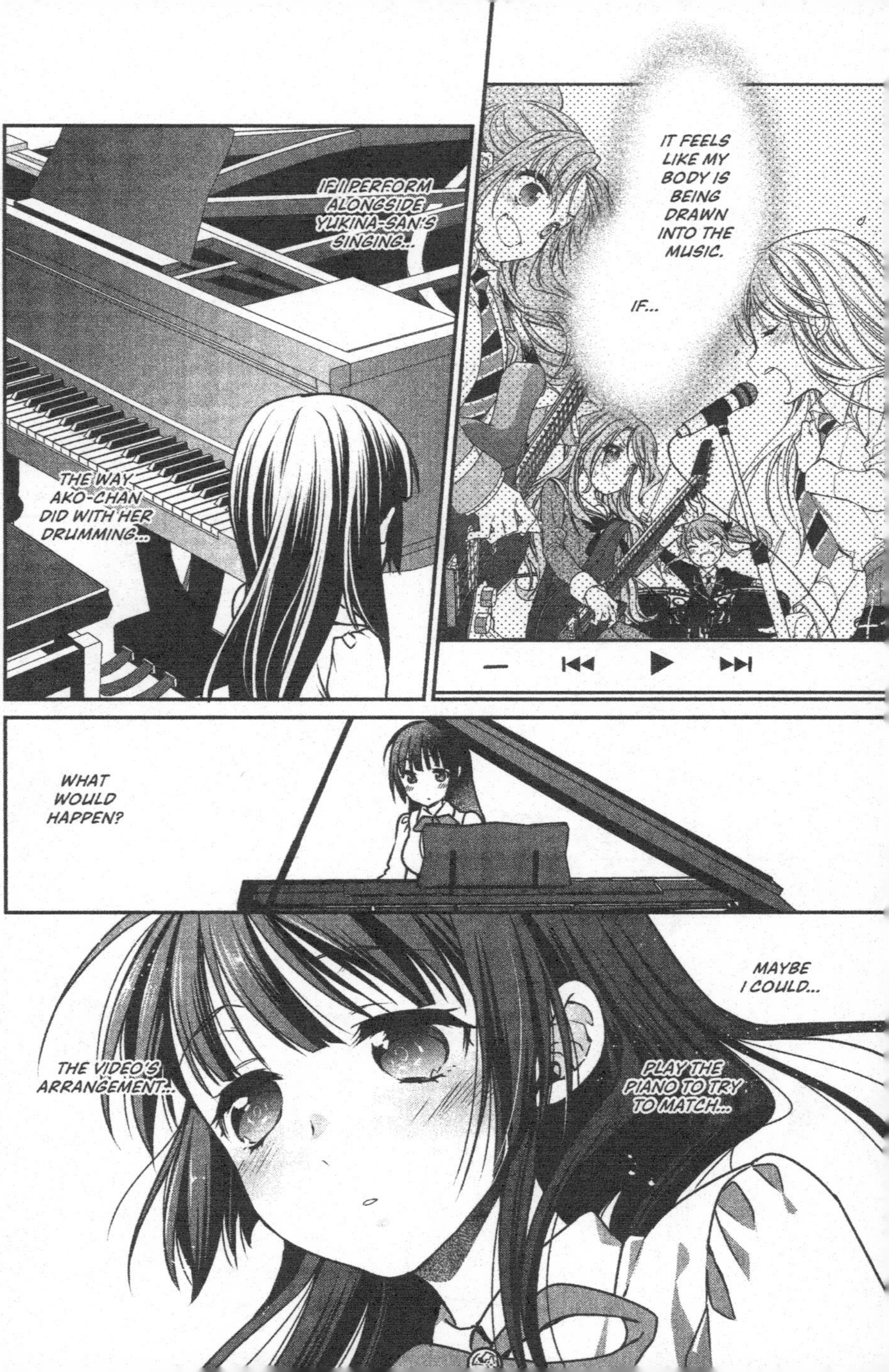
IT FEELS LIKE MY BODY IS BEING DRAWN INTO THE MUSIC.
IF...
IF I PERFORM ALONGSIDE YUKINA-SAN'S SINGING...
THE WAY AKO-CHAN DID WITH HER DRUMMING...
WHAT WOULD HAPPEN?
MAYBE I COULD...
PLAY THE PIANO TO TRY TO MATCH...
THE VIDEO'S ARRANGEMENT...

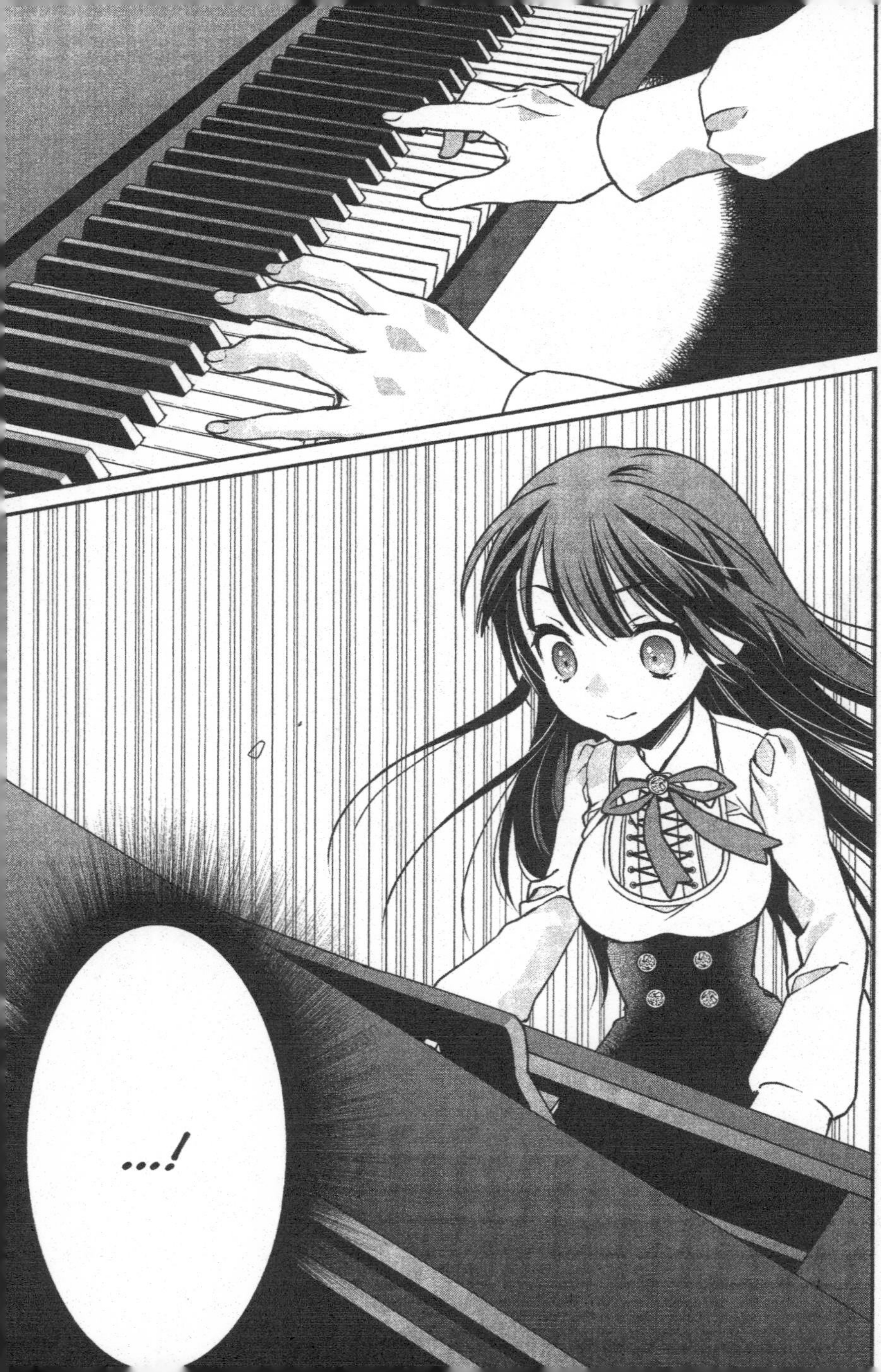
...!

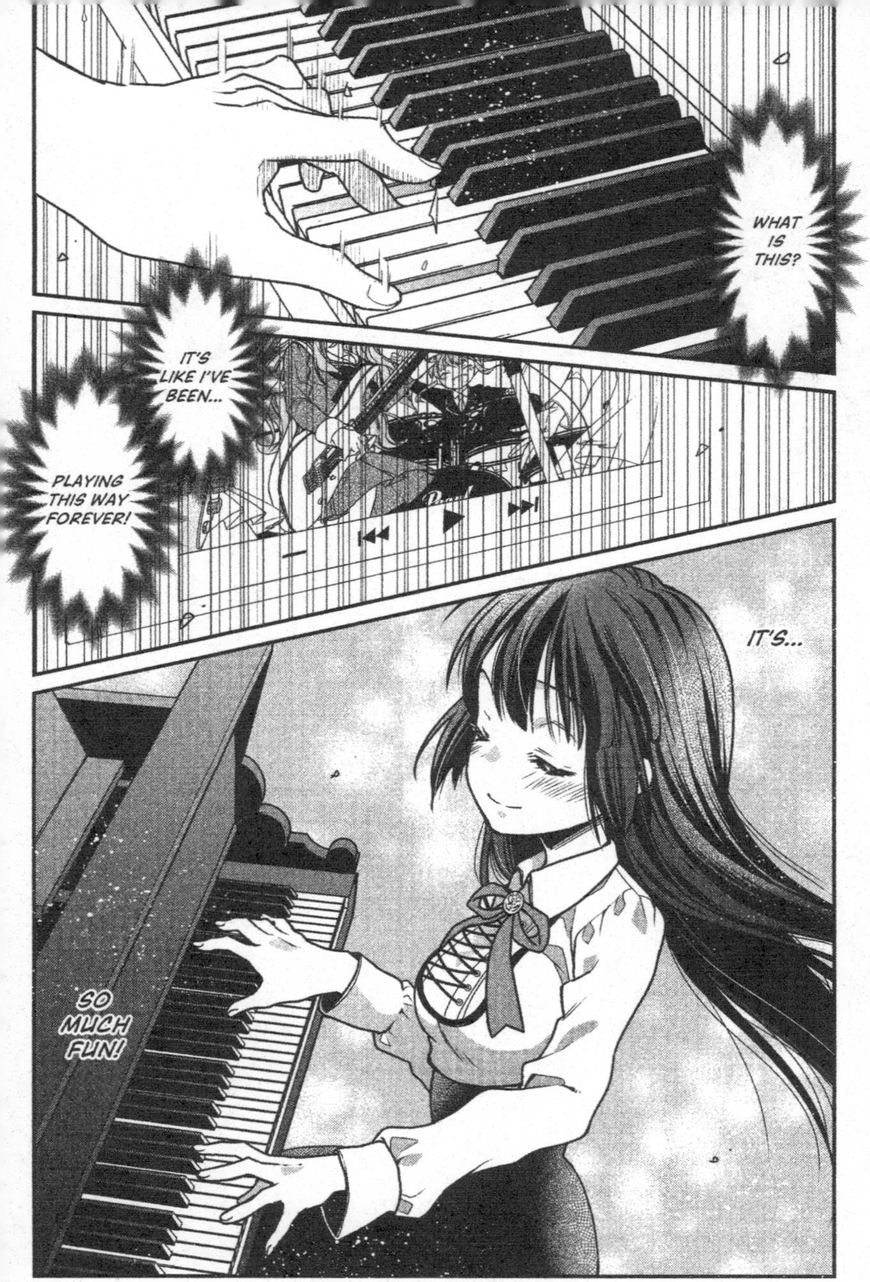
WHAT IS THIS?
IT'S LIKE I'VE BEEN...
PLAYING THIS WAY FOREVER!
IT'S...
SO MUCH FUN!

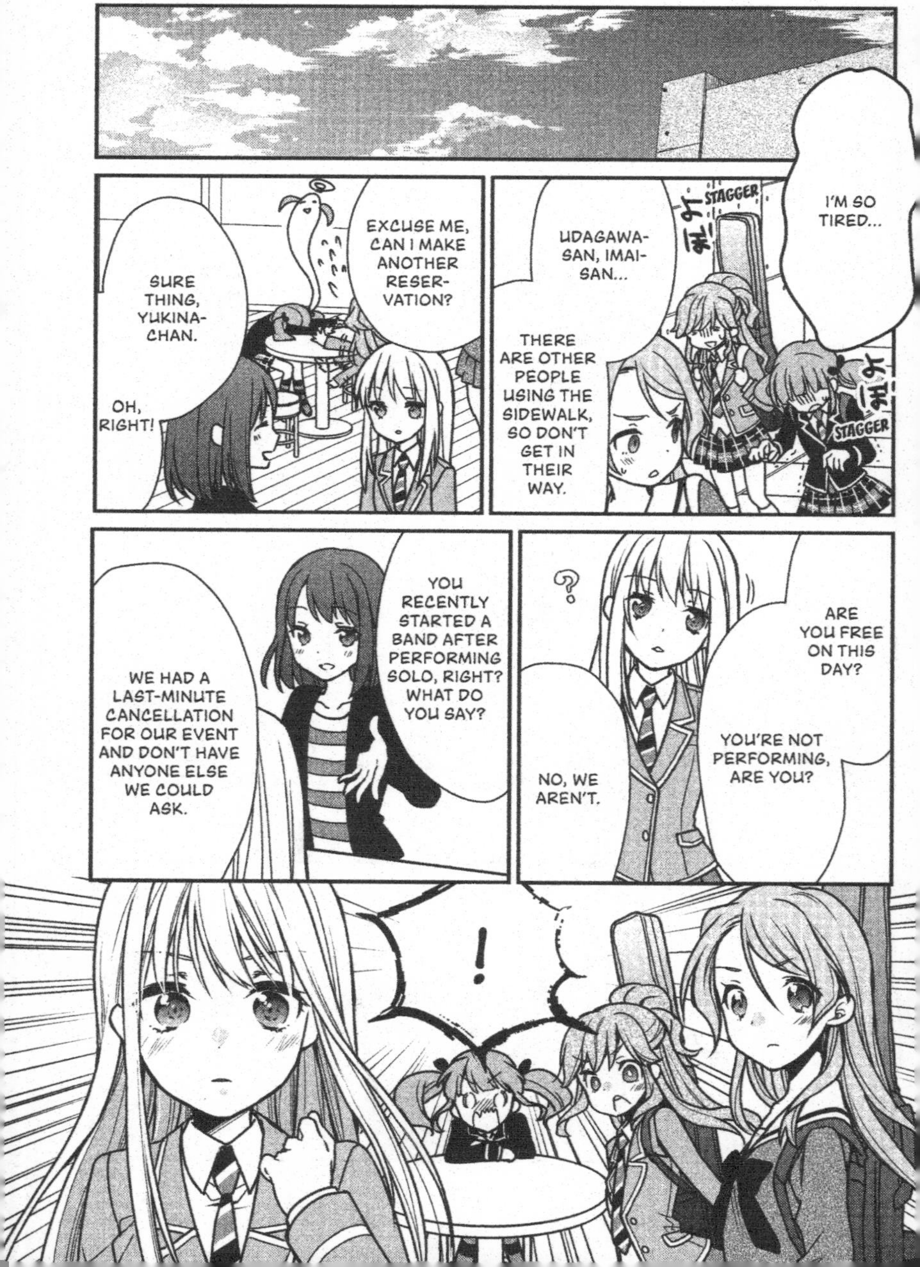
I'M SO TIRED...
STAGGER
UDAGAWA-SAN, IMAI-SAN...
THERE ARE OTHER PEOPLE USING THE SIDEWALK, SO DON'T GET IN THEIR WAY.
STAGGER
EXCUSE ME, CAN I MAKE ANOTHER RESER-VATION?
SURE THING, YUKINA-CHAN.
OH, RIGHT!
ARE YOU FREE ON THIS DAY?
YOU'RE NOT PERFORMING, ARE YOU?
NO, WE AREN'T.
YOU RECENTLY STARTED A BAND AFTER PERFORMING SOLO, RIGHT? WHAT DO YOU SAY?
WE HAD A LAST-MINUTE CANCELLATION FOR OUR EVENT AND DON'T HAVE ANYONE ELSE WE COULD ASK.
!

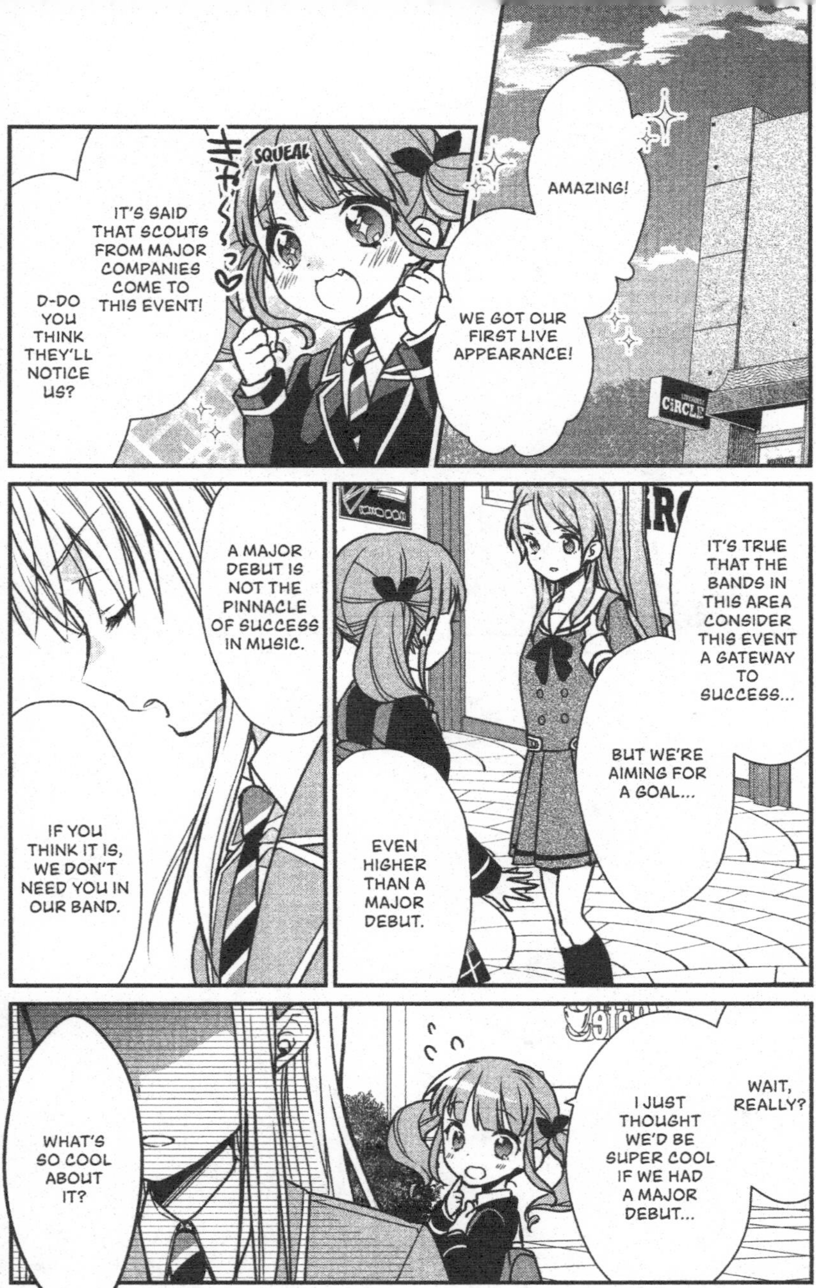
AMAZING!
WE GOT OUR FIRST LIVE APPEARANCE!
CiRCLE
SQUEAL
IT'S SAID THAT SCOUTS FROM MAJOR COMPANIES COME TO THIS EVENT!
D-DO YOU THINK THEY'LL NOTICE US?
IT'S TRUE THAT THE BANDS IN THIS AREA CONSIDER THIS EVENT A GATEWAY TO SUCCESS...
BUT WE'RE AIMING FOR A GOAL...
EVEN HIGHER THAN A MAJOR DEBUT.
A MAJOR DEBUT IS NOT THE PINNACLE OF SUCCESS IN MUSIC.
IF YOU THINK IT IS, WE DON'T NEED YOU IN OUR BAND.
WAIT, REALLY?
I JUST THOUGHT WE'D BE SUPER COOL IF WE HAD A MAJOR DEBUT...
WHAT'S SO COOL ABOUT IT?

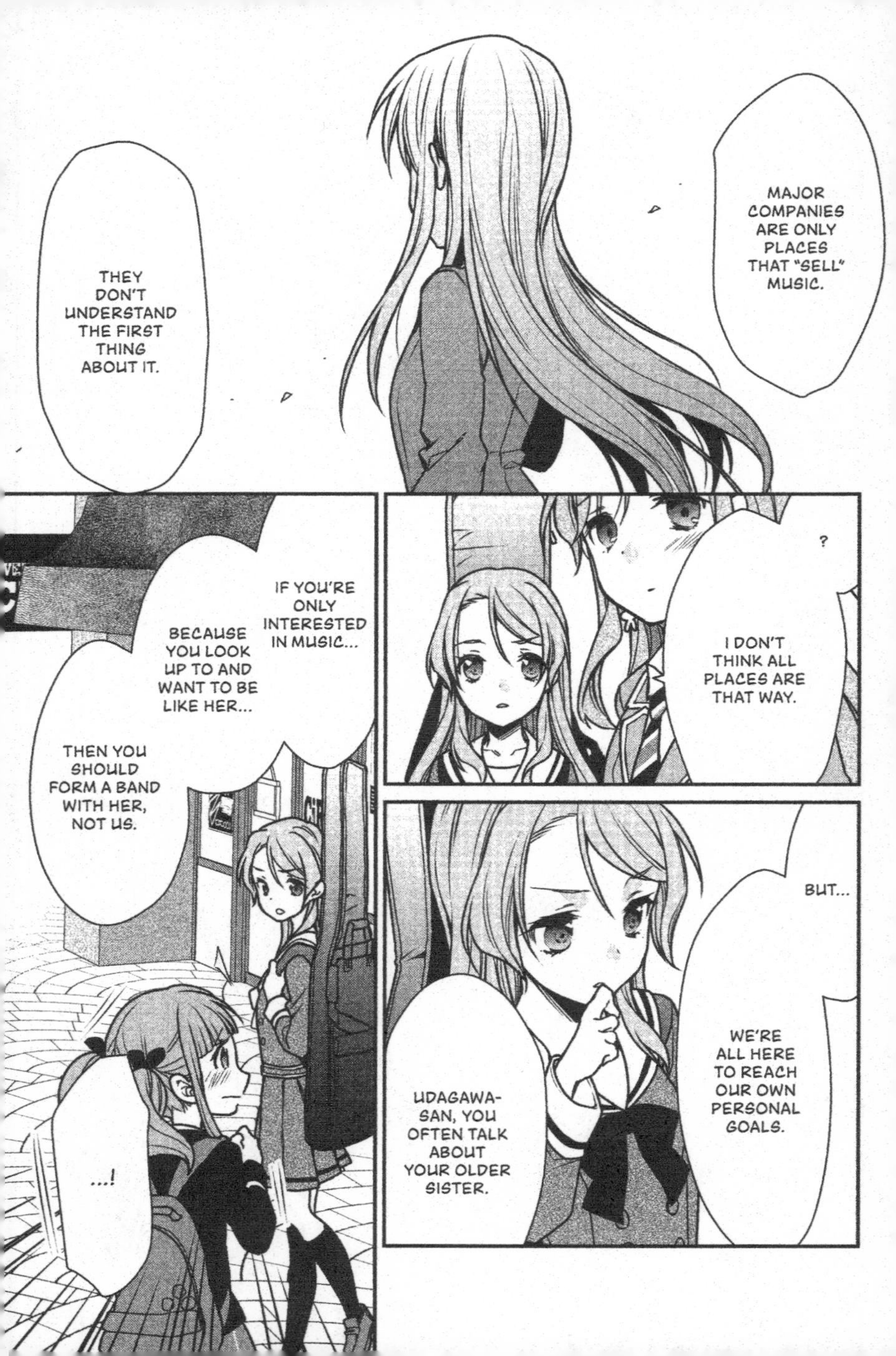
MAJOR COMPANIES ARE ONLY PLACES THAT "SELL" MUSIC.
THEY DON'T UNDERSTAND THE FIRST THING ABOUT IT.
?
I DON'T THINK ALL PLACES ARE THAT WAY.
BUT...
WE'RE ALL HERE TO REACH OUR OWN PERSONAL GOALS.
UDAGAWA-SAN, YOU OFTEN TALK ABOUT YOUR OLDER SISTER.
IF YOU'RE ONLY INTERESTED IN MUSIC...
BECAUSE YOU LOOK UP TO AND WANT TO BE LIKE HER...
THEN YOU SHOULD FORM A BAND WITH HER, NOT US.
...!

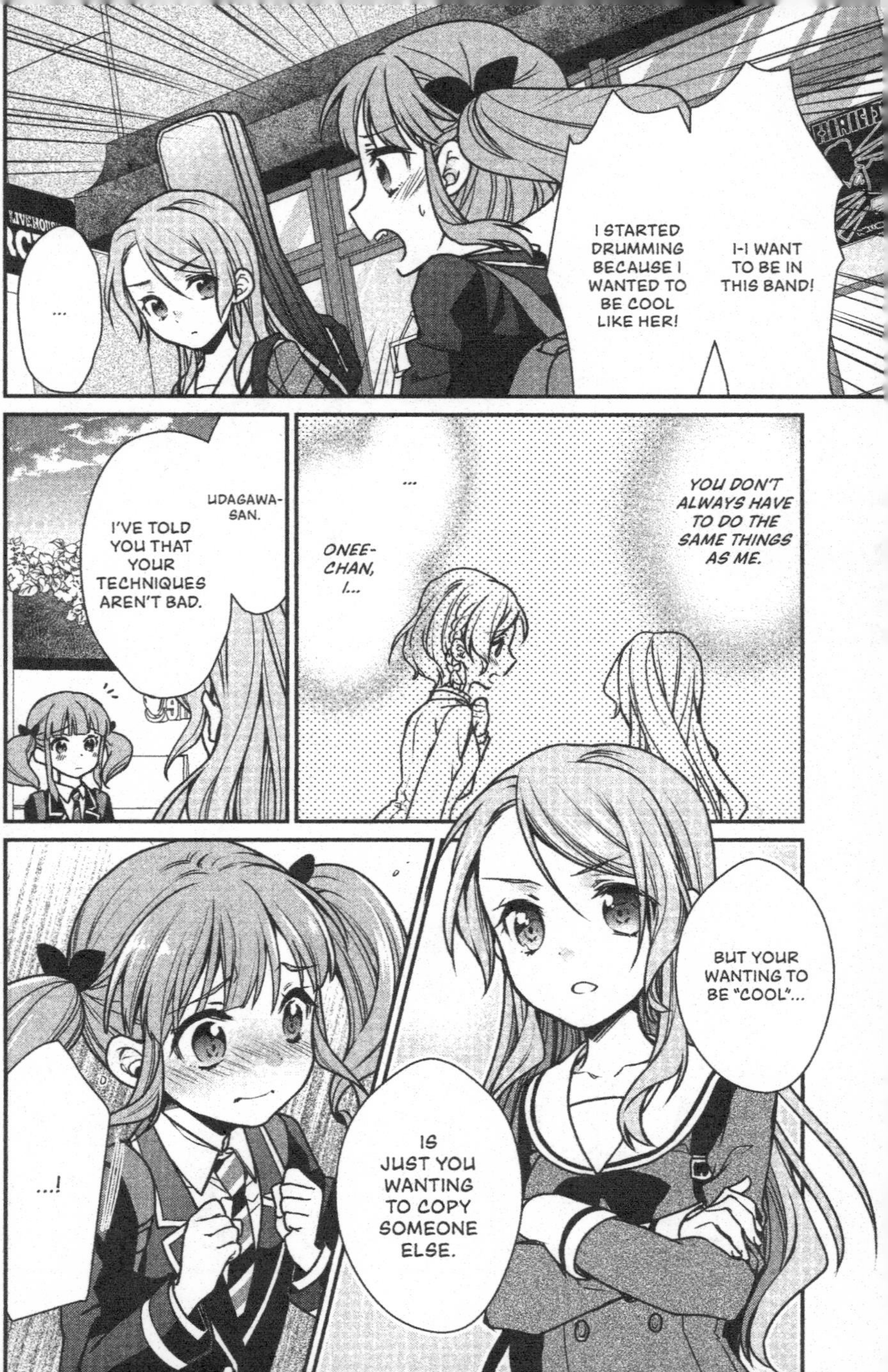
I-I WANT TO BE IN THIS BAND!
I STARTED DRUMMING BECAUSE I WANTED TO BE COOL LIKE HER!
...
YOU DON'T ALWAYS HAVE TO DO THE SAME THINGS AS ME.
...
ONEE-CHAN, I...
UDAGAWA-SAN.
I'VE TOLD YOU THAT YOUR TECHNIQUES AREN'T BAD.
BUT YOUR WANTING TO BE "COOL"...
IS JUST YOU WANTING TO COPY SOMEONE ELSE.
...!

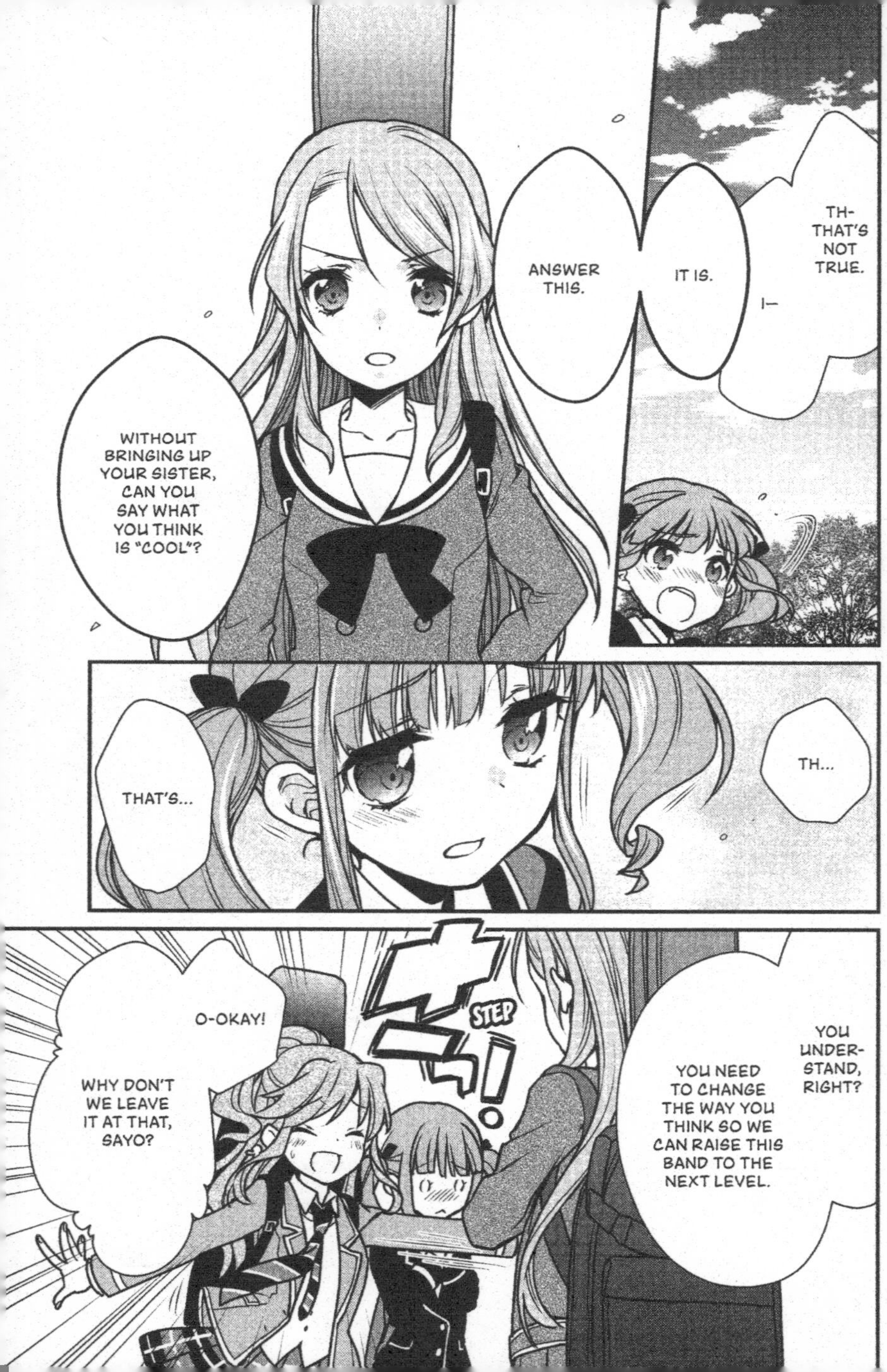
TH- THAT'S NOT TRUE.
I—
IT IS.
ANSWER THIS.
WITHOUT BRINGING UP YOUR SISTER, CAN YOU SAY WHAT YOU THINK IS "COOL"?
TH...
THAT'S...
YOU UNDER-STAND, RIGHT?
YOU NEED TO CHANGE THE WAY YOU THINK SO WE CAN RAISE THIS BAND TO THE NEXT LEVEL.
STEP
O-OKAY!
WHY DON'T WE LEAVE IT AT THAT, SAYO?

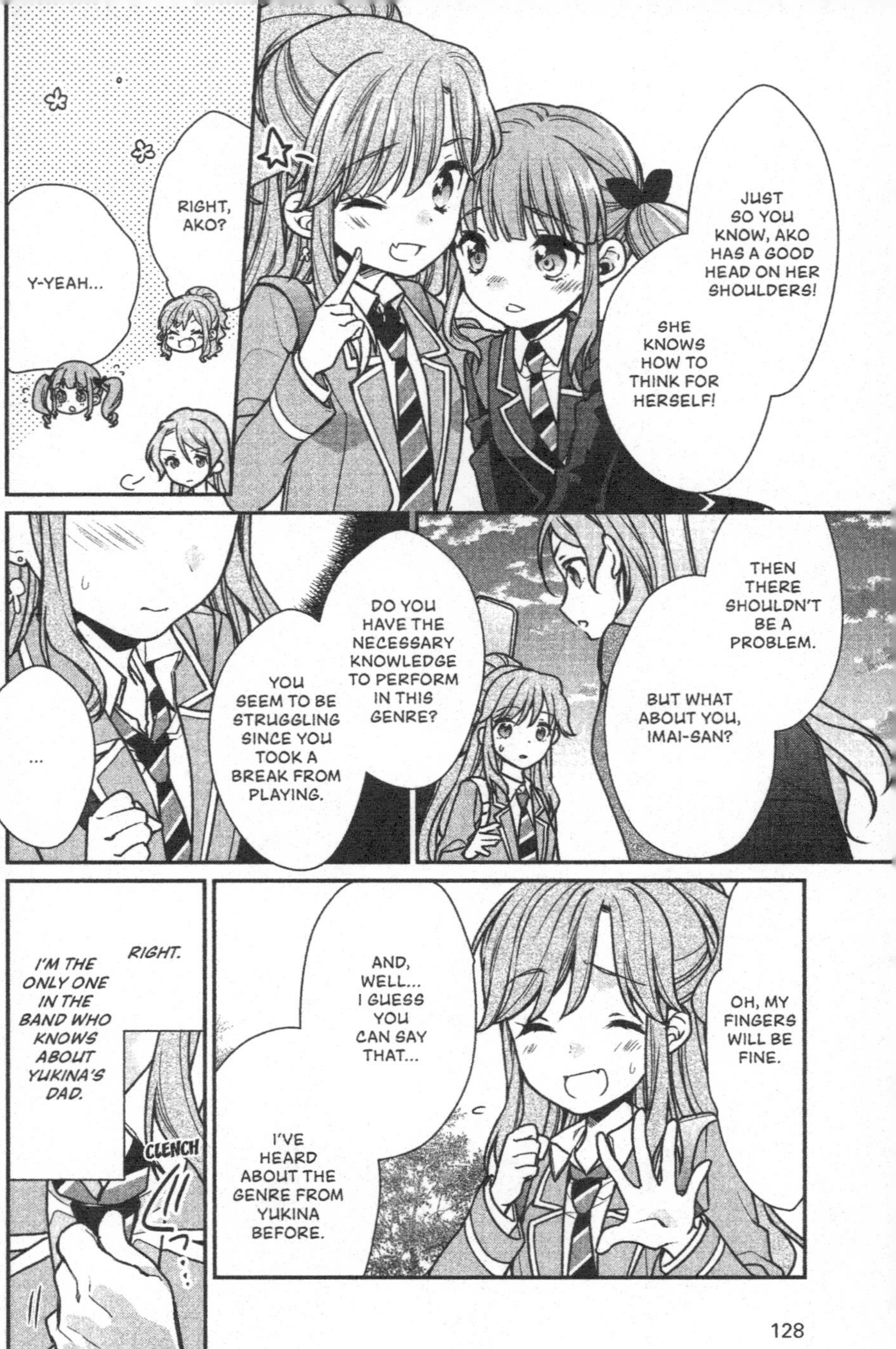
JUST SO YOU KNOW, AKO HAS A GOOD HEAD ON HER SHOULDERS!
SHE KNOWS HOW TO THINK FOR HERSELF!
RIGHT, AKO?
Y-YEAH...
THEN THERE SHOULDN'T BE A PROBLEM.
BUT WHAT ABOUT YOU, IMAI-SAN?
DO YOU HAVE THE NECESSARY KNOWLEDGE TO PERFORM IN THIS GENRE?
YOU SEEM TO BE STRUGGLING SINCE YOU TOOK A BREAK FROM PLAYING.
...
OH, MY FINGERS WILL BE FINE.
AND, WELL... I GUESS YOU CAN SAY THAT...
I'VE HEARD ABOUT THE GENRE FROM YUKINA BEFORE.
RIGHT.
I'M THE ONLY ONE IN THE BAND WHO KNOWS ABOUT YUKINA'S DAD.
CLENCH

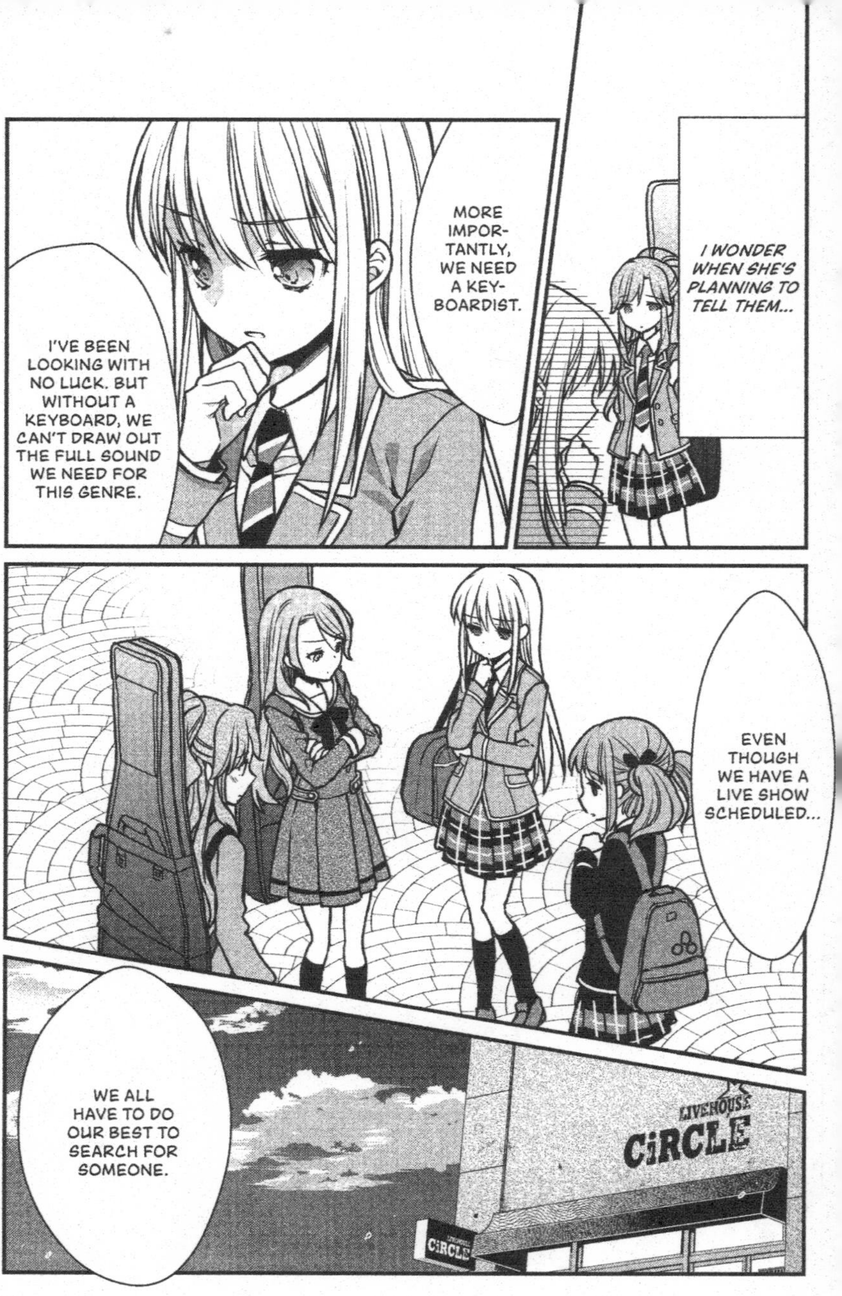
I WONDER WHEN SHE'S PLANNING TO TELL THEM...
MORE IMPORTANTLY, WE NEED A KEYBOARDIST.
I'VE BEEN LOOKING WITH NO LUCK. BUT WITHOUT A KEYBOARD, WE CAN'T DRAW OUT THE FULL SOUND WE NEED FOR THIS GENRE.
EVEN THOUGH WE HAVE A LIVE SHOW SCHEDULED...
WE ALL HAVE TO DO OUR BEST TO SEARCH FOR SOMEONE.
LIVEHOUSE CiRCLE

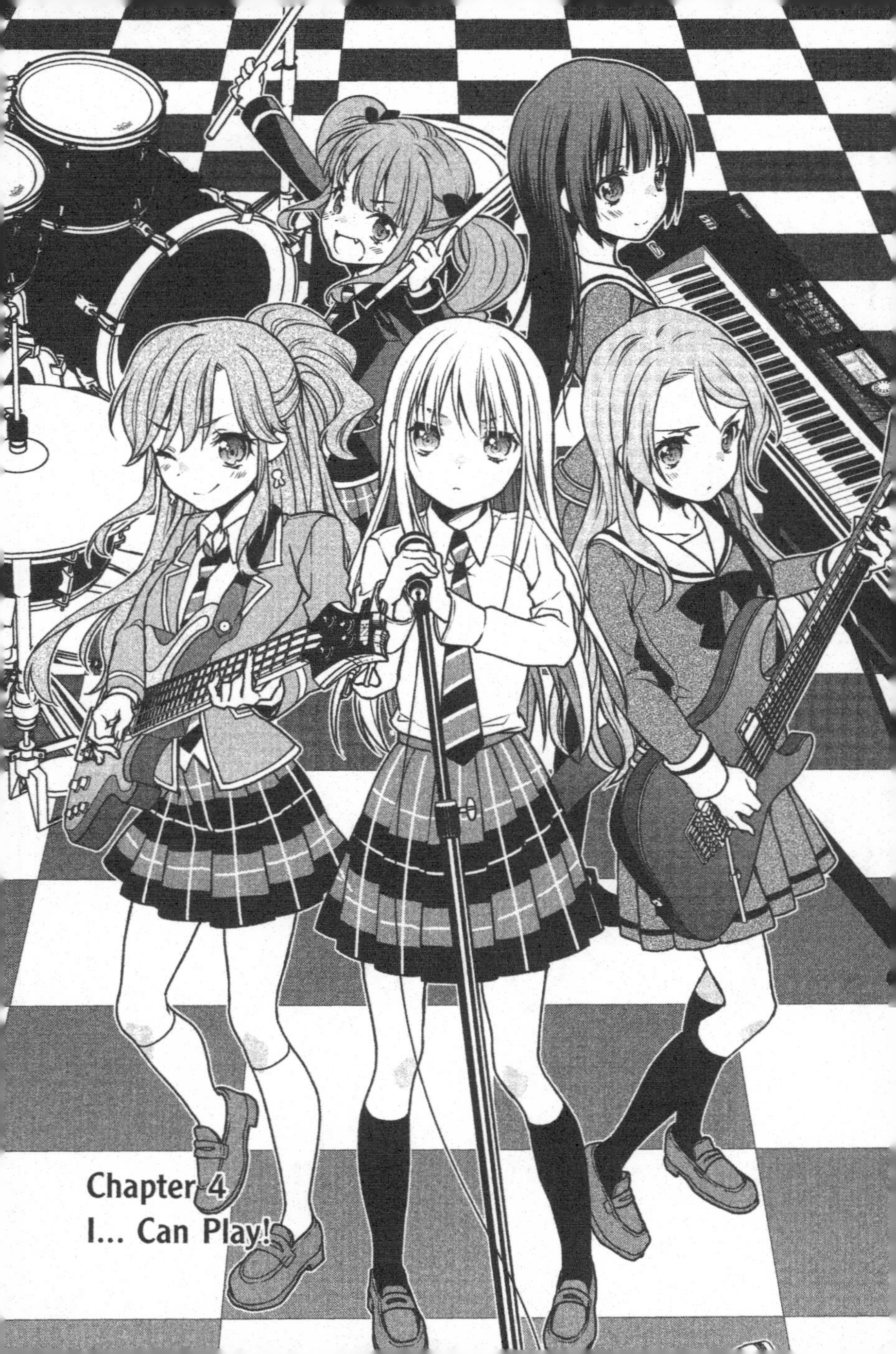

Chapter 4
I... Can Play!

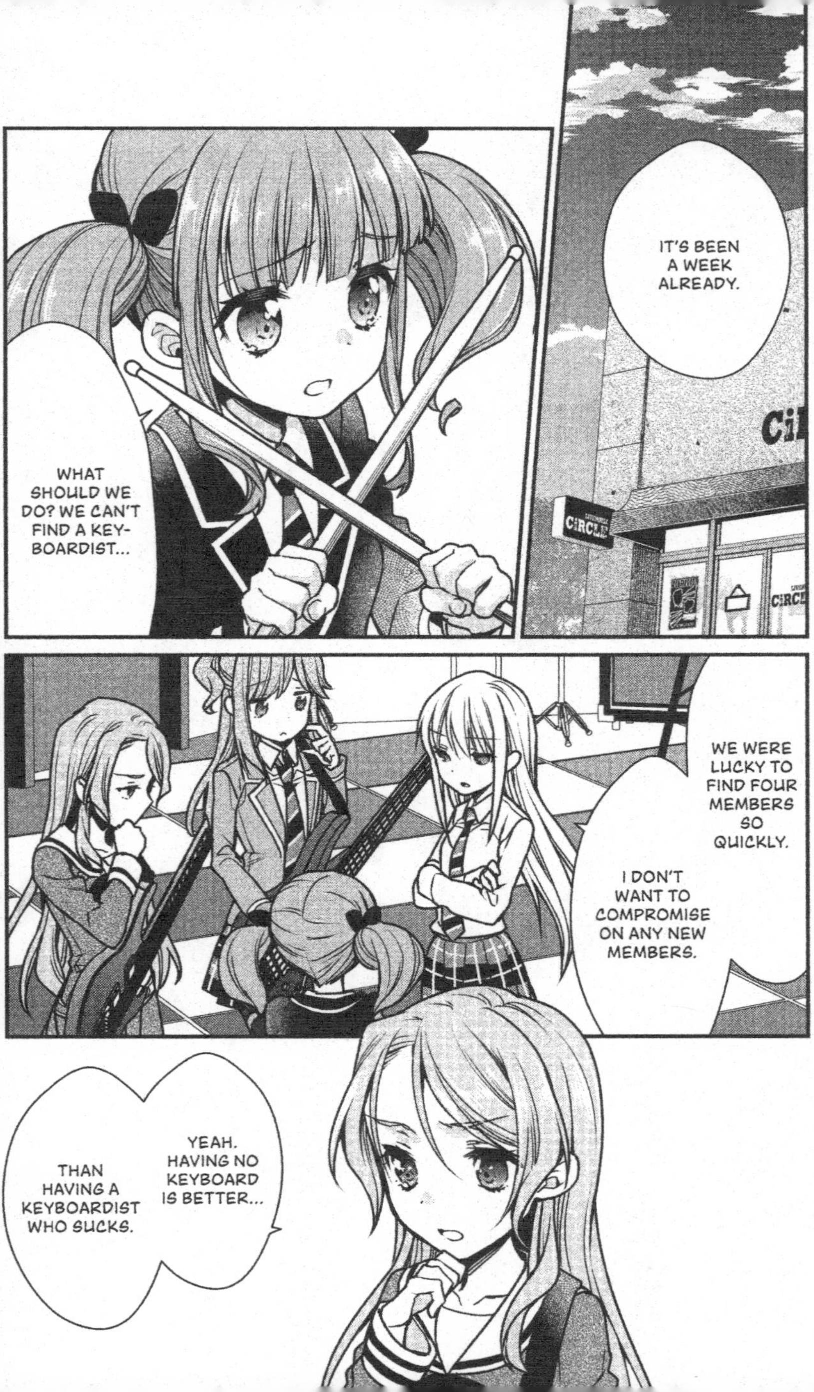
IT'S BEEN A WEEK ALREADY.
CiRCLE
WHAT SHOULD WE DO? WE CAN'T FIND A KEY-BOARDIST...
WE WERE LUCKY TO FIND FOUR MEMBERS SO QUICKLY.
I DON'T WANT TO COMPROMISE ON ANY NEW MEMBERS.
YEAH. HAVING NO KEYBOARD IS BETTER...
THAN HAVING A KEYBOARDIST WHO SUCKS.

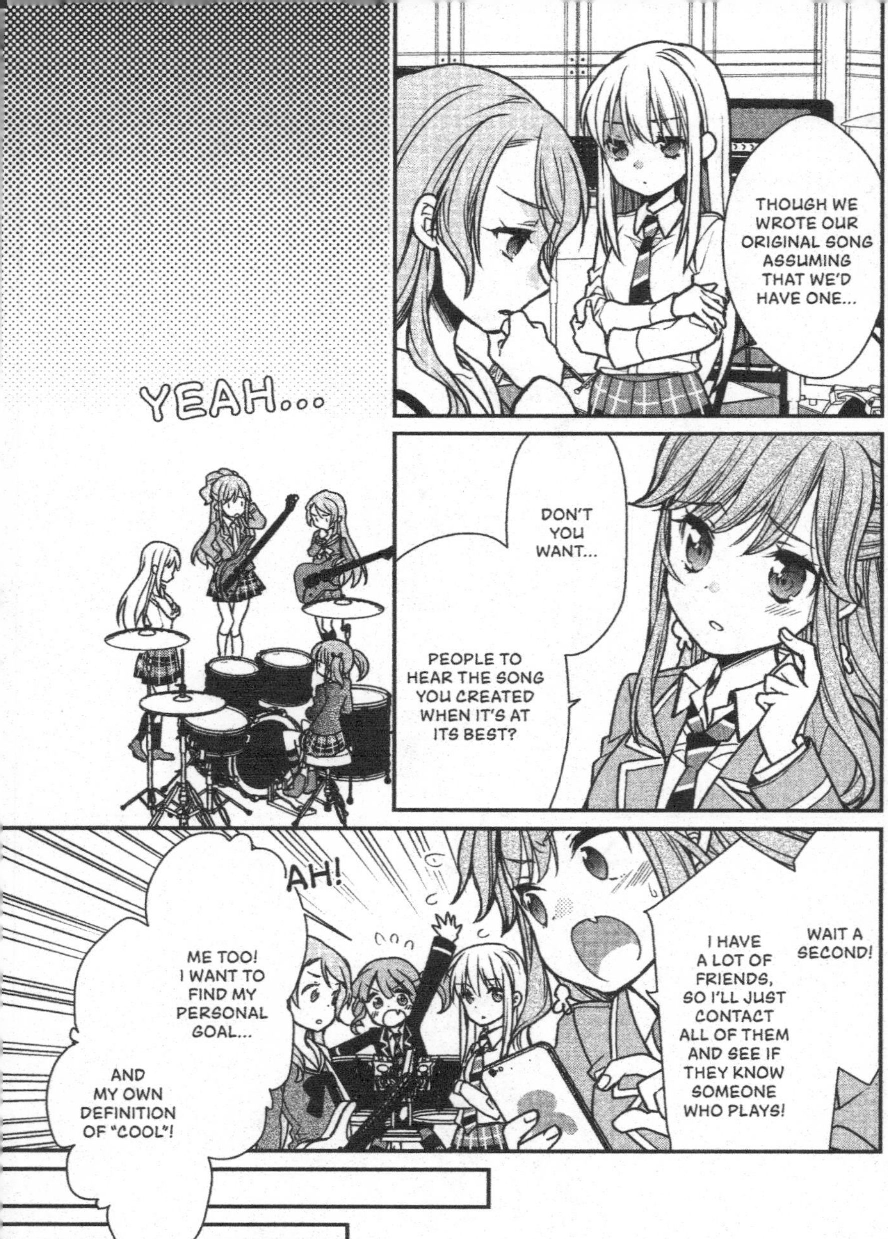
THOUGH WE WROTE OUR ORIGINAL SONG ASSUMING THAT WE'D HAVE ONE...
YEAH...
DON'T YOU WANT...
PEOPLE TO HEAR THE SONG YOU CREATED WHEN IT'S AT ITS BEST?
WAIT A SECOND!
I HAVE A LOT OF FRIENDS, SO I'LL JUST CONTACT ALL OF THEM AND SEE IF THEY KNOW SOMEONE WHO PLAYS!
AH!
ME TOO! I WANT TO FIND MY PERSONAL GOAL...
AND MY OWN DEFINITION OF "COOL"!

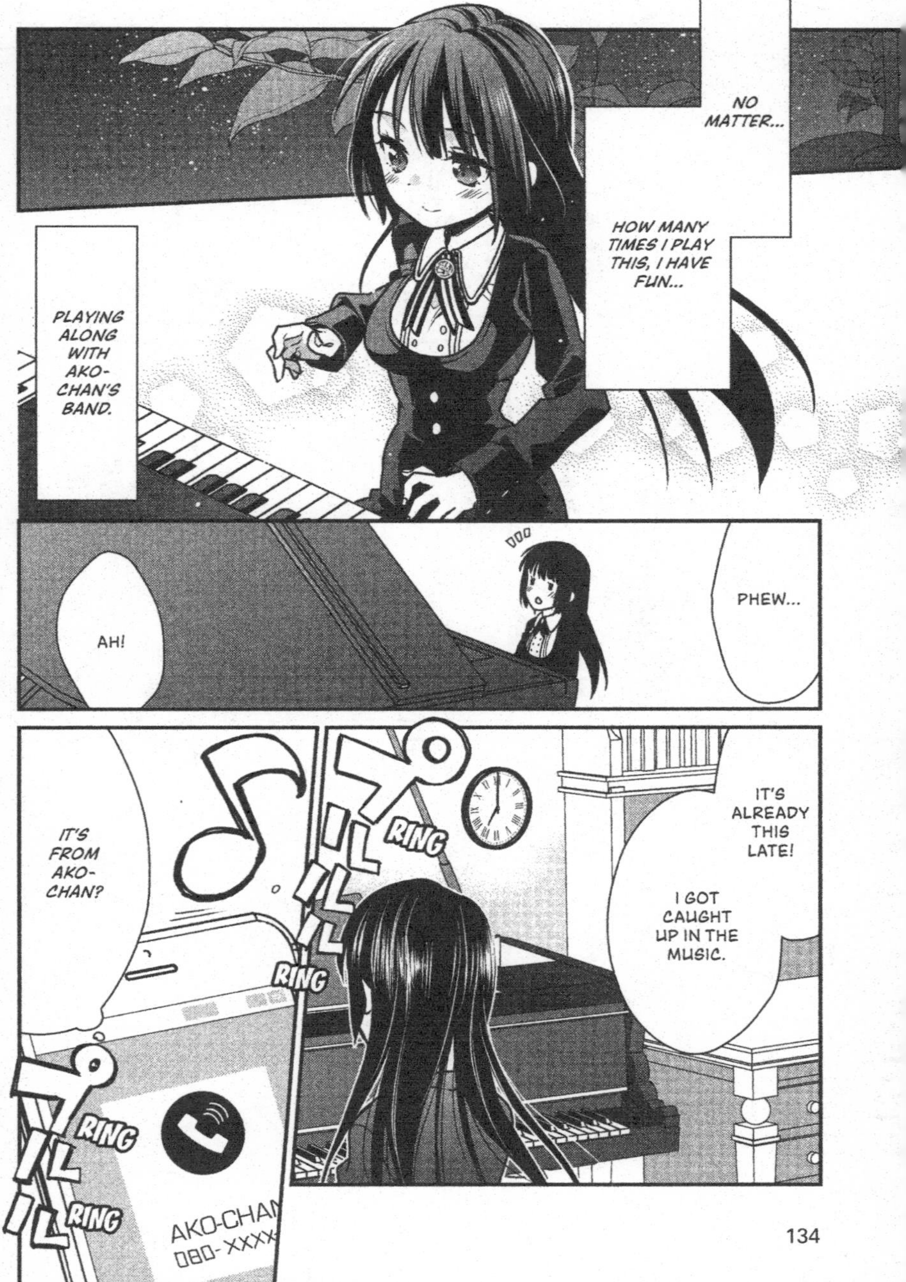
NO MATTER...
HOW MANY TIMES I PLAY THIS, I HAVE FUN...
PLAYING ALONG WITH AKO-CHAN'S BAND.
PHEW...
AH!
IT'S ALREADY THIS LATE!
I GOT CAUGHT UP IN THE MUSIC.
RING
RING
IT'S FROM AKO-CHAN?
RING
RING
AKO-CHAN
080-XXXX

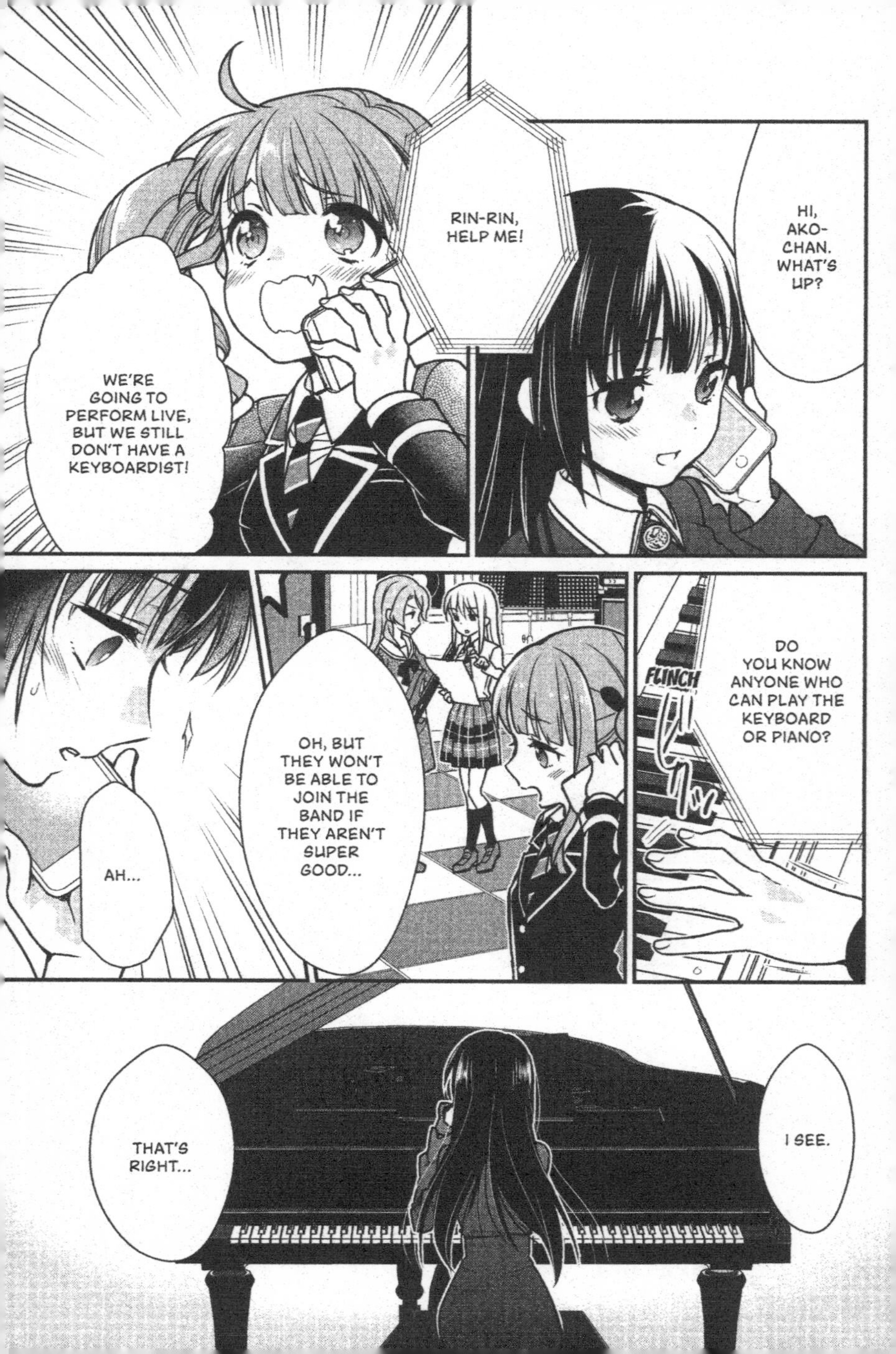
HI, AKO-CHAN. WHAT'S UP?
RIN-RIN, HELP ME!
WE'RE GOING TO PERFORM LIVE, BUT WE STILL DON'T HAVE A KEYBOARDIST!
DO YOU KNOW ANYONE WHO CAN PLAY THE KEYBOARD OR PIANO?
FLINCH
OH, BUT THEY WON'T BE ABLE TO JOIN THE BAND IF THEY AREN'T SUPER GOOD...
AH...
I SEE.
THAT'S RIGHT...

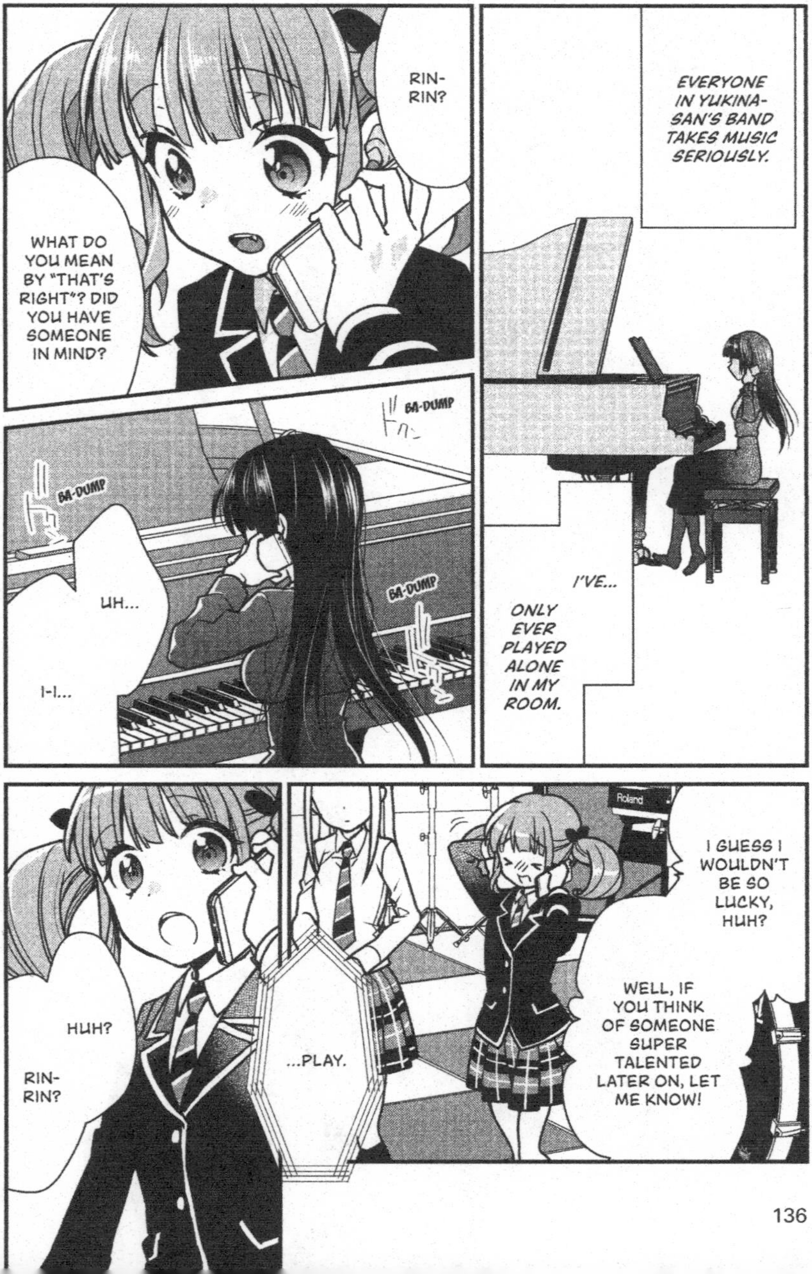
EVERYONE IN YUKINA-SAN'S BAND TAKES MUSIC SERIOUSLY.
I'VE...
ONLY EVER PLAYED ALONE IN MY ROOM.
RIN-RIN?
WHAT DO YOU MEAN BY "THAT'S RIGHT"? DID YOU HAVE SOMEONE IN MIND?
BA-DUMP
BA-DUMP
BA-DUMP
UH...
I-I...
I GUESS I WOULDN'T BE SO LUCKY, HUH?
WELL, IF YOU THINK OF SOMEONE SUPER TALENTED LATER ON, LET ME KNOW!
Roland
...PLAY.
HUH?
RIN-RIN?

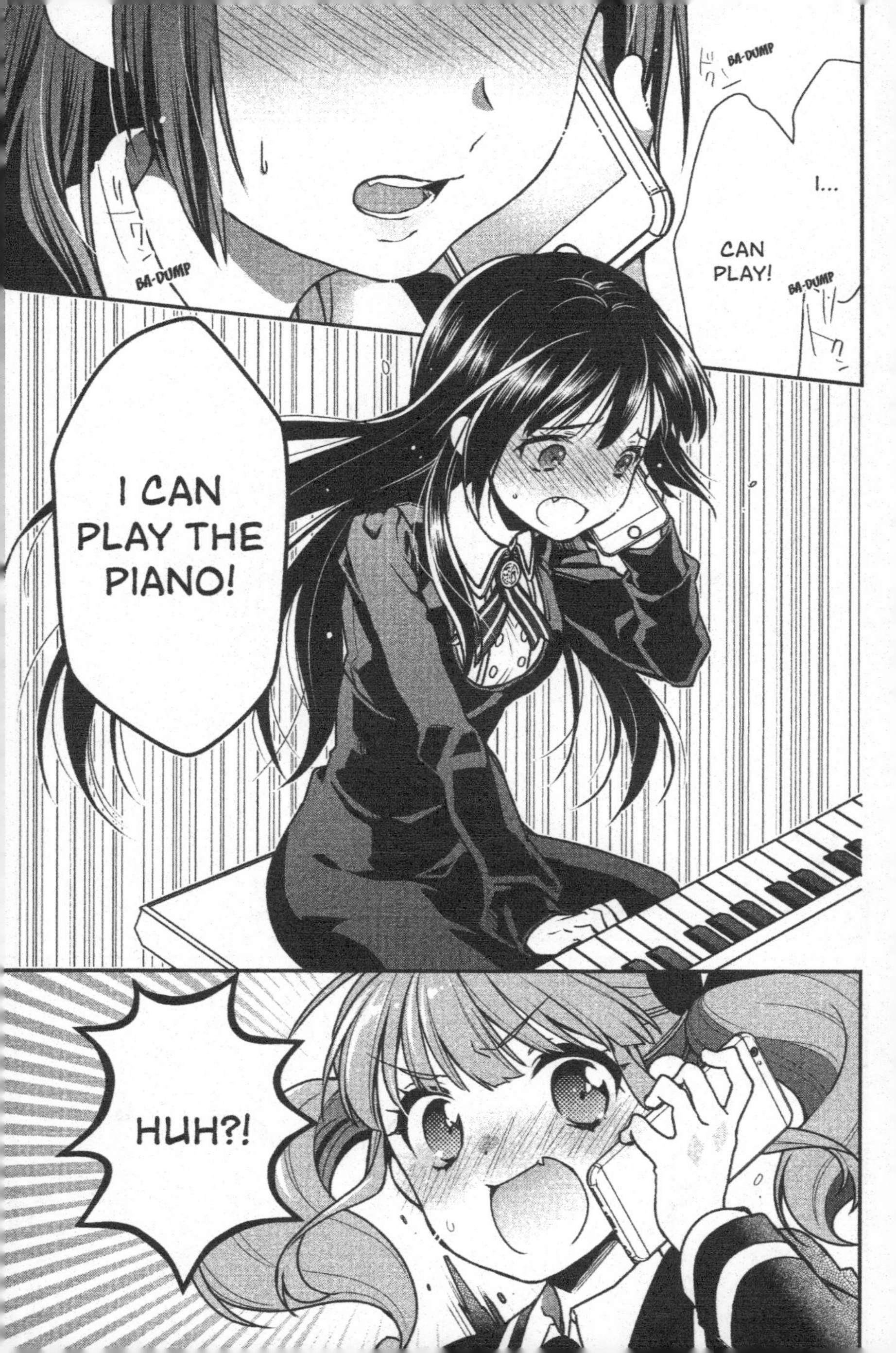
BA-DUMP
I...
CAN PLAY!
BA-DUMP
BA-DUMP
I CAN PLAY THE PIANO!
HUH?!

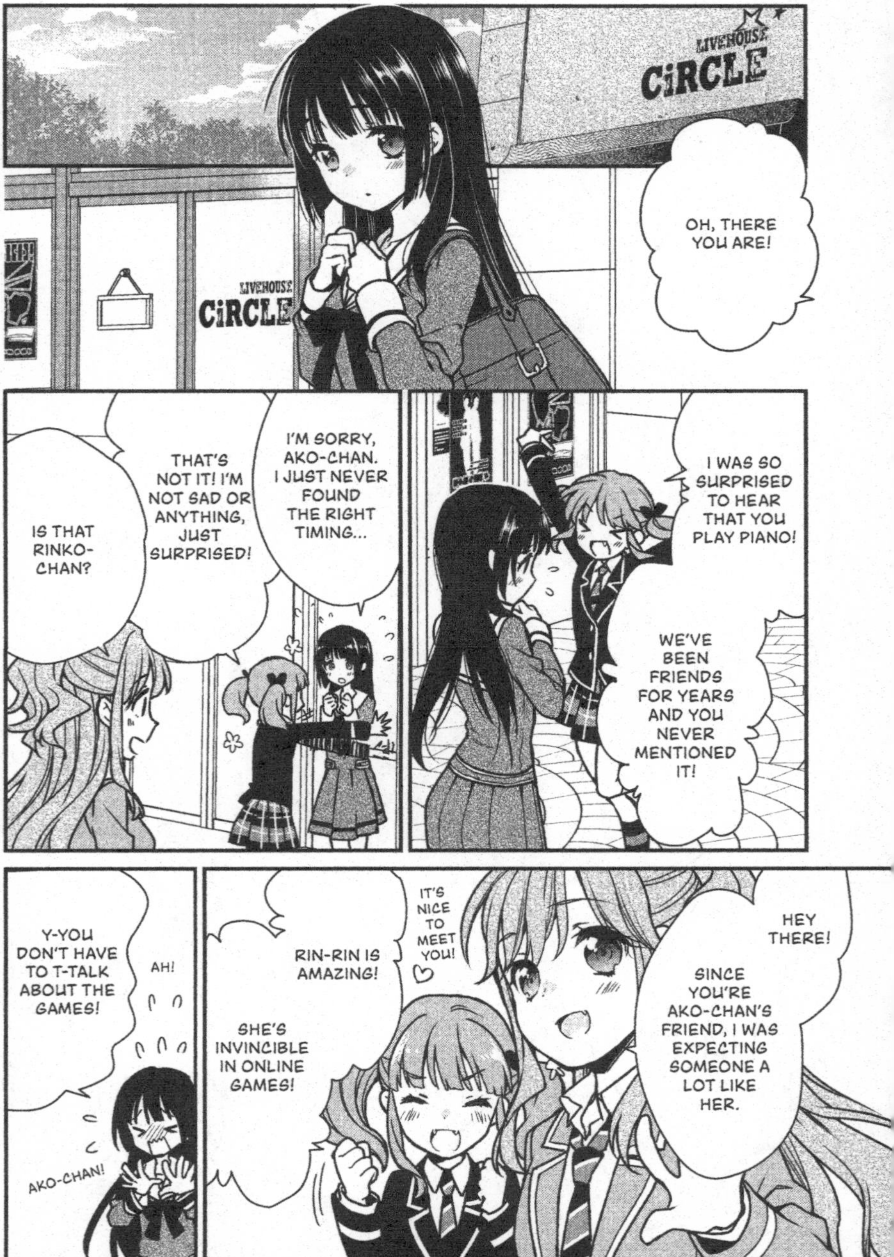
LIVEHOUSE CiRCLE
LIVEHOUSE CiRCLE
OH, THERE YOU ARE!
I WAS SO SURPRISED TO HEAR THAT YOU PLAY PIANO!
WE'VE BEEN FRIENDS FOR YEARS AND YOU NEVER MENTIONED IT!
I'M SORRY, AKO-CHAN. I JUST NEVER FOUND THE RIGHT TIMING...
THAT'S NOT IT! I'M NOT SAD OR ANYTHING, JUST SURPRISED!
IS THAT RINKO-CHAN?
HEY THERE!
SINCE YOU'RE AKO-CHAN'S FRIEND, I WAS EXPECTING SOMEONE A LOT LIKE HER.
IT'S NICE TO MEET YOU!
RIN-RIN IS AMAZING!
SHE'S INVINCIBLE IN ONLINE GAMES!
Y-YOU DON'T HAVE TO T-TALK ABOUT THE GAMES!
AH!
AKO-CHAN!

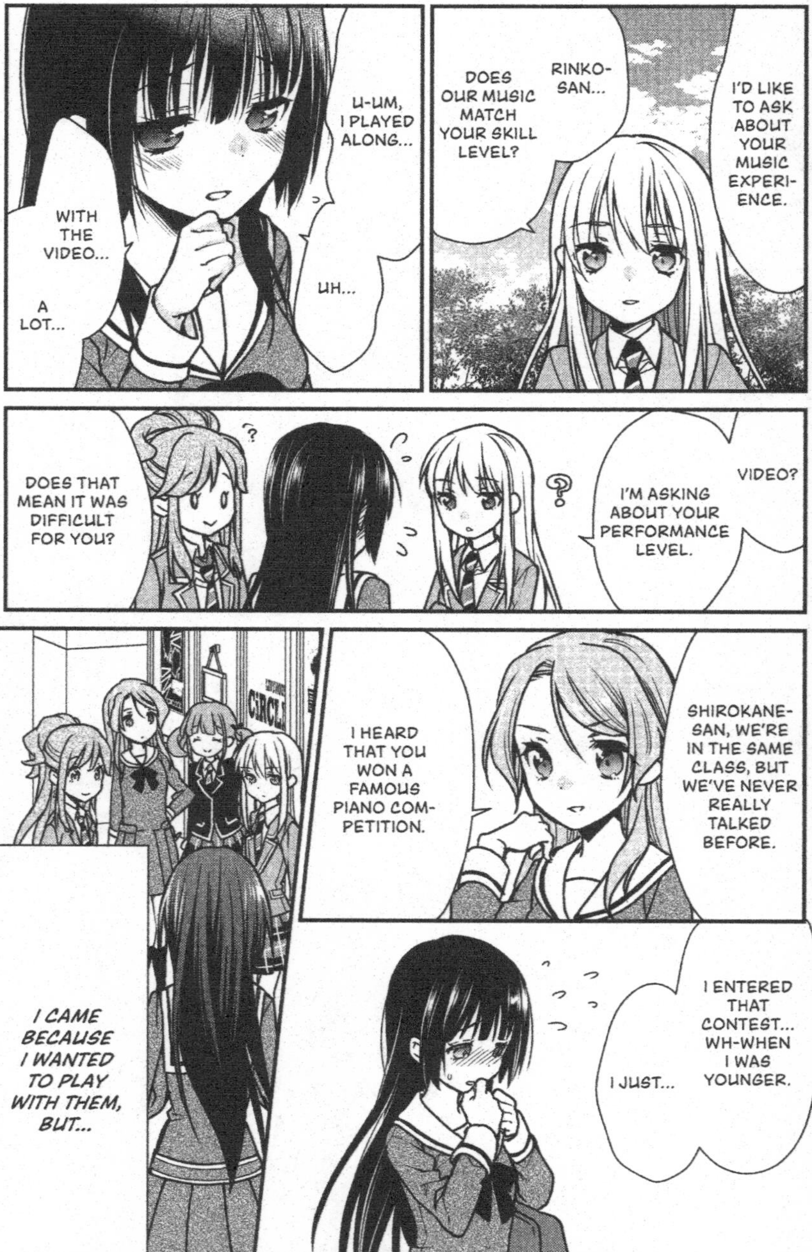
RINKO-SAN...
I'D LIKE TO ASK ABOUT YOUR MUSIC EXPERIENCE.
DOES OUR MUSIC MATCH YOUR SKILL LEVEL?
UH...
U-UM, I PLAYED ALONG...
WITH THE VIDEO...
A LOT...
VIDEO?
I'M ASKING ABOUT YOUR PERFORMANCE LEVEL.
DOES THAT MEAN IT WAS DIFFICULT FOR YOU?
SHIROKANE-SAN, WE'RE IN THE SAME CLASS, BUT WE'VE NEVER REALLY TALKED BEFORE.
I HEARD THAT YOU WON A FAMOUS PIANO COMPETITION.
I ENTERED THAT CONTEST... WH-WHEN I WAS YOUNGER.
I JUST...
I CAME BECAUSE I WANTED TO PLAY WITH THEM, BUT...

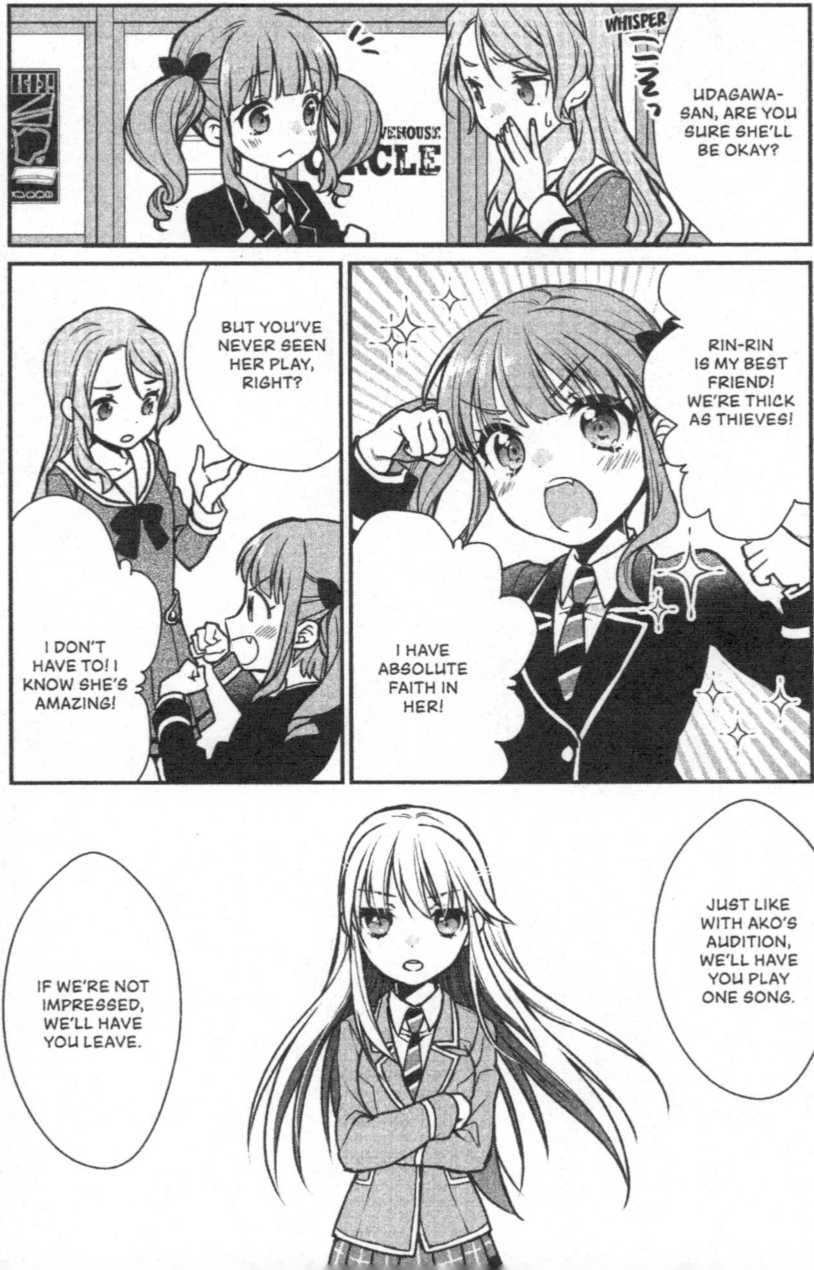
WHISPER
UDAGAWA-SAN, ARE YOU SURE SHE'LL BE OKAY?
RIN-RIN IS MY BEST FRIEND! WE'RE THICK AS THIEVES!
I HAVE ABSOLUTE FAITH IN HER!
BUT YOU'VE NEVER SEEN HER PLAY, RIGHT?
I DON'T HAVE TO! I KNOW SHE'S AMAZING!
JUST LIKE WITH AKO'S AUDITION, WE'LL HAVE YOU PLAY ONE SONG.
IF WE'RE NOT IMPRESSED, WE'LL HAVE YOU LEAVE.

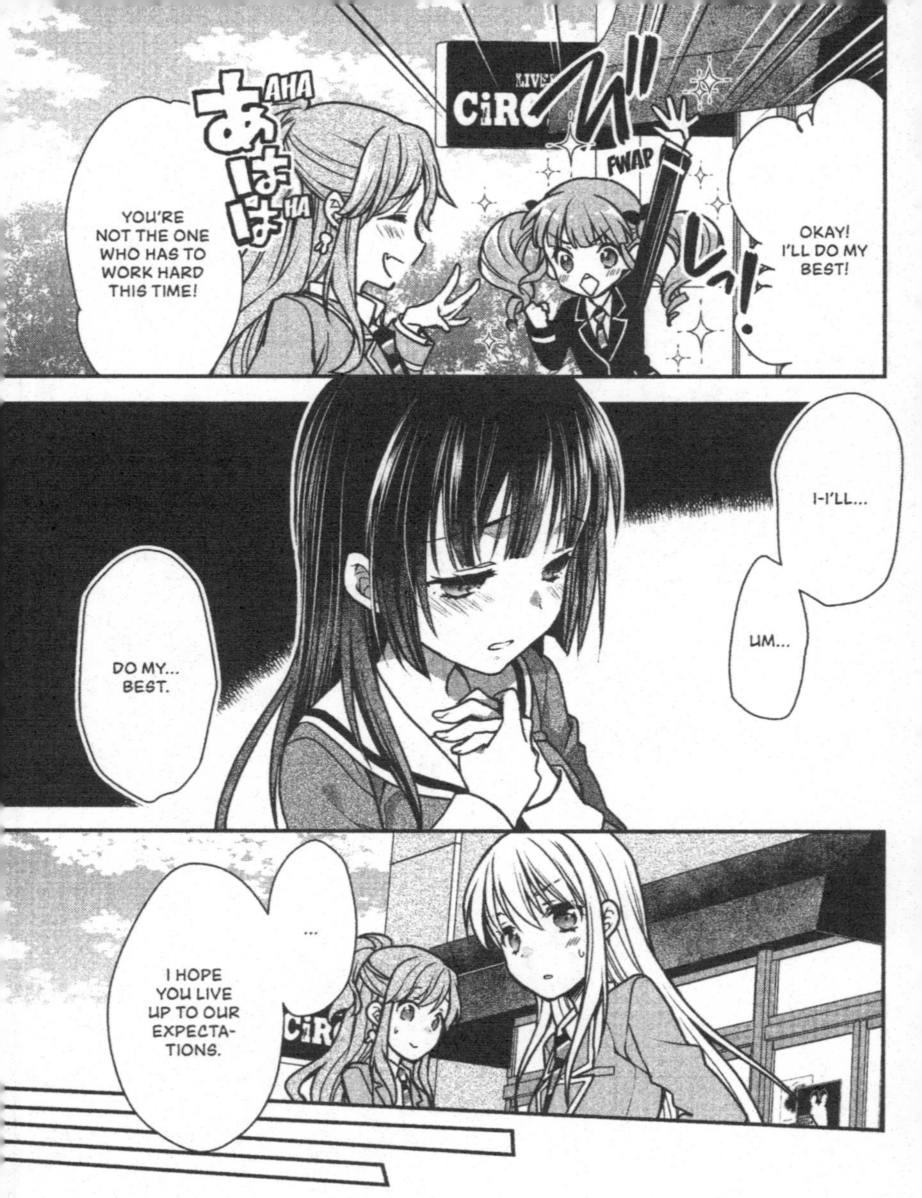
OKAY! I'LL DO MY BEST!
FWAP
AHA
HA
YOU'RE NOT THE ONE WHO HAS TO WORK HARD THIS TIME!
I-I'LL...
UM...
DO MY... BEST.
...
I HOPE YOU LIVE UP TO OUR EXPECTATIONS.

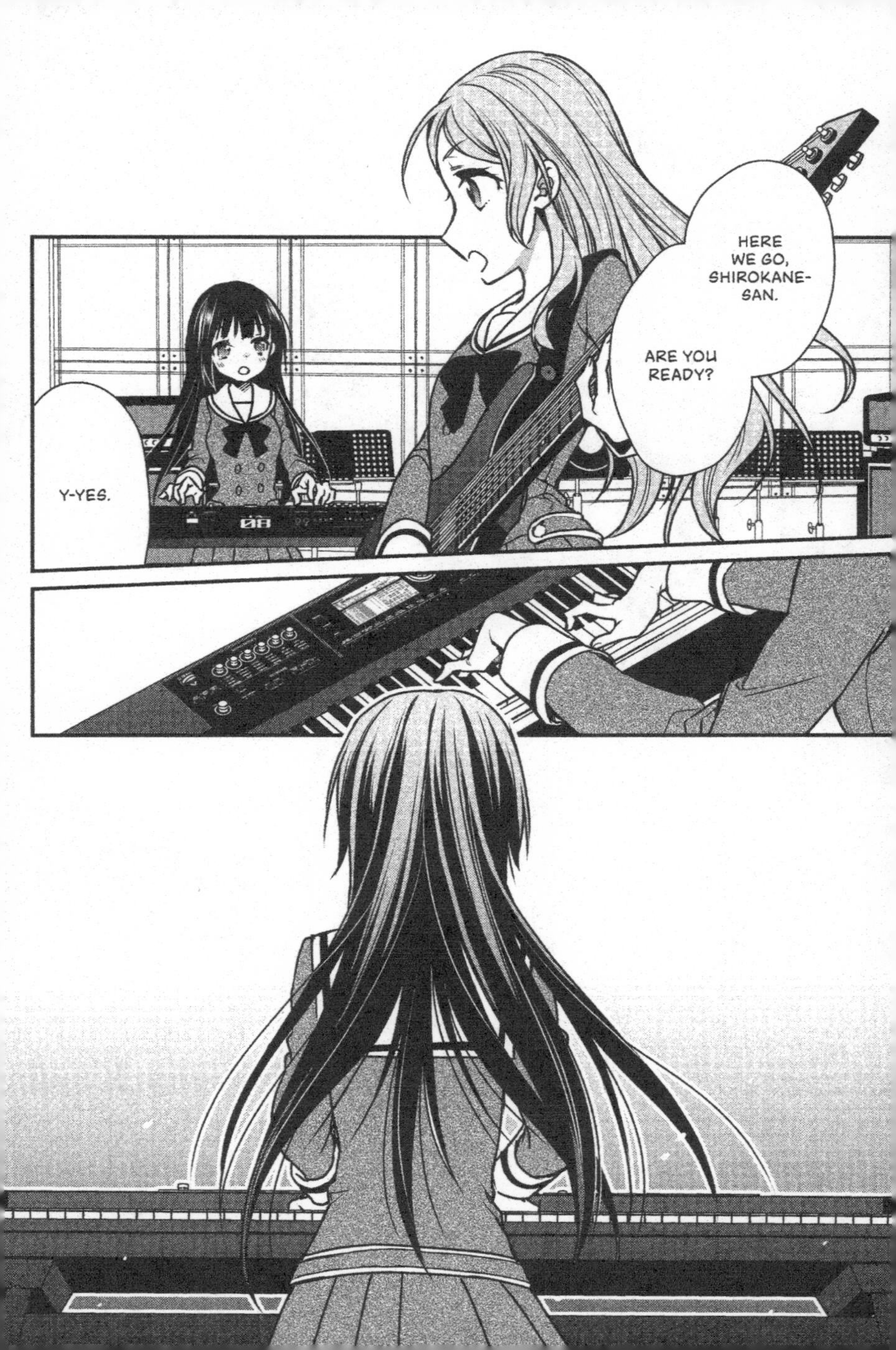
HERE WE GO, SHIROKANE-SAN.
ARE YOU READY?
Y-YES.

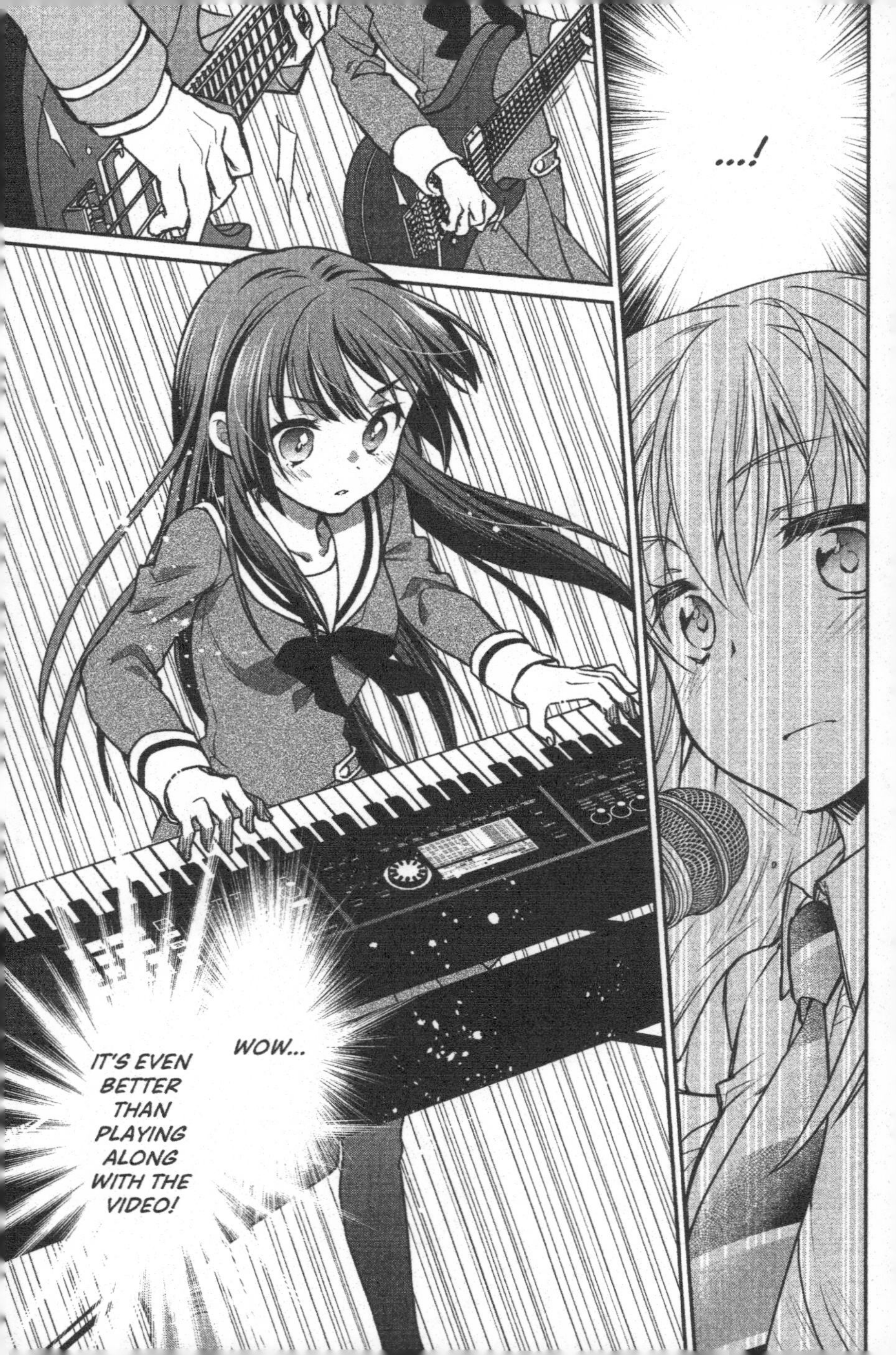
...!
WOW...
IT'S EVEN BETTER THAN PLAYING ALONG WITH THE VIDEO!

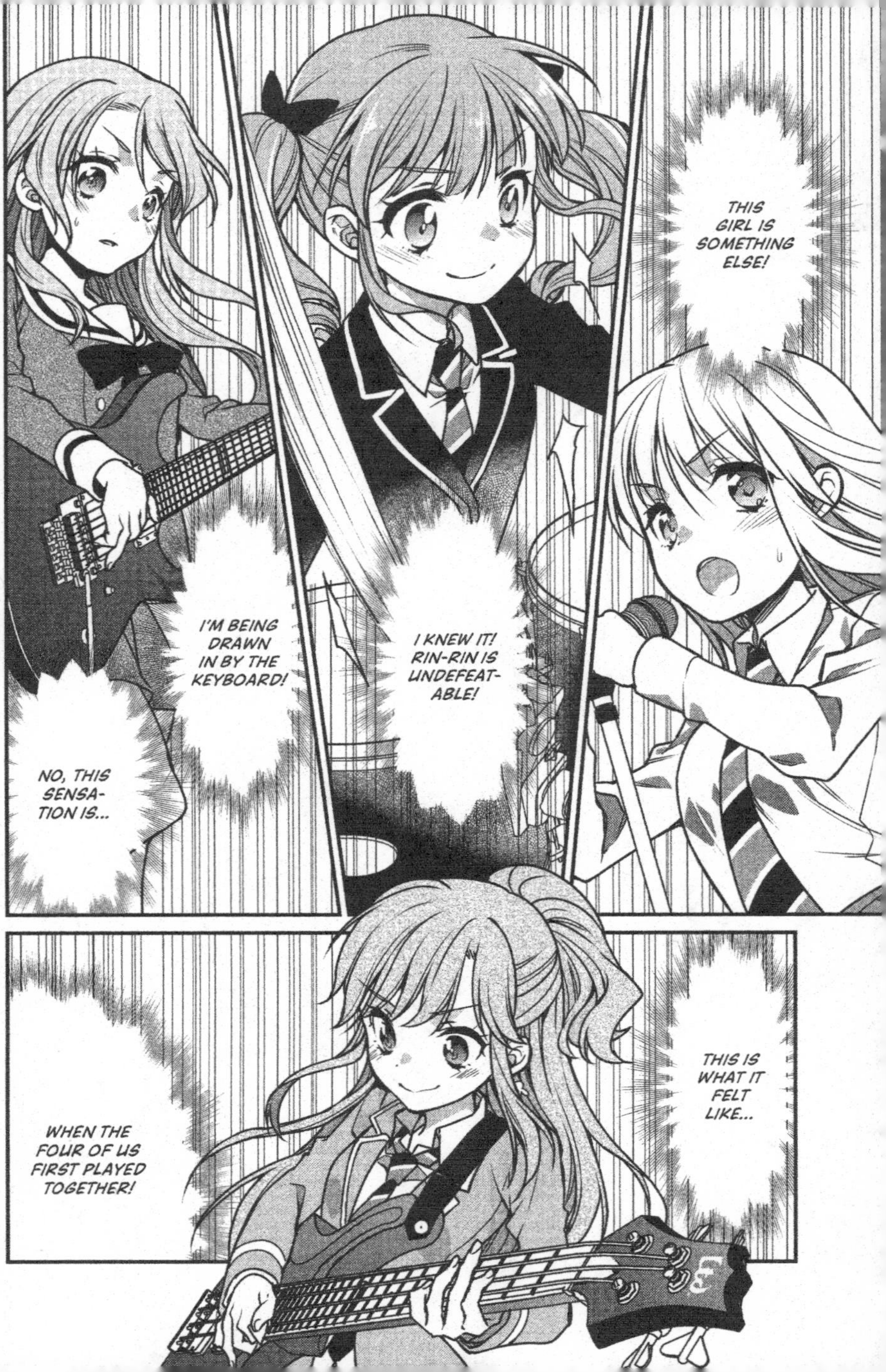
THIS GIRL IS SOMETHING ELSE!
I KNEW IT! RIN-RIN IS UNDEFEAT-ABLE!
I'M BEING DRAWN IN BY THE KEYBOARD!
NO, THIS SENSA-TION IS...
THIS IS WHAT IT FELT LIKE...
WHEN THE FOUR OF US FIRST PLAYED TOGETHER!

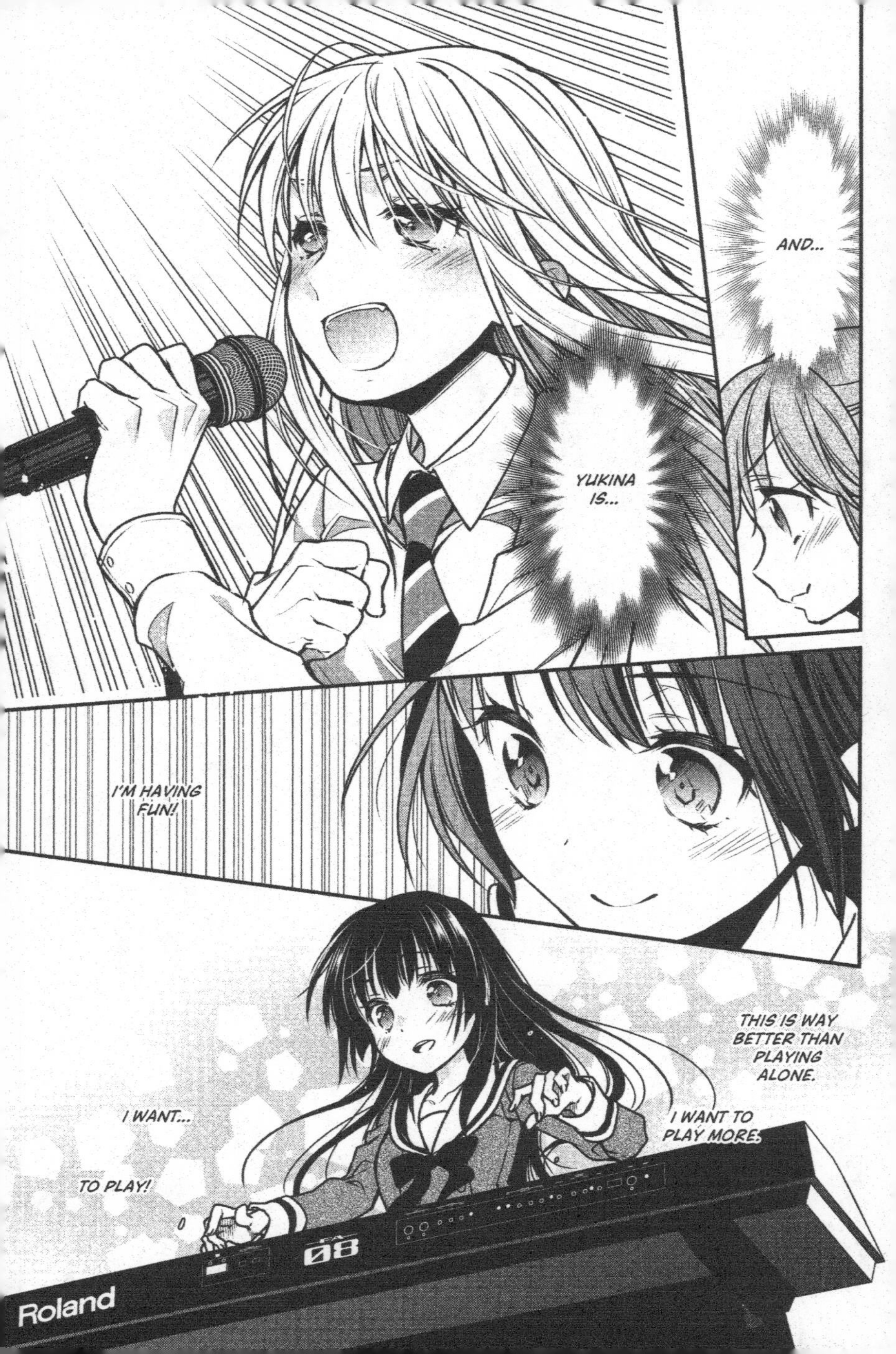
AND...
YUKINA IS...
I'M HAVING FUN!
THIS IS WAY BETTER THAN PLAYING ALONE.
I WANT TO PLAY MORE.
I WANT...
TO PLAY!
08
Roland

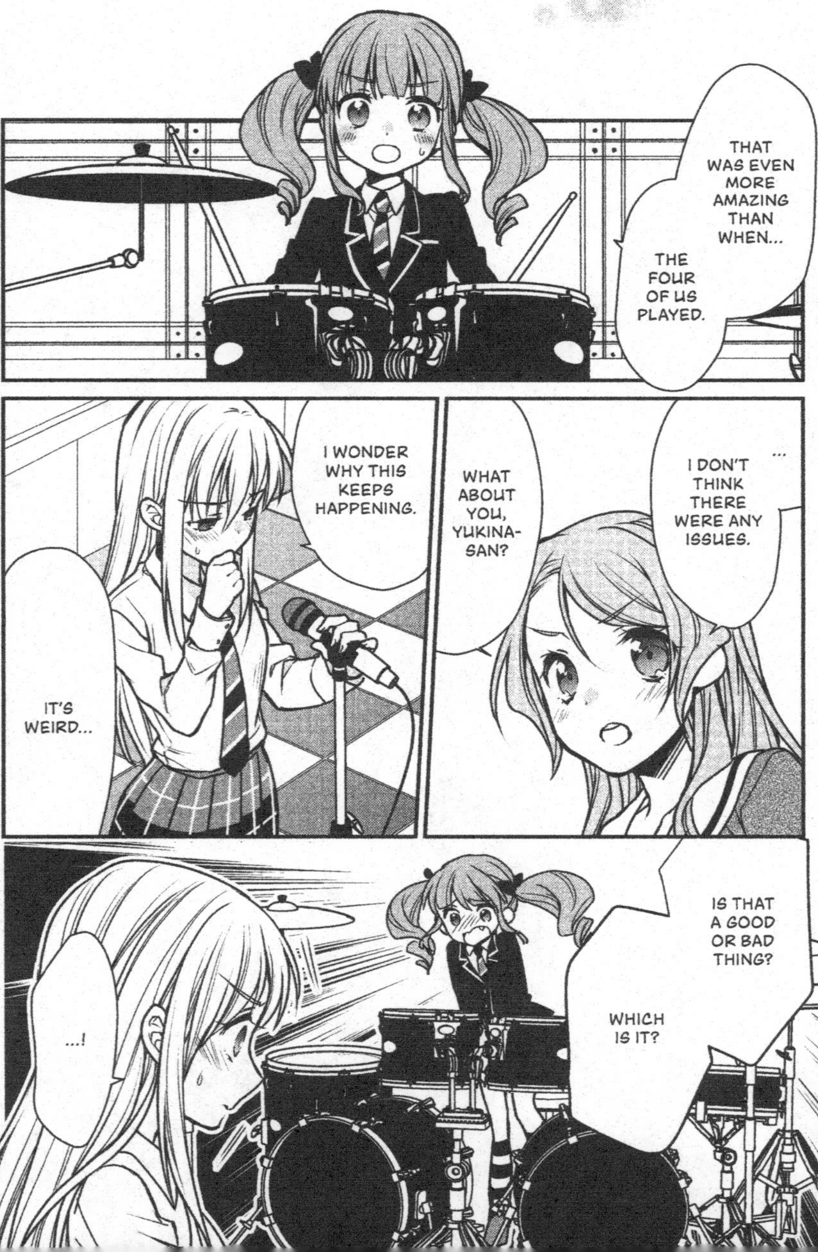
THAT WAS EVEN MORE AMAZING THAN WHEN...
THE FOUR OF US PLAYED.
...
I DON'T THINK THERE WERE ANY ISSUES.
WHAT ABOUT YOU, YUKINA-SAN?
I WONDER WHY THIS KEEPS HAPPENING.
IT'S WEIRD...
IS THAT A GOOD OR BAD THING?
WHICH IS IT?
...!

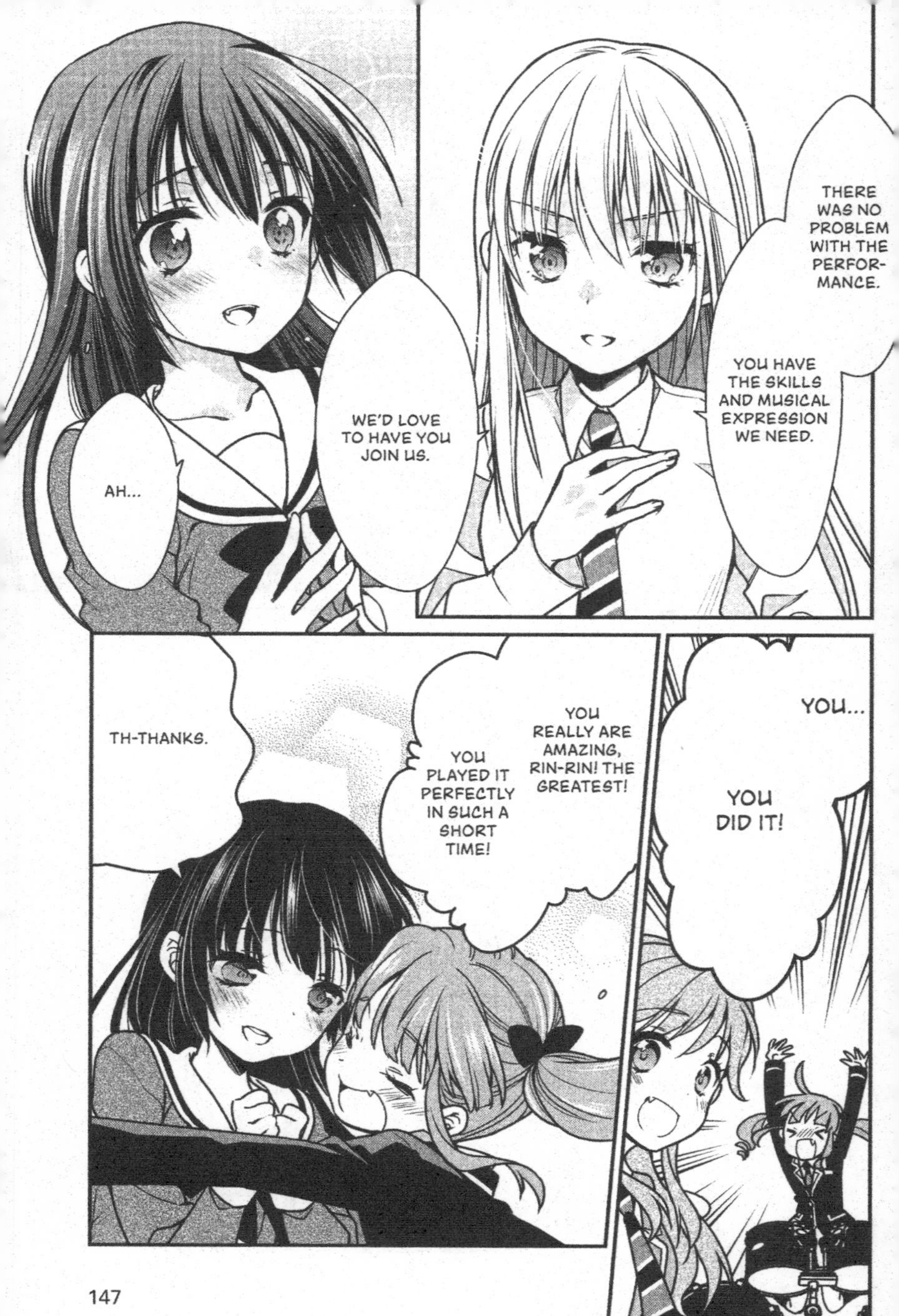
THERE WAS NO PROBLEM WITH THE PERFORMANCE.
YOU HAVE THE SKILLS AND MUSICAL EXPRESSION WE NEED.
WE'D LOVE TO HAVE YOU JOIN US.
AH...
YOU...
YOU DID IT!
YOU REALLY ARE AMAZING, RIN-RIN! THE GREATEST!
YOU PLAYED IT PERFECTLY IN SUCH A SHORT TIME!
TH-THANKS.

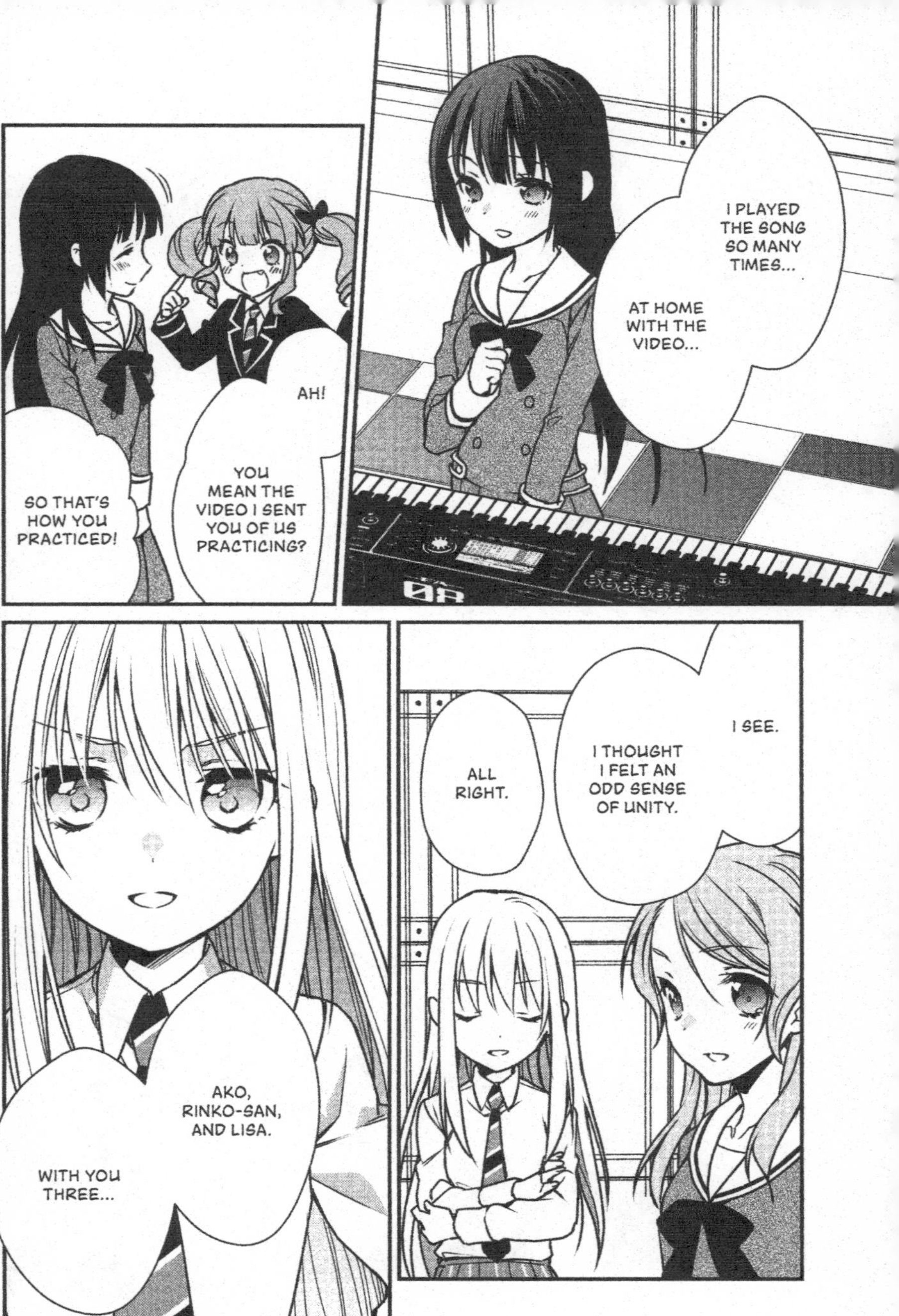
I PLAYED THE SONG SO MANY TIMES...
AT HOME WITH THE VIDEO...
AH!
YOU MEAN THE VIDEO I SENT YOU OF US PRACTICING?
SO THAT'S HOW YOU PRACTICED!
I SEE.
I THOUGHT I FELT AN ODD SENSE OF UNITY.
ALL RIGHT.
AKO, RINKO-SAN, AND LISA.
WITH YOU THREE...

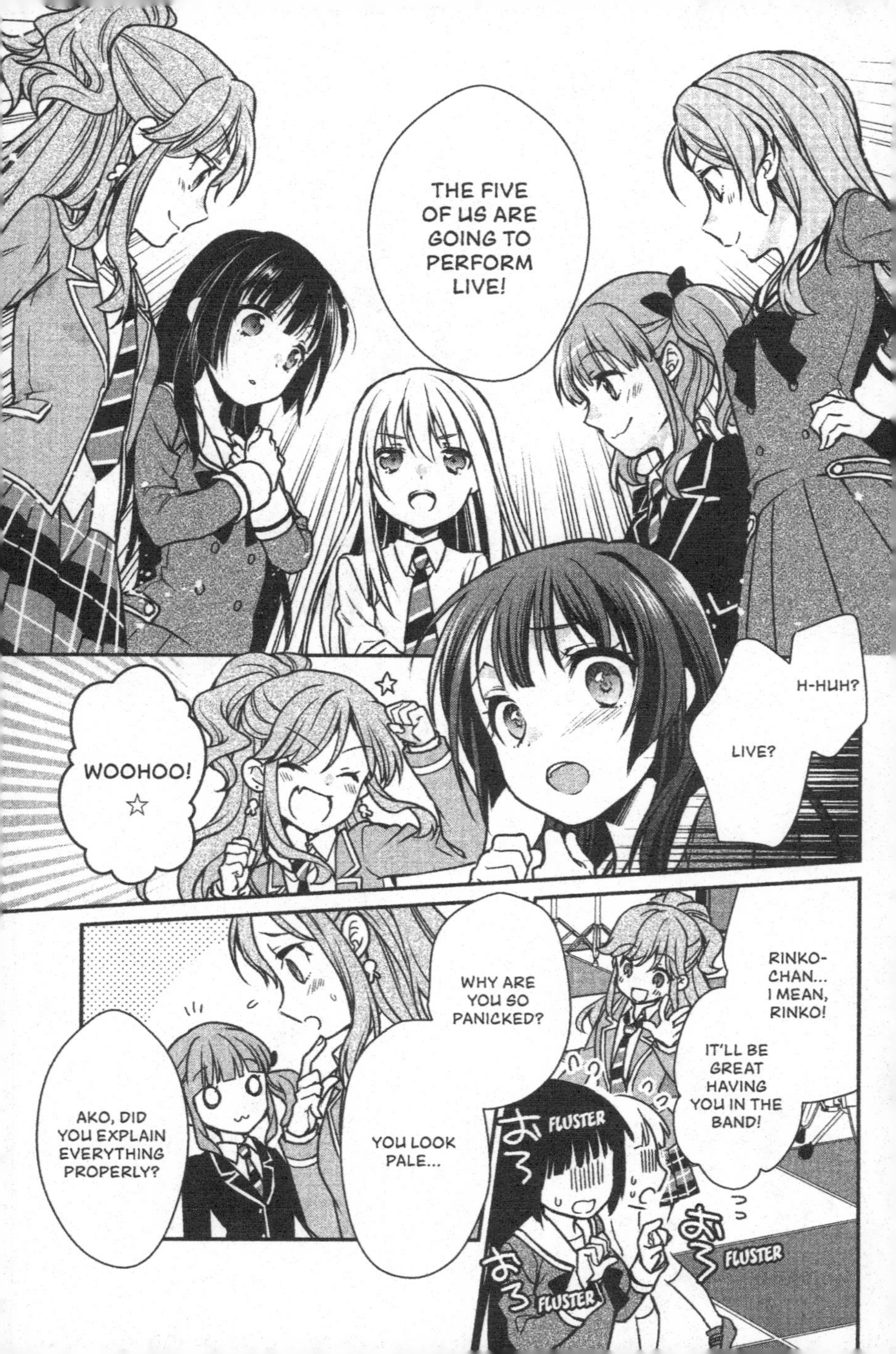
THE FIVE OF US ARE GOING TO PERFORM LIVE!
H-HUH?
LIVE?
WOOHOO! ☆
RINKO-CHAN... I MEAN, RINKO!
IT'LL BE GREAT HAVING YOU IN THE BAND!
おろ FLUSTER
おろ FLUSTER
おろ FLUSTER
WHY ARE YOU SO PANICKED?
YOU LOOK PALE...
AKO, DID YOU EXPLAIN EVERYTHING PROPERLY?

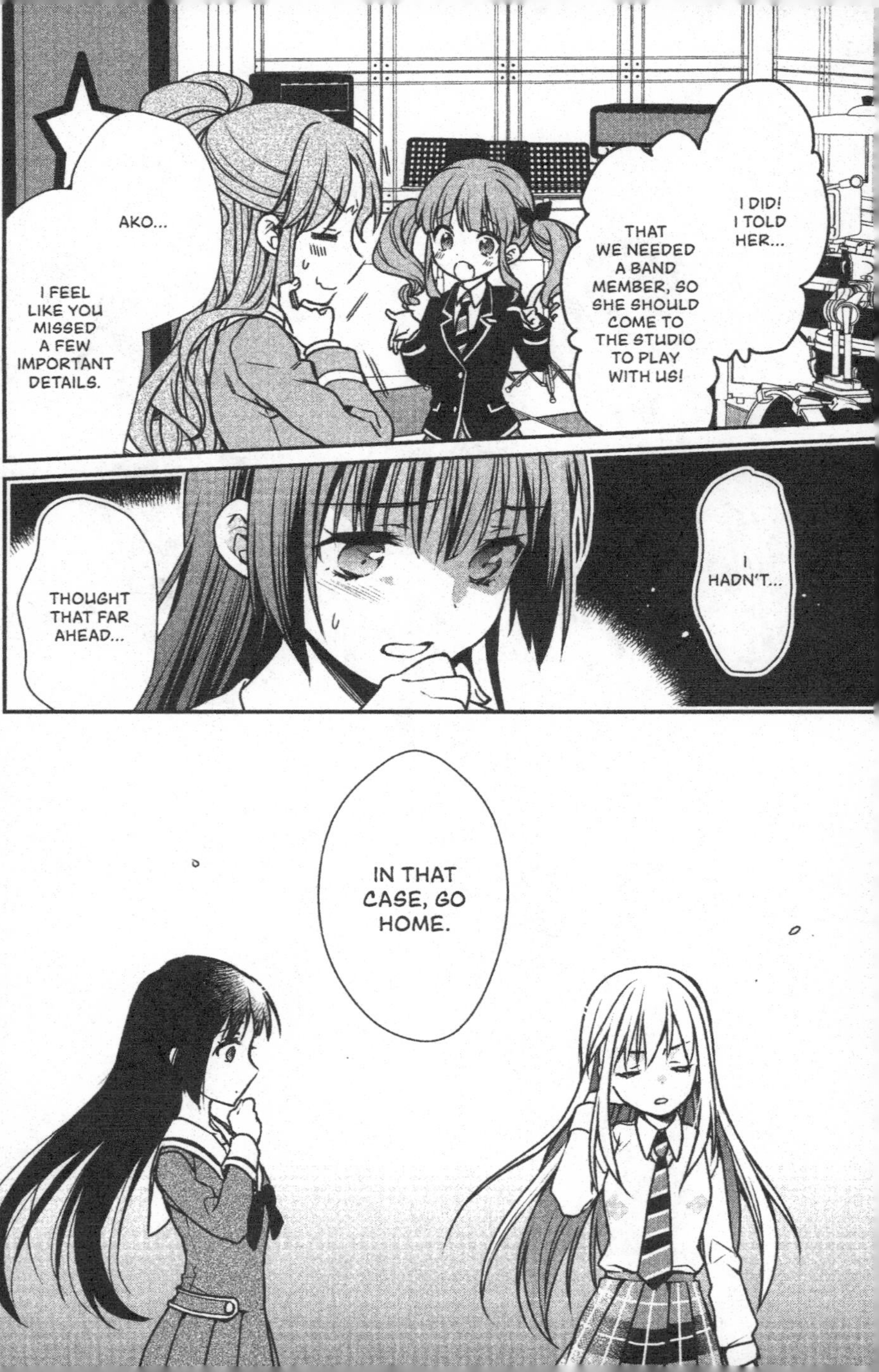
I DID! I TOLD HER...
THAT WE NEEDED A BAND MEMBER, SO SHE SHOULD COME TO THE STUDIO TO PLAY WITH US!
AKO...
I FEEL LIKE YOU MISSED A FEW IMPORTANT DETAILS.
I HADN'T...
THOUGHT THAT FAR AHEAD...
IN THAT CASE, GO HOME.

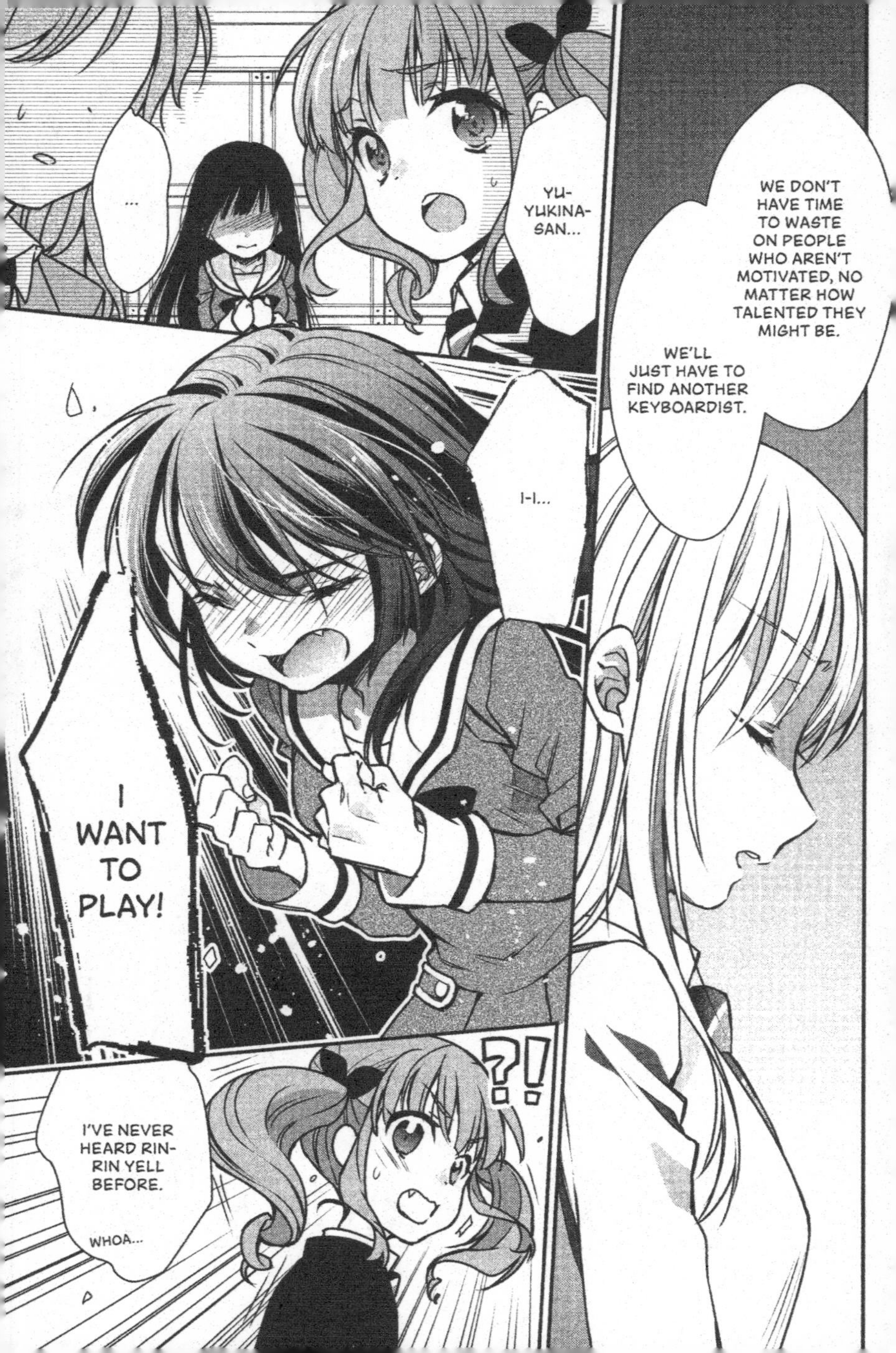
WE DON'T HAVE TIME TO WASTE ON PEOPLE WHO AREN'T MOTIVATED, NO MATTER HOW TALENTED THEY MIGHT BE.
WE'LL JUST HAVE TO FIND ANOTHER KEYBOARDIST.
YU-YUKINA-SAN...
...
I-I...
I WANT TO PLAY!
?!
I'VE NEVER HEARD RIN-RIN YELL BEFORE.
WHOA...

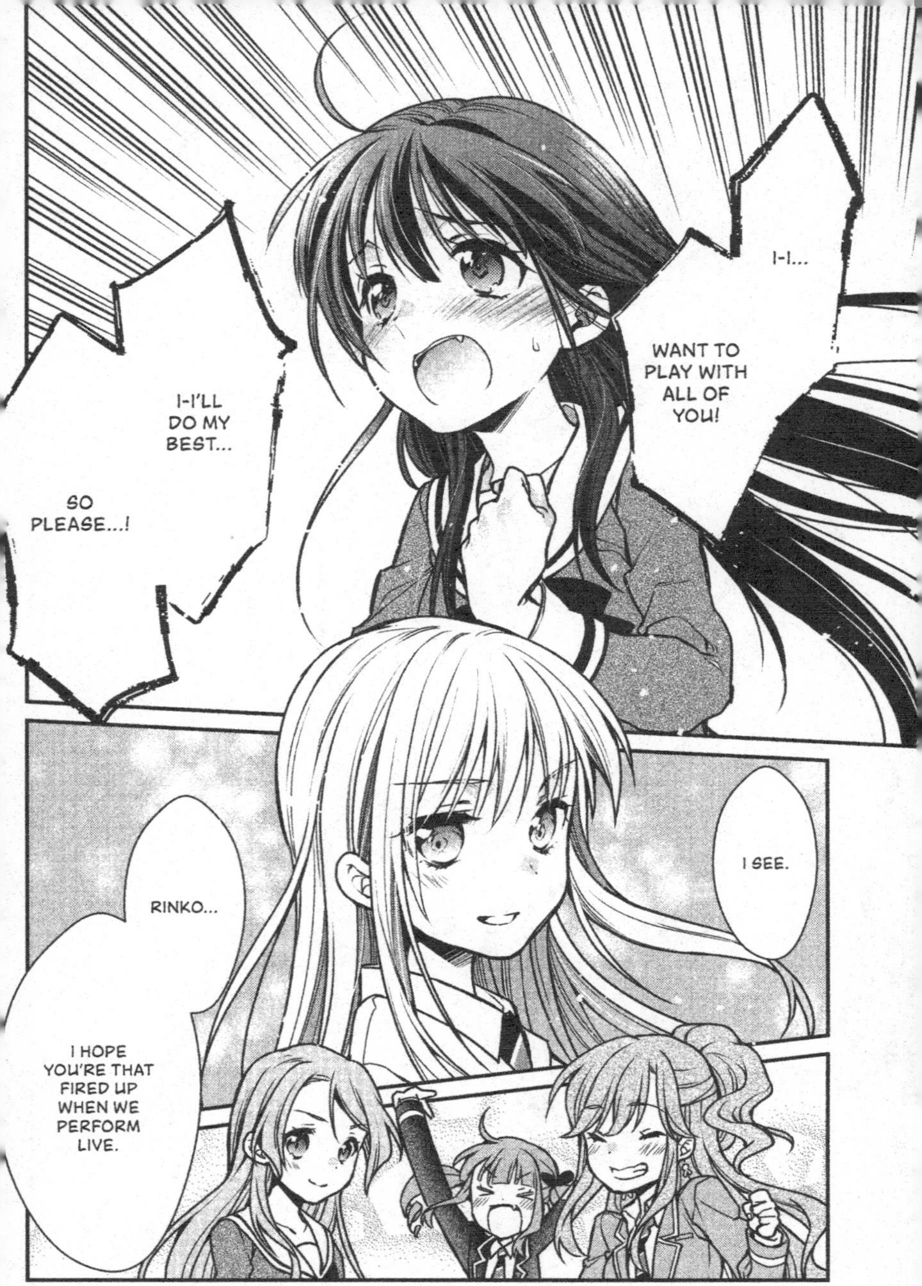
I-I...
WANT TO PLAY WITH ALL OF YOU!
I-I'LL DO MY BEST...
SO PLEASE...!
I SEE.
RINKO...
I HOPE YOU'RE THAT FIRED UP WHEN WE PERFORM LIVE.

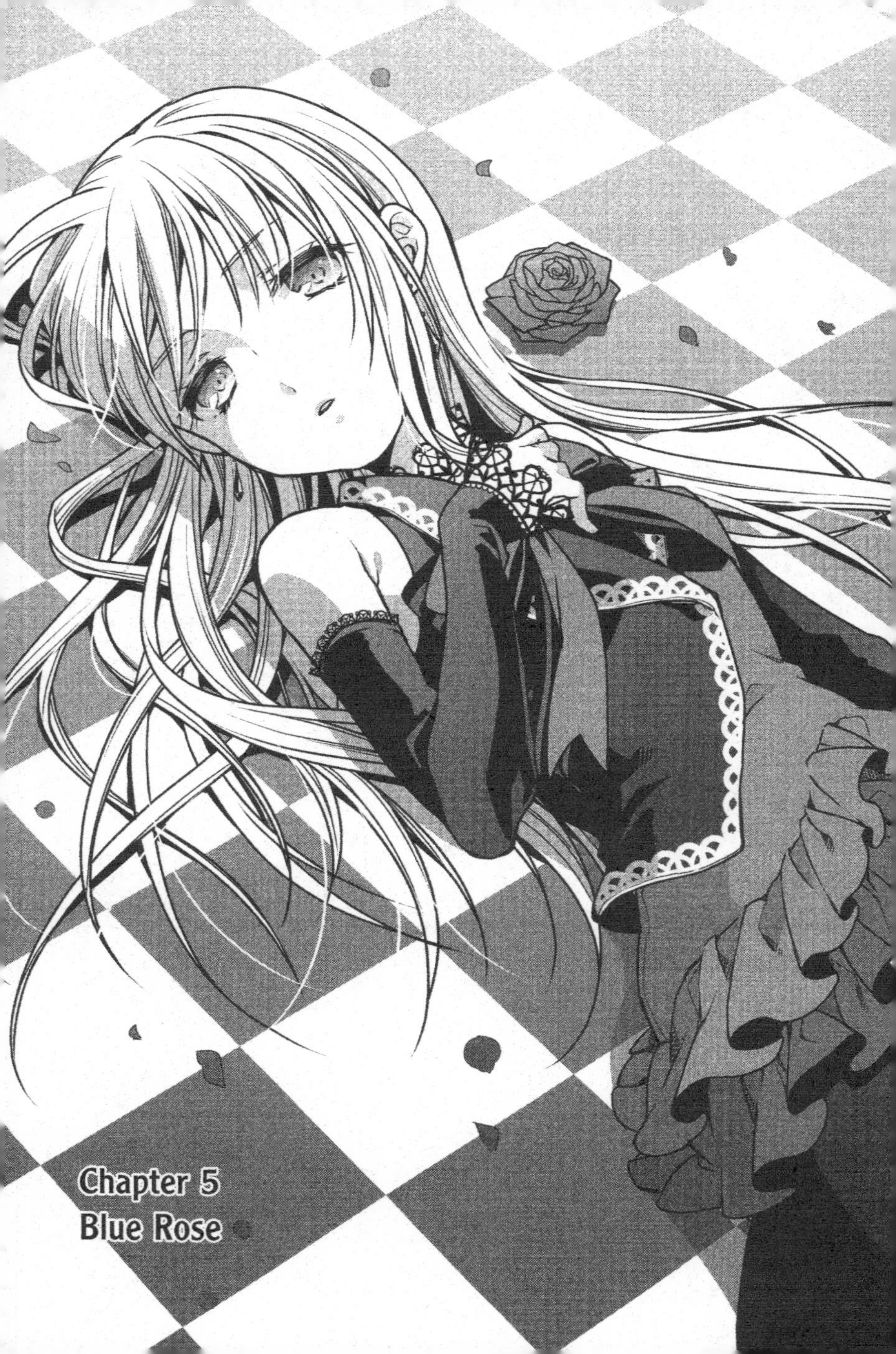
Chapter 5
Blue Rose

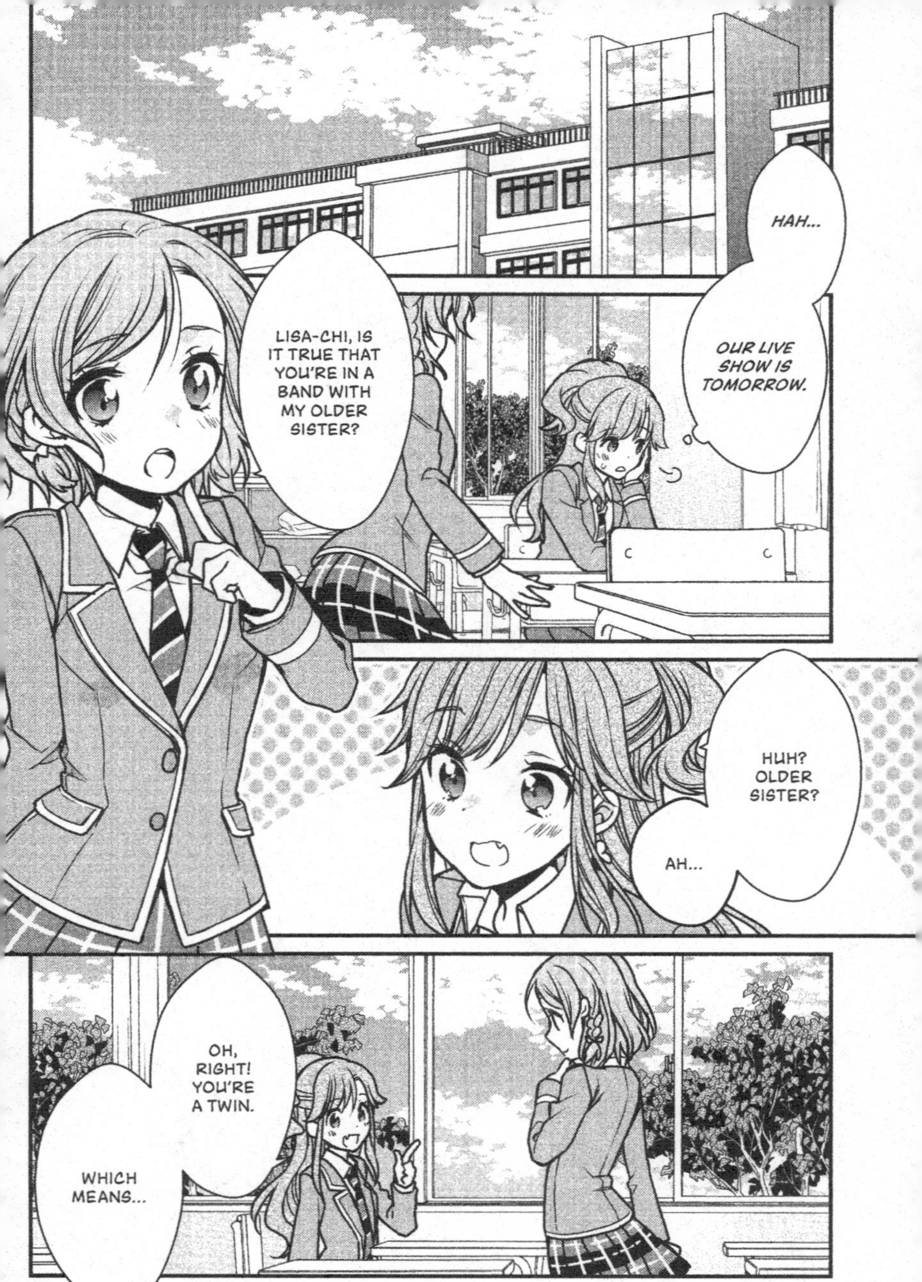
HAH...
OUR LIVE SHOW IS TOMORROW.
LISA-CHI, IS IT TRUE THAT YOU'RE IN A BAND WITH MY OLDER SISTER?
HUH? OLDER SISTER?
AH...
OH, RIGHT! YOU'RE A TWIN.
WHICH MEANS...

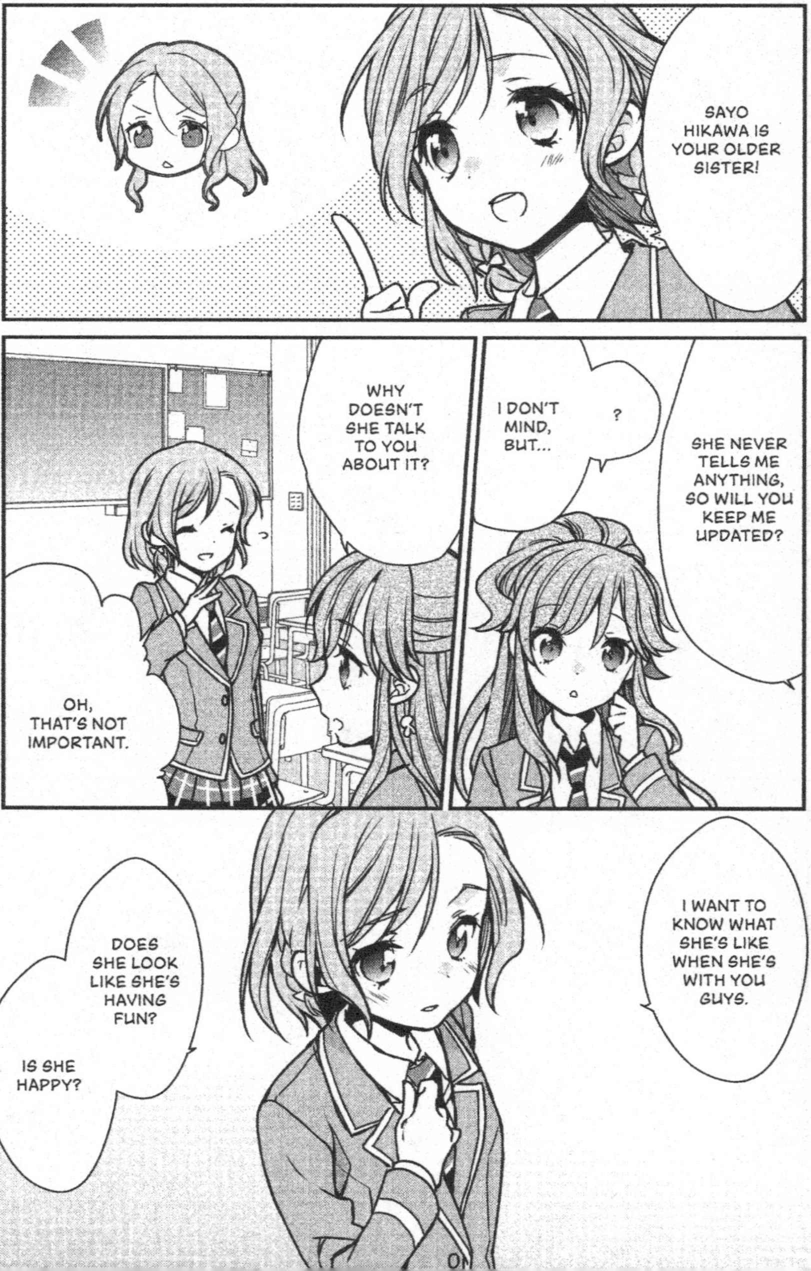
SAYO HIKAWA IS YOUR OLDER SISTER!
SHE NEVER TELLS ME ANYTHING, SO WILL YOU KEEP ME UPDATED?
?
I DON'T MIND, BUT...
WHY DOESN'T SHE TALK TO YOU ABOUT IT?
OH, THAT'S NOT IMPORTANT.
I WANT TO KNOW WHAT SHE'S LIKE WHEN SHE'S WITH YOU GUYS.
DOES SHE LOOK LIKE SHE'S HAVING FUN?
IS SHE HAPPY?

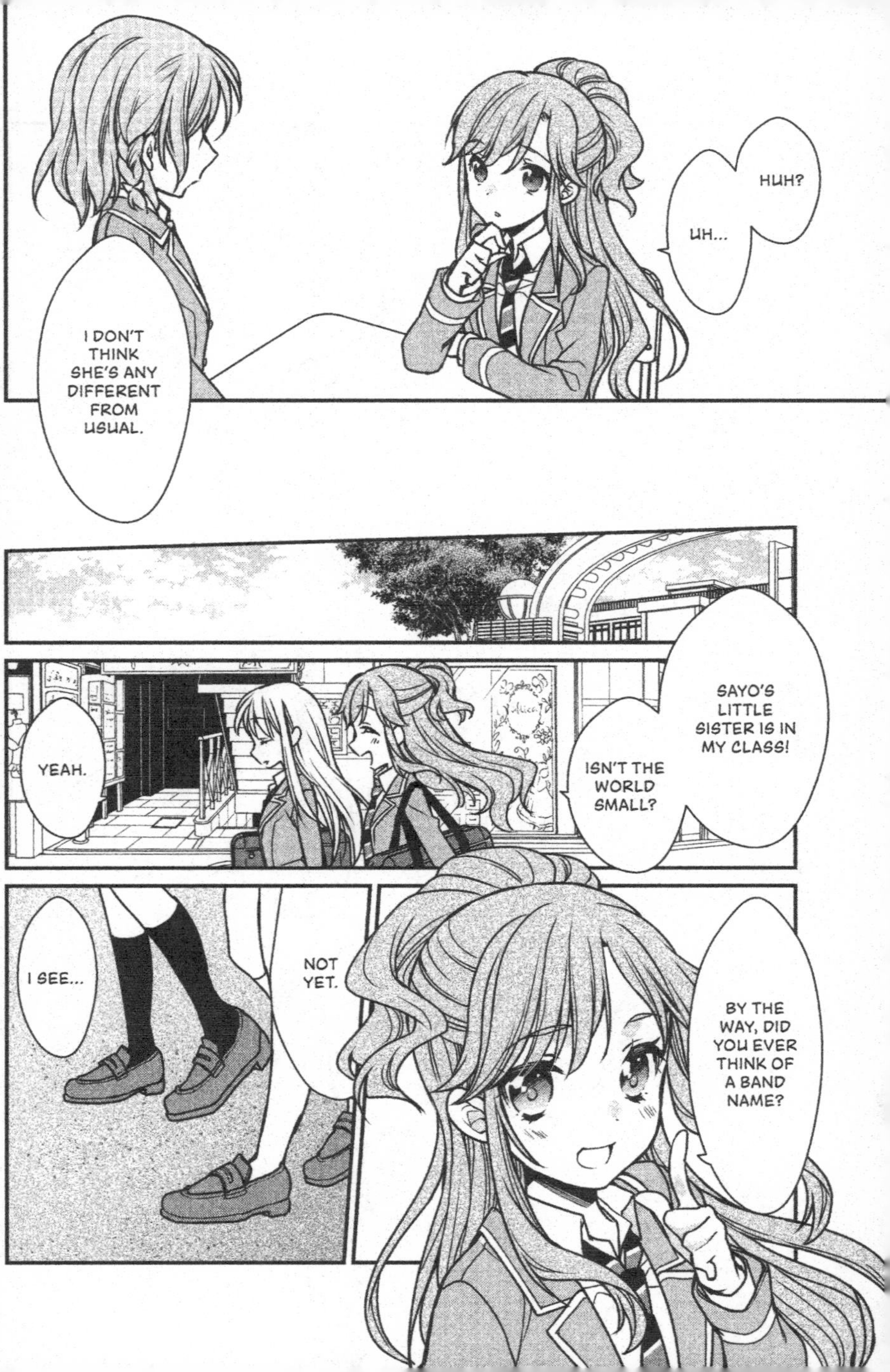
HUH?
UH...
I DON'T THINK SHE'S ANY DIFFERENT FROM USUAL.
SAYO'S LITTLE SISTER IS IN MY CLASS!
ISN'T THE WORLD SMALL?
YEAH.
BY THE WAY, DID YOU EVER THINK OF A BAND NAME?
NOT YET.
I SEE...

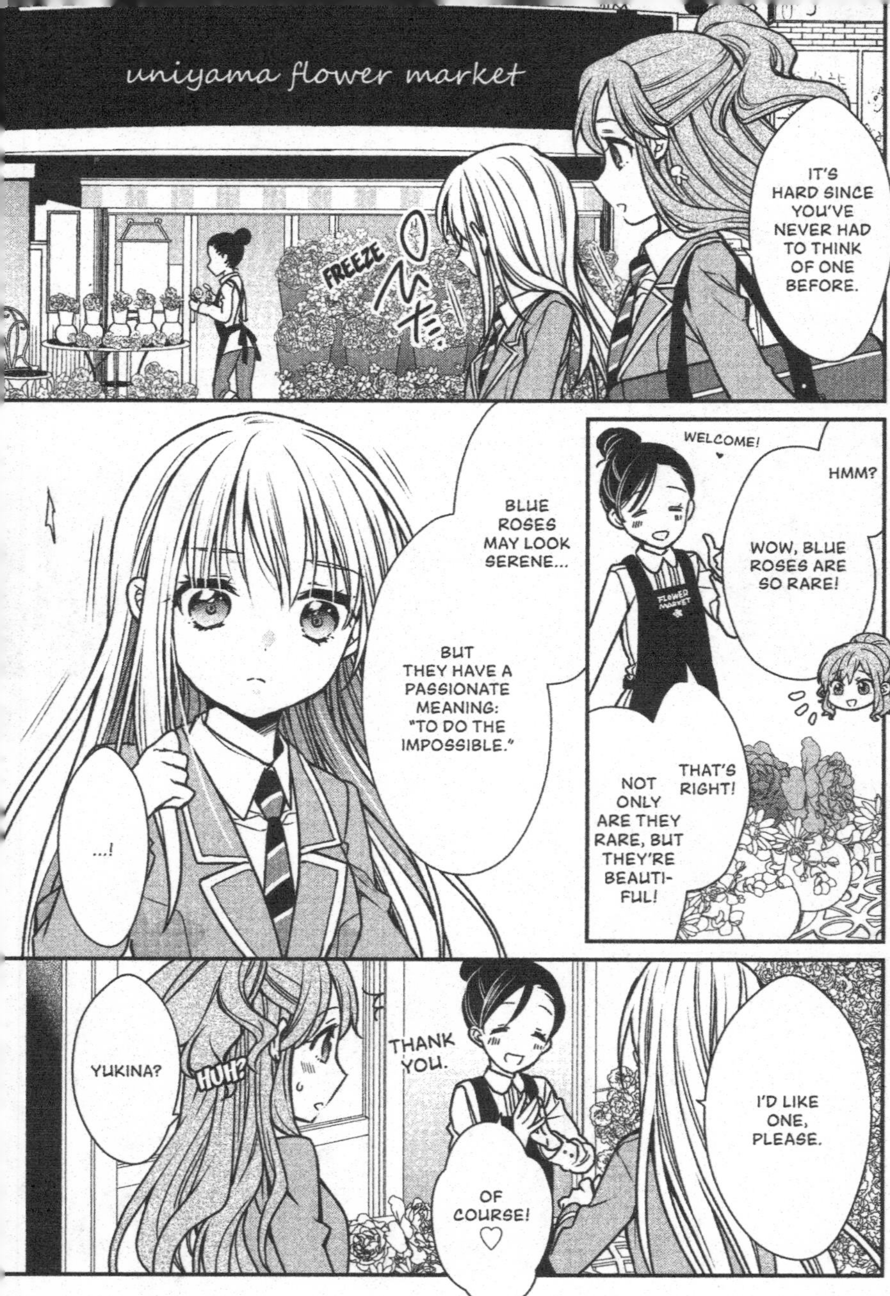
IT'S HARD SINCE YOU'VE NEVER HAD TO THINK OF ONE BEFORE.
uniyama flower market
FREEZE
HMM?
WELCOME! ♥
WOW, BLUE ROSES ARE SO RARE!
THAT'S RIGHT!
NOT ONLY ARE THEY RARE, BUT THEY'RE BEAUTIFUL!
FLOWER MARKET
BLUE ROSES MAY LOOK SERENE...
BUT THEY HAVE A PASSIONATE MEANING: "TO DO THE IMPOSSIBLE."
...!
I'D LIKE ONE, PLEASE.
THANK YOU.
OF COURSE! ♡
HUH?
YUKINA?

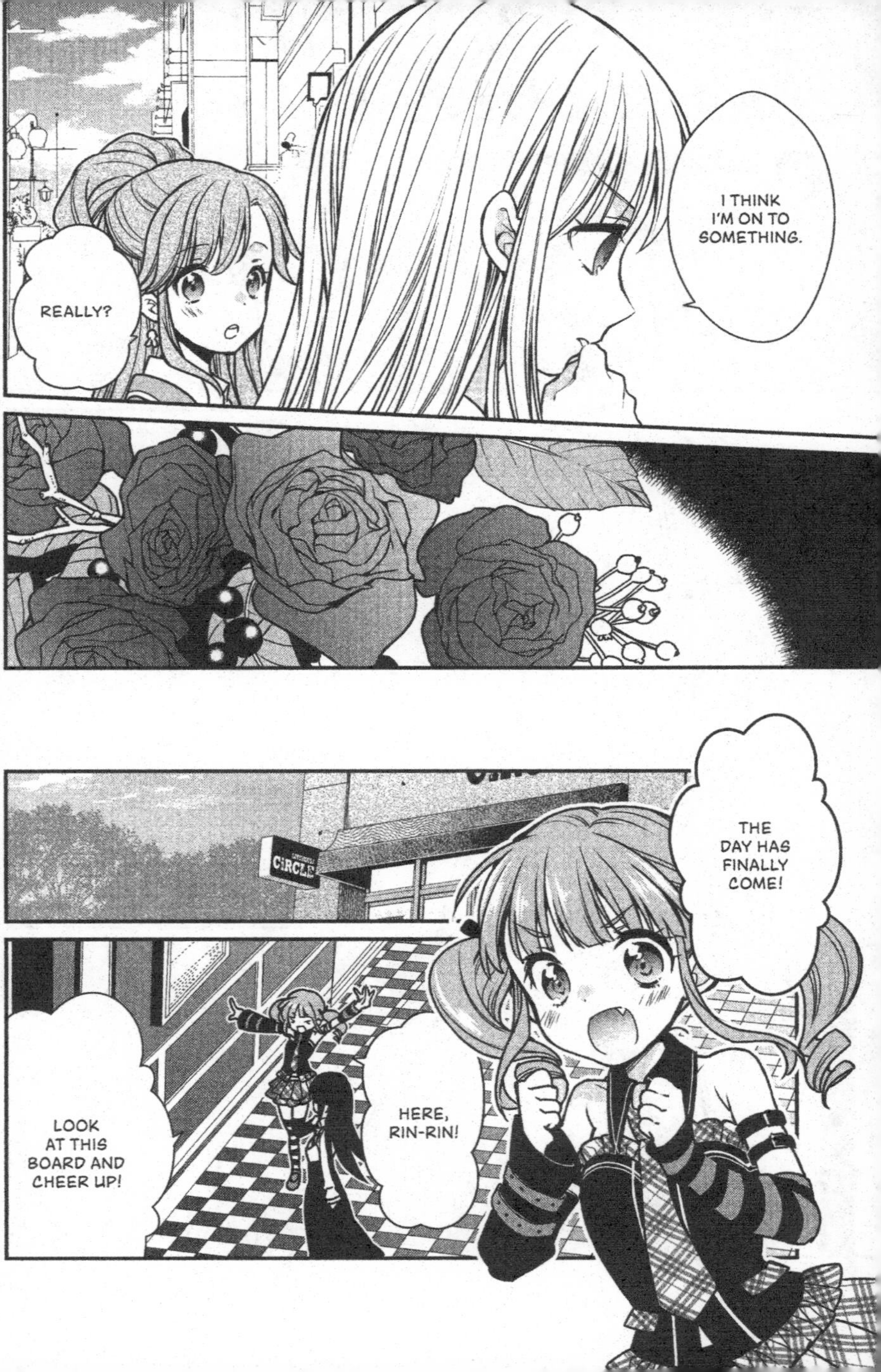
I THINK I'M ON TO SOMETHING.
REALLY?
THE DAY HAS FINALLY COME!
CiRCLE
HERE, RIN-RIN!
LOOK AT THIS BOARD AND CHEER UP!

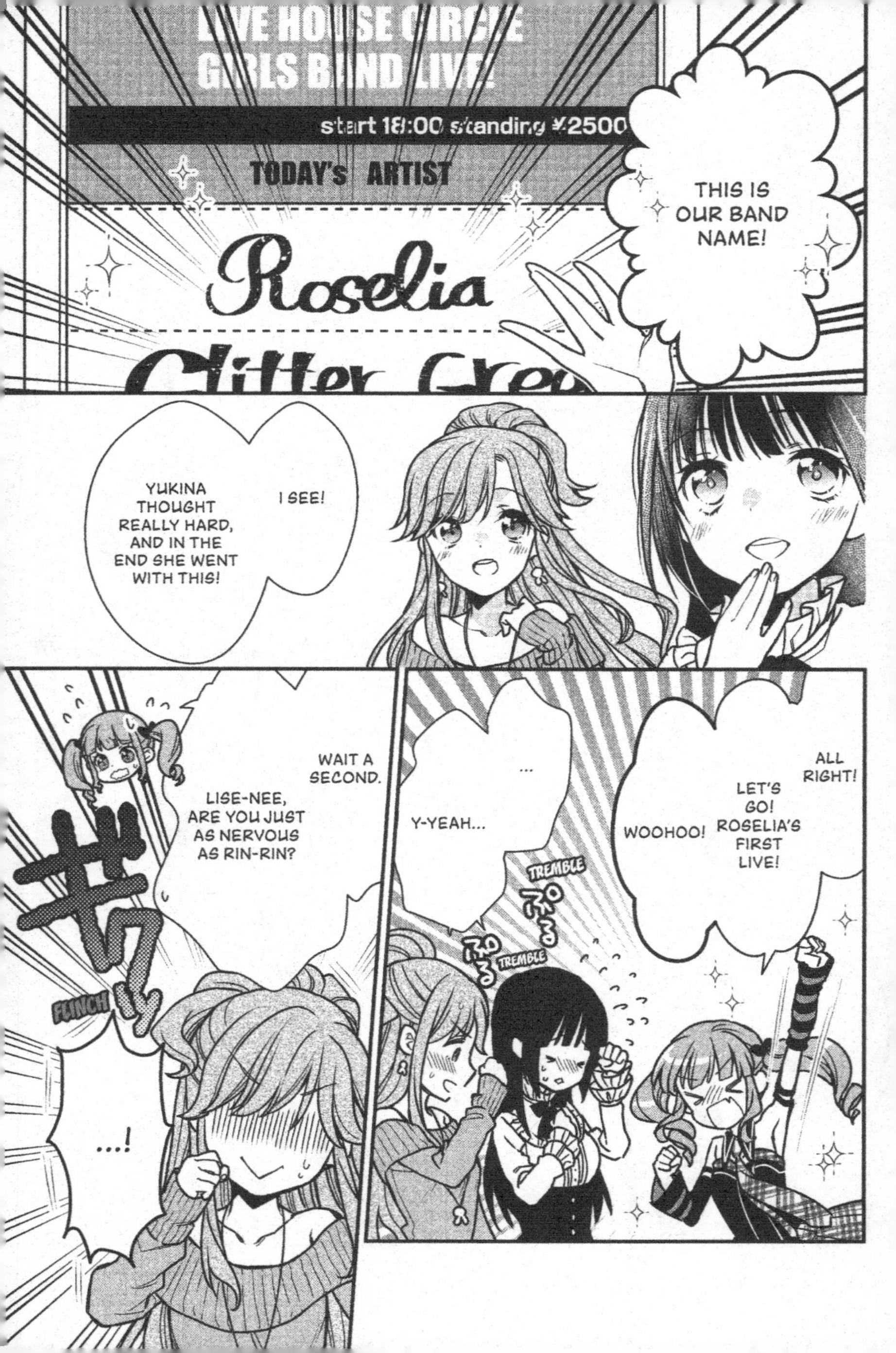
LIVE HOUSE CIRCLE
GIRLS BAND LIVE!
start 18:00 standing ¥2500
TODAY's ARTIST
Roselia
THIS IS OUR BAND NAME!
I SEE!
YUKINA THOUGHT REALLY HARD, AND IN THE END SHE WENT WITH THIS!
ALL RIGHT!
LET'S GO! ROSELIA'S FIRST LIVE!
WOOHOO!
...
Y-YEAH...
TREMBLE
TREMBLE
WAIT A SECOND.
LISE-NEE, ARE YOU JUST AS NERVOUS AS RIN-RIN?
FLINCH
...!

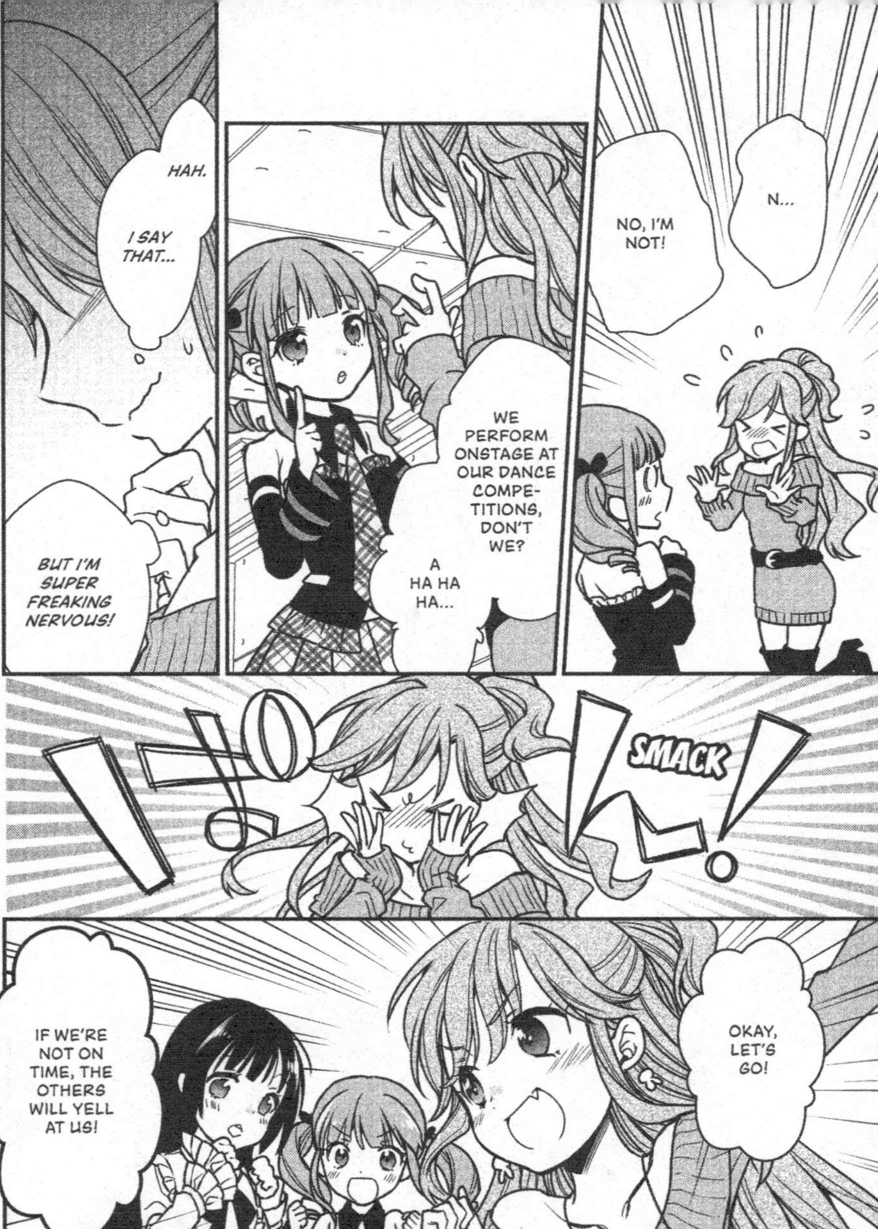
N...
NO, I'M NOT!
WE PERFORM ONSTAGE AT OUR DANCE COMPE-TITIONS, DON'T WE?
A HA HA HA...
HAH.
I SAY THAT...
BUT I'M SUPER FREAKING NERVOUS!
SMACK
OKAY, LET'S GO!
IF WE'RE NOT ON TIME, THE OTHERS WILL YELL AT US!

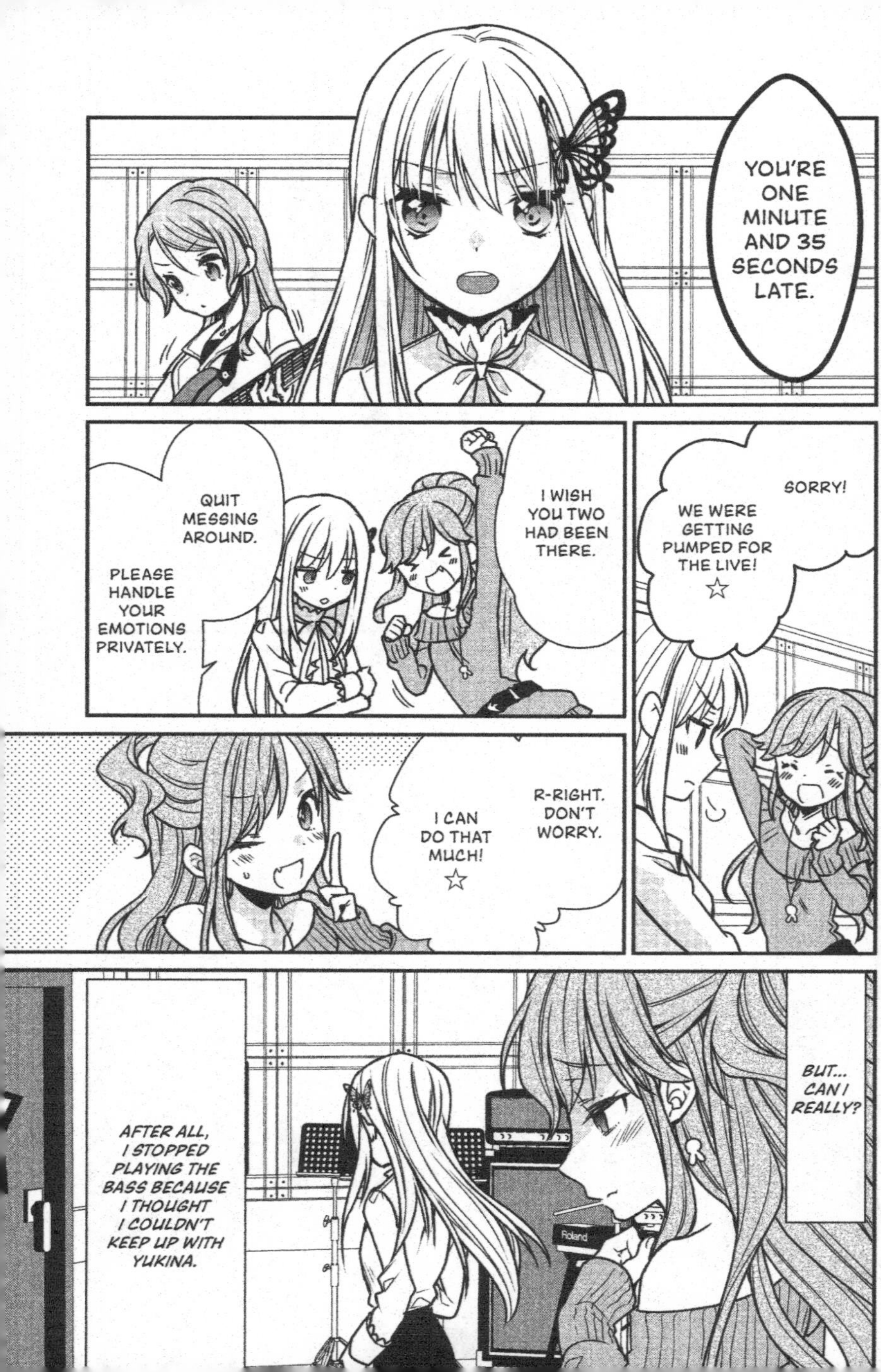
YOU'RE ONE MINUTE AND 35 SECONDS LATE.
SORRY!
WE WERE GETTING PUMPED FOR THE LIVE! ☆
I WISH YOU TWO HAD BEEN THERE.
QUIT MESSING AROUND.
PLEASE HANDLE YOUR EMOTIONS PRIVATELY.
R-RIGHT. DON'T WORRY.
I CAN DO THAT MUCH! ☆
BUT... CAN I REALLY?
Roland
AFTER ALL, I STOPPED PLAYING THE BASS BECAUSE I THOUGHT I COULDN'T KEEP UP WITH YUKINA.

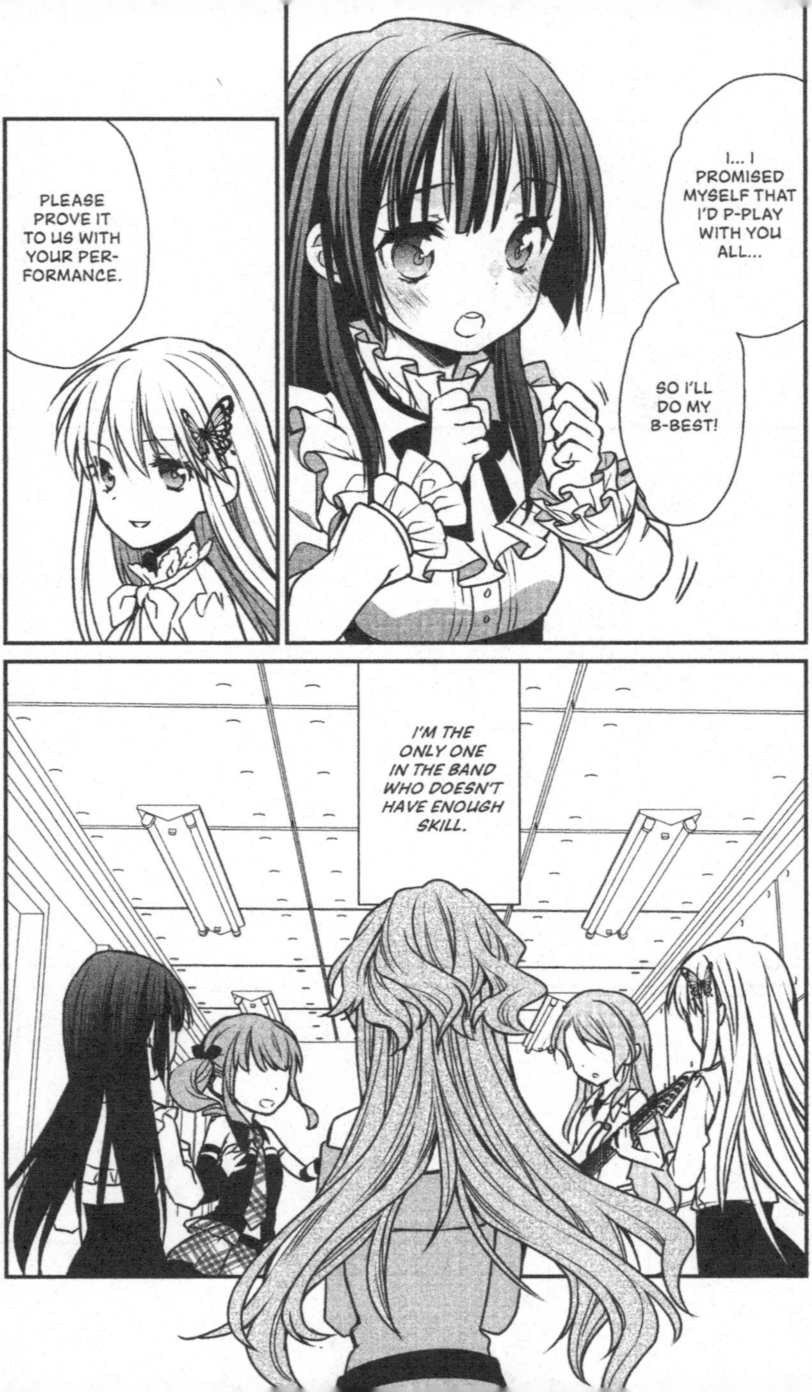
I... I PROMISED MYSELF THAT I'D P-PLAY WITH YOU ALL...
SO I'LL DO MY B-BEST!
PLEASE PROVE IT TO US WITH YOUR PER-FORMANCE.
I'M THE ONLY ONE IN THE BAND WHO DOESN'T HAVE ENOUGH SKILL.

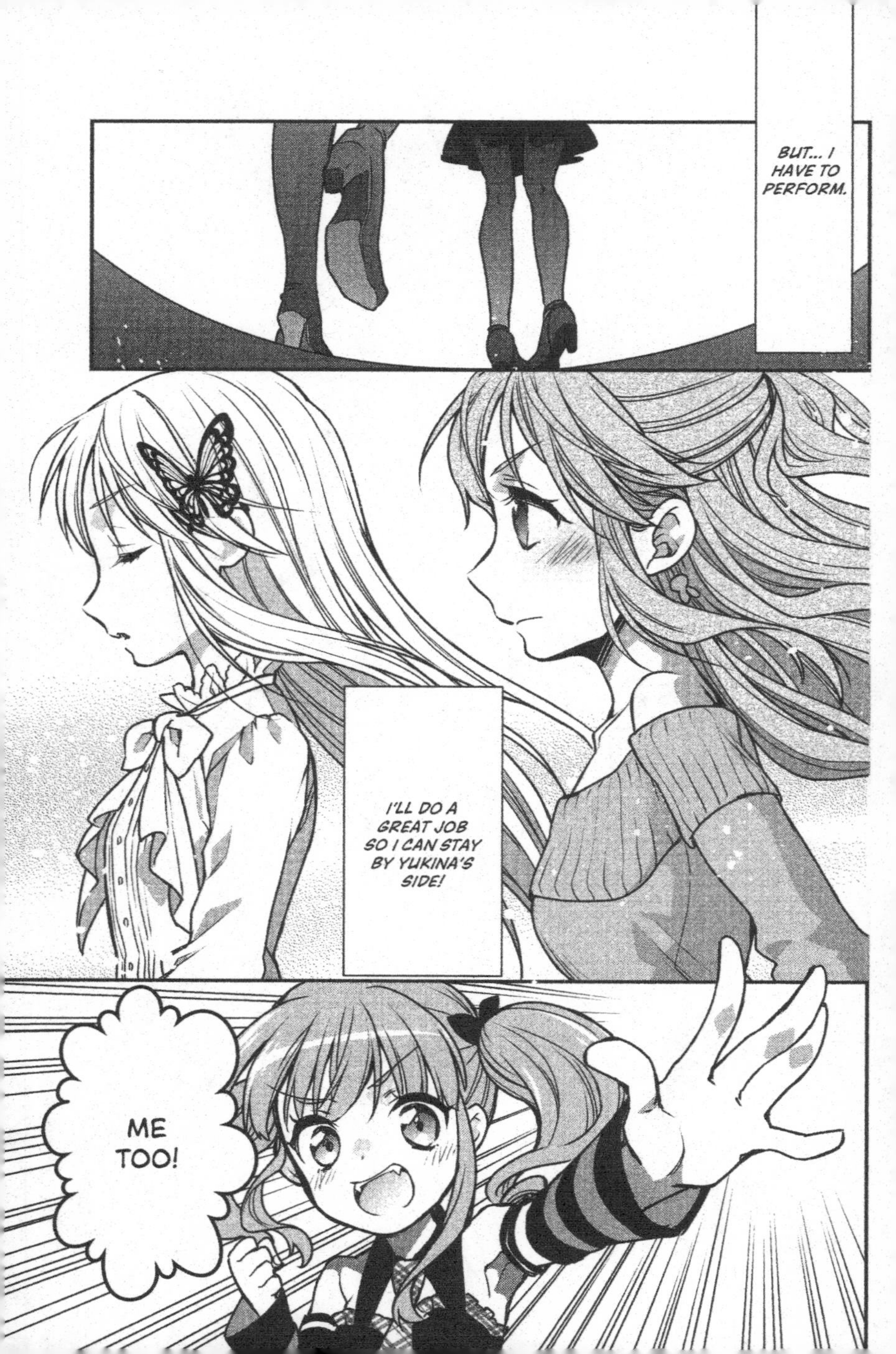
BUT... I HAVE TO PERFORM.
I'LL DO A GREAT JOB SO I CAN STAY BY YUKINA'S SIDE!
ME TOO!

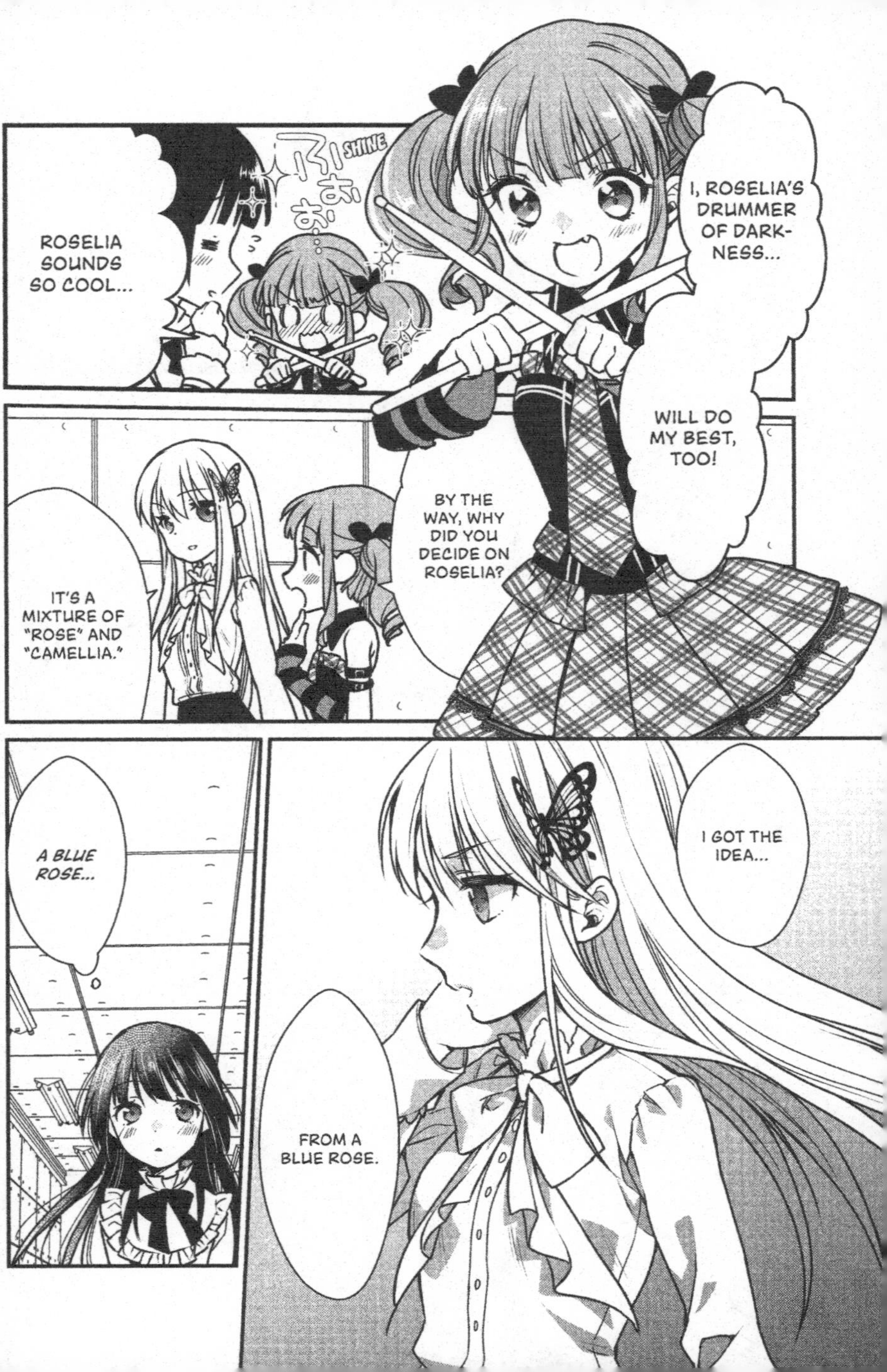
ROSELIA SOUNDS SO COOL...
SHINE
I, ROSELIA'S DRUMMER OF DARK-NESS...
WILL DO MY BEST, TOO!
BY THE WAY, WHY DID YOU DECIDE ON ROSELIA?
IT'S A MIXTURE OF "ROSE" AND "CAMELLIA."
I GOT THE IDEA...
FROM A BLUE ROSE.
A BLUE ROSE...

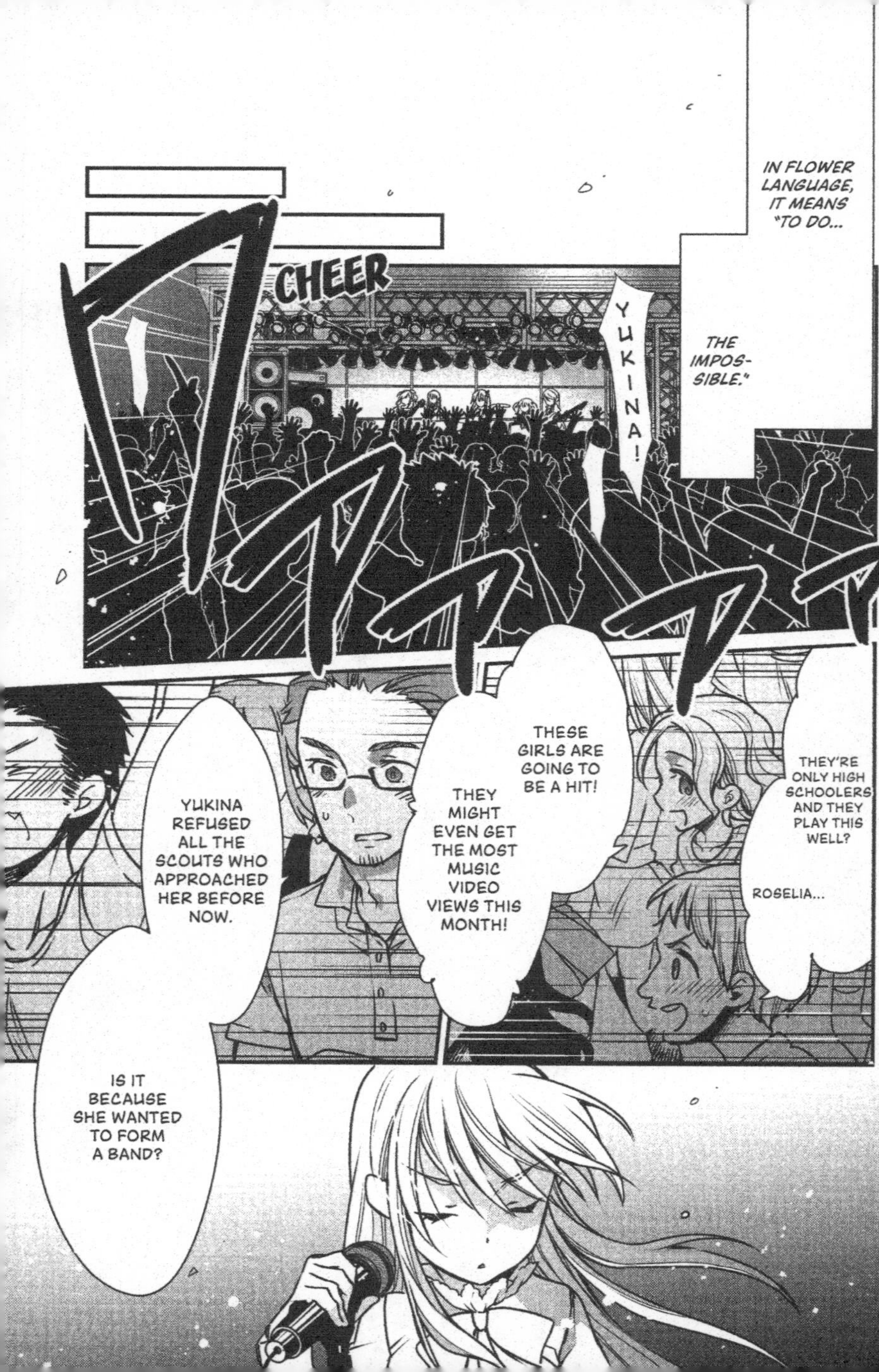
IN FLOWER LANGUAGE, IT MEANS "TO DO...
THE IMPOS-SIBLE."
YUKINA!
CHEER
THEY'RE ONLY HIGH SCHOOLERS AND THEY PLAY THIS WELL?
ROSELIA...
THESE GIRLS ARE GOING TO BE A HIT!
THEY MIGHT EVEN GET THE MOST MUSIC VIDEO VIEWS THIS MONTH!
YUKINA REFUSED ALL THE SCOUTS WHO APPROACHED HER BEFORE NOW.
IS IT BECAUSE SHE WANTED TO FORM A BAND?

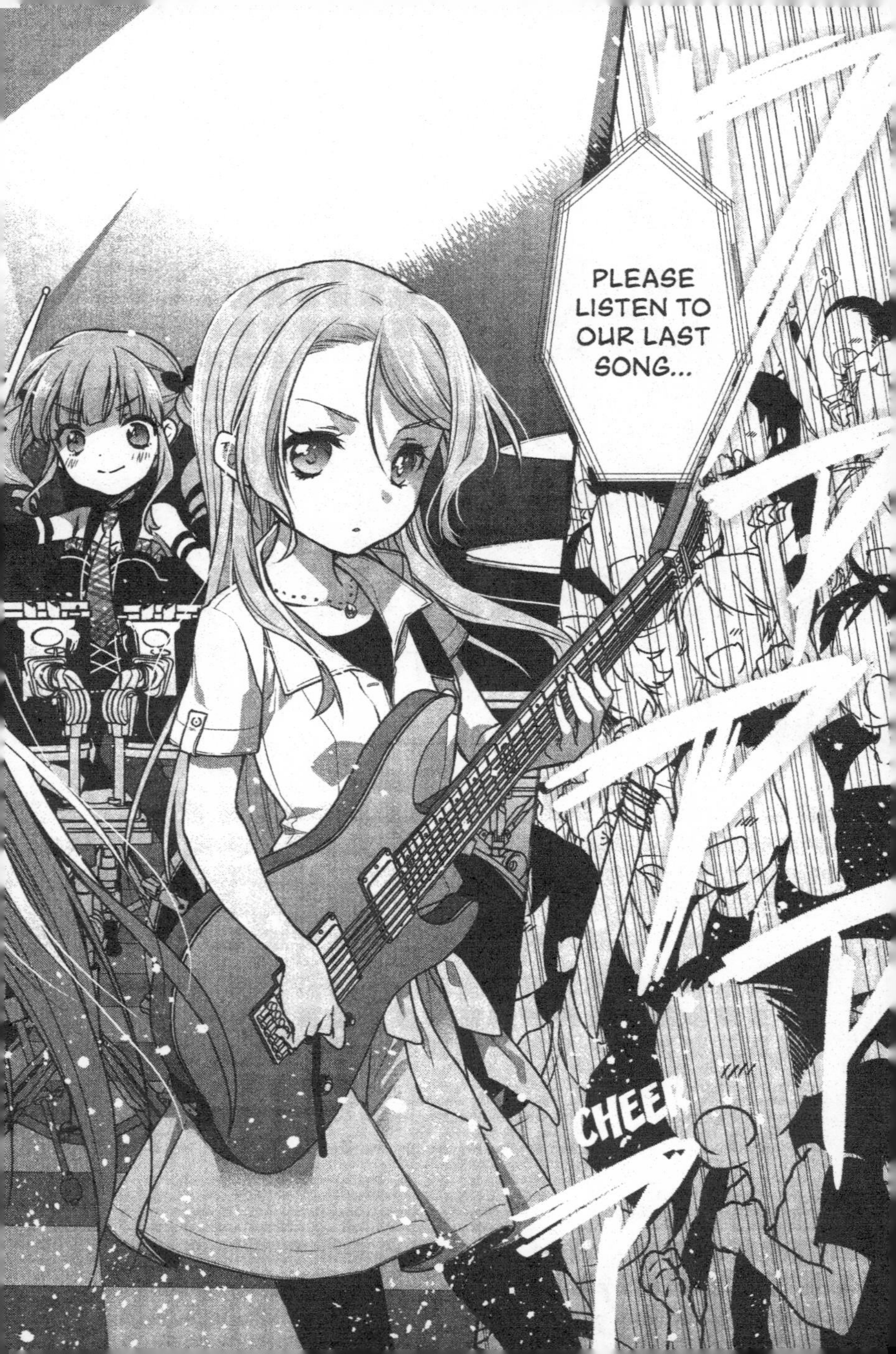
PLEASE LISTEN TO OUR LAST SONG...
CHEER

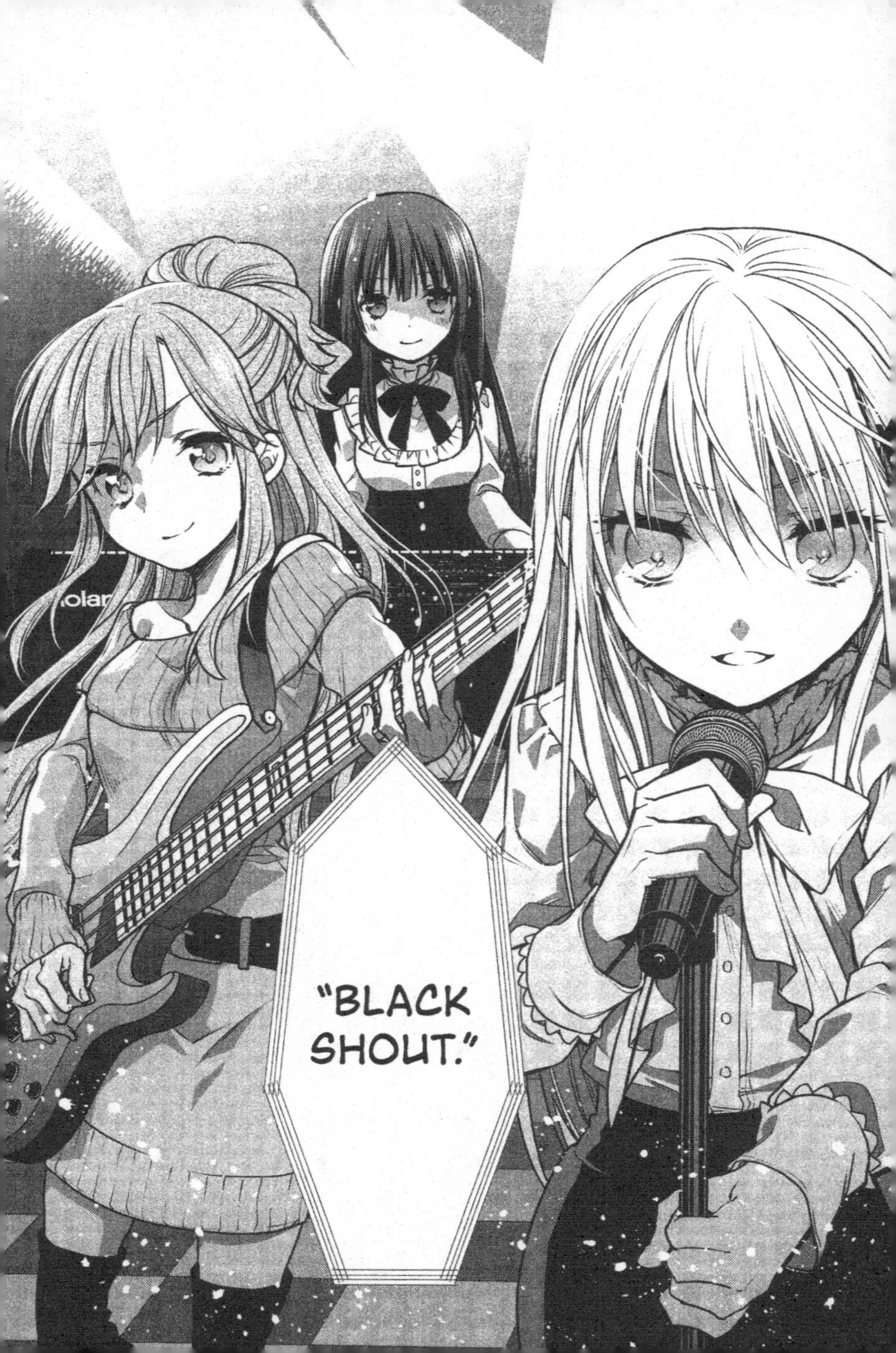
"BLACK SHOUT."

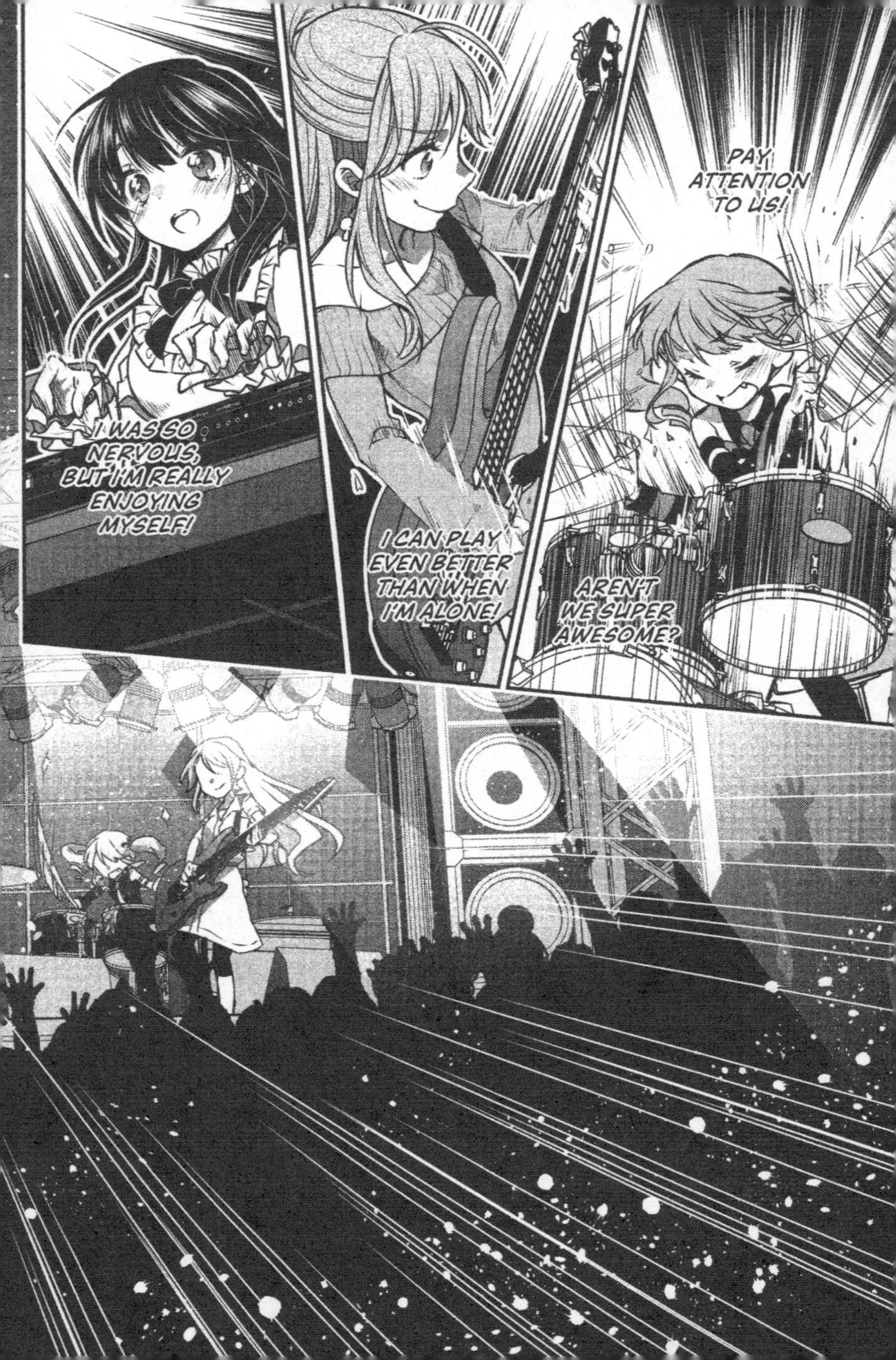
PAY ATTENTION TO US!
AREN'T WE SUPER AWESOME?
I CAN PLAY EVEN BETTER THAN WHEN I'M ALONE!
I WAS SO NERVOUS, BUT I'M REALLY ENJOYING MYSELF!

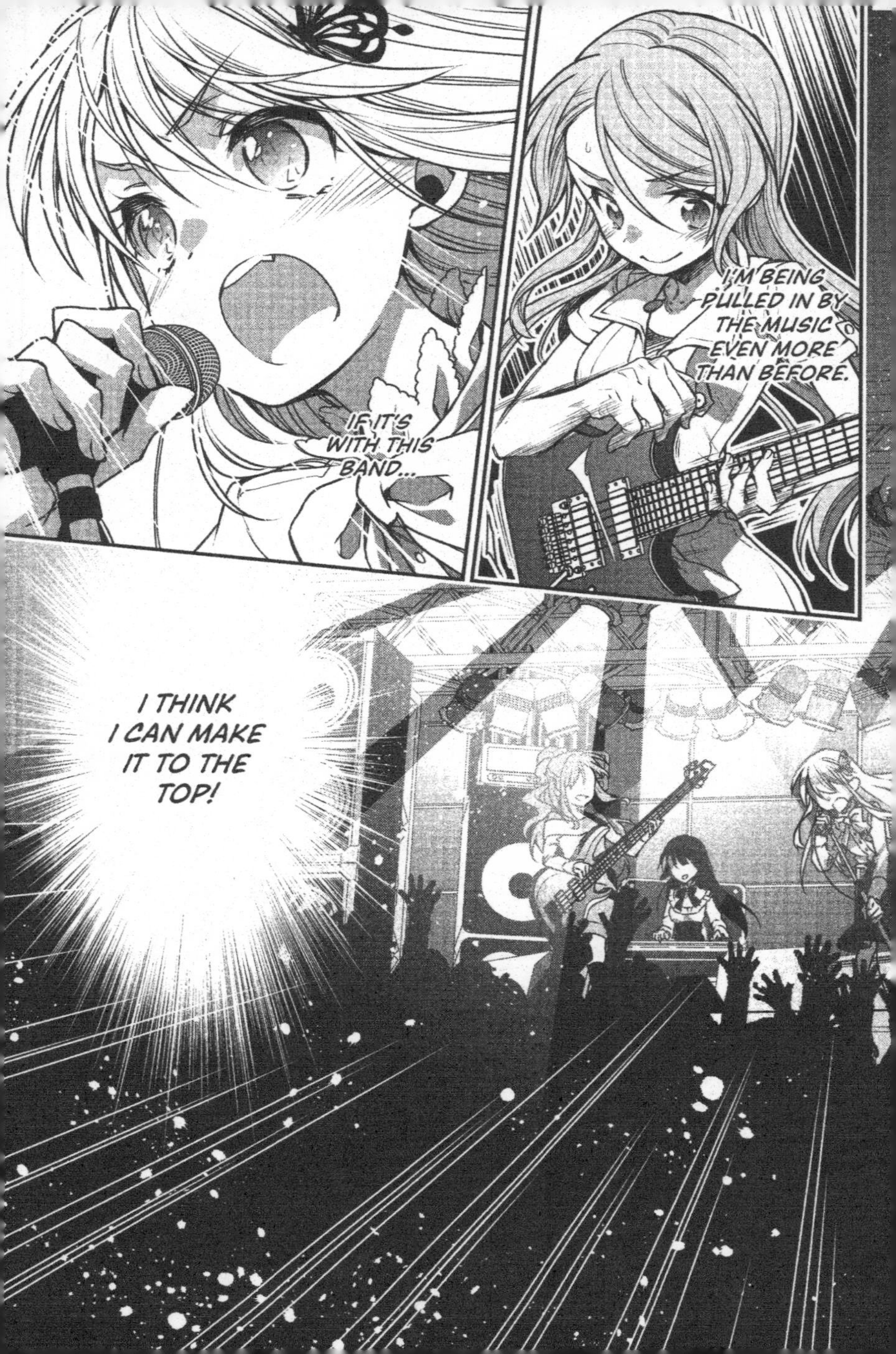
I'M BEING PULLED IN BY THE MUSIC EVEN MORE THAN BEFORE.
IF IT'S WITH THIS BAND...
I THINK I CAN MAKE IT TO THE TOP!

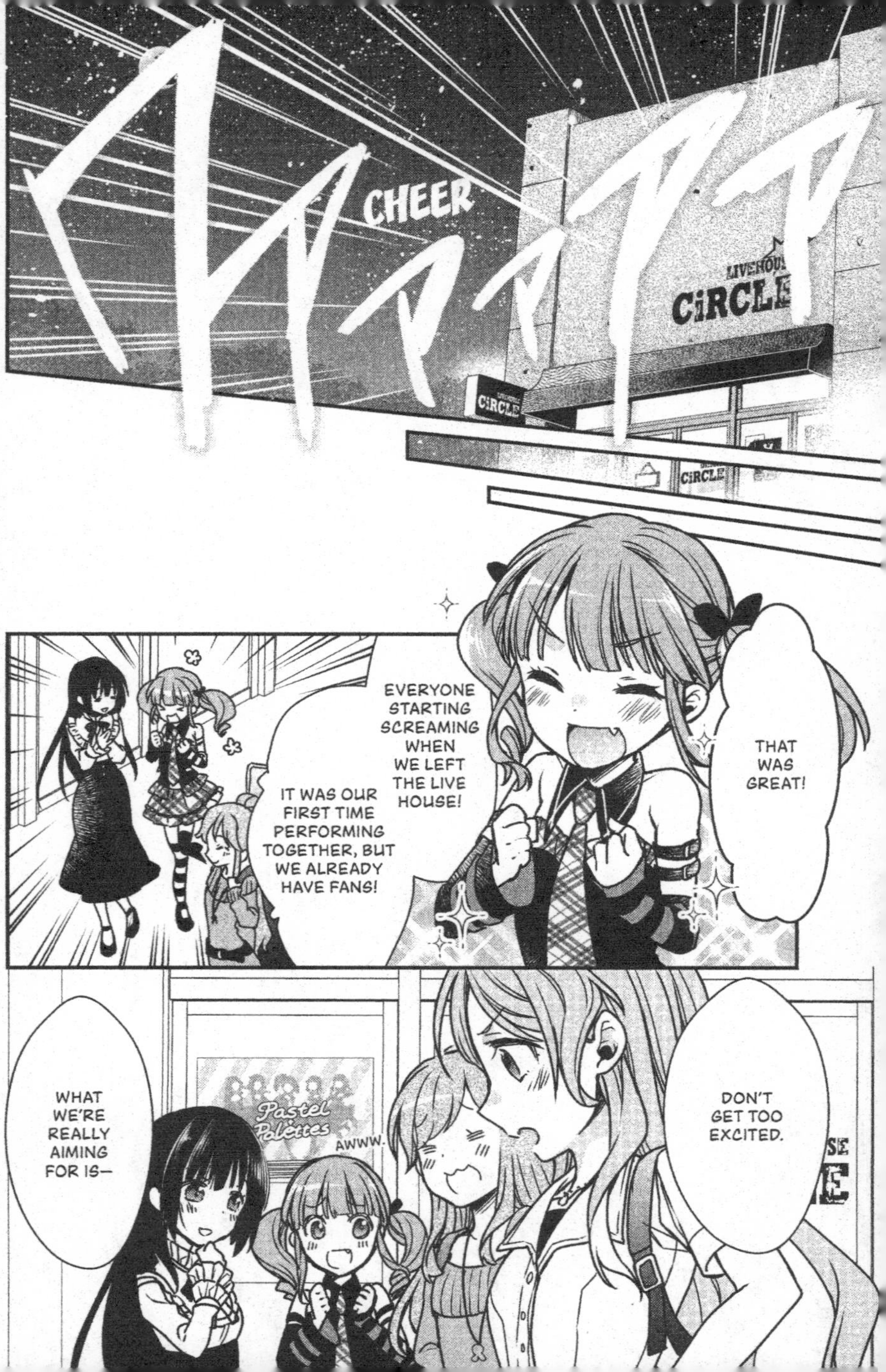
CHEER
CiRCLE
THAT WAS GREAT!
EVERYONE STARTING SCREAMING WHEN WE LEFT THE LIVE HOUSE!
IT WAS OUR FIRST TIME PERFORMING TOGETHER, BUT WE ALREADY HAVE FANS!
DON'T GET TOO EXCITED.
AWWW.
Pastel Palettes
WHAT WE'RE REALLY AIMING FOR IS—

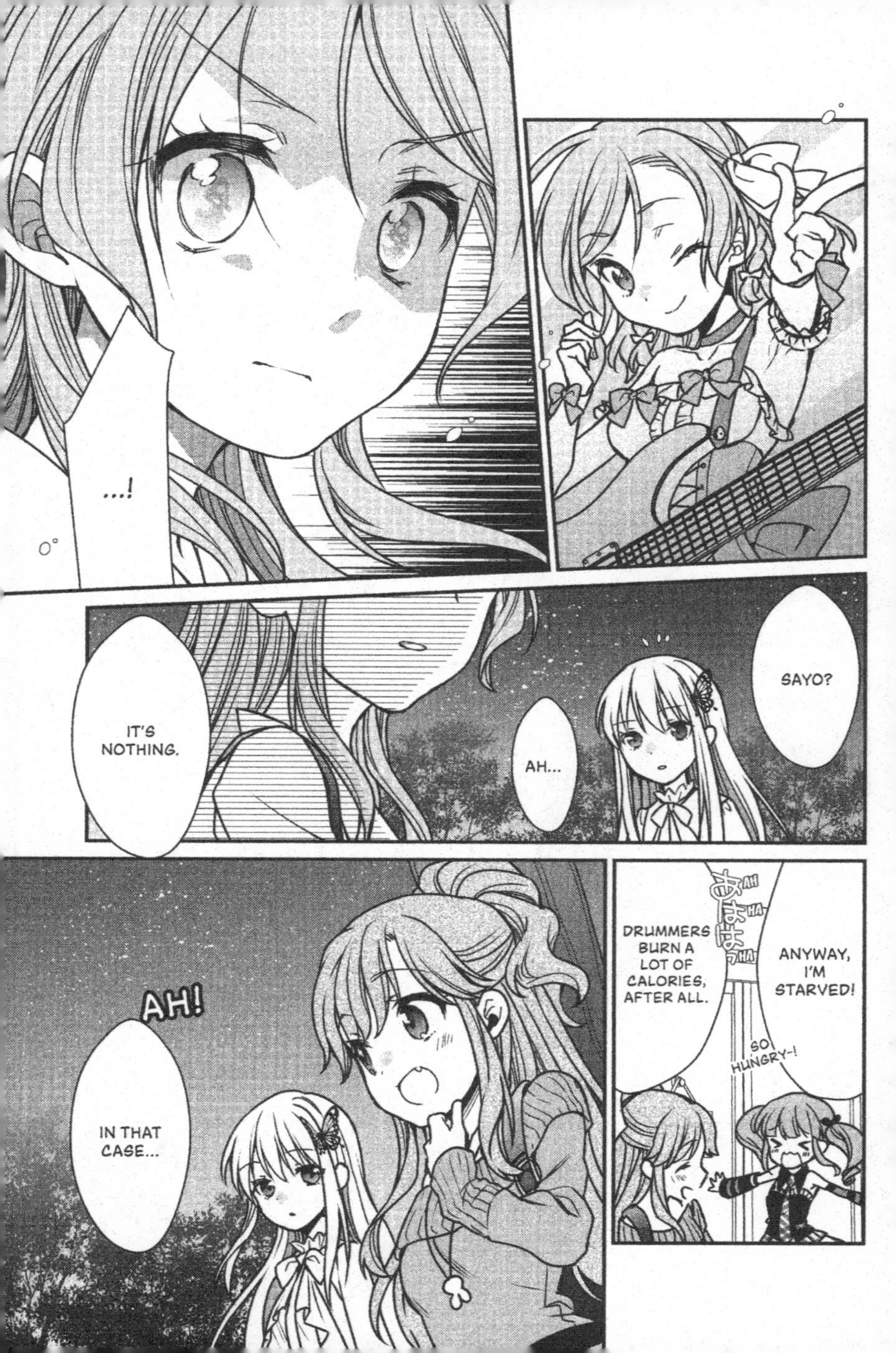

...!
SAYO?
AH...
IT'S NOTHING.
ANYWAY, I'M STARVED!
AH HA HA
DRUMMERS BURN A LOT OF CALORIES, AFTER ALL.
SO HUNGRY-!
AH!
IN THAT CASE...

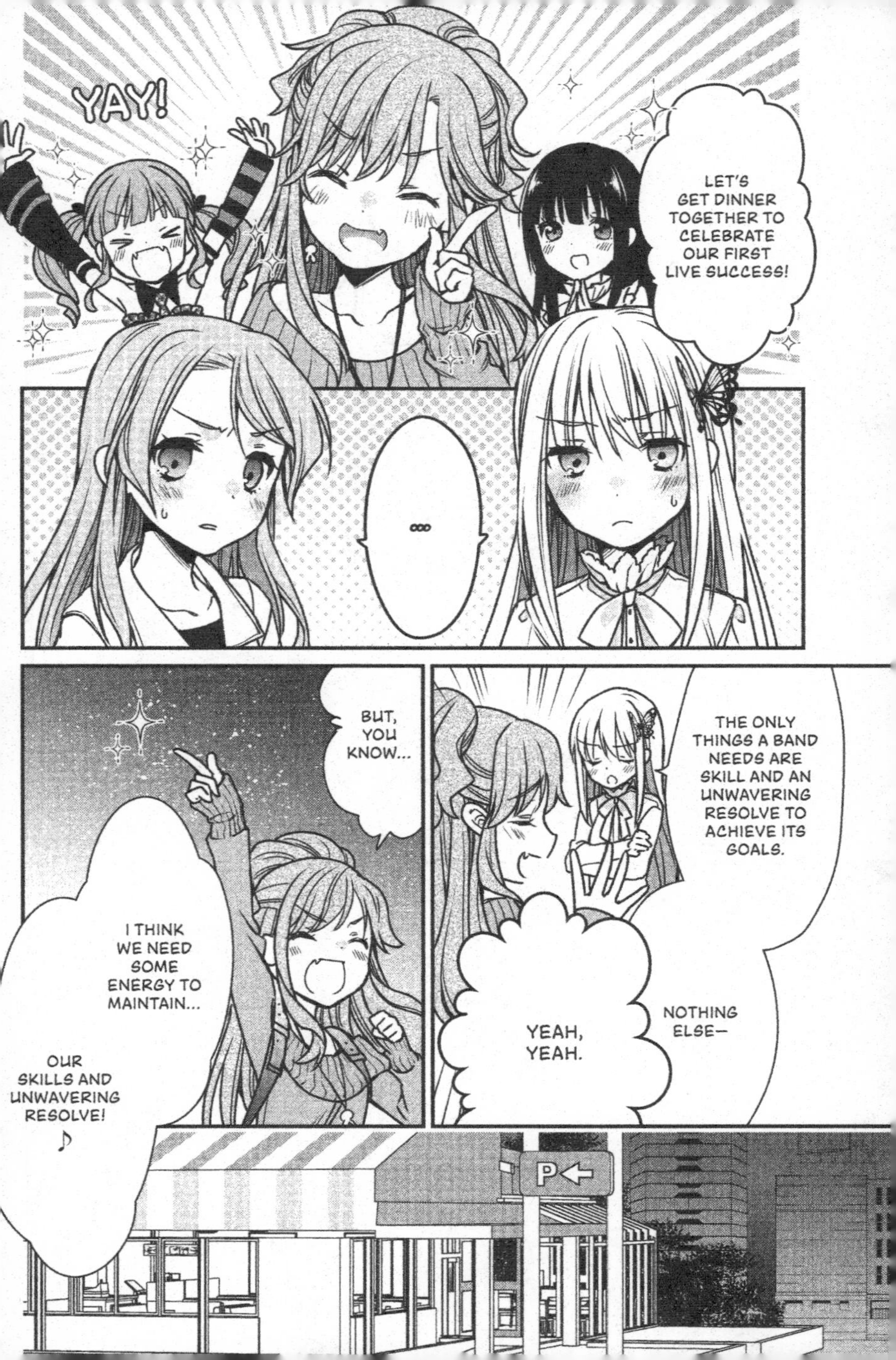
LET'S GET DINNER TOGETHER TO CELEBRATE OUR FIRST LIVE SUCCESS!
YAY!
...
THE ONLY THINGS A BAND NEEDS ARE SKILL AND AN UNWAVERING RESOLVE TO ACHIEVE ITS GOALS.
NOTHING ELSE—
YEAH, YEAH.
BUT, YOU KNOW...
I THINK WE NEED SOME ENERGY TO MAINTAIN...
OUR SKILLS AND UNWAVERING RESOLVE! ♪

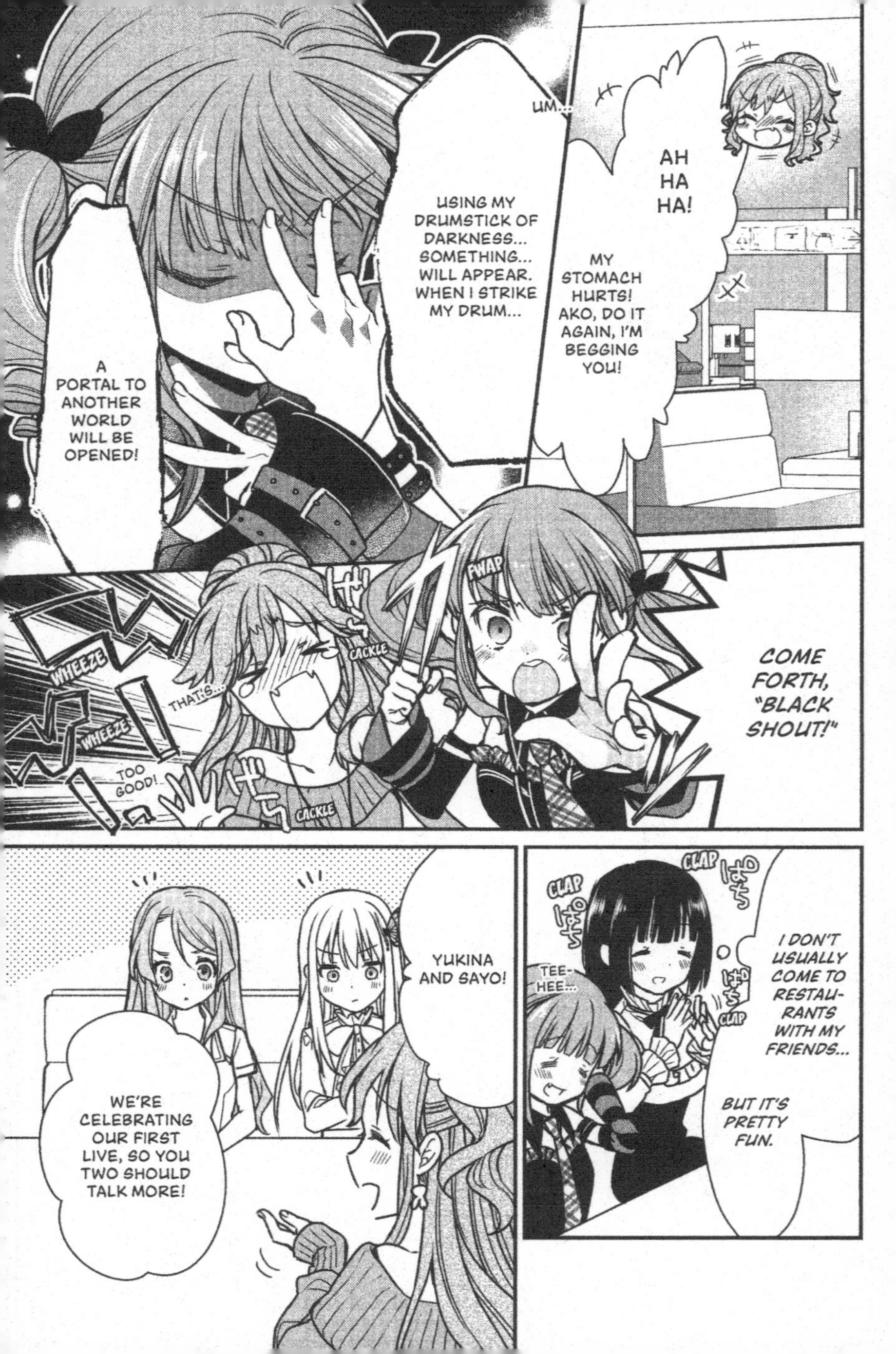
AH HA HA!
MY STOMACH HURTS! AKO, DO IT AGAIN, I'M BEGGING YOU!
UM...
USING MY DRUMSTICK OF DARKNESS... SOMETHING... WILL APPEAR. WHEN I STRIKE MY DRUM...
A PORTAL TO ANOTHER WORLD WILL BE OPENED!
COME FORTH, "BLACK SHOUT!"
FWAP
CACKLE
THAT'S...
WHEEZE
WHEEZE
TOO GOOD!
CACKLE
CLAP
CLAP
I DON'T USUALLY COME TO RESTAURANTS WITH MY FRIENDS...
BUT IT'S PRETTY FUN.
CLAP
TEE-HEE...
YUKINA AND SAYO!
WE'RE CELEBRATING OUR FIRST LIVE, SO YOU TWO SHOULD TALK MORE!

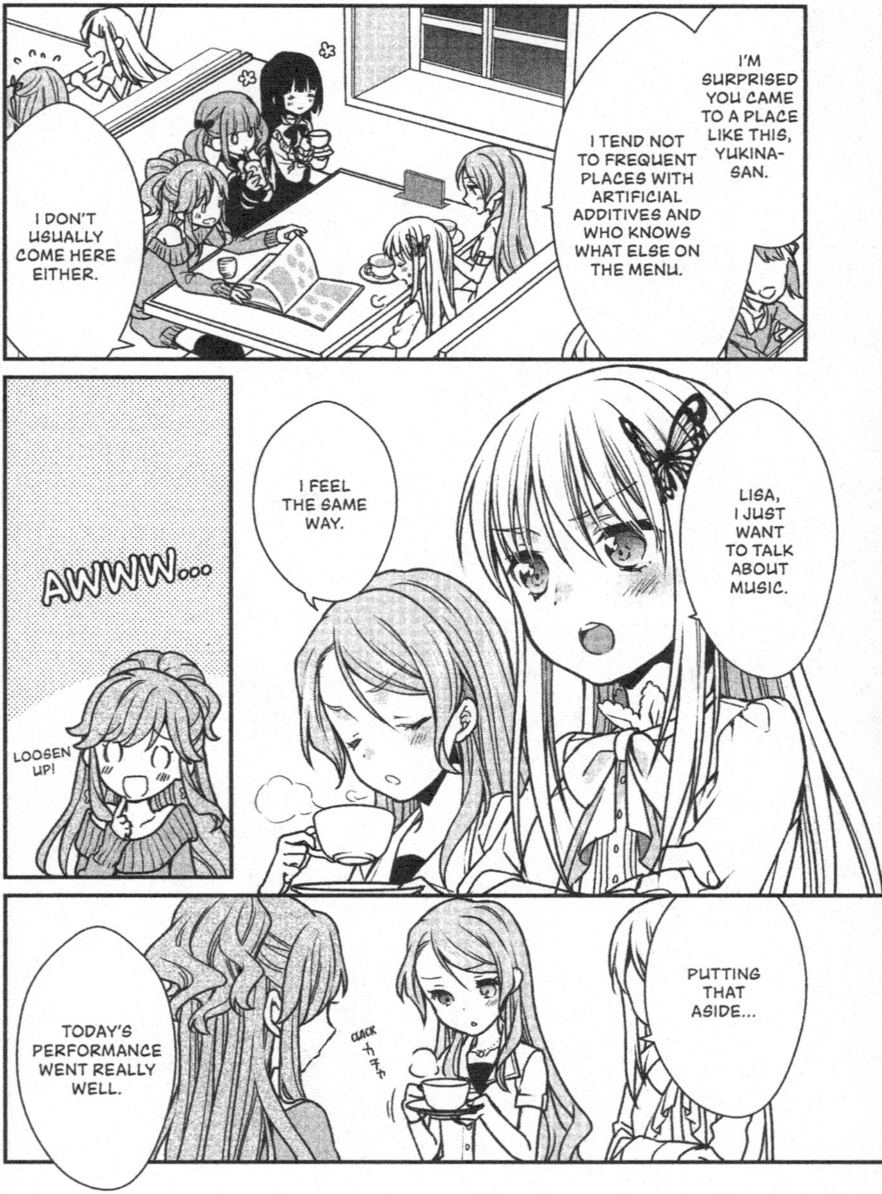
I'M SURPRISED YOU CAME TO A PLACE LIKE THIS, YUKINA-SAN.
I TEND NOT TO FREQUENT PLACES WITH ARTIFICIAL ADDITIVES AND WHO KNOWS WHAT ELSE ON THE MENU.
I DON'T USUALLY COME HERE EITHER.
LISA, I JUST WANT TO TALK ABOUT MUSIC.
I FEEL THE SAME WAY.
AWWW...
LOOSEN UP!
PUTTING THAT ASIDE...
CLACK
TODAY'S PERFORMANCE WENT REALLY WELL.

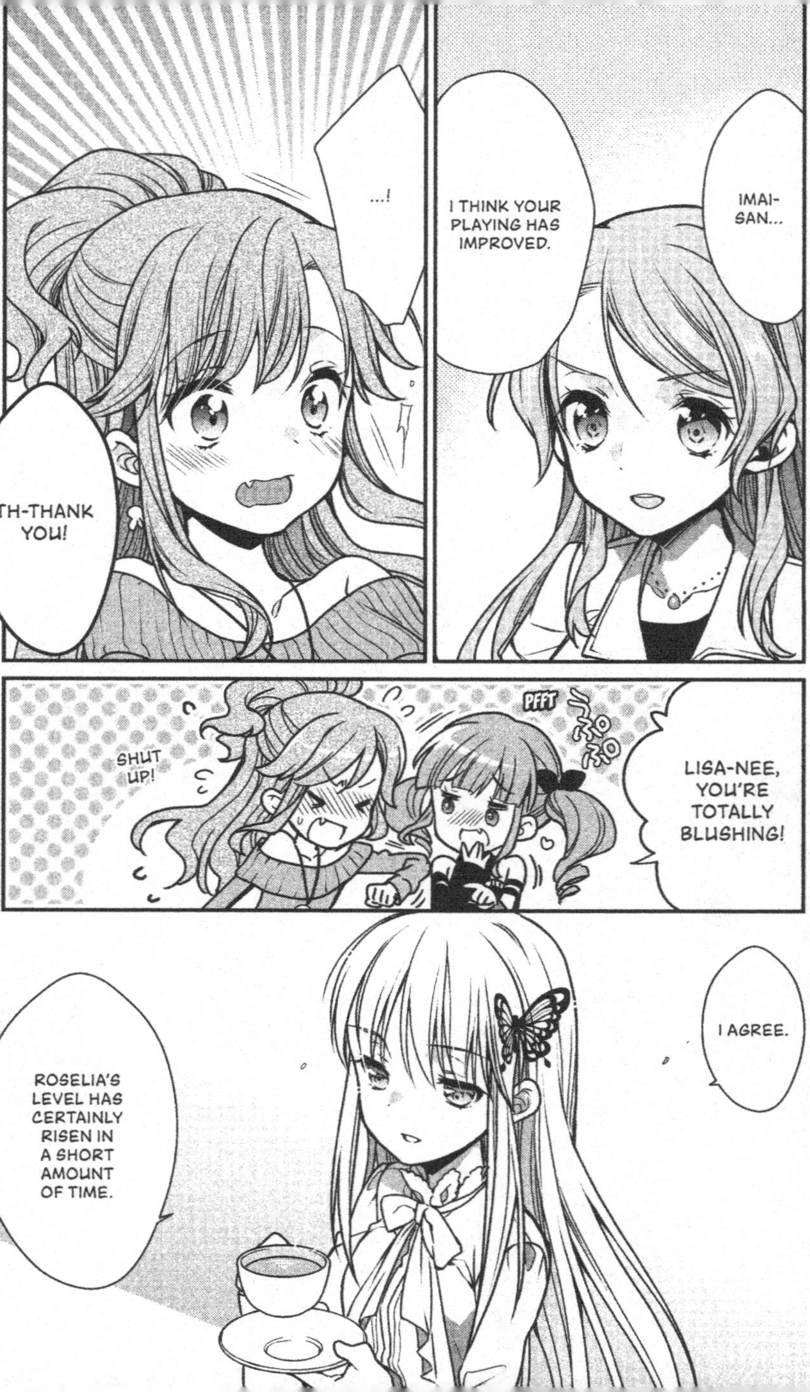
IMAI-SAN...
I THINK YOUR PLAYING HAS IMPROVED.
...!
TH-THANK YOU!
LISA-NEE, YOU'RE TOTALLY BLUSHING!
PFFT
SHUT UP!
I AGREE.
ROSELIA'S LEVEL HAS CERTAINLY RISEN IN A SHORT AMOUNT OF TIME.

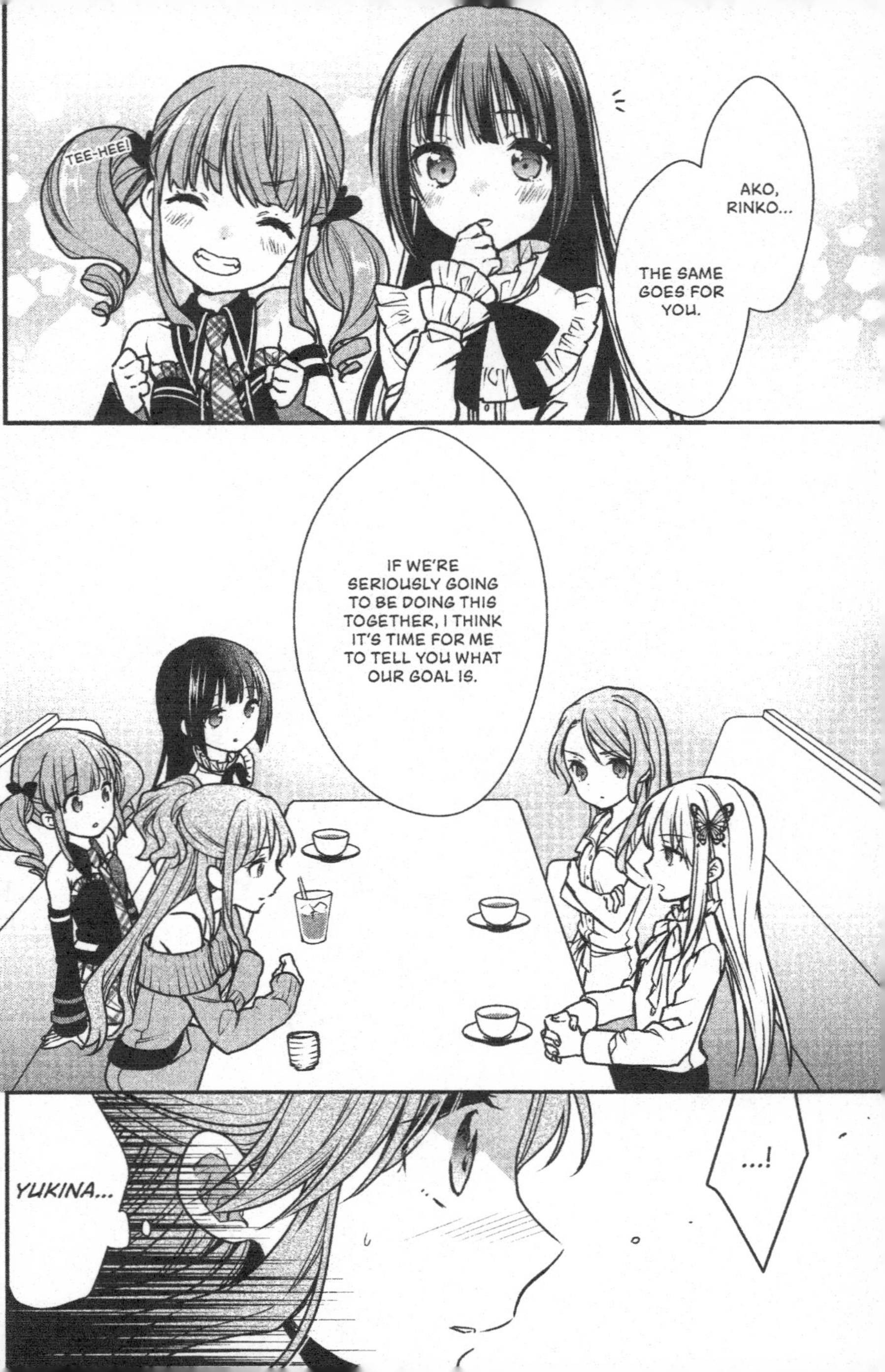
AKO, RINKO... THE SAME GOES FOR YOU.
TEE-HEE!
IF WE'RE SERIOUSLY GOING TO BE DOING THIS TOGETHER, I THINK IT'S TIME FOR ME TO TELL YOU WHAT OUR GOAL IS.
...!
YUKINA...

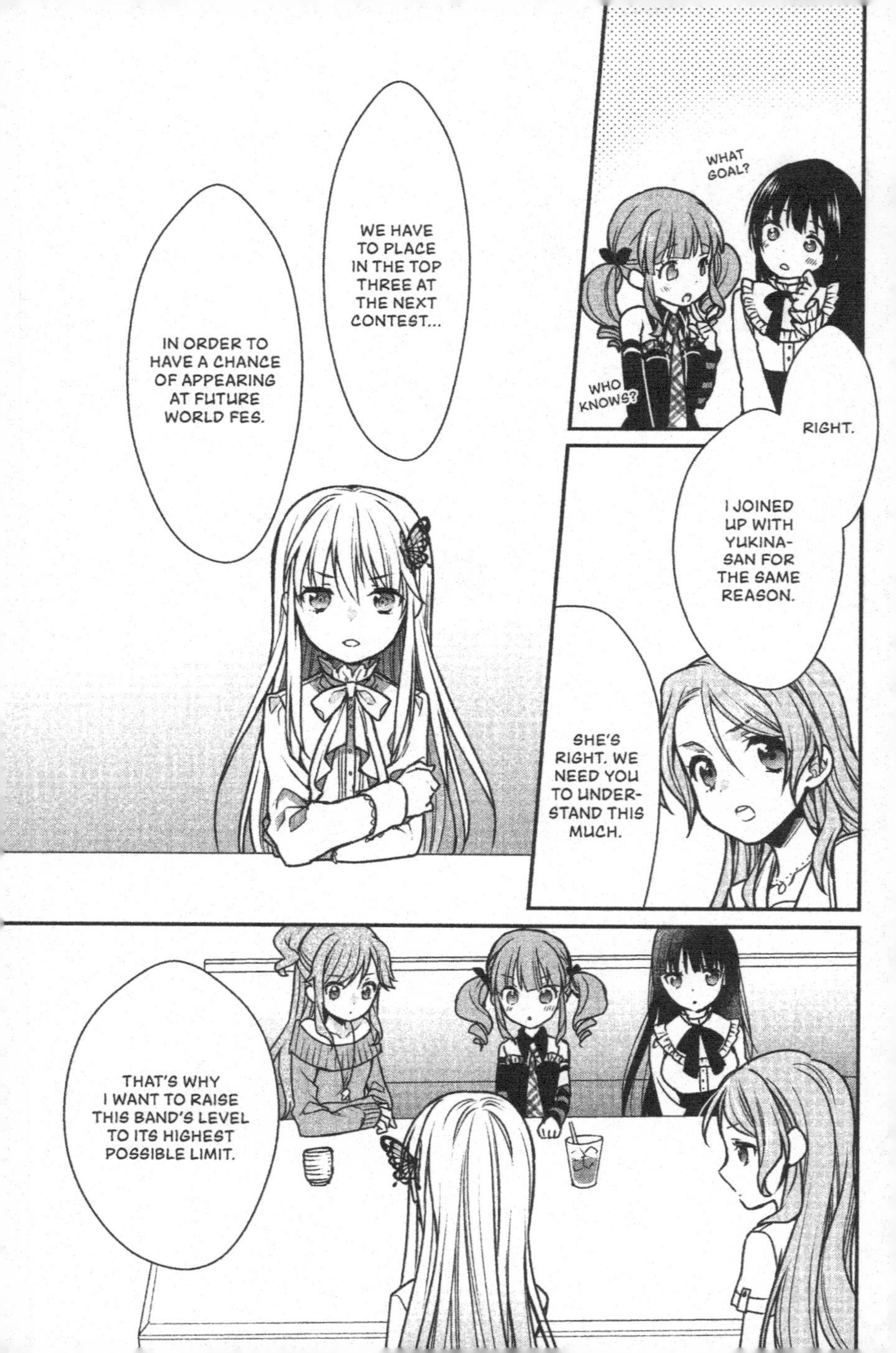
WHAT GOAL?
WHO KNOWS?
RIGHT.
I JOINED UP WITH YUKINA-SAN FOR THE SAME REASON.
SHE'S RIGHT. WE NEED YOU TO UNDER-STAND THIS MUCH.
WE HAVE TO PLACE IN THE TOP THREE AT THE NEXT CONTEST...
IN ORDER TO HAVE A CHANCE OF APPEARING AT FUTURE WORLD FES.
THAT'S WHY I WANT TO RAISE THIS BAND'S LEVEL TO ITS HIGHEST POSSIBLE LIMIT.

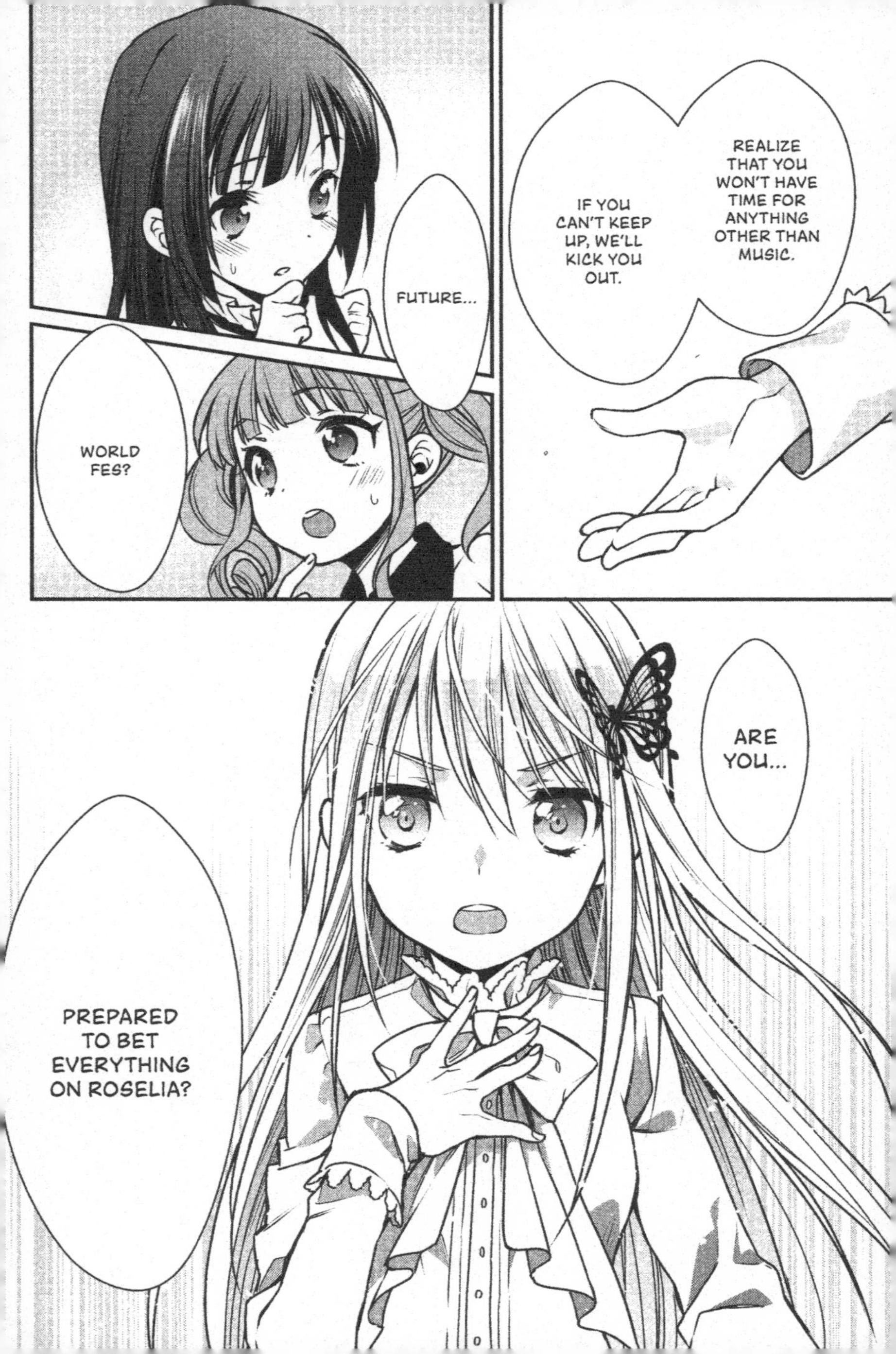
REALIZE THAT YOU WON'T HAVE TIME FOR ANYTHING OTHER THAN MUSIC.
IF YOU CAN'T KEEP UP, WE'LL KICK YOU OUT.
FUTURE...
WORLD FES?
ARE YOU...
PREPARED TO BET EVERYTHING ON ROSELIA?

BanG Dream! Girls Band Party! Roselia Stage

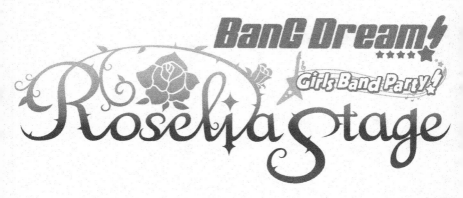

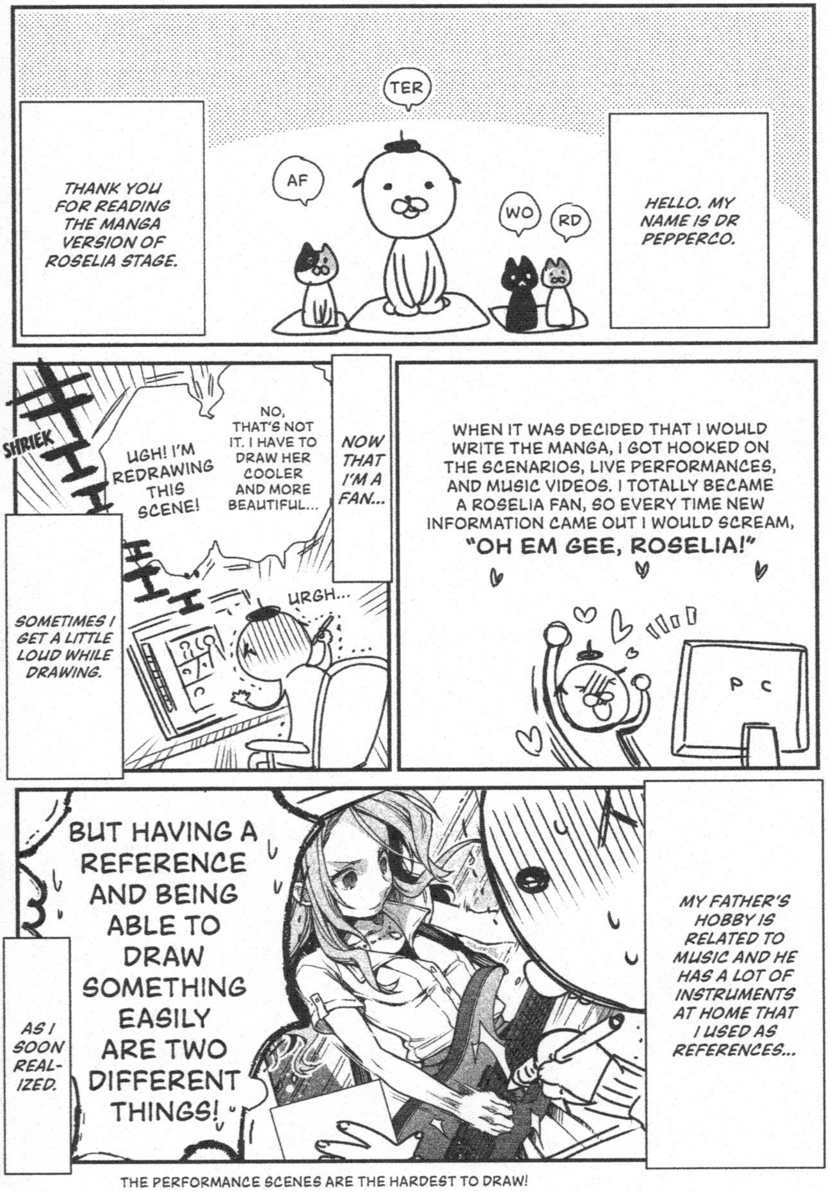
HELLO. MY NAME IS DR PEPPERCO.
AF
TER
WO
RD
THANK YOU FOR READING THE MANGA VERSION OF ROSELIA STAGE.
WHEN IT WAS DECIDED THAT I WOULD WRITE THE MANGA, I GOT HOOKED ON THE SCENARIOS, LIVE PERFORMANCES, AND MUSIC VIDEOS. I TOTALLY BECAME A ROSELIA FAN, SO EVERY TIME NEW INFORMATION CAME OUT I WOULD SCREAM,
"OH EM GEE, ROSELIA!"
PC
NOW THAT I'M A FAN...
NO, THAT'S NOT IT. I HAVE TO DRAW HER COOLER AND MORE BEAUTIFUL...
UGH! I'M REDRAWING THIS SCENE!
SHRIEK
URGH...
SOMETIMES I GET A LITTLE LOUD WHILE DRAWING.
MY FATHER'S HOBBY IS RELATED TO MUSIC AND HE HAS A LOT OF INSTRUMENTS AT HOME THAT I USED AS REFERENCES...
BUT HAVING A REFERENCE AND BEING ABLE TO DRAW SOMETHING EASILY ARE TWO DIFFERENT THINGS!
AS I SOON REAL-IZED.

THE PERFORMANCE SCENES ARE THE HARDEST TO DRAW!

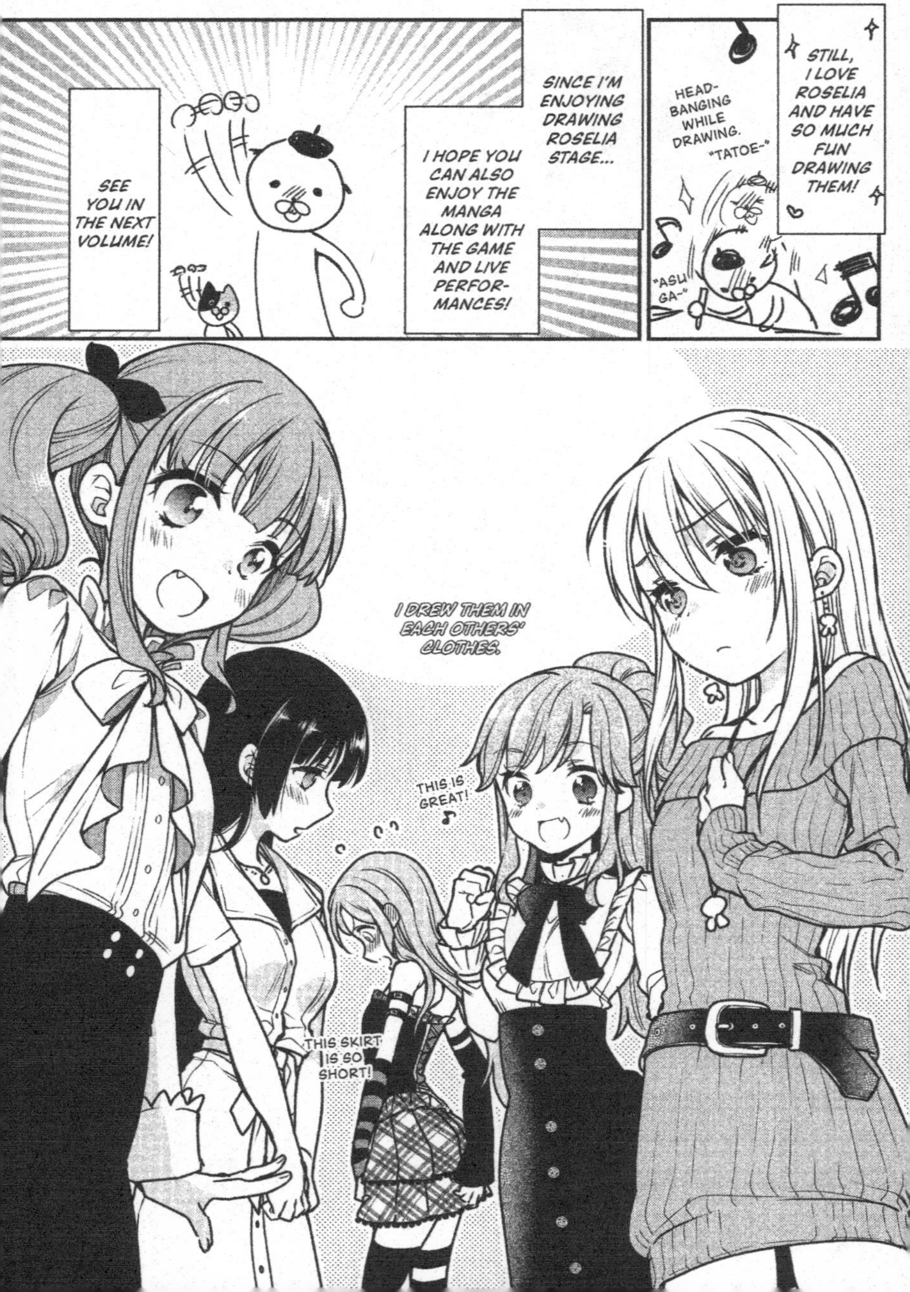
STILL, I LOVE ROSELIA AND HAVE SO MUCH FUN DRAWING THEM!
HEAD-BANGING WHILE DRAWING.
"TATOE-"
"ASU GA-"
SINCE I'M ENJOYING DRAWING ROSELIA STAGE...
I HOPE YOU CAN ALSO ENJOY THE MANGA ALONG WITH THE GAME AND LIVE PERFORMANCES!
SEE YOU IN THE NEXT VOLUME!
I DREW THEM IN EACH OTHERS' CLOTHES.
THIS IS GREAT!
THIS SKIRT IS SO SHORT!

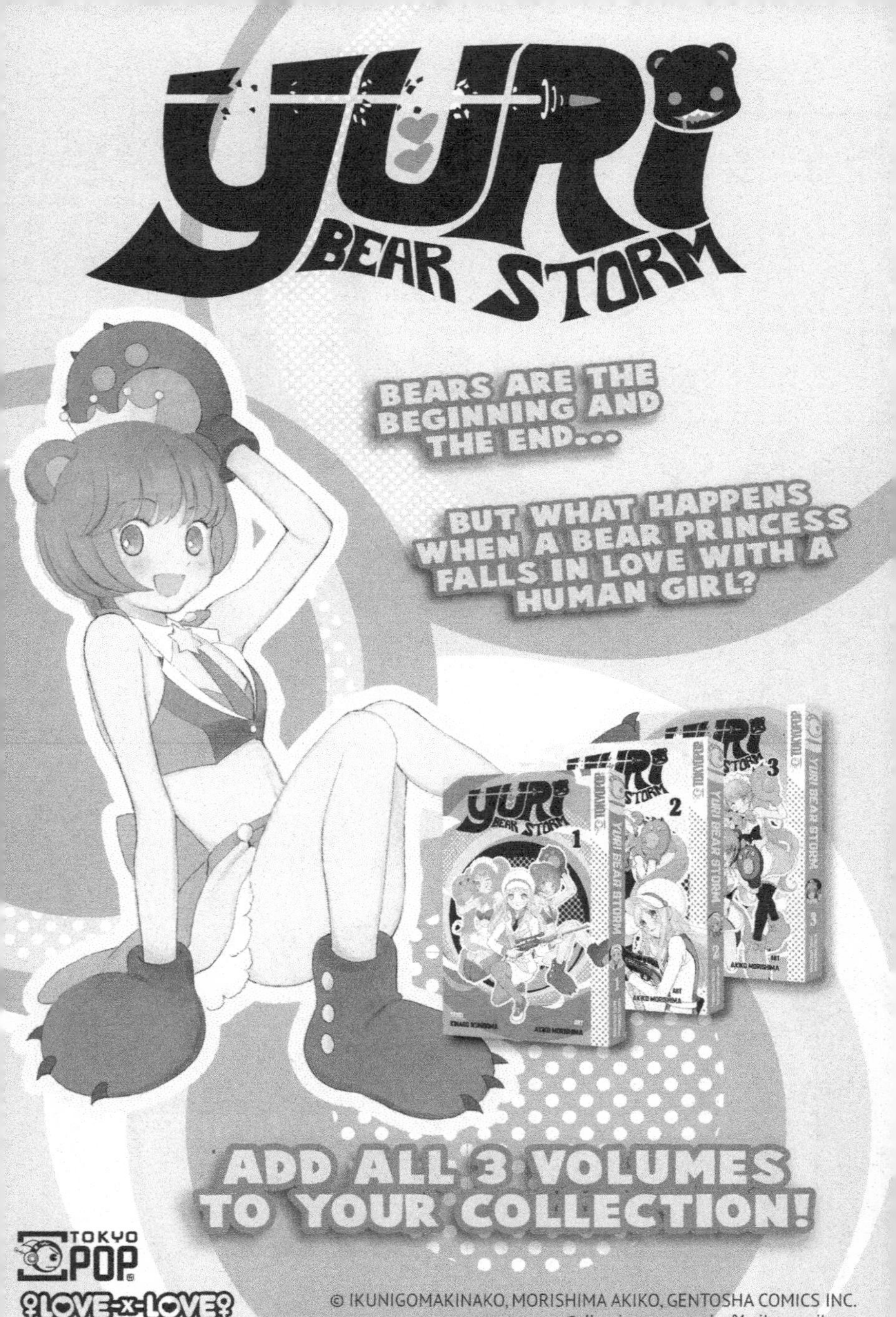
YURI BEAR STORM
BEARS ARE THE BEGINNING AND THE END...
BUT WHAT HAPPENS WHEN A BEAR PRINCESS FALLS IN LOVE WITH A HUMAN GIRL?
ADD ALL 3 VOLUMES TO YOUR COLLECTION!
TOKYO POP
LOVE x LOVE

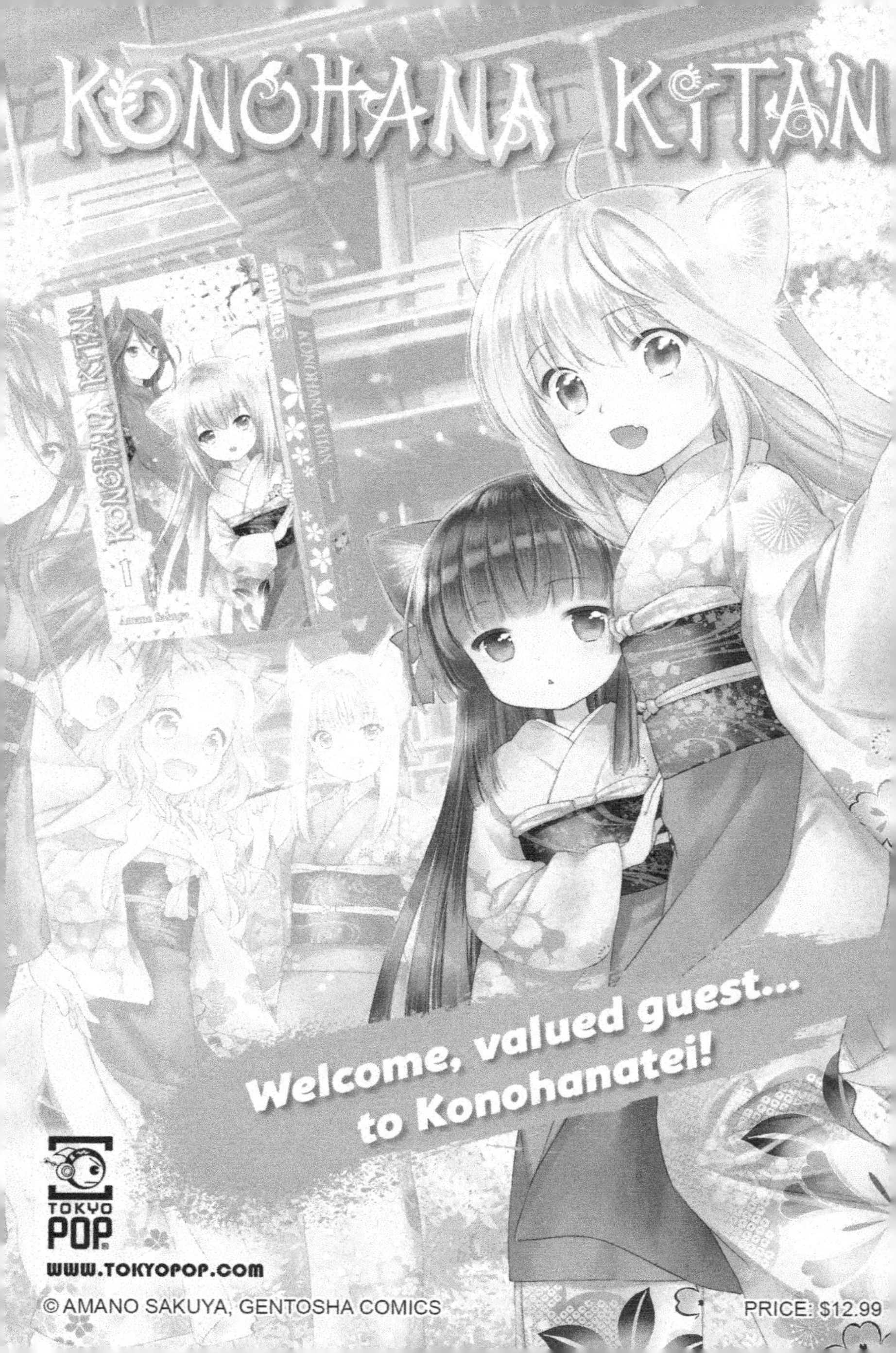
KONOHANA KITAN
KONOHANA KITAN
1
Amano Sakuya
KONOHANA KITAN
Welcome, valued guest...
to Konohanatei!
TOKYO POP
WWW.TOKYOPOP.COM
© AMANO SAKUYA, GENTOSHA COMICS
PRICE: $12.99

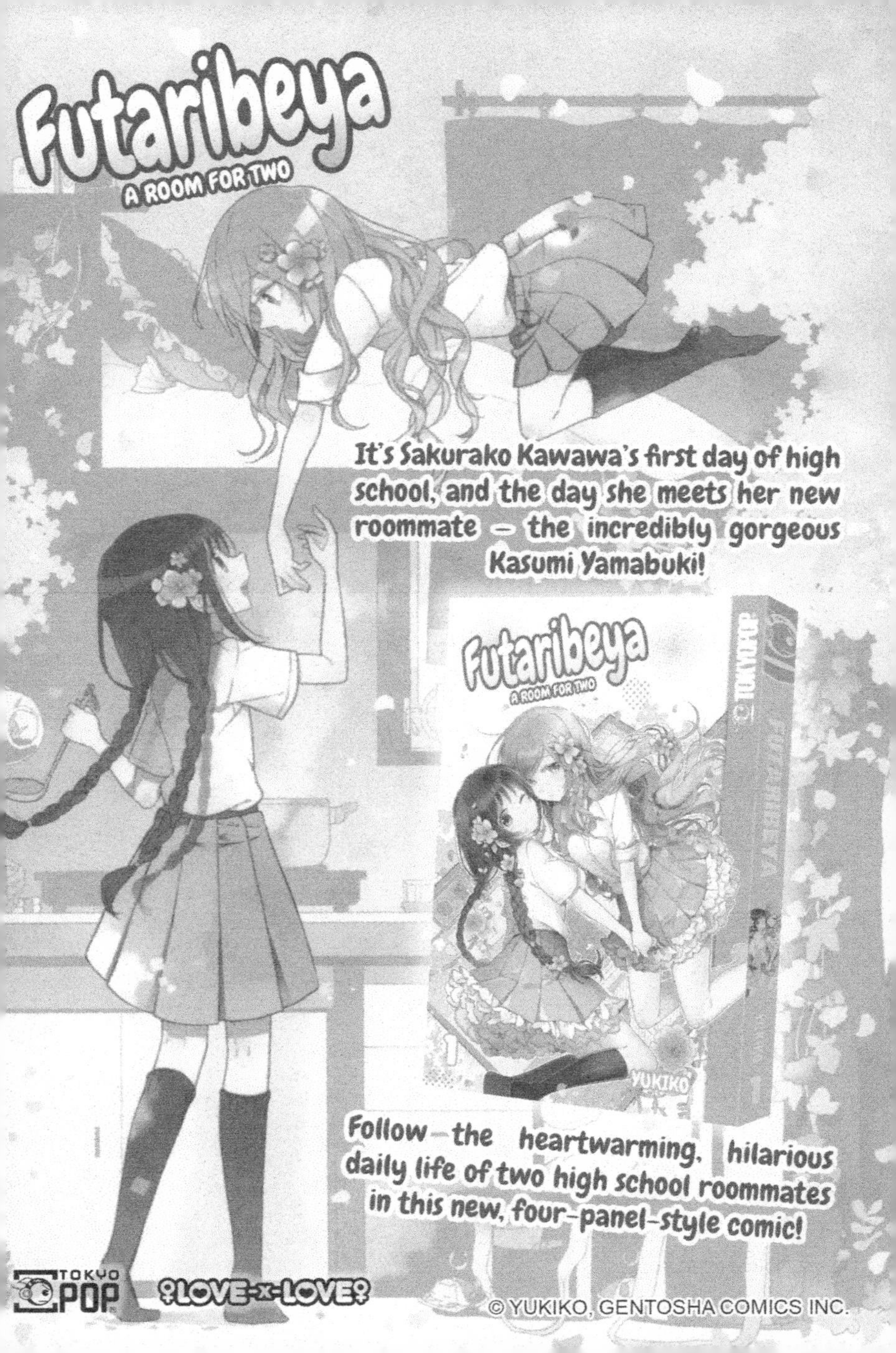
Futaribeya
A ROOM FOR TWO
It's Sakurako Kawawa's first day of high school, and the day she meets her new roommate – the incredibly gorgeous Kasumi Yamabuki!
Futaribeya
A ROOM FOR TWO
1
YUKIKO
TOKYOPOP
Follow the heartwarming, hilarious daily life of two high school roommates in this new, four-panel-style comic!
TOKYOPOP
LOVE x LOVE
© YUKIKO, GENTOSHA COMICS INC.

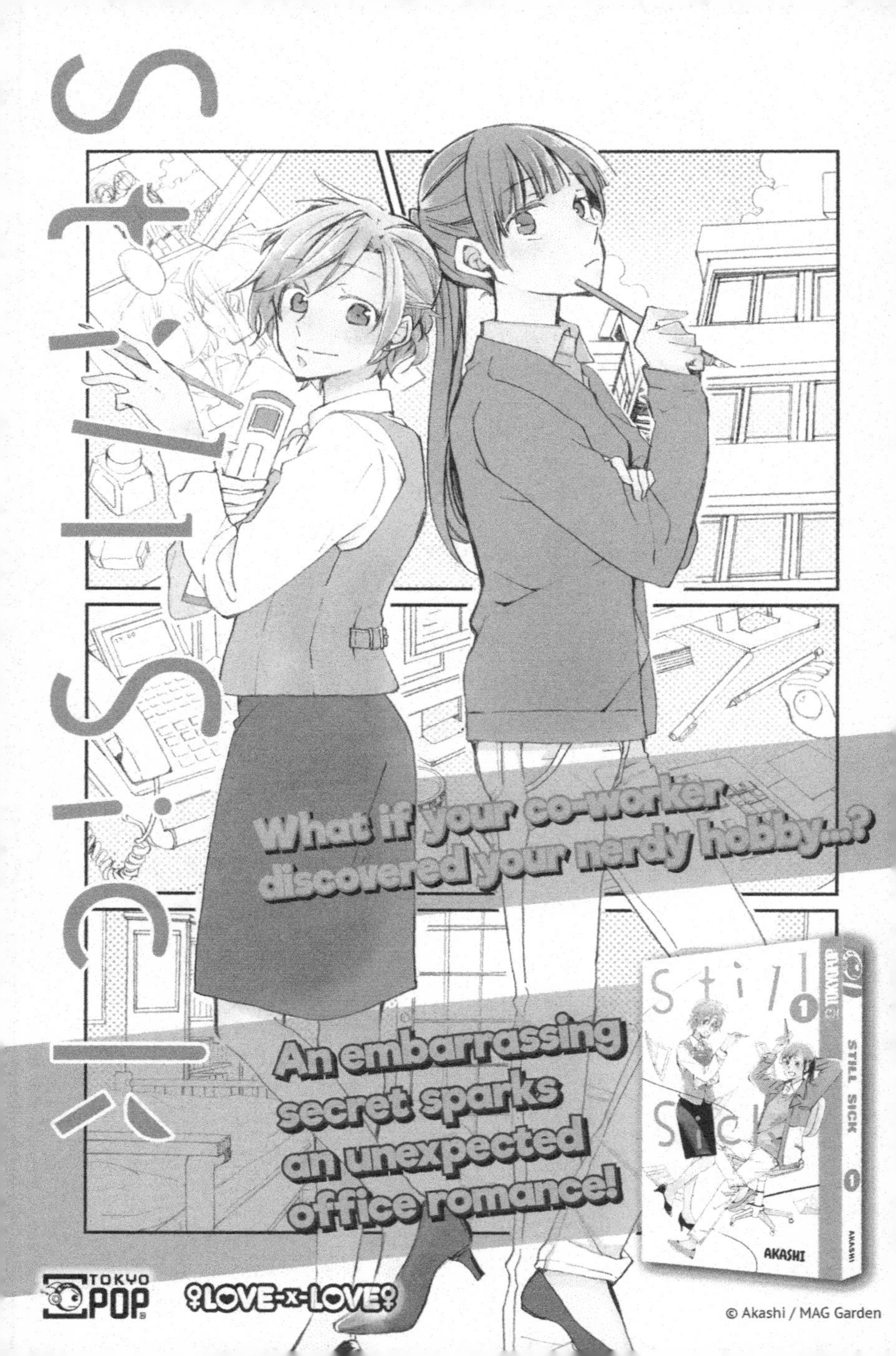

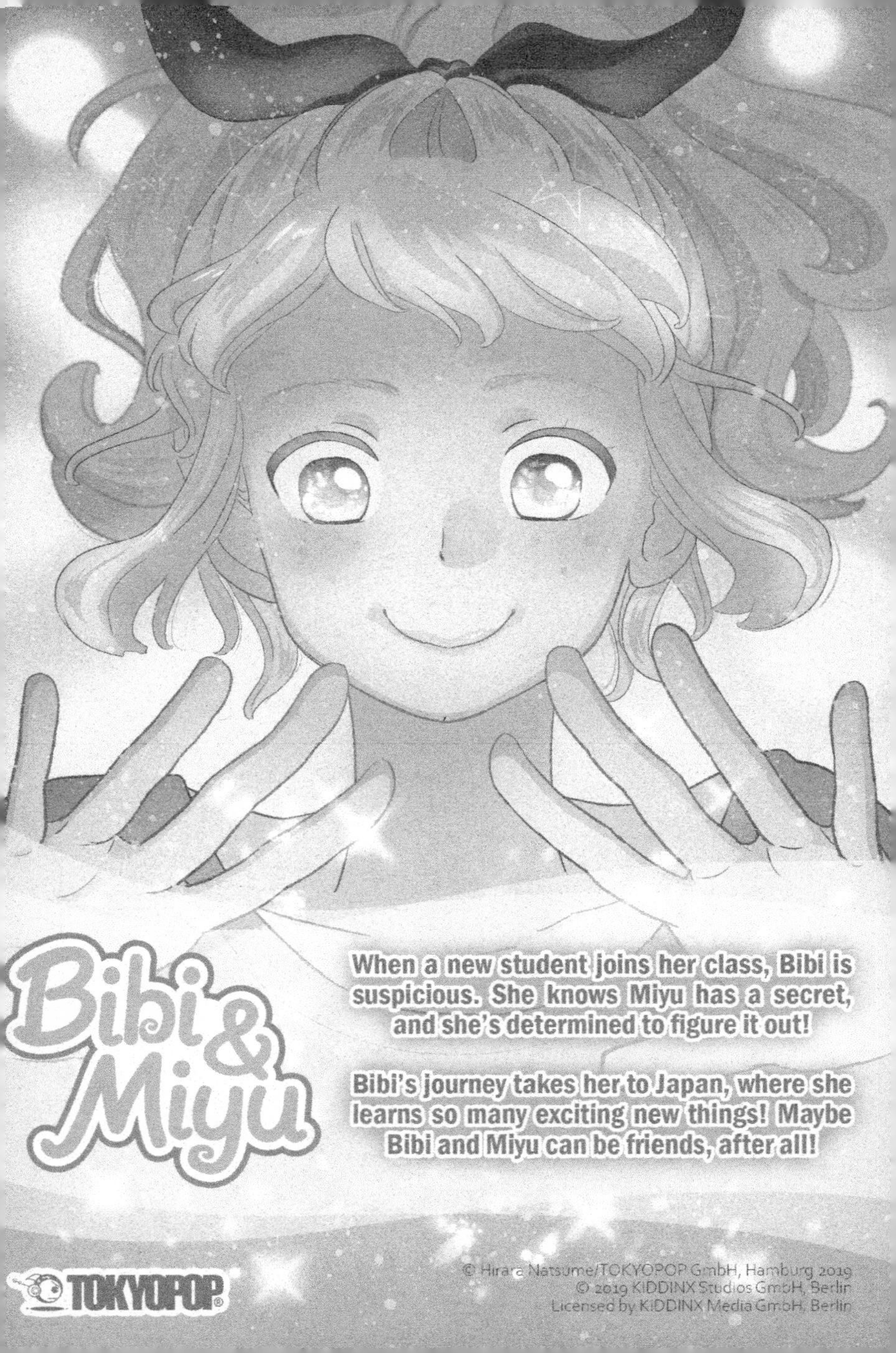
Bibi & Miyu
When a new student joins her class, Bibi is suspicious. She knows Miyu has a secret, and she's determined to figure it out!
Bibi's journey takes her to Japan, where she learns so many exciting new things! Maybe Bibi and Miyu can be friends, after all!
TOKYOPOP
© Hirara Natsume/TOKYOPOP GmbH, Hamburg 2019
© 2019 KIDDINX Studios GmbH, Berlin
Licensed by KIDDINX Media GmbH, Berlin

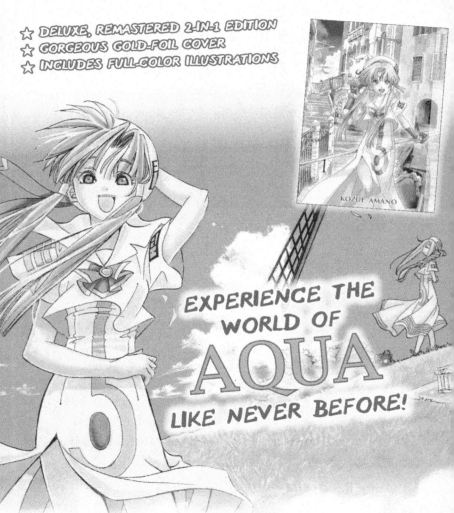
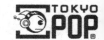

SCARLET SOUL

Long ago, an ancient hero sealed away the underworld. Now, with that sacred barrier broken, it's up to Rin and the mysterious demon Aghyr to restore balance to the Kingdom of Nohmur!

SCARLET SOUL

KIRA YUKISHIRO

1

TOKYO POP ♀LOVE-x-LOVE♂

Breath of Flowers

IN THE LANGUAGE OF FLOWERS, EVERY BLOSSOM IS UNIQUE

BEING A TEEN IS HARD. IT'S EVEN HARDER WHEN YOU'RE HIDING A SECRET...

BanG Dream! Girls Band Party! Roselia Stage, Volume 1
Manga by Dr pepperco

Editor - Lena Atanassova
Marketing Associate - Kae Winters
Translator - Katie Kimura
Copy Editor - Massiel Gutierrez
QC - Daichi Nemoto
Licensing Specialist - Arika Yanaka
Original Cover Design - Hajime Sasaki (LALA HANDS)
Retouching and Lettering - Vibrraant Publishing Studio
Editor-in-Chief & Publisher - Stu Levy

A  Manga

TOKYOPOP and 🌀 are trademarks or registered trademarks of TOKYOPOP Inc.

TOKYOPOP inc.
5200 W Century Blvd
Suite 705
Los Angeles, CA 90045 USA

E-mail: info@TOKYOPOP.com
Come visit us online at www.TOKYOPOP.com

f www.facebook.com/TOKYOPOP
www.twitter.com/TOKYOPOP
www.pinterest.com/TOKYOPOP
www.instagram.com/TOKYOPOP

ISBN: 978-1-4278-6360-7
First TOKYOPOP Printing: June 2020
10 9 8 7 6 5 4 3 2 1

STO

THIS IS THE BACK OF THE BOOK!

How do you read manga-style? It's simple! Let's practice -- just start in the top right panel and follow the numbers below!

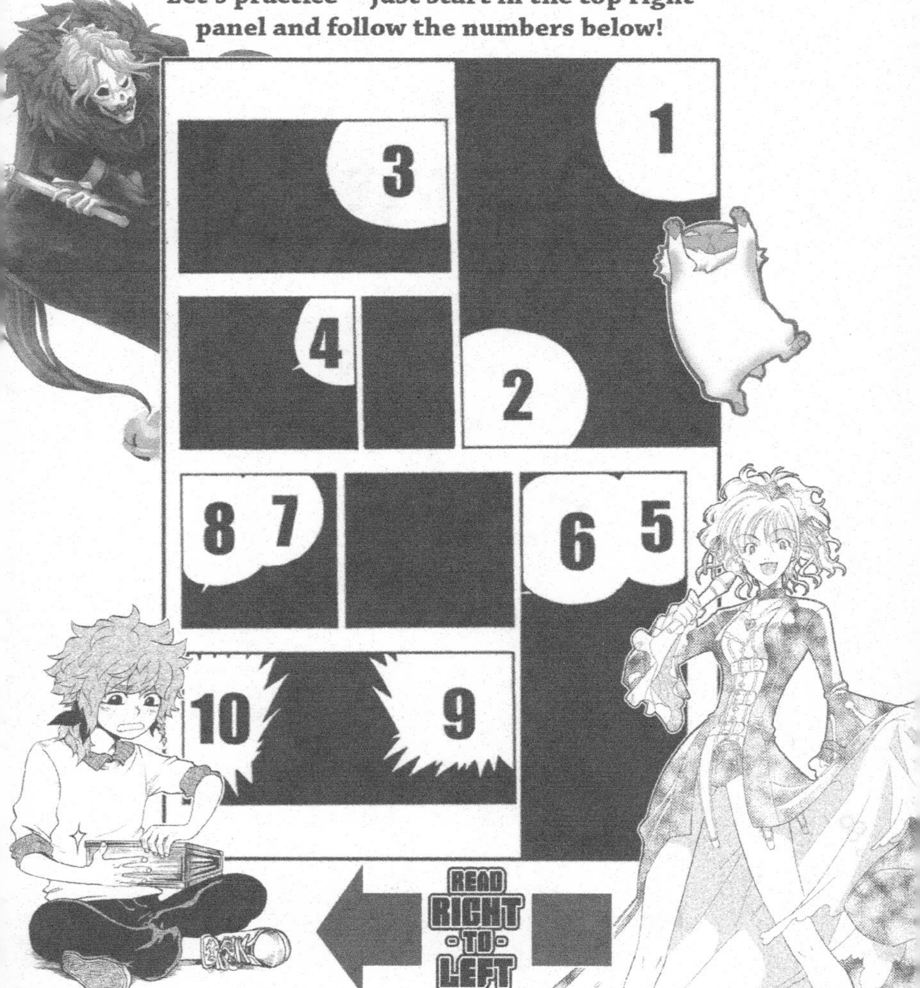
1
2
3
4
5
6
7
8
9
10
READ
RIGHT
-TO-
LEFT

Crimson from ***Kamo*** / Fairy Cat from ***Grimms Manga Tales***
Morrey from ***Goldfisch*** / Princess Ai from ***Princess Ai***